VISUAL QUICKSTART GUIDE

PREMIERE 6

FOR MACINTOSH AND WINDOWS

Antony Bolante

 Peachpit Press

Visual QuickStart Guide
Premiere 6 for Macintosh and Windows
Antony Bolante

Peachpit Press
1249 Eighth Street
Berkeley, CA 94710
(510) 524-2178
(800) 283-9444
(510) 542-2221 (fax)

Find us on the World Wide Web at
http://www.peachpit.com

Published by Peachpit Press, a division of Addison Wesley Longman

Copyright © 2001 by Antony Bolante

Editor: Wendy Sharp
Production coordinator: Connie Jeung-Mills
Copyeditor: Kathy Simpson
Compositors: Myrna Vladic, Rick Gordon, Deborah Roberti
Indexer: Rebecca Plunkett
Cover design: The Visual Group

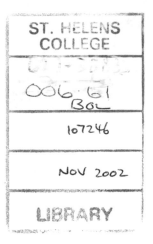
Notice of Rights
All rights reserved. No part of this book may be reproduced or transmitted in any form by
any means, electronic, mechanical, photocopying, recording, or otherwise, without the prior
written permission of the publisher. For information on getting permission for reprints and
excerpts, contact Gary-Paul Prince at Peachpit Press.

Notice of Liability
The information in this book is distributed on an "As Is" basis, without warranty. While every
precaution has been taken in the preparation of the book, neither the author nor Peachpit
Press shall have any liability to any person or entity with respect to any loss or damage caused
or alleged to be caused directly or indirectly by the instructions contained in this book or by
the computer software and hardware products described in it.

Trademarks
Visual QuickStart Guide and its marks are registered trademarks of Peachpit Press.

Adobe, Adobe Premiere, Adobe After Effects, Adobe Photoshop, and Adobe Illustrator are
either registered trademarks or trademarks of Adobe Systems Incorporated in the United
States and/or other countries.

Throughout this book trademarked names are used. Rather than put a trademark symbol in every
occurrence of a trademarked name, we state we are using the names only in an editorial fashion
and to the benefit of the trademark owner with no intention of infringement of copyright.

ISBN: 0-201-72207-0

 Printed on recycled paper

9 8 7 6 5 4 3

Printed and bound in the United States of America.

Dedication

To my parents, Gaspar and Marlene Bolante.

Thank You

Everyone who helped with the first edition. I hope the new one does you proud.

The folks at PeachPit Press: Hannah Onstad Latham, who put me on the path; Kathy Simpson who rights the wrongs; Myrna Vladic, Debbie Roberti, and Rick Gordon, who make it all look good.

Marjorie Baer, for her confidence, encouragement, and advice.

Wendy Sharp, who's not my editor; I'm her author.

Grant Balfour, for planting the tree. And Kim McShane, his silent partner.

The good people at the Bean There cafe.

Atsuko Yamagishi, for her love and support.

My family, of course.

TABLE OF CONTENTS

Chapter 14: Motion Settings   **413**

Chapter 15: Creating Output   **443**

Premiere:
The Big Picture

Fade in. A keyboard sits in front of what looks like a beige pizza box with a computer screen sitting on top. On the screen, a small, grainy movie plays jerkily. Superimpose titles in steady succession: Macintosh IIsi. QuickTime 1.0. Premiere l.0. 1991.

From the first scene, you could see where this movie was headed. Programs like Premiere hinted at the computer's potential for democratizing the video medium. The benefits the computer brought to number-crunching, word-processing, and publishing would inevitably reach video. What once could be achieved only on high-priced, high-end equipment would one day be done on a desktop. The low end was ascending.

Now desktop video is realizing its potential. Just as digital tools ushered in a desktop publishing revolution years ago, new technology is sparking a desktop video revolution. Increased computing power has made digital filmmaking a reality; innovations like the DV video format have brought high-quality imaging to the masses; and the rapidly expanding bandwidth of the Web provides new presentation venues.

Premiere has long been a useful tool for editing digital video, audio, still images, and text on the desktop. If you've followed Premiere's development over this decade of evolution, you know that it's able to fulfill its promise better than ever before. Whether you've chosen Premiere to create programs for multimedia, video broadcast, or the Web, you've chosen this book because you're eager to get started.

The Visual QuickStart Series

Chances are that you're already familiar with Peachpit Press' *QuickStart* series of books. They're known for their concise style, step-by-step instructions, and ample illustrations.

The *Premiere 6 Visual QuickStart Guide* distills a dense, multifaceted program in the time-tested *QuickStart* tradition. If the book looks a little thick for a "concise" guide, consider that it contains literally hundreds of screen shots that clearly illustrate every task. Like other books in this series, the *Premiere 6 Visual QuickStart Guide* strives to be quick without failing to guide.

Using This Book

Though the text restricts itself to the task at hand, it doesn't hesitate to give you critical background information, usually in the form of sidebars. *Sidebars* set aside useful information that helps you understand the concepts behind the task. If you are already familiar with the concept, feel free to skip ahead; if not, look to the sidebars for some grounding. Also keep an eye out for tips, which point out shortcuts, pitfalls, and tricks of the trade.

Chapters are organized to present topics as you encounter them in a typical editing project, though the task-oriented format and thumb tabs let you jump to the topic that you need.

The arrangement of chapters does diverge from the editing process in one notable area: video capture. Although capturing video takes place at the beginning of an editing project, the book doesn't address it until Chapter 16. This is because you don't have to capture your own video to edit in Premiere; you simply have to put footage on your hard drive. In addition, capture has a lot in common with the end of the process: outputting the program to tape. Both procedures require the same hardware: a deck or camera and a FireWire/iLink or capture card, and both procedures use similar video and audio settings. For this reason, I discuss video capture after discussing output.

Speaking of settings, you'll find a detailed explanation of video and audio settings in Chapter 18. These pervasive technical topics are compiled in the final chapter, which also serves as a mini handbook for digital video.

Using Premiere, of course, touches on a multitude of related topics: formats, editing aesthetics, special effects, audio sweetening, Web delivery, and on and on. Explaining the fundamentals and background of each of these areas is far outside the scope of this book (and even books that don't have the word *quick* in their title). Nevertheless, this guide tries to provide enough information to keep you moving and point you in new directions.

How Premiere Works

Premiere is digital nonlinear editing software. A breakdown of this description can give you clues about how it works.

Digital—Premiere manipulates digital media: digital video and audio, scanned images, and digitally created artwork and animation stored in several formats. Regardless of the particular format, these materials are stored as files on your computer's hard disk. Strictly speaking, Premiere doesn't convert analog video and audio to digital form, although it does contain controls that do so in conjunction with built-in or add-on hardware, such as your FireWire/ iLink connection or capture card.

Because Premiere works with graphical references to the source files and not with the files themselves, digital editing is also called nondestructive editing.

Nonlinear—Editing in Premiere is described as nonlinear because your sources are not constrained to a linear medium, such as videotape. In other words, you can access any source clip instantly, without shuttling tape, and you can change the sequence of clips in the program without rerecording.

Software—As a software-only package, Premiere can import and export digital files. To acquire and export material to and from videotape, however, Premiere relies on built-in or add-on hardware.

Terminology: Digital and Analog

When you record audio and video, sound and light are converted to electrical signals. *Analog* media record these signals as continuously changing values. *Digital* media, on the other hand, record audio and video as a series of specific, discrete values. A playback device converts these values back to audio and video. The accuracy of each conversion greatly influences the picture and sound quality.

Because digital recordings use discrete values, it's easy to reproduce them exactly, time after time. Also, you can take advantage of the computer's ability to manipulate these values—which means you can more easily alter the sound, color, and brightness, and add effects.

To help you picture the difference between analog and digital, imagine copying a picture and then copying the copy. Analog is like copying the picture freehand. Every mistake is magnified in each successive copy. Digital is like having a connect-the-dots version of the picture. Each copy is exactly the same. And as long as you use enough dots, the picture looks pretty good.

Editing Strategy: Offline and Online Editing

Any project, it can be argued, begins at the same point: the end. Setting your output goal determines the choices you make to achieve it. Therefore, the editing strategy that you develop always proceeds from the same question: What is my output goal (**Figure i.1**)?

Whether your animation is destined for film, broadcast video, CD-ROM, or the Web, familiarize yourself with the specifications of your output goal, such as frame size, frame rate, and file format. Often, you must reconcile your output goal with the capabilities and limitations of your system. These factors help determine your postproduction path, particularly whether you perform offline editing or online editing.

Online editing results in the final video program. You can online-edit in Premiere if your system is capable of acquiring, processing, and delivering your program at final-output quality. The higher the image quality, however, the greater the system requirements. To achieve your output goal, you may need a fast processor; a high-end capture card; and large, fast hard drives. If your system doesn't meet your output requirements, use another system for the online edit, and use Premiere for your offline edit.

Offline editing prepares projects for an online edit. In an offline edit, you edit with low-quality versions of the video. Rather than produce a final program at output quality, you produce an accurate draft version.

The completed offline edit can produce a kind of transcription of all your edits, known as an *edit decision list* (EDL). You can use the EDL and source tapes to re-create your program quickly and easily in a traditional tape-based online-editing suite. You could also use your offline edit to conform to a film edit.

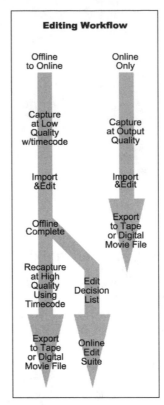

Figure i.1 This flow chart outlines the typical offline and online editing strategies.

(Sidebar) OFFLINE/ONLINE EDITING

Alternatively, you can offline- and online-edit on the same system. Because lower-quality clips are smaller, more of them fit on your hard drive, and your computer can process them faster. For the online edit, you can recapture only the clips that you used in the program at the final-output quality. Premiere automatically uses the high-quality clips in your final program, and no re-editing is required.

For an offline edit to succeed, you must have some way to accurately match your low-quality offline clips with their high-quality counterparts. Without a frame-accurate reference, there's no way to easily reproduce the program you created in the offline edit. That frame-accurate reference is known as *timecode*.

Timecode numbers identify each frame of video on a source tape. Premiere and other video equipment use timecode to track each edit in the offline edit and accurately re-create it in the online edit. Without timecode, an EDL would be meaningless, and recapturing clips would be impossible. You can learn more about timecode in Chapters 17 and 18.

Your Desktop Editing Suite

All nonlinear editing systems use a graphical interface that to some degree refers to their predecessors: film- and tape-based editing tools. Yet as these traditional tools yield to newer technologies, the metaphors lose much of their meaning. These days, many editors have never seen a film splicer or a traditional video-editing suite. Nevertheless, it may help you to understand what Premiere does if you realize what it's designed to replace.

Before programs like Premiere, offline editing was synonymous with inexpensive, but very

limited, editing equipment. In a typical offline suite, you would create a simple *cuts-only* edit (no dissolves or other transitions), using low-quality copies of the camera originals called *window dubs*. In a window dub, timecode numbers have been recorded over the picture. (It's not actual timecode; it's a "picture" of the timecode.) When editing was complete, you could painstakingly transcribe the timecode numbers at the beginning and end of each shot to create the edit decision list.

Only after you were armed with an EDL would you proceed to an online suite, with its expensive decks and special equipment. At this stage, you would finally be able to add transitions, effects, titles, and mix audio.

Programs like Premiere blur the line between online and offline editing by offering the online features at the offline stage (and price):

A/B roll editing—In a traditional tape-editing suite, any transition other than a cut required two sources: an *A roll* and a *B roll*. As the two tapes played, a video switcher could mix the signal from tape A with tape B to record on the master tape. This way, you could create dissolves, wipes, and other effects. If two scenes were on the same source tape, it had to be copied onto the B roll before dissolves and other transitions could be performed (unless you had a deck with a preread feature, but that's another story). And all this was possible only in an expensive online editing suite. Premiere allows you to accomplish A/B roll effects in the offline stage (and at an offline price).

Audio mixing and sweetening—Just as a traditional offline suite permitted only simple cuts-only video editing, audio editing was usually limited to simple volume control. Better audio editing was left to the online edit or even a separate audio post session. Premiere allows you to do complex audio editing and effects from the start, including audio processing to adjust the level, placement, and character of the sound. You can set audio in points based on audio samples, which are more precise than video frames. In addition, you can fade, boost, mix, and pan almost unlimited tracks of audio. The new audio mixer even resembles a traditional mixing board. Moreover, you can *sweeten* the audio, subtly correcting the sound and adding special effects.

Digital video effects (DVE)—DVE is the generic term for a device used to process the video signal digitally, in real time, to accomplish all kinds of visual effects. DVEs can rotate, resize, and move an image; change the colors; and add other visual effects. Premiere's effects and motion settings can achieve the same results, as well as many effects you won't find in a DVE. Though they take more time to process on the desktop, these kinds of visual effects used to be unavailable outside an online suite.

Character generator (CG)—A CG is used to create text for video, usually to superimpose over other images. Premiere's title window brings the tools and ease of desktop publishing to character generation for video.

Edit decision list (EDL) import/export—This feature produces a transcription of the edits in the program so that it can be reproduced on another system—typically, a traditional higher-end system. Alternatively, it can read an EDL from another system.

Batch capture—Batch capture uses timecode references to capture the proper clips automatically from a log or offline edit.

Workflow

Apart from taking an offline or online editing path, you should look at your editing workflow as proceeding from simple to complex. Though you don't need to adhere rigidly to the following outline, gradually fleshing out the program is usually more efficient than plunging into effects, going back again to rough cutting, and then discovering the effects should be redone. In fact, the Premiere workspace options reflect an incremental process, optimizing the interface for editing, audio editing, and effects editing. See "Selecting an Initial Workspace" in Chapter 2 to learn how to set up the editing layout you prefer; see Chapters 10 and 11 to learn how to optimize the workspace for audio and effects editing.

Logging—The most tedious (and, therefore, the most neglected) part of the editing process involves watching your source tapes and noting the *selects*—the shots you want to use in the program. Premiere's capture window and device control can make the logging process close to painless. If your tape has timecode, your log can serve as a *batch list*, which is a list of timecode start and end numbers that can be used to automate the capture process.

Capture—If you're using an IEEE 1394 (FireWire or iLink) connection, capture simply involves transferring video from your camera or deck to the hard drive. Analog sources require a capture device, which can digitize the video. If you have timecode and device control, Premiere can capture shots from a batch list automatically.

Import—At this point, you add to a Premiere project the footage you want to use. You can import a variety of digital media: video, audio, stills, image sequences, and so on. Your project uses references to the source footage, not the footage itself.

Basic edit/rough cutting—Arrange and adjust the sequence of clips into an edited program, using a variety of flexible and powerful editing tools.

Preview—Watch your program at any time, with or without transitions or special effects.

Fine-tuning/fine cutting—Use the trimming mode and other editing tools to refine the edits in the program.

Effects and character generation—Add titles, superimpose clips, add motion or video and audio effects, and animate effects over time.

Audio sweetening—Use subframe editing to cut audio more accurately. Use the fader and audio mixer to fade and pan audio. Use audio effects to enhance the audio or add special effects.

Output—Export the finished program directly to tape, or save a file for playback on other computers or over the Web.

New Features

If you're a Premiere user who moved from version 4 to 5, you will be relieved to discover that you won't have to make such a radical adjustment this time around. Premiere 6 doesn't overhaul the interface the way that version 5 did. Nevertheless, the interface has significant enhancements and improvements. Users who were a little disappointed with Premiere 5—most notably, with its lack of native DV support—will be happy with its added functionality. Overall, Premiere 6 has grown out of an awkward transitional phase and has reestablished itself as a leading NLE. The most notable of its new and enhanced features include:

Direct support of IEEE 1394 (FireWire, iLink)—Premiere 6 includes preset project settings for DV, device control, support for nonsquare pixels, DV file interchange

support, and the capability to preview the program on an NTSC monitor.

Web-optimized export options—These options simplify exporting video for Web delivery by including Windows media export (for Windows) and integrating Terran's Media Cleaner Lite and Advanced RealMedia export engine.

Enhanced program markers—You can embed HTML links or chapter markers for DVD.

Audio Mixer—This feature emulates a traditional mixing board to execute real-time fades and pans. The audio mixer includes mixing-board-style controls, VU meters, and automation options.

Enhanced effects—Premiere has added 30 After Effects plug-ins, which you can keyframe in the timeline with tools similar to those in Adobe After Effects, including an Effect Controls palette.

Enhanced windows—You can reconfigure, add, or expand the features of all the major windows. The Project window includes a split panel for bins and footage items; the Monitor and clip window controls are redesigned; the timeline includes improved tools and more convenient buttons.

New timeline menu and menu commands—The menu bar and commands have been reorganized, and a Timeline menu added, making it easier to find the command you need.

Expanded contextual menus—The contextual menus include more commands and functions so you can access them more quickly.

Workspace options—You can choose between A/B or single-track style editing. Other options apply to other phases of the editing process, such as audio and effects editing, and allow you to create a custom workspace.

Visualization tools—A full-fledged storyboard feature lets you generate a sequence from the storyboard automatically with the Automate to Timeline feature. A Settings Viewer window allows you to evaluate and compare your capture, project, and output settings.

New and improved palettes—The Commands palette has been improved, with features similar to those of Photoshop's Command palette. A new History palette (another Photoshop feature) allows you to undo actions more selectively.

Integration—Premiere 6 provides greater consistency with other Adobe programs, particularly After Effects. An Edit Original command allows you to open source footage in the program in which it was created and update the changes in your Premiere project.

The Dynamic Media Suite

Though Premiere is dedicated to editing video, you can use it to bring together a range of digital media. And while Premiere's features sometimes overlap with other types of software, the ideal workflow includes tools specialized for each job. For this reason, Adobe hopes that you will use Premiere together with Photoshop, Illustrator, and After Effects as a suite of tools. In fact, these products are sometimes offered together as "The Dynamic Media Collection."

In addition to selling their programs as a set, the folks at Adobe are trying their best to make the programs work as a set. As these software packages have matured, they have also become more integrated. Over time, it has become easier to move files from one program to the other without performing intermediate steps or sacrificing elements of your work. Even the interfaces have grown more consistent with one another. (Although the landscape is similar, however, the customs aren't always the same. You may find that some shared features don't always have exactly the same procedure or keyboard shortcut.)

Your familiarity with other Adobe programs may give you a head start on learning Premiere. If you're thinking about buying Premiere or other Adobe programs, you may find their consistency or bundled pricing appealing. In any case, Adobe's eye toward product integration may be an important consideration for you.

Figure i.2 The differences between the Mac and Windows versions of Premiere are superficial. This window on the Mac...

Figure i.3 ... looks nearly the same on a Windows machine.

Macintosh and Windows

Premiere is widely available for both the Macintosh and Windows systems, and it functions nearly the same way on both platforms. Except where noted, the information in this book applies to both versions. The book features screen shots from both systems, and includes both Mac and Windows keyboard shortcuts and instructions in the text. With very few exceptions, you'll find that Premiere works the same on both systems. Apart from a few cosmetic differences, the windows are also strikingly similar (**Figures i.2** and **i.3**).

When a process or window differs between the two versions of the program, that fact is clearly noted. Otherwise, you'll find that the most significant differences are at the desktop level of the two operating systems, not in the program itself. The book does assume that you are familiar with your operating system and can use its conventions to make selections, access menu options, and manage files.

✔ Tip

- In case you're wondering, Premiere shares its code with both platforms. This means that if you take a few precautions, you can easily transfer projects and most other related files between the Windows and Mac versions.

Minimum System Requirements

To use Premiere 6, your system must meet these minimum requirements.

Macintosh requirements

◆ Power PC processor

◆ Apple System software OS 8.1 or later (or 7.5.1 with Radius VideoVision only)

◆ 32 MB of application RAM

◆ 30 MB of available hard disk space required for installation

◆ CD-ROM drive

Recommended:

◆ Multi-processor system

◆ Apple QuickTime 4.0 or later (installed with Premiere)

◆ 48 MB or more of application RAM

◆ Large-capacity hard disk or disk array

◆ QuickTime-compatible video capture card

◆ 24-bit color display adapter

Windows 95, 98, and NT 4.0 requirements

◆ Intel Pentium-class processor (or 100% compatible)

◆ Microsoft Windows 95, Windows 98, or Windows NT 4.0

◆ 32 MB of RAM installed

◆ 60 MB of available hard disk space for installation (30 MB for application)

◆ 256-color video display adapter and compatible monitor

◆ CD-ROM drive

Recommended:

◆ Multi-processor system (Windows NT only)

◆ 64 MB or more of RAM (128 MB recommended)

◆ Large-capacity hard drive or hard disk array

◆ 24-bit color display adapter

◆ Microsoft Video for Windows-compatible or Apple QuickTime for Windows-compatible video capture card

◆ Apple QuickTime for Windows 4.0 or Microsoft DirectX Media 5.1 (optionally installed with Premiere), or other video software supported by video capture hardware

◆ Sound card (if your video capture card does not contain onboard sound circuitry)

Requirements for Built-In DV Support

If you plan to use Premiere 6 to edit video footage in the DV format, your system must meet these minimum requirements.

Macintosh requirements

◆ 300MHz PowerPC processor

◆ Apple FireWire 2.4 or later

◆ QuickTime-compatible FireWire (IEEE 1394) interface

◆ Large-capacity hard disk capable of sustaining 5 MB/second

Windows requirements

◆ 500MHz Pentium-class processor

◆ Windows 2000 Pro, Windows 98 Second Edition, or Windows Me

◆ Microsoft DirectX-compatible IEEE 1394 interface

◆ Large-capacity hard disk capable of sustaining 5 MB/second

Digital Video

Digital video is a generic term that can refer to any video signal stored in digital form. A digital signal can be stored on certain tape formats or on other digital storage devices, such as a computer hard drive. Video stored in analog formats (VHS, Hi8, or BetacamSP) can be *digitized*, or converted to a digital signal. A video capture device—usually, a *capture card* that you install in your computer—is required to make the conversion. Capture cards vary greatly in quality and price.

It's also possible to copy video from an analog format to a digital format. Many DV cameras have analog inputs that you can use to copy analog video to DV.

Suggested System

These features aren't required, but they can make working with Premiere a lot more satisfying.

Faster processor—The faster your system can make calculations, the faster it can process the frames of video and create effects.

Additional RAM—Like all programs, Premiere relies partly on RAM for performance and stability. In addition, the number of frames you can watch via the RAM preview feature (which allows you to render sequences containing transitions and effects quickly) depends entirely on the amount of RAM you can allocate to Premiere.

Larger hard drives—Video files are notoriously large. Five minutes of DV footage, for example, consumes more than a gigabyte of storage. Ample storage space allows you to work with more footage and with high-quality footage.

Faster hard drives—Your system's capability to play back footage smoothly relies partly on how quickly information can be read from the drives. Generally speaking, higher-quality footage requires faster drives. Drive arrays (RAIDs) use multiple drives to increase the overall transfer speed. To use DV footage, for example, your drives should sustain a data rate of around 5 MB per second.

24-bit displays—It almost goes without saying that it's best to work in Millions of Colors (Mac) or True Colors (Windows).

Larger or multiple displays—Premiere's interface can take up a lot of screen space. A large monitor can be more comfortable to work with. Many users like to spread out over two monitors, though others may find that arrangement to be overkill.

DV or Not DV

DV stands for *digital video* but actually refers to a specific type of signal that can be stored in certain formats. The introduction of DV in recent years has helped drive the desktop video revolution. Consumer DV cameras are not only affordable, but also capture remarkably high-quality images. Just as important, it's a simple matter to transfer footage from a DV camera to a computer for editing and effects.

You may encounter several flavors of DV. Though all these formats record the same type of DV signal, each records it in a slightly different way:

MiniDV—often called simply DV. It's the consumer version, used by the DV cameras offered by consumer electronics vendors.

DVCam—Sony's professional variation of DV. It records a DV signal at a different track pitch, which uses more tape and results in a more reliable signal. It's used by Sony's professional line of cameras and decks, which can also read miniDV.

DVCPro—Panasonic's professional variety, which records the signal at an even greater track pitch and uses a more durable metal particle tape. Panasonic's equipment also supports DVCPro50, which doubles the standard data rate to achieve better color reproduction and more detail.

As far as capturing video in Premiere is concerned, it doesn't matter which format you're using. But you should understand the difference when you're choosing other equipment, such as cameras, decks, and tapes. Though the essential DV signals are the same, the quality and cost of the equipment differs greatly, and it's not interchangeable.

Professional System Additions

Other additions can elevate your editing system to a more professional level:

Video capture/playback device—As you already know, your computer needs a FireWire or iLink connection (aka IEEE 1394 terminal) and a similarly equipped camera or deck if you want to capture and output video in the DV format. If you want to capture material from an analog source (VHS, Hi8, or BetacamSP), you may opt for an add-on capture card, such as a Targa card or Media100QX. You'll also need a deck to play and record tapes in your format of choice.

NTSC monitor—*NTSC monitor* is a fancy way of saying a really good video monitor, with professional inputs and excellent color reproduction. Video monitors and computer monitors display images differently, so if your work is destined for video or broadcast, a good NTSC monitor will allow you to judge it more accurately. A video capture device typically supports both your computer and video monitor. By the way, *NTSC* stands for the National Television Standards Committee, which develops the television standards used in North America and Japan; its name describes everything that meets those standards.

Third-party plug-ins—A multitude of third-party developers offer software plug-ins that expand Premiere's capabilities. These products can include improved or additional effects and transitions, audio effects, "matchback" tools to create EDLs for film, and tools that allow you to better evaluate the video signal.

Hardware acceleration—If rendering speed and turnaround time are of paramount importance, you may want to invest in a Premiere system bundled with hardware to accelerate effects rendering. Matrox and Pinnacle offer Premiere bundles that render common effects in real time.

System Configurations

As the preceding sections suggest, your Premiere setup can be simple or elaborate. As long as your computer meets the minimum requirements, you can simply install Premiere and start editing. On the other hand, your system might include a television monitor and a camera or deck. DV-based systems are increasingly popular. Here's how a few common configurations might look.

DV camera configuration (Figure i.4)—In this setup, a DV camera is used to transfer source video to your computer's hard drive via a IEEE 1394 terminal (aka FireWire or iLink). The completed edited project can be played back and recorded to a tape in the camera.

Analog capture configuration (Figure i.5.)—In this setup, the computer is equipped with a qualifying video capture card (such as a Targa 2000) to digitize video from an analog source (VHS, Hi8, or BetacamSP). The capture card converts the signal from analog to digital so that it can be stored on the hard drive.

Enhanced DV Configuration (Figure i.6)—In this setup, several recommended options have been added to the system. An external FireWire drive provides additional storage space for media; a dedicated playback and record deck reduces wear on the camera's tape transport; an NTSC monitor displays the program as it will appear on a television screen; and external speakers provide the audio.

✔ Tip

■ Looking for a complete system? Several vendors offer preconfigured editing systems. You may find their pricing and service agreements attractive. If not, you can at least see the equipment they select for their packages, which may help you put together your own.

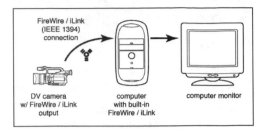

Figure i.4 This simple configuration includes a computer equipped with IEEE 1394 (FireWire or iLink) and a DV camera.

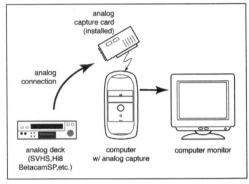

Figure i.5 This configuration includes a computer equipped with an Adobe-certified capture card and an analog video deck.

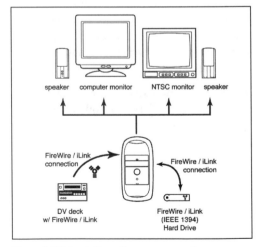

Figure i.6 This configuration uses several recommended options, such as a television monitor, speakers, external hard drive, and deck.

PREMIERE BASICS

Before embarking on a journey, it can be useful to survey the landscape and learn a few local customs. In this chapter, you'll get oriented to Premiere's interface, and catch a glimpse of what's to come. In addition, you'll learn a few things about the basic workings of the Premiere interface: how to use contextual menus, keyboard shortcuts, commands, and palettes (including Premiere's new History palette), and how to undo mistakes. Once you've familiarized yourself with this little "travel guide," you can get your passport stamped in Chapter 2.

PREMIERE BASICS

Taking a Look at the Interface

Rather than take a window-by-window, button-by-button approach, this book addresses each window and tool as dictated by the editing process. Nevertheless, an overview of the interface can help orient you before you take a closer look.

Most of your editing takes place in three primary windows, which leaves a little room for some helpful palettes as well (**Figure 1.1**).

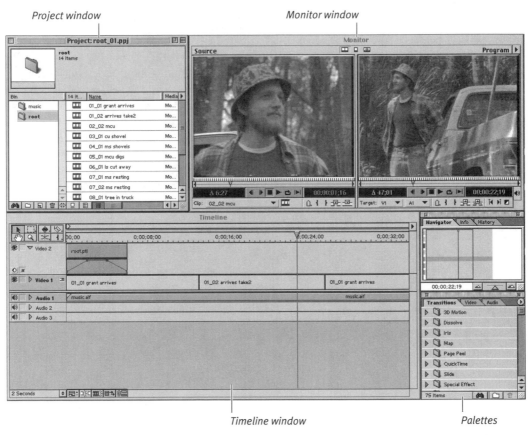

Figure 1.1 Most of your editing takes place in three primary windows, which leaves screen space for several helpful palettes.

Figure 1.2 The Monitor window doubles as the trimming window.

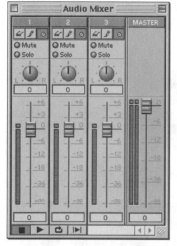

Figure 1.3 The new audio mixer emulates a traditional mixing board.

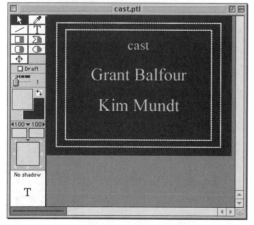

Figure 1.4 The title window lets you create text and graphics.

The *Project window* lists and organizes the source clips that you want to use. It displays important information about each clip; you can also use this information to sort the clips in the window.

The *Monitor window* displays the source clips in the left pane, or *source view*, and displays the clips in your program in the right pane, or *program view*. It also contains playback and editing controls, and it doubles as the trimming-mode window.

The *Timeline window* graphically represents your program as video and audio clips arranged in time. The timeline includes an assortment of editing tools that help you arrange and adjust the clips in the program.

Palettes—including Information, Navigator, Transitions, Effect Controls, History, and Commands—appear in tabbed windows and provide useful tool sets.

Glancing at Secondary Windows

As your project progresses, you'll call upon various other windows and features to fine-tune edits, mix audio, and add effects, as well as capture video, export edit decision lists, and compare video and audio settings.

The *trimming mode* is a mode of the Monitor window that provides special controls for fine-tuning in and out points (**Figure 1.2**). (See Chapter 7.)

The *audio mixer*, which emulates a traditional mixing board, allows you to fade and pan audio tracks in real time (**Figure 1.3**). (See Chapter 10.)

The *title window* allows you to create text and graphics for use in your program (**Figure 1.4**). (See Chapter 12.)

continues on next page

GLANCING AT SECONDARY WINDOWS

Though it was mentioned in the previous section, the new *Effect Controls* palette deserves special attention. Now, you can control effects in Premiere in much the same way as you do in Adobe After Effects (**Figure 1.5**).

The *Motion Settings dialog box* is an elaborate control center that provides extensive tools for animating a clip in two-dimensional space (**Figure 1.6**). (See Chapter 14.)

Another extensive dialog box, *Transparency Settings,* allows you to specify and adjust various keying effects, such as a chroma key or alpha key (**Figure 1.7**). (See Chapter 13.)

Figure 1.5 The new Effect Controls palette helps you view and adjust the effects you apply to clips in the program.

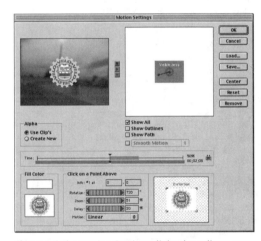

Figure 1.6 The Motion Settings dialog box allows you to animate clips.

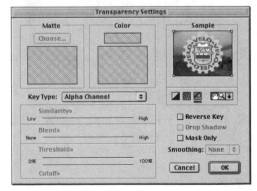

Figure 1.7 The Transparency Settings dialog box allows you to apply keying effects.

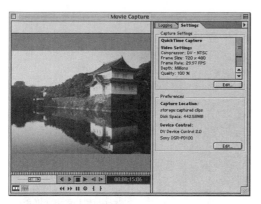

Figure 1.8 The enhanced Movie Capture window controls video capture.

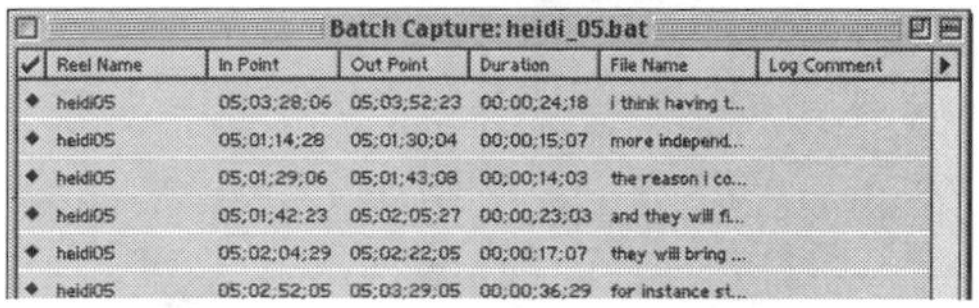

Figure 1.9 A batch list allows you to automate the capture process.

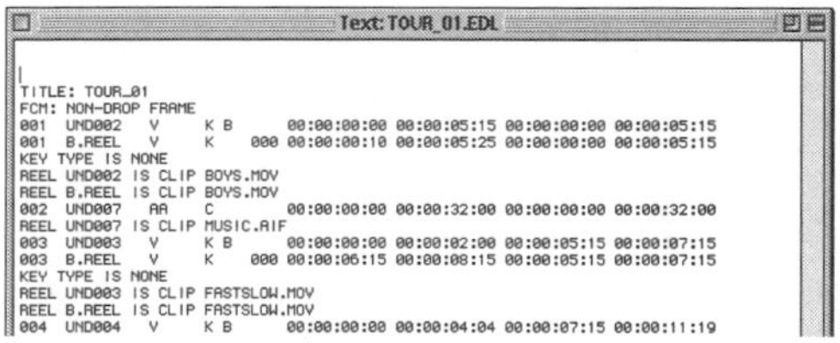

Figure 1.10 The edit decision list can be used by other systems to re-create the project in an online suite.

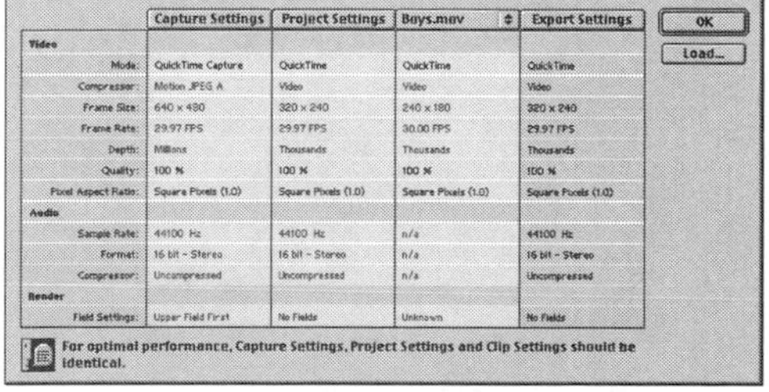

Figure 1.11 The Settings Viewer lets you compare settings.

The *Movie Capture window* controls the capture of video (**Figure 1.8**). (See Chapter 16.)

A couple of windows show useful lists. A *batch list* contains a list of timecode in and out points that can be used to automate the capture process (**Figure 1.9**). (See Chapter 17 for more about batch capture.) An *edit decision list* (or EDL) lists every editing event in the program, in terms of in and out points. Various online edit controllers can import the list directly (**Figure 1.10**). (See Chapter 15 for more about EDLs.)

Finally, the *Settings Viewer* displays capture, project, and export settings so that you can easily compare and evaluate them (**Figure 1.11**). (See Chapter 2.)

GLANCING AT SECONDARY WINDOWS

Using Palettes

Premiere 5 redesigned windows and palettes to use the screen space more efficiently. Premiere 6 refines and enhances the ways palettes work and organize information, particularly in the Commands, Effects, and Transitions palettes. The current version also introduces the History palette to Premiere. This section deals with the features common to all of Premiere's palettes. Individual palettes are discussed in more detail later.

You'll find that Premiere's palettes are consistent with those in other Adobe programs, such as Photoshop, Illustrator, and After Effects. As in other Adobe programs, you can group palettes or dock them so that they're attached to one another.

To display or hide windows and palettes:

◆ From the Window menu, choose the name of the window or palette that you want to display or hide (**Figure 1.12**).

To display a palette in a group:

◆ In the palette group, click the palette tab to make the palette visible in front of other palettes in that group (**Figure 1.13**).

Figure 1.12 Choose Window > and select a window to show or hide. Here, the Timeline window is highlighted.

Figure 1.13 Click a tab to bring the palette to the front.

Figure 1.14 Drag a palette to another group...

Figure 1.15 ...to make it part of the group.

Figure 1.16 Drag one palette to the bottom of another.

To move a palette to another group:

◆ Drag a palette tab to another group (**Figure 1.14**).

The palette tab appears in the same window as the group (**Figure 1.15**).

To dock palettes:

1. Drag a palette tab to the bottom of another palette.

2. When the bottom of the destination palette is highlighted, release the mouse button (**Figure 1.16**).

The two palettes connect and will move as one palette (**Figure 1.17**).

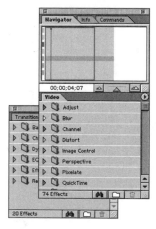

Figure 1.17 The dragged palette docks to the other palette.

To separate docked palettes:

◆ In a docked palette, drag a palette tab away from the other palettes (**Figure 1.18**).

The palette separates from the others (**Figure 1.19**).

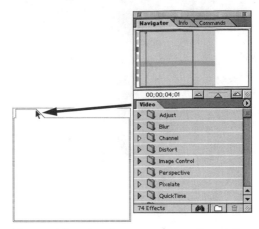

Figure 1.18 Drag the tab away to separate the palettes.

Figure 1.19 The palette is separated from the others.

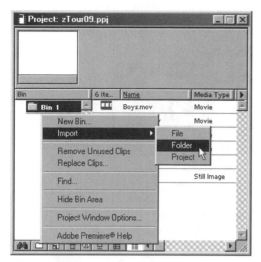

Figure 1.20 Ctrl -click (Mac) or right-click (Windows) to view a contextual menu that relates to the area you're clicking.

Using Contextual Menus

In addition to accessing commands from the menu bar at the top of the screen, you can use contextual menus. Though contextual menus are part of both Windows and Mac operating systems, not all Mac users are familiar with them.

As the name suggests, *contextual menus* can appear in a particular context or area of the screen. In other words, the contextual menu for a clip in the timeline contains commands that relate to clips in the timeline; the contextual menu for the bin panel of the Project window contains commands that relate to it, and so on. The contextual menus in Premiere 6 have been expanded to include a more complete set of commands.

To access a contextual menu:

1. Position the pointer on the appropriate window or item, and Ctrl -click (Mac) or right-click (Windows).

   A menu relating to the window or item appears (**Figure 1.20**).

2. Choose a command from the menu as you would from any other menu, and release the mouse button.

   Premiere executes the command.

✔ Tip

- Even the most loyal Mac users appreciate a two-button mouse when using the Ctrl key is inconvenient. If you've never used a PC-style mouse, the left button works like the single button on a Mac mouse. Clicking the right button accesses contextual menus (just as if you Ctrl -clicked with a Mac mouse). The right button also opens contextual menus in other menus and on the Finder level.

USING CONTEXTUAL MENUS

Using Keyboard Shortcuts

One way to increase your speed and efficiency is to take advantage of keyboard shortcuts. In this book, I mention the most commonly used keyboard shortcuts, but you may want to expand your repertoire. If the Quick Reference Card that comes with Premiere isn't handy, you can view the keyboard shortcuts by using the Help menu. If you activate the Tool Tips feature, positioning the pointer over a tool or button will reveal its name and shortcut.

To view the keyboard shortcuts:

1. Choose Help > Keyboard Shortcuts (Macintosh) or Help > Keyboard (Windows) (**Figure 1.21**).

   Premiere launches your browser and opens the Help feature (**Figure 1.22**).

   To find a keyboard shortcut, click a topic to view shortcuts in that category, or type a keyword to find a shortcut.

2. Exit the Help feature.

Figure 1.21 Choose Help > Keyboard Shortcuts.

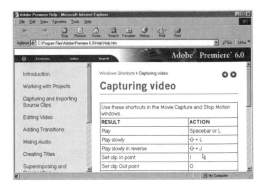

Figure 1.22 The Help feature launches in a browser window.

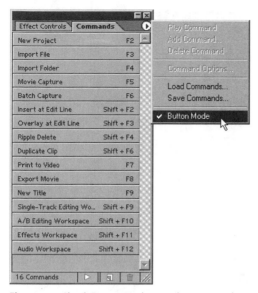

Figure 1.23 Check Button Mode to make commands operate as buttons; uncheck it to make them appear as a selectable list.

Using the Commands Palette

In addition to using keyboard shortcuts, you can save time by using the Commands palette. This palette can spare you from hunting down a command buried in sub-menus and permits you to create custom shortcuts.

Premiere 6 sports an enhanced Commands palette, which is more consistent with that palette in other Adobe programs. You can create and save sets of commands for different phases of editing and load the set as needed.

The commands in the palette work like buttons when the palette is set to button mode. When button mode is inactive, you can also add, delete, and modify commands in the palette.

To toggle button mode:

1. If the Commands palette is not visible, click the Commands tab in a grouped palette or choose Window > Show Commands.

   The Commands palette appears, and is selected.

2. In the palette menu, choose Button Mode to toggle button mode on and off (**Figure 1.23**).

   Checking Button Mode makes commands appear as buttons; unchecking it makes them appear as a selectable list and makes other palette-menu options available.

To use a command:

1. If the Commands palette is not visible, click the Commands tab in a grouped palette or choose Window > Show Commands.

2. *Do any of the following:*

   ▲ When button mode is active, click a command (**Figure 1.24**).

   ▲ When button mode is inactive, select a command and then click the Play button  (**Figure 1.25**).

   ▲ Press the keyboard equivalent listed next to the command in the palette.

   Premiere executes the command.

To create a command button:

1. If the Commands palette is not visible, click the Commands tab in a grouped palette or choose Window > Show Commands.

2. In the palette menu, choose Button Mode to uncheck it (**Figure 1.26**).

   The commands no longer appear as buttons.

Figure 1.24 In button mode, simply click a command button.

Figure 1.25 When button mode is off, select a command and click the play button.

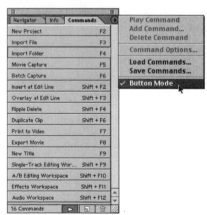

Figure 1.26 Turn off button mode, by unchecking Button Mode.

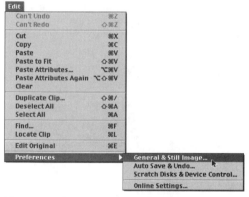

Figure 1.27 Click the Add Command button.

Figure 1.28 Choose a command from the main menu bar.

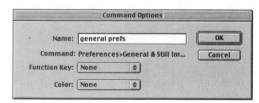

Figure 1.29 The command appears in the Command Options dialog box.

3. In the Commands palette, click the Add Command button [icon] (**Figure 1.27**).

The Command Options dialog box appears.

4. In the Name field, enter a name for the new command.

5. From the main menu bar, choose the command that you want to save for the new command button (**Figure 1.28**).

The command you selected appears in the Command Options dialog box (**Figure 1.29**).

continues on next page

6. To assign a keyboard shortcut for the new command button, choose an available shortcut from the Function Key pull-down menu (**Figure 1.30**).

7. To assign a color to the button, choose a color from the Color pull-down menu (**Figure 1.31**).

8. Click OK to close the Command Options dialog box and create the button.

The new command appears in the Commands palette.

9. In the palette menu, choose Button Mode.

Commands in the palette appear as buttons.

To delete a command button:

1. If the Commands palette is not visible, click the Commands tab in a grouped palette or choose Window > Show Commands.

2. In the palette menu, choose Button Mode to uncheck it.

The commands no longer appear as buttons.

3. In the Commands palette, select a command.

4. Click the delete button (**Figure 1.32**).

The selected command is removed from the list (**Figure 1.33**).

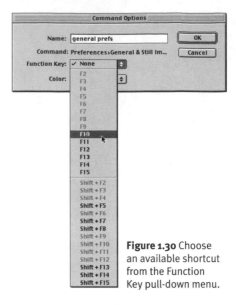

Figure 1.30 Choose an available shortcut from the Function Key pull-down menu.

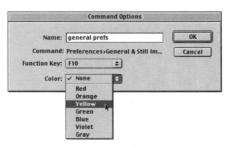

Figure 1.31 Use the Color pull-down menu to assign a color to the button in the palette.

Figure 1.32 Select a command and click the delete button...

Figure 1.33 ...to remove the command.

To save a command set:

1. In the palette menu, choose Save Commands (**Figure 1.34**).

   The Save Commands dialog box appears.

2. Specify a name and destination for the saved set (**Figure 1.35**).

3. Click Save.

To load a command set:

1. In the palette menu, choose Load Commands.

   The Load Commands dialog box appears.

2. Locate and select a saved command set.

3. Click Open.

   The loaded command set becomes the current command set in the palette.

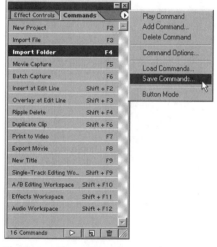

Figure 1.34 Choose Save Commands.

Figure 1.35 In the Save Commands dialog box, specify a name and destination for the saved set.

Correcting Mistakes

Many people judge a program not only by how much it can do, but also by how much it can undo. Premiere allows up to 99 levels of undo. In other words, you can negate up to 99 of your most recent actions. If you change your mind yet again, you can redo the last undone action.

Premiere 6 introduces a History palette, which lists your recent actions, so it's easier to choose exactly how many steps back you'd like to take. This new feature is covered in the following section.

When undoing can't solve the problem, you may want to revert to the last saved version of the project or open an archived version.

To undo an action:

◆ Choose Edit > Undo (**Figure 1.36**), or press ⌘-Z (Mac) or Ctrl-Z (Windows).

If the last action can't be undone, the menu displays the grayed entry Can't Undo.

To redo an action:

◆ Choose Edit > Redo (**Figure 1.37**), or press Shift-⌘-Z (Mac) or Shift-Ctrl-Z (Windows).

If the last action can't be redone, the menu displays the grayed entry Can't Redo.

Figure 1.36 Choose Edit > Undo to negate the preceding action.

Figure 1.37 Choose Edit > Redo to restore an undone action.

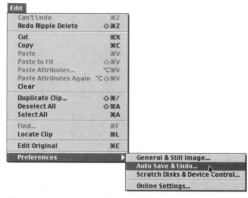

Figure 1.38 Choose Edit > Preferences > Auto Save & Undo.

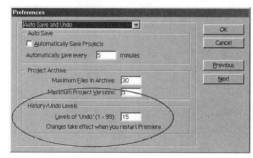

Figure 1.39 The Auto Save and Undo panel of the Preferences dialog box appears.

To set the levels of undo:

1. Choose Edit > Preferences > Auto Save & Undo (**Figure 1.38**).

    The Auto Save and Undo panel of the Preferences dialog box appears (**Figure 1.39**).

2. In the History Undo Levels section of the dialog box, enter the number for Levels of Undo.

3. Click OK to close the Preferences dialog box.

4. If necessary, save the current project, quit, and then restart Premiere to make the changes take effect.

Using the History Palette

If you're familiar with Adobe's other programs, you know that the History palette is like a super-undo, or a time machine. The History palette lists your recent actions; each new action is added to the bottom of the list. By looking at the list, you can see exactly what you did—and exactly where you went wrong. Clicking an action negates all the subsequent actions listed below. You can even negate particular events in the list. When you resume editing, the undone actions are removed from the list, and history is rewritten.

To use the History palette:

1. In a grouped palette, click the History tab to make the History palette visible.

   The palette lists the most recent actions, with the most recent action at the bottom of the list (**Figure 1.40**).

2. Click the last action you want to retain (**Figure 1.41**).

   Actions below the selected action become dimmed in the list. The project reverts to the state it was in at the time the selected action was taken. You can reselect different items.

3. If you are satisfied with your choice, resume other editing tasks.

   The dimmed actions disappear (**Figure 1.42**), and subsequent actions are added to the list.

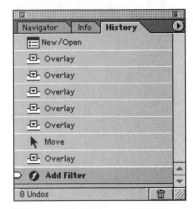

Figure 1.40 The History palette lists actions, the most recent at the bottom.

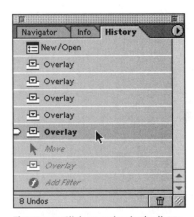

Figure 1.41 Click an action in the list to return the project to the state it was in at that time.

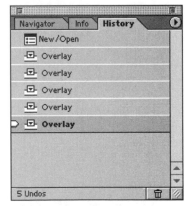

Figure 1.42 In the History palette, the dimmed actions disappear.

USING THE HISTORY PALETTE

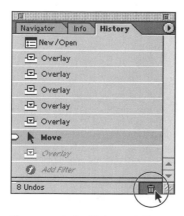

Figure 1.43 In the History palette, select an action and (Option)-click (Mac) or (Alt)-click (Windows) the delete button to undo that action.

To delete a particular action:

1. In the History palette, select an action in the list.

2. *Do one of the following:*

   ▲ (Option)-click (Mac) or (Alt)-click (Windows) the delete button 🗑 (**Figure 1.43**).

   ▲ Click the delete button 🗑 and then click Yes.

   ▲ From the palette menu, choose Delete.

   The action is removed from the list and is undone in the project.

✔ Tips

■ The History palette doesn't list every move you make, just actions that affect the project itself.

■ Selecting Revert eliminates all the states listed in the History palette since the project was last saved.

USING THE HISTORY PALETTE

STARTING
A PROJECT

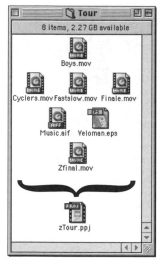

Figure 2.1 A project file is a detailed set of instructions that refers to—but doesn't contain—source files. Your hard drive must contain both the project (a small file) and the source files to which it refers (larger files).

When you're editing with Adobe Premiere, you're creating a detailed set of instructions, called a *project* (**Figure 2.1**).

A project lists all the clips that you intend to use in your edited video program. It also contains all your editing decisions, including the arrangement of the clips, transitions, audio levels, and effects.

You can compare a project with a recipe or a musical score. Just as sheet music refers to instruments and indicates when they should play, the project refers to media files and when they should play. A project doesn't contain the files themselves—only references to those files, called *clips*. As a result, you never alter the source files directly. Hence, editing in Premiere is sometimes referred to as *nondestructive editing*.

Because it is simply a detailed set of instructions, a project is a small file, often less than 1 MB. The source files, on the other hand, tend to take up a lot more drive space. In terms of our metaphor, you can slip sheet music into your pocket, but the actual orchestra is considerably more bulky.

In this chapter, you learn to start a new project, choose audio and video settings, and import a variety of source files as clips.

Selecting an Initial Workspace

When you launch Premiere for the first time, the first thing you see after the splash screen is the Initial Workspace dialog box (**Figure 2.2**). This screen prompts you to choose between A/B Editing and Single-Track Editing. If you're not already familiar with these terms, you may find the text in the dialog box less than illuminating. The message that does come across is that new users should choose A/B editing, and more experienced editors should use single-track editing. Though this advice serves as an adequate rule of thumb, more information will help you make an informed choice. Read on.

The workspace you choose determines how Premiere depicts the program in the Timeline window. Though both layouts can achieve similar results, each one represents a different editing style—particularly when it comes to transitions.

In the A/B roll layout, transitions (such as dissolves and wipes) are represented in three tracks of the timeline: an A track, a B track, and a transitions track (**Figure 2.3**). This layout visually portrays a traditional A/B-roll editing suite. As you learned in the introduction, a traditional A/B roll suite creates dissolves and wipes by playing two source tapes (A and B) simultaneously, and creates transitions between the two via a video switcher. The tracks in the A/B workspace correspond to this editing model: Clips playing at the same time overlap in the timeline, and a transition acts as the switcher.

As the Initial Workspace dialog box suggests, the A/B layout is easy to understand visually, because all the footage involved in the transition is visible in the timeline.

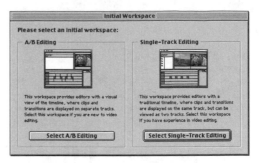

Figure 2.2 The first time you launch Premiere, you must choose an initial workspace, according to the style of editing you prefer.

Video Track 1A

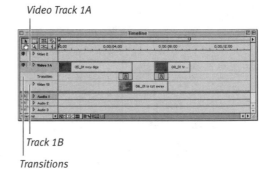

Track 1B

Transitions

Figure 2.3 In the A/B editing workspace, you view and edit transitions in three tracks of the timeline: video A, video B, and a transitions track.

Figure 2.4 In the single-track editing workspace, you view and edit transitions in a single track of the timeline.

Figure 2.5 You can expand the single-track editing workspace to resemble the A/B format for viewing purposes.

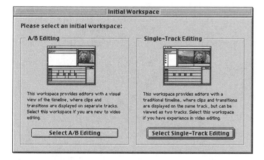

Figure 2.6 When you launch the program for the first time, you must choose your preferred editing method in the Initial Workspace dialog box.

In a single-track editing workspace, you apply transitions between clips in a single track (**Figure 2.4**). The frames that overlap in the A/B view are not visible in a single-track view. Because the frames that are being used to create the transition don't appear in the timeline, it can be more difficult to understand how to define a transition, how to plan for it, and how to adjust it.

You should understand how both methods work, but single-track editing offers several practical advantages over A/B editing. I favor single-track editing, and this book focuses mainly on the single-track editing workspace. But if you're not yet feeling like an expert, don't worry: The single-track editing workspace also has a track mode feature, which lets you view (although not edit) your project in an A/B roll format (**Figure 2.5**). That way, you can edit like the pros and still sneak a peek at an A/B-style representation.

For more about using transitions, see Chapter 8.

To specify an initial workspace:

1. Launch Premiere for the first time (or after having deleted the Preferences file).

   After the program launches, the Initial Workspace dialog box appears (**Figure 2.6**).

2. In the Initial Workspace dialog box, select an option:

   A/B Editing—The Video 1 track includes A, B, and transition tracks.

   Single-Track Editing—Clips and transitions are added to a single Video 1 track.

   The dialog box closes, and Premiere opens. The workspace you selected becomes the default, and you will not be prompted to choose an initial workspace again unless you throw away Premiere's Preferences file.

To change the current workspace:

◆ With Premiere running, choose
Window > Workspace > and then choose
an option:

A/B Editing—The Video 1 track
includes A, B, and transition tracks.

Single-Track Editing—Clips and transitions are added to a single Video 1 track.

The workspace changes according to
your selection. You may also choose other
workspace options, which are optimized
for audio and effects editing. (See
Chapter 10 for more information about
audio editing; see Chapter 11 for more
about effects editing).

✔ Tips

■ You select and use workspaces differently
in Premiere 6 than you did in Premiere 5.
But even though tracks work slightly differently in Premiere 6, the principles of
A/B and single-track editing remain
the same.

■ When you launch a program for the first
time, it creates a file in the Preferences
folder inside the System folder. At times,
the Preferences file becomes corrupted,
causing the program to malfunction.
Deleting the Preferences file forces the
program to create a new, uncorrupted file.
If you delete Premiere's Preferences file,
you'll have to reset the initial workspace.

Figure 2.7
If the program is already running, choose File ›
New Project.

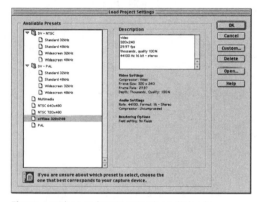

Figure 2.8 The Load Project Settings dialog box appears.

Starting a New Project

You can start a new project either when you launch Premiere or after Premiere is running. You can have only one project open at a time, however.

Unless you delete the Preferences file, you have to set the initial workspace only when you launch Premiere for the first time. Thereafter, the window that appears when you open Premiere depends on the preference you set. By default, Premiere opens a dialog box for you to choose audio and video settings. But you can set Premiere to start with an open dialog box or a new project, or simply to start without initiating anything.

The following task outlines how to start a project without detailing specific settings. Later sections explain how to set the default startup window and how to choose audio and video settings.

To start a new project:

1. *Do either of the following:*

   ▲ Double-click the Premiere icon or its alias to launch the program.

   or

   ▲ With Premiere running, choose File > New Project (**Figure 2.7**).

   The Load Project Settings dialog box opens (**Figure 2.8**).

2. In the Available Presets section, select the name of the preset that is most appropriate for your project.

   A description of the preset's audio and video settings appears on the right side of the dialog box.

   continues on next page

STARTING A NEW PROJECT

3. Click OK.

An untitled Project window opens, as well as several associated windows, such as the Monitor window and Timeline window. The layout (**Figure 2.9**) reflects the choice of initial workspace that you made earlier. (See "Selecting an Initial Workspace" earlier in this chapter.)

To launch Premiere without starting a new project:

1. Double-click the Premiere icon or its alias.

The Load Project Settings dialog box appears.

2. Click Cancel.

Premiere starts without opening a project. From this point, you can open a new or existing project, or use one of Premiere's features that doesn't require an open project.

✔ Tips

■ You don't have to open a project to capture clips, open and view clips, get properties for a clip, use the Data Rate Analyzer, or batch-process clips.

■ You can have only one project open at a time. If you start a new project without saving the current project, Premiere prompts you to save the current project.

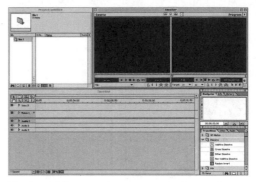

Figure 2.9 When you choose preset project settings, a new project and its associated windows appear.

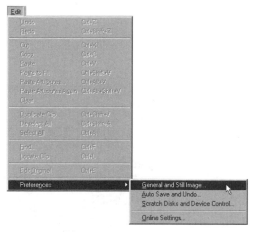

Figure 2.10 Choose Edit > Preferences > General and Still Image.

Figure 2.11 The General and Still Image panel of the Preferences dialog box appears.

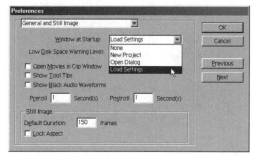

Figure 2.12 Choose an option from the Window at Startup pull-down menu.

Setting the Startup Screen

You can set the screen that opens when you launch Premiere. You can have the program prompt you to set new project settings, open an existing project, or load saved project settings.

On the other hand, you can have Premiere start up without initiating a project. You might choose this option if you don't have a standard procedure or if you frequently use features that don't require an open project, such as title creation or batch capture.

To set the default screen for startup:

1. Choose Edit > Preferences > General and Still Image (**Figure 2.10**).

   The General and Still Image panel of the Preferences dialog box appears (**Figure 2.11**).

2. From the Window at Startup pull-down menu, choose an option (**Figure 2.12**):

   None—opens Premiere without initiating a project.

   New Project—opens the Project Settings dialog box, where you can create and save new project settings.

   Open Dialog—opens the Open File dialog box, where you can select a project or other file.

   Load Settings (the default)—opens the Load Project Settings dialog box, where you can select preset project settings.

3. Click OK to close the dialog box.

   The next time you launch Premiere, it opens the window you specified.

Specifying Project Settings

Project settings determine how Premiere processes the audio and video as you edit your program. You can choose built-in preset settings, which are optimized for several common scenarios, such as editing video in the DV format, or you can create custom settings to fit your particular needs.

Generally, you want to use project settings that allow you to edit and view your work quickly and easily, and to prevent undue processing time. Your choices are based partly on your source material and partly on your computer's ability to process and play back video and audio.

Usually, the project settings match the settings of the source video. If you're editing DV footage, for example, your project settings should match DV's video and audio characteristics. If your system uses a capture card, your project settings should match the settings supported by your particular card. You can set the project to play back at a relatively low quality, however, so that your computer can process edits and effects faster.

In addition to your source material, consider your output goal. If you plan to record the program to videotape directly from the timeline, specify settings that match or exceed the output quality you want.

The following sections first explain how to select a built-in preset and then explain each of the video and audio settings in more detail. This chapter also introduces you to the Settings Viewer, which makes it easy to compare the capture, project, and export settings.

✔ Tips

- Because you must deal with video and audio settings at every step in the editing process, the final chapter of this book consolidates an explanation of video and audio settings. Consult it whenever you need additional information about a setting.

- Various video and audio settings control characteristics such as frame size, frame rate, compression, and audio quality. You must select video and audio settings at each major phase of the editing process: capturing video, editing the program, and exporting the project. *Pay special attention to how the settings you choose at each phase interact with the others*. DV-based projects are easy: if you want to shoot, edit, and export DV format video, your capture, project, and export settings will all match.

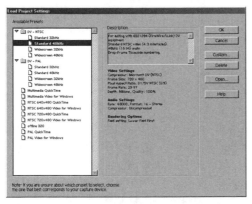

Figure 2.13 The Load Project Settings dialog box presents a choice of built-in or custom-made project presets.

Choosing Built-In Presets

By default, launching Premiere opens the Load Project Settings dialog box. Starting a new project also opens the Load Project Settings dialog box. This dialog box allows you to make choices from a list of preset project settings (**Figure 2.13**). You can also access controls to create and save a custom preset; that topic is covered in later sections of this chapter.

The right side of the Load Project Settings dialog box lists preset project settings that you can use. When you select a preset from the list, a description of the settings appears on the left side of the dialog box. The built-in presets include project settings optimized for using common types of source footage, particularly DV:

DV – NTSC folder—contains presets for DV footage shot in NTSC, the video standard used in North America, Japan, and other countries.

DV – PAL folder—contains presets for DV footage shot in PAL, the standard in most of Europe.

These folders each contain the following four options:

Standard 32kHz—for DV footage shot in television's standard 4:3 aspect ratio, using 32kHz audio, one of two audio sample rates supported by most DV cameras.

Standard 48kHz—for DV footage shot in television's standard 4:3 aspect ratio, using 48kHz audio.

Widescreen 32kHz—for DV footage shot in a 16:9 aspect ratio, which is supported by some DV cameras and equipment, using 32kHz audio.

continues on next page

Widescreen 48kHz—for DV footage shot in a 16:9 aspect ratio, which is supported by some DV cameras and equipment, using 48kHz audio.

The other non-DV-based presets don't directly correspond to a particular standard and may not be as useful. Learn about each video and audio setting to determine whether one of these presets is appropriate for your project. In any case, they can be useful as general guidelines for creating your own preset.

To select a built-in preset:

1. To open the Load Project Settings dialog box, choose File > New Project, or press ⌘-N (Mac) or Ctrl-N (Windows) (**Figure 2.14**).

   The Load Project Settings dialog box appears.

2. In the Available Presets section, click a preset to select it (**Figure 2.15**).

   A description of the preset appears in the Description section of the dialog box. To open and close a folder in the list, click the triangle next to the folder.

3. Click OK to use the setting and start a project.

✔ Tip

■ If you're not sure whether your DV footage was shot with 32kHz or 48kHz audio, check your camera's documentation, or analyze the clip with Premiere's Properties feature (see "Viewing Clip Properties," in Chapter 3). QuickTime Pro can also tell you a clip's audio sample rate.

Figure 2.14
Choose File > New Project or press ⌘-N (Mac) or Ctrl-N (Windows).

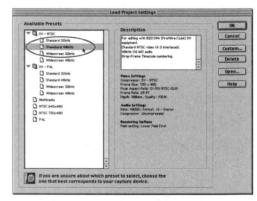

Figure 2.15 Click a preset to select it. A detailed description of the settings appears in the Description area.

Selecting Custom Project Settings

This chapter deals with the settings that determine how Premiere processes clips while you edit. Other settings control the attributes of captured clips (see Chapter 16) and the final rendered movie (see Chapter 15). In other words, the project settings do not affect the qualities of the source clips or an exported movie file.

You specify project settings in the Project Settings dialog box (Macintosh) or New Project Settings dialog box (Windows). (For the sake of brevity, I'll just refer to this as the Project Settings dialog box in the following pages.) You can set Premiere to open this dialog box when you launch the program, or you can access it from the Load Project Settings dialog box.

At the top of the Project Settings dialog box is a pull-down menu that allows you to view the five categories of settings: General, Video, Audio, Keyframe and Rendering, and Capture. This chapter deals with the first four categories, leaving capture settings for Chapter 16.

If you're new to digital video, the number of options can be daunting at first. Don't worry; making a choice is not as hard as it looks. And even if you make a wrong choice or change your mind, you can change the settings at any time. This chapter provides enough information to keep you moving; for more complete explanations of each setting, consult Chapter 18.

To open the Project Settings dialog box:

1. *Do either of the following:*

▲ In the Load Project Settings dialog box, click Custom (**Figure 2.16**).

or

▲ While Premiere is running, choose Project > Project Settings > General (**Figure 2.17**).

The General panel of the Project Settings dialog box opens (**Figure 2.18**).

In the Current Settings section of the General panel, you can view a summary of the current settings.

2. To view and adjust other project settings, *do one of the following:*

▲ Choose a settings category from the pull-down menu at the top of the dialog box (**Figure 2.19**).

▲ Click Next to see the next settings category.

▲ Click Previous to see the previous settings category.

3. If you are satisfied with your settings, *do either of the following:*

▲ Click OK to close the dialog box and begin a new project.

or

▲ Click Save to save the current settings as a preset (explained in "Saving Custom Settings as a Preset" later in this chapter.)

✔ Tips

■ You can also use the Project > Project Settings menu to access any of the other panels of the Project Settings dialog box, such as Video or Audio.

■ If you've decided that one of the built-in presets works for you, you can skip the following sections on settings and get right to editing.

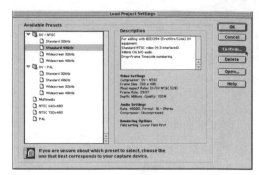

Figure 2.16 To create custom settings, you can click Custom in the Load Project Settings dialog box...

Figure 2.17 ...or choose Project > Project Settings > General.

Figure 2.18 The Project Settings dialog box appears.

Figure 2.19 Use the pull-down menu at the top of the dialog box, or click the Next and Previous buttons to view each setting category. When you finish specifying settings, click OK.

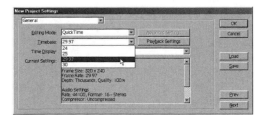

Figure 2.20 Choose how frames are calculated by choosing an option from the Timebase pull-down menu.

Specifying General Settings

The general settings dictate the basic properties of the program, including the way that Premiere processes video, the timebase, the time count, and advanced settings provided by third-party manufacturers. The General settings panel also displays a summary of the current settings.

To specify general settings:

1. *Do either of the following:*
   ▲ In the Project Settings dialog box, choose General from the top pull-down menu.

   or

   ▲ Choose Project > Project Settings > General.

   The Project Settings dialog box displays the General settings.

2. From the Editing Mode pull-down menu, choose a video format (or *architecture*). The most common formats include:

   QuickTime—the movie-playing format available for both the Mac and Windows platforms.

   Video for Windows—the movie-playing format available only for the Windows platform.

3. From the Timebase pull-down menu, choose an option that specifies how the project calculates video frames (**Figure 2.20**):

   24—Film frame rate

   25—PAL video frame rate

   29.97—True NTSC frame rate, intended for television

   30—Full-motion video not intended for television

   continues on next page

4. From the Time Display pull-down menu, choose an option that specifies how Premiere displays the frame count (**Figure 2.21**):

24 fps Timecode—standard film.

25 fps Timecode—PAL video.

30 fps Drop-Frame Timecode—NTSC video using drop-frame timecode, used by standard DV.

30 fps Non Drop-Frame Timecode—NTSC video using non-drop-frame timecode.

Frames/Samples—video frames and audio samples, useful in audio editing.

Feet + Frames 16mm—16mm film, which is 40 frames per foot.

Feet + Frames 35mm—35mm film, which is 16 frames per foot.

5. If you are using third-party hardware, such as a capture card, click the Advanced Settings button.

Your options are determined by your hardware.

6. If available, click Playback Settings to access a dialog box to set up an output device and specify other playback options (**Figure 2.22**).

This button is available if you have installed plug-ins that provide additional playback options. Consult the manufacturer's documentation to set up these options.

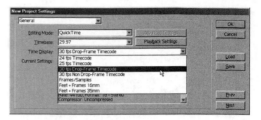

Figure 2.21 Choose how Premiere displays the frame count in the Time Display pull-down menu.

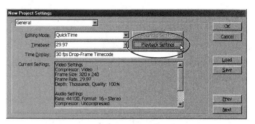

Figure 2.22 Click Advanced Settings to access hardware-specific options; click Playback Settings if you're using plug-ins that provide additional playback options.

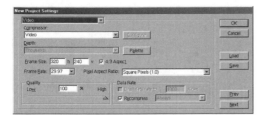

Figure 2.23 The Video panel of the Project Settings dialog box determines how the program processes video.

Figure 2.24 To set the video compression scheme used to process the program's video, choose an option from the Compressor pull-down menu.

Specifying Video Settings

Video settings determine the video compression scheme (or *codec*), amount of compression, color depth, and frame size of the program that you play back. In most cases, choose the settings that match your source video footage.

This section explains video settings in two parts. The first task covers only the essential video settings, which must be specified for any editing project. The second task covers settings that pertain to manipulating compression and color depth. For most programs, adjusting the latter settings isn't necessary. These settings become more useful when you export your program.

To specify video settings:

1. *Do either of the following:*

   ▲ In the Project Settings dialog box, choose Video Settings from the top pull-down menu.

   or

   ▲ Choose Project > Settings > Video.

   The Project Settings dialog box displays the video settings (**Figure 2.23**).

2. Choose a codec from the Compressor pull-down menu (**Figure 2.24**).

   Generally, the codec that matches your video footage is the best choice. If you have a hardware capture card, consult the documentation included with the card to select the codec designed for use with your card. For more detailed descriptions of the available codecs, see Chapter 18.

   continues on next page

3. Choose the color bit depth from the Depth pull-down menu.

256—8-bit color, results in a limited and grainy-looking color range.

Thousands—16-bit color, suitable for some mulitmedia.

Millions—24-bit color, results in the best image quality.

Millions +—32-bit color, preserves transparency information in an alpha channel.

For most projects, Millions is appropriate.

4. For Frame Size, type the pixel height and width of the video frame (**Figure 2.25**).

In most cases, choose the frame size that matches your source video.

5. From the Pixel Aspect Ratio pull-down menu, choose the pixel aspect ratio that matches your source video.

The most common settings include:

Square Pixels (1.0)—for video captured with lower-end capture cards.

D1/DV NTSC (0.9)—for standard DV footage or footage captured with higher-end capture cards.

6. From the Frame Rate pull-down menu, choose the rate at which the project will play back, in frames per second (**Figure 2.26**).

In most cases, choose the frame rate that matches your source footage.

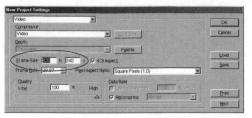

Figure 2.25 In the Frame Size fields, enter the dimensions of the project video. Set the pixel aspect ratio that matches your source footage in the Pixel Aspect Ratio pull-down menu. Enter the dimensions of the project video in the Frame Size fields.

Figure 2.26 In most cases, choose the frame rate that matches your source footage from the Frame Rate pull-down menu.

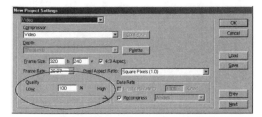

Figure 2.27 You can adjust the quality of the image in percentage increments or by using the slider.

To specify other video settings:

1. In the Video panel of the Project Settings dialog box, click Palette to make or load a color palette.

   Palettes are useful for exporting movies with a limited number of colors for multimedia applications. Ignore this setting for a typical video project.

2. To set the amount of compression, *do either of the following:*

   ▲ In the Quality field, type an image quality for the specified compressor.

   or

   ▲ Use the Quality slider to set the image quality (**Figure 2.27**).

   This setting is most useful for exporting a movie file.

3. To limit the video data rate, check the Limit Data Rate To checkbox, if available, and type the upper limit of the rate of data transfer, expressed in kilobytes per second.

   If you choose to limit the data rate, check the Recompress checkbox to ensure that Premiere processes previews at or under the specified rate; then, from the pull-down menu, choose one of the following options:

   Always—recompresses frames, even if they are already under the specified limit.

   Maintain Data Rate—recompresses only frames that are above the specified limit.

SPECIFYING VIDEO SETTINGS

Specifying Audio Settings

Audio settings control the attributes of the audio that the program plays back. When you choose Audio in the Project Settings dialog box, you can select a data rate, format, type of audio codec, audio interleave, and processing options. Again, it's usually a good idea to match your source audio's settings. When your source audio files differ, choose the audio quality based on your output goal.

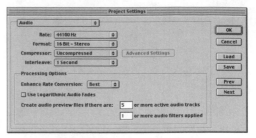

Figure 2.28 The Audio panel of the Project Settings dialog box determines the properties of the audio in your project.

To specify audio settings:

1. *Do either of the following:*

   ▲ In the Project Settings dialog box, choose Audio from the top pull-down menu.

   or

   ▲ Choose Project > Settings > Audio.

   The Project Settings dialog box displays the audio settings (**Figure 2.28**).

2. From the Rate pull-down menu, choose an audio sample rate.

   The most common settings include:

   32000 Hz—equivalent to one of the sample rates recorded by most DV cameras.

   44100 Hz—equivalent to the sample rate used by CD audio.

   48000 Hz—equivalent to one of the sample rates used by many DV cameras.

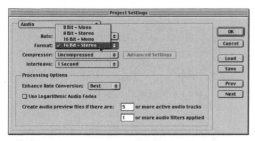

Figure 2.29 From the Format pull-down menu, choose a bit rate and format for your project's audio.

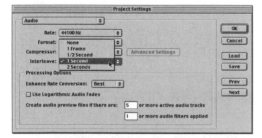

Figure 2.30 For most purposes, 1 Second is the most appropriate option in the Interleave pull-down menu.

3. Specify the audio's bit depth and format by choosing the appropriate option from the Format pull-down menu (**Figure 2.29**).

   8 Bit – Mono—produces a reduced dynamic range with a single channel.

   8 Bit – Stereo—produces a reduced dynamic range with separate right and left channels.

   16 Bit – Mono—produces the greatest dynamic range with a single channel.

   16 Bit – Stereo—produces the greatest dynamic range with separate right and left channels.

4. From the Compressor pull-down menu, choose an audio codec.

   In most cases, leave this menu set to Uncompressed. Audio Compression and Advanced options are most useful for exporting a movie file. For an explanation of each codec, see Chapter 18.

5. From the Interleave pull-down menu, choose a method of inserting the audio information among video frames (**Figure 2.30**).

   1 Second is appropriate in most cases. (For an explanation, see "Enhanced Rate Conversion and Audio Interleave," in Chapter 18.)

To specify audio processing options:

1. In the Audio panel of the Project Settings dialog box, specify how you want Premiere to convert the audio source's sample rate to the sample rate that you specified in the project settings by choosing an option from the Enhance Rate Conversion pull-down menu (**Figure 2.31**):

   Off—doesn't use enhanced methods for converting sample rates.

   Good—uses a better, but slower, method for converting sample rates.

   Best—uses the best, but slowest, method for converting sample rates.

2. To process audio gain levels by using a logarithmic scale, check the Use Logarithmic Audio Fades checkbox (**Figure 2.32**).

   Logarithmic fades more closely simulate how the human ear perceives audio gain increases and decreases, but take longer to process.

3. To specify when Premiere creates audio preview files, enter values for the following (**Figure 2.33**):

   ▲ The number of active audio tracks required before an audio preview is created

   ▲ The number of audio filters required before an audio preview is created

   See Chapter 9 for more about previewing video and audio.

Figure 2.31 In the Enhance Rate Conversion pull-down menu, you can specify how your project conforms the audio sample rates of source audio with the project's sample rate.

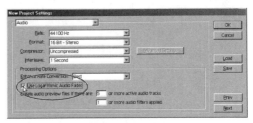

Figure 2.32 Check Use Logarithmic Audio Fades to make Premiere process audio fades using a logarithmic scale.

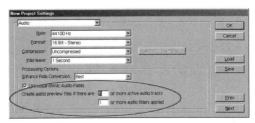

Figure 2.33 Enter values to set when Premiere creates audio preview files.

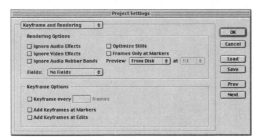

Figure 2.34 The Keyframe and Rendering panel includes options that determine how Premiere renders preview files and compresses video. At this point, pay special attention to the rendering options.

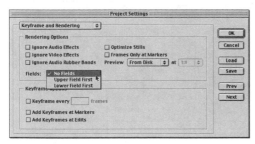

Figure 2.35 Specify how video fields are processed by making a choice from the Fields pull-down menu.

Specifying Keyframe and Rendering Settings

Keyframe and rendering settings work in conjunction with the video settings to determine how frames of the program are processed and played back. Rendering options become especially important when you begin previewing the program and rendering effects (covered in Chapter 9).

Keyframe options determine how certain types of video compression are applied. Keyframe options are more pertinent when you are exporting a movie file; they are not usually important as project settings.

To specify rendering options:

1. *Do either of the following:*
   ▲ In the Project Settings dialog box, choose Keyframe and Rendering from the top pull-down menu.

   or

   ▲ Choose Project > Settings > Keyframe and Rendering.

   The Project Settings dialog box displays the keyframe and rendering options (**Figure 2.34**).

2. Specify how Premiere processes video fields by choosing an option from the Fields pull-down menu (**Figure 2.35**):

   No Fields—for video under full-screen size, or progressive scan video.

   Upper Field First—for interlaced video with field-one dominance.

   Lower Field First—for interlaced video with field-two dominance, such as DV footage.

   For an explanation, see the section, "Interlaced and Progressive Scan Video," in Chapter 18.

continues on next page

SPECIFYING KEYFRAME AND RENDERING SETTINGS

3. Activate several optional settings by checking the ones you want (**Figure 2.36**):

Ignore Audio Effects—to play back program audio without the effects of applied filters.

Ignore Video Effects—to play back program video without the effects of applied filters.

Ignore Audio Rubber Bands—to play back program audio without the effects of fading and panning (see Chapter 10).

Optimize Stills—to allow Premiere to process still-image files more efficiently. Uncheck this checkbox if exported video exhibits playback problems.

Frames Only At Markers—to play back only frames that are located at markers in the timeline. (For more information about markers, see Chapter 6.) This option does not affect keyframes.

To specify keyframe options:

◆ In the Keyframe Options section of the Keyframe and Rendering panel of the Project Settings dialog box, check any of the following options (**Figure 2.37**):

Keyframe Every—to set the interval of frames at which the codec inserts keyframes. Enter a number in the field. (For more information about compression and keyframes, refer to Chapter 18.)

Add Keyframes At Markers—to create a keyframe for each marked frame. (For more information about markers, see Chapter 6.)

Add Keyframes At Edits—to create a keyframe for the first frame of each clip in the program.

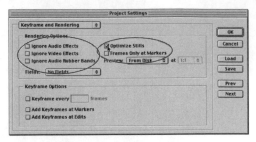

Figure 2.36 You can change how Premiere previews video and audio by checking the appropriate checkboxes.

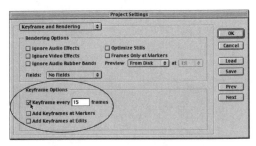

Figure 2.37 To influence how certain compression schemes compress video, you can control how keyframes are used.

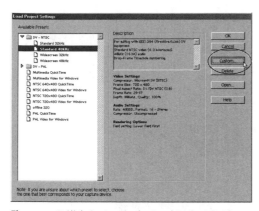

Figure 2.38 Click Custom in the Load Project Settings dialog box...

Figure 2.39 ... or choose Project › Project Settings › General.

Figure 2.40 The General panel of the Project Settings dialog box appears. Specify your custom settings for each settings category (as explained in the previous sections), and click Save.

Saving Custom Settings as a Preset

Even if you're comfortable selecting project settings, making those choices still can be a chore. Fortunately, you can save different settings as presets that appear in the Load Project Settings dialog box. You can also delete presets from the list.

To save settings:

1. *Do either of the following:*
   ▲ In the Load Project Settings dialog box, click Custom (**Figure 2.38**).

   or

   ▲ Choose Project > Project Settings > General (**Figure 2.39**).

   The General panel of the Project Settings dialog box appears (**Figure 2.40**).

2. Specify the project settings, as explained in the previous sections.

3. In the Project Settings dialog box, click Save.

   The Save Project Settings dialog box appears.

   continues on next page

SAVING CUSTOM SETTINGS AS A PRESET

4. Type a name for your settings, as well as an accurate description that summarizes your choices (**Figure 2.41**).

5. Click OK to close the dialog box.

6. Click OK to close the Project Settings dialog box and start your project.

From now on, your saved preset appears in the Available Presets section of the Load Project Settings dialog box. When this preset is selected, the description appears in the Description area (**Figure 2.42**).

✔ Tip

■ You can also click the Load button in the Project Settings dialog box to open the Load Project Settings dialog box.

Figure 2.41
In the Save Project Settings dialog box, enter a description of your custom settings, and enter a name for the preset. Click OK to save the preset.

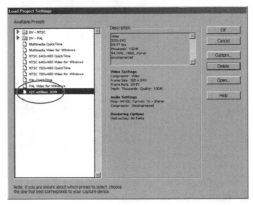

Figure 2.42 Your custom preset appears in the Load Project Settings dialog box.

Figure 2.43 If you're using video files that don't match the DV presets, you might try these settings for Mac/QuickTime projects.

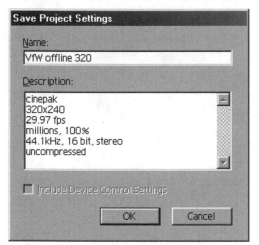

Figure 2.44 Try using these settings for Windows/Windows Media projects.

Using Suggested Settings for Multimedia

Previous versions of Adobe Premiere kindly suggested using a preset setting in case you were unsure which to choose. Although the current version provides several presets, it doesn't offer this comforting advice. Nevertheless, you may still be unsure which settings will work for you. **Figures 2.43** and **2.44** show a few suggestions that work well for most systems using less-than-full-screen, square-pixel images, such as ones you might download from the Web or use in multimedia projects. These suggestions should get you started until you become more at ease selecting your own settings.

✔ Tip

- The multimedia preset uses Cinepak as the compressor. Though Cinepak's small file sizes make it a popular choice for rendering movies for multimedia, it is relatively slow to compress and may delay previews. The zTour project included with Premiere, for example, uses source video in the Cinepak format. A preview of the project using the QuickTime "video" codec rendered eight times faster than a preview using the Cinepak codec.

Using the Settings Viewer

Because you revisit essentially the same video and audio settings when you capture video, start a project, and export a movie file, it would be useful to see them all at the same time and compare them with your source-footage settings. Well, Premiere 6 lets you do just that with the new Settings Viewer.

To use the Settings Viewer:

1. Choose Project > Settings Viewer (**Figure 2.45**).

   The Settings Viewer opens. Compare the video and audio settings for capture, project, source clips, and export (**Figure 2.46**).

2. *Do any of the following:*
   - ▲ To view the settings for a different source file, choose a file from the pull-down menu (**Figure 2.47**).
   - ▲ To adjust capture, project, or export settings, click the appropriate button (**Figure 2.48**).
   - ▲ To load a preset project setting, click Load.

3. Click OK to close the Settings Viewer.

Figure 2.45
Choose Project >
Settings Viewer.

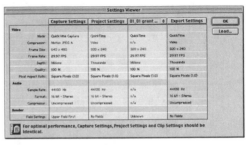

Figure 2.46 Compare settings in the Settings Viewer.

Figure 2.47 To view settings for other clips in the project, select one from the pull-down menu.

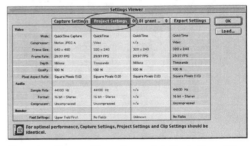

Figure 2.48 To modify settings, click the button at the top of the appropriate column.

USING THE SETTINGS VIEWER

Figure 2.49 Choose File > Save As to save the project under a new name or in a new location.

Figure 2.50 In the Save As dialog box, specify a name and destination for the project file.

Figure 2.51 Choose File > Revert to return the project to the state it was in when you last saved it.

Figure 2.52 Premiere asks you if you're sure you want to discard your changes. Click OK to revert to the last saved version of the project.

Saving Projects

Because your project file embodies all your editing decisions, protecting it from possible mishaps is crucial. As with any important file, you should save your project often and keep backups. Premiere can help you protect your project by automatically saving it to the Project-Archive folder. In the event of a system crash or file corruption, you can retrieve one of the archived copies.

To save a project:

1. To save a project, *do one of the following:*

    ▲ Choose File > Save to save the project under the current name and location or to save the project for the first time.

    ▲ Choose File > Save As (**Figure 2.49**) to save the project under a new name or location and continue working on the new copy of the project.

    ▲ Choose File > Save a Copy to save a copy of the current project and continue working on the current project.

    Choosing Save As and Save a Copy opens the Save File As or Save a Copy As dialog box, respectively.

2. If you are prompted by a dialog box, specify a name and destination for the project (**Figure 2.50**).

3. Click OK to close the Save File As dialog box and save the file.

To revert to the last saved version of a project:

1. Choose File > Revert (**Figure 2.51**). Premiere prompts you to confirm your choice (**Figure 2.52**).

2. Click OK to confirm that you want to revert to the last saved version.

    The project returns to the state that it was in when you last saved it.

Saving Projects Automatically

Premiere can back up your project automatically, as frequently as you choose. Backup files are saved in a folder called Project-Archive inside the Premiere folder. Backup files use the original project name followed by a tilde and a number (project.ppj~2, project.ppj~3, and so on).

To set automatic save:

1. Choose File > Preferences > Auto Save and Undo (**Figure 2.53**).

   The Auto Save and Undo panel of the Preferences dialog box opens.

2. Check the Automatically Save Projects checkbox, and type the time interval at which you want Premiere to save the current project (**Figure 2.54**).

3. For Maximum Files to Archive, enter the number of copies of all projects that will be saved automatically in the Project-Archive folder.

   After Premiere saves the number of copies that you specified, it deletes the oldest project to make room for the newest copy.

4. For Maximum Project Versions, enter the number of versions of each project that you want Premiere to automatically save.

5. Click OK to close the Preferences dialog box.

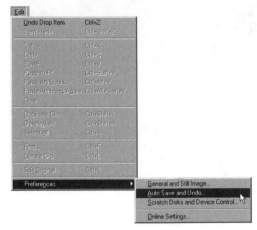

Figure 2.53 Choose File > Preferences > Auto Save and Undo.

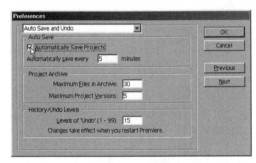

Figure 2.54 Check Automatically Save Projects, and type a number in the Automatically Save Every field to set the time interval of automatic saves. In the Maximum Files in Archive and Maximum Project Versions fields, type numbers to set the number of files and versions to be saved.

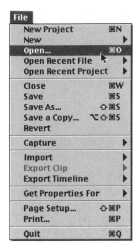

Figure 2.55
Choose File > Open.

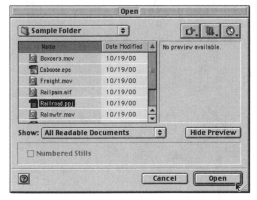

Figure 2.56 In the Open dialog box, select a project file and click Open.

Opening Projects

You can open projects created in Adobe Premiere 5.1c or later. You can also open Premiere projects that were created on other computer platforms, provided that you follow a few guidelines (outlined in your Adobe Premiere User Guide).

To open a project:

1. In Premiere, choose File > Open (**Figure 2.55**).

   The Open dialog box appears (**Figure 2.56**).

2. Select the project file that you want to open.

3. Click Open.

To open an archived project:

1. Choose File > Open.

   The Open dialog box appears.

2. Locate the Premiere folder, and open the Project-Archive folder (**Figure 2.57**).

3. Select the archived project that you want to use and click Open.

   The selected project opens.

To open a recent project:

◆ Choose File > Open Recent Project, and choose the name of a recently open project (**Figure 2.58**).

   The project opens.

Figure 2.57 To open an archived project file, locate it in the Project-Archive folder inside the Premiere folder.

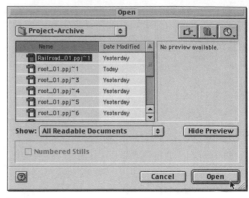

Figure 2.58 You can open a recently used project quickly by choosing File > Open Recent Project > and selecting a project from the menu.

Locating Missing and Offline Files

As you learned at the beginning of this chapter, a project is simply a set of instructions that refer to files on a drive. When you open a project, Premiere looks for the files to which the project refers. If the source files have been moved, deleted, or renamed since the project was last saved, Premiere may have trouble finding them. Premiere attempts to locate the missing clips and prompts you to confirm its choice. (Premiere also attempts to find missing preview files; see Chapter 8.)

Sometimes, the project refers to a file that is not currently available, also known as *offline*. Fortunately, you can tell Premiere to insert a blank placeholder, or *offline clip*, to stand in for the clip. Although an offline file can't allow you to view the file it replaces, it permits the project to remember the name of the file and recall how you used it in your program.

Just as Premiere can create placeholders for files that have been moved offline, you can create placeholders for files that you don't have but expect to use later. Later, you can swap the project's reference to the offline file with a reference to the source file, thereby replacing the placeholder with the actual clip.

✔ Tip

■ In this context, the term *offline* means unavailable, or not on a drive. Don't confuse offline clips with the term *offline editing* (discussed in the introduction).

To open a project with missing files:

1. Choose File > Open.

   The Open dialog box appears.

2. Locate a project, and click OK.

   If files are missing, the Locate File dialog box opens (**Figure 2.59**).

3. To find a file, *do either of the following*:

   ▲ Allow Premiere to locate a file with the same name as the missing file automatically.

   or

   ▲ Manually locate the missing file or its replacement.

4. Select a file, and click one of the following buttons:

   Select (Mac) or **OK** (Windows)—to replace the missing file with the selected file.

   Offline—to replace the missing file with an offline file.

   All Offline—to replace all missing files with offline files, without prompting you for confirmation.

   Skip—to remove the missing clip from the project. All instances of the clip disappear from the project, including the edited program.

   Skip All—to remove all missing clips from the project, without prompting you for confirmation.

5. Repeat steps 3 and 4 each time you are prompted to locate a missing file.

   Once you account for all missing files, the project opens.

6. Save the project to update the status of the missing clips.

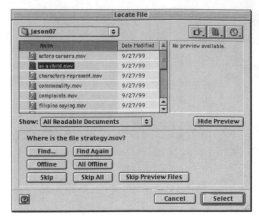

Figure 2.59 If Premiere can't find the files associated with the project you're trying to open, the Locate File dialog box appears.

✔ Tip

■ Click Skip or Skip All only if you are sure that you want to remove the clip from the project.

Figure 2.60
In the Project window, click the Create Item button.

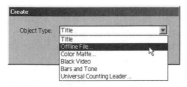

Figure 2.61
In the Create dialog box, choose Offline File.

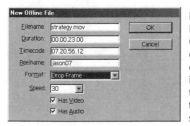

Figure 2.62
In the New Offline File dialog box, enter the information that matches the actual source file.

Figure 2.63
In the Speed pull-down menu, choose the rate appropriate to the source clip.

To create an offline file:

1. In the Project window, click the Create Item button ⬛ (**Figure 2.60**).
   The Create dialog box appears.

2. From the Object Type pull-down menu, choose Offline File (**Figure 2.61**).
   The New Offline File dialog box appears (**Figure 2.62**).

3. Enter information that matches that of the missing file, as follows:
   Filename—the name of the missing file.
   Duration—the length of the missing file.
   Timecode—the timecode in point of the missing file, if timecode is present.
   Reel Name—the name of the reel, or tape, that contains the source file.

4. From the Format pull-down menu, choose the timecode format used by the missing file, if it contains timecode:
   Drop Frame—encoded with drop-frame timecode, used by most DV cameras.
   Non-Drop Frame—encoded with non-drop-frame timecode.
   For an explanation of timecode, see "Drop Frame and Non-Drop Frame Timecode," in Chapter 18.

5. From the Speed pull-down menu, choose the frame rate that matches your missing file (**Figure 2.63**):
   24—for clips that use a standard film frame rate.
   25—for PAL video.
   30—for NTSC video.

   continues on next page

6. Check either or both of the following checkboxes:

   Has Video—to use video from the missing source file.

   Has Audio—to use audio from the missing source file.

7. Click OK to close the dialog box.

To replace an offline file in a project:

1. In the Project window, double-click the offline file (**Figure 2.64**).

   The File Offline dialog box appears (**Figure 2.65**).

2. In the File Offline dialog box, click Locate.

   The Locate File dialog box appears.

3. Select the source file and click Select.

   The file replaces the offline file (**Figure 2.66**).

4. Save the project to reflect the change.

Figure 2.64 To replace an offline file with the source file, double-click the offline file in the Project window.

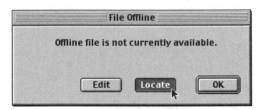

Figure 2.65 In the File Offline dialog box, click Locate to search for the missing file.

Figure 2.66 The offline file no longer acts as a surrogate and is replaced by the actual source file.

LOCATING MISSING AND OFFLINE FILES

IMPORTING AND MANAGING CLIPS

Once you've selected video and audio settings for your project, it's time to begin adding the material you want to use in it—a process called *importing*.

You can import a wide variety of source media files as clips: movie files in various formats; audio files; still images, including bitmapped and EPS files; numbered image sequences; even other Premiere project files. As you learned in the previous chapters, a clip merely refers to the source media file. Therefore, altering the clip in the project doesn't change the source, and you can import the same file more than once.

All the clips you intend to use in the program are listed in the Project window. The longer and more complex the project, however, the lengthier and more unwieldy the list becomes. Fortunately, the new and improved Project window includes features that help you keep your clips organized and easy to find.

In this chapter, you learn to import clips into your project and how to use the Project window to view, sort, and organize them.

Working with the Project Window

When you open a project, Premiere assembles an array of windows, according to the initial workspace you specified (or how it looked when you last saved the project). In the top-left corner of your workspace, you'll find the Project window. As its name suggests, the Project window is fundamental; although you can close other windows, closing the Project window closes the project.

The Project window is the receptacle of all the clips you intend to use in the program. Accordingly, it's vital that the clips in the Project window be organized, easy to find, and easy to evaluate. Premiere 6's new Project window helps you do just that (**Figure 3.1**).

By default, the left side of the window contains bins; the right side shows the clips contained in the selected bin. This arrangement makes it much easier to organize and locate even a large number of clips without consuming a lot of screen space.

To help you change the view options or access common commands quickly, several buttons are conveniently located at the bottom of the Project window. As you can in all the primary windows, you can also access commands associated with the window from an integrated fly-out menu named after the window— in this case, the Project window menu.

The preview area displays vital information about selected bins and clips, as well as a sample image. You can play back movie files in the preview area. In addition, you can set any frame of a movie clip to represent the clip in the Project window views.

The Project window is central to importing and managing clips in your project—the tasks explained in the following sections.

Figure 3.1 The new Project window looks different and works better than it did in previous versions.

Clips and Bins (Not Files and Folders)

Premiere often employs film-editing metaphors. Film editors use bins to store and organize their clips. The film dangles from hangers into a bin until the editor pulls a strip of film down and adds it to the sequence. Premiere's bins may be less tactile than film bins are, but they are also a lot less messy.

If you've never seen a film bin, you might compare clips stored in bins with files stored in folders on a drive. In fact, bins were called folders in older versions of Premiere. If you import a folder of files, the folder appears in the project as a bin containing clips.

Unlike some other editing programs, Premiere saves bins as part of the project, not as separate files.

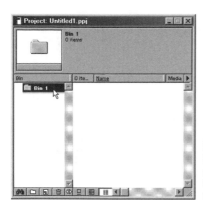

Figure 3.2
Select
a bin in
the Project
window.

Figure 3.3 Choose File > Import > File.

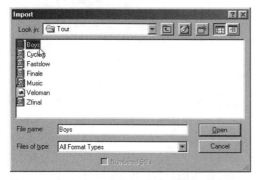

Figure 3.4 In the Import dialog box, double-click the name of the file to import a single file.

Importing Clips

When you want to use a file in your project, you import the file as a clip. You can import one clip at a time, several clips at a time, or an entire folder of clips. You can even import another project into the current project.

Clips can be as big as 4,000 pixels tall by 4,000 pixels wide, and Premiere can support a variety of video and audio formats. Over time, Adobe and other manufacturers undoubtedly will offer plug-in software modules to provide additional file-format support.

To import a file as a clip in the project:

1. In the Project window, click the bin in which you want to import a clip to select it (**Figure 3.2**).

   The bin appears highlighted, and the clip area displays the current contents of the bin.

2. Choose File > Import > File (**Figure 3.3**). The Import dialog box appears.

3. To import a single file, *do either of the following* (**Figure 3.4**):

   ▲ Double-click the name of the file.

   or

   ▲ Select a file and click Open.

   The dialog box closes, and the clip appears in the bin of the Project window.

To import multiple files:

1. In the Project window, click the bin in which you want to import a clip to select it.

    The bin appears highlighted, and the clip area displays the current contents of the bin.

2. Choose File > Import > File.

    The Import dialog box appears.

3. To import multiple files, *do one of the following:*
    - ▲ (Mac) Shift -click each file you want to import.
    - ▲ (Windows) Ctrl -click each file you want to import (**Figure 3.5**).
    - ▲ (Windows) Shift -click the first and last files to select a range of files.

4. Click Open.

    The files appear as clips in the selected bin of the Project window (**Figure 3.6**).

To import a folder of clips as a bin:

1. In the Project window, click the bin in which you want to import a clip to select it (**Figure 3.7**).

    The bin appears highlighted, and the clip area displays the current contents of the bin.

2. Choose File > Import > Folder, or press Shift -⌘-I (Mac) or Shift -Ctrl-I (Windows) (**Figure 3.8**).

    The Choose a Folder dialog box opens.

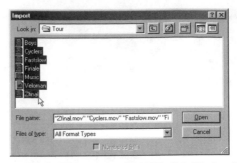

Figure 3.5 Shift -click (Mac) or Ctrl -click (Windows) multiple clips to import them.

Figure 3.6 The files appear as clips in the selected bin in the Project window.

Figure 3.7 Select a bin in the Project window.

Figure 3.8 Choose File > Import > Folder.

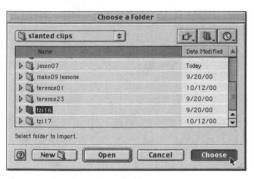

Figure 3.9 In the Choose a Folder dialog box, select a folder of clips and click Choose.

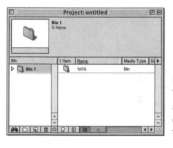

Figure 3.10
The folder appears as a bin of clips inside the selected bin.

Figure 3.11
You can drag the bin into the bin area of the Project window...

Figure 3.12
... so that it appears in the bin area and is no longer inside another bin.

3. Select a folder of clips and click Choose (**Figure 3.9**).

   You will not be able to select or view individual files, only folders. The folder appears in the selected bin of the Project window (**Figure 3.10**).

4. If you want, drag the imported folder into the bin panel of the Project window (**Figures 3.11** and **3.12**).

✔ Tip

- There are many ways to import files, and chances are that you'll be doing a lot of importing. Now's a good time to learn (or create) shortcuts for the import command. Use a contextual menu, keyboard shortcuts, or the Commands palette to save time and mouse hand strain. Instead of choosing File > Import > File, you can simply double-click an empty part of the clip area of the Project window.

Aspect Ratio

By default, Premiere scales a clip to conform to your project settings, particularly the image aspect ratio (usually, 4:3) and pixel aspect ratio (square or nonsquare, depending on the format). If you prefer, you can preserve the original aspect ratio of a still image (discussed later in this chapter) or a video clip. For a more detailed explanation of image aspect ratio and pixel aspect ratio, see Chapter 18.

IMPORTING CLIPS

Importing Projects

In Premiere, a project can contain a single edited program sequence; and as you know, you can have only one project open at a time. Ergo, one project equals one program sequence. There's a workaround for this restriction, however: You can import a project into the current project. This way, you can still work on a large project in sections and later bring them together into a single timeline.

The clips of the imported project appear in a bin in the current project. The bin is named after the imported project. You can insert the imported project's program sequence at the beginning, at the end, or at the edit line of the current project. Any tracks needed to accommodate the imported project are added to the current project.

To import another project into the current project:

1. In the Project window, click the bin in which you want to import a clip to select it (**Figure 3.13**).

    The bin appears highlighted, and the clip area displays the current contents of the bin.

2. Choose File > Import > Project (**Figure 3.14**).

    The Import Project dialog box appears.

Figure 3.13
Select a bin in the Project window.

Figure 3.14
Choose File > Import > Project.

Figure 3.15 In the Import Project dialog box, select another Premiere project, and click Open.

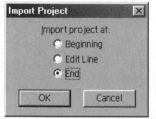

Figure 3.16
Choose a location for the imported project sequence to begin in the timeline of the current project.

3. In the Import Project dialog box, select another Premiere project, and click Open (**Figure 3.15**).

A second, smaller Import Project dialog box opens.

4. Click a radio button to determine where the imported project begins in the current project (**Figure 3.16**).

Beginning—inserts the project at the beginning of the current project.

Edit Line—inserts the project at the edit line of the current project.

End—inserts the project at the end of the current project.

5. Click OK to import the project.

The imported clips appear in a bin that uses the same name as the imported project; the imported project sequence is inserted at the specified point in the current project.

IMPORTING PROJECTS

Importing Digital Audio

If you're using the Mac OS, you can import all or part of a track from an audio CD. QuickTime directly converts the track on the CD to an AIFF file. Because this process converts the audio digitally, it prevents the quality loss associated with the conventional digitizing process (in which the CD audio is played back, delivered as an analog signal, and digitized again). Moreover, a digital conversion can take less time than playing the track in real time.

To import an audio CD track (Mac OS only):

1. In the Project window, click the bin in which you want to import a clip to select it.

   The bin appears highlighted, and the clip area displays the current contents of the bin.

2. Make sure that an audio CD is inserted into your computer.

3. In Premiere, choose File > Open (**Figure 3.17**).

   The Open dialog box appears.

4. Navigate to the audio CD, select a track, and click Open (**Figure 3.18**).

   The Save Translated File As dialog box appears.

5. Enter a name and destination for the AIFF file that you want to create and import.

6. Click Options to open the audio settings (**Figure 3.19**).

   The Audio CD Import Options dialog box appears (**Figure 3.20**).

Figure 3.17
Choose File > Open.

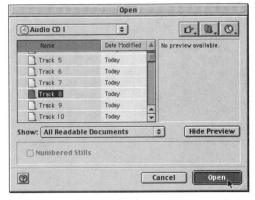

Figure 3.18 In the Open dialog box, select an audio track, and click Open.

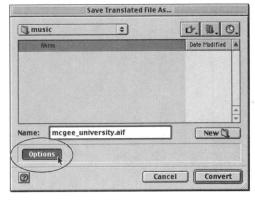

Figure 3.19 Click the Options button.

Figure 3.20 In the Audio CD Import Options dialog box, choose settings for the converted audio file, and click OK.

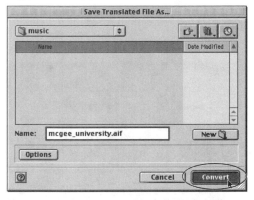

Figure 3.21 In the Save Translated File As dialog box, click Convert.

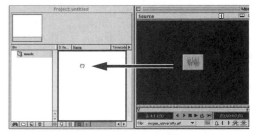

Figure 3.22 To add the audio to the current project, drag the audio from the source view of the Monitor window to the appropriate bin in the Project window.

7. Choose the following options:

▲ From the Rate pull-down menu, choose a sample rate.

44.100 kHz is equivalent to the CD's sample rate.

▲ In the Size section, click a radio button to specify the bit depth.

16 bit is equivalent to the CD's bit depth.

▲ In the Use section, click a radio button to specify mono or stereo.

Stereo matches most CD tracks.

8. To preview and select a portion of the track, *do one of the following:*

▲ To preview the track, click Play.

or

▲ To select a portion of the audio track, enter the start and end times for the audio or drag the beginning and ending sliders.

9. Click OK to exit the Audio CD Import Options dialog box and return to the Save Translated File As dialog box.

10. Click Convert (**Figure 3.21**).

After the CD audio is converted and saved to the location you specified, it appears in the selected bin and in the source view of the Monitor window.

11. To add the audio to the current project, drag the audio from the source view of the Monitor window to the appropriate bin in the Project window, or press ⌘-J (Mac) or Ctrl-J (Windows) (**Figure 3.22**).

The audio is not part of the project until it is listed in a bin of the Project window.

✔ **Tip**

■ A 44,100 kHz, 16-bit stereo track consumes about 5 MB per minute. A three-minute song at CD quality takes up 15 MB.

IMPORTING DIGITAL AUDIO

Importing Still Images

Although individual images are only single frames, you can set them to play back in the program for any duration. Also, if the aspect ratio of the still doesn't match the project's aspect ratio (usually, 4:3), you must specify whether Premiere should maintain the still image's original proportions or resize it to fit the screen.

To set the default duration for still images before you import them:

1. Choose Edit > Preferences > General and Still Image (**Figure 3.23**).

   The General and Still Image panel of the Preferences dialog box opens.

2. In the Still Image section, type a default duration for still images (**Figure 3.24**).

   Hereafter, all still images imported into the project use the default duration. Still images that are already in the project or program remain unaffected. You can change the duration of a still-image clip at any time (see Chapter 4).

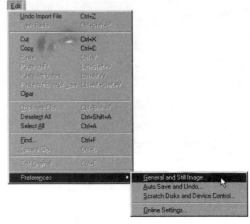

Figure 3.23 Choose Edit > Preferences > General & Still Image.

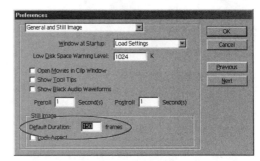

Figure 3.24 Enter a default duration for imported still images. Here, the duration is 150 frames.

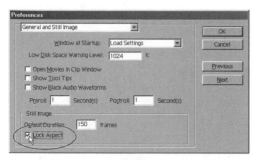

Figure 3.25 Check Lock Aspect to keep the aspect ratio of the source image; uncheck it to conform its aspect ratio to that of the project.

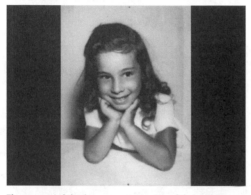

Figure 3.26 If the image aspect ratio of the still image and that of the project differ, locking the aspect ratio can result in borders.

Figure 3.27 Not locking the aspect ratio can distort the image.

To lock the aspect ratios of still images before you import them:

1. Choose Edit > Preferences > General and Still Image. The General and Still Image panel of the Preferences dialog box appears.

2. In the Still Image section, *do either of the following* (**Figure 3.25**):

   ▲ To keep the aspect ratio of the still image, check the Lock Aspect checkbox.

   or

   ▲ To resize still images to fit the aspect ratio defined by your project settings, uncheck Lock Aspect.

   Unless the aspect ratio matches that of the project, still images with a locked aspect may appear with a border, while resized still images may appear distorted (**Figures 3.26** and **3.27**).

Importing Illustrator Files

Premiere can rasterize Illustrator files—a process that converts the path-based (vector) art to Premiere's pixel-based (bitmapped) format. The program antialiases the art, so that edges appear smooth; it also interprets blank areas as an alpha channel premultiplied with white.

You can import Illustrator art up to 2,000 by 2,000 pixels. Set crop marks in the Illustrator file to define the dimensions of the art that will be rasterized by Premiere (**Figures 3.28** and **3.29**).

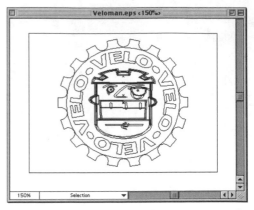

Figure 3.28 An image viewed in Illustrator as artwork only...

Figure 3.29 ...appears rasterized and antialiased in Premiere.

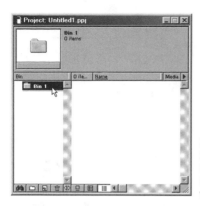

Figure 3.30
Select a
bin in the
Project
window.

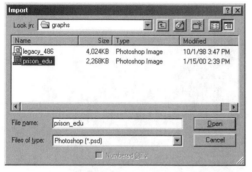

Figure 3.31 Locate the layered Photoshop file, and click Open.

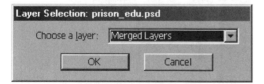

Figure 3.32 The Layer Selection dialog box opens.

Importing Photoshop Files

Premiere can import files created in Photoshop 3.0 or later. You can even import a single layer from a multiple-layer Photoshop file. Premiere also recognizes an alpha channel in a Photoshop file, so you can use it to define transparent areas (see Chapter 12).

To import separate Photoshop layers:

1. In the Project window, click the bin in which you want to import a clip to select it (**Figure 3.30**).

   The bin appears highlighted, and the clip area displays the current contents of the bin.

2. Choose File > Import > File .

   The Import dialog box appears.

3. Locate a layered Photoshop file to import, and click Open (**Figure 3.31**).

   The Layer Selection dialog box opens (**Figure 3.32**).

continues on next page

4. Choose an option from the pull-down menu (**Figure 3.33**):

▲ Choose Merged Layers to import the image after merging all layers into a single layer.

▲ Select a layer to import the single layer as a clip.

5. Click OK.

Depending on your choice, the single layer or merged layer appears in the selected bin.

✔ Tip

■ Being able to open individual layers from Photoshop files can be a time-saver. When you create a sequence of graphics that "builds," for example, you don't have to create individual images for each part of the build. Instead, you can import each layer from a single Photoshop file (**Figure 3.34**).

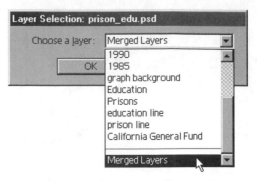

Figure 3.33 Choose Merged Layers to import all the layers as a single file, or select the name of an individual layer.

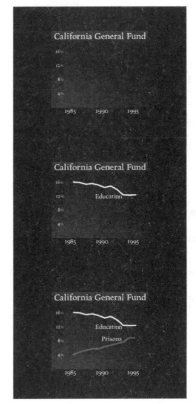

Figure 3.34 You can create each graphic element separately as layers in Photoshop, import individual layers, and then successively fade each one up to build the final image.

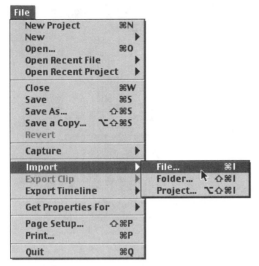

Figure 3.35 Choose File > Import > File.

Importing Still-Image Sequences

In addition to (and sometimes instead of) a single movie file, many programs export movies as a sequence of still images. Don't worry—Premiere has no trouble importing a numbered sequence as a single clip.

In Windows, confirm that each image in the numbered sequence has the correct extension and that the filenames contain an equal number of digits at the end (seq000.bmp, seq001.bmp, and seq002.bmp, for example).

In the Mac OS, confirm that each image in the sequence has the same filename, followed by an equal number of digits seq000, seq001, and seq002, for example).

To import numbered still images as a single clip:

1. Confirm that the sequence of stills uses the naming convention required by your platform (see the preceding section).

2. In the Project window, click the bin in which you want to import a clip to select it.

3. Choose File > Import > File (**Figure 3.35**). The Import dialog box appears.

   continues on next page

4. Select the first file in the numbered sequence.

5. Check the Numbered Stills checkbox (**Figure 3.36**).

6. Click Open.

The image sequence appears in the selected bin as a single clip (**Figure 3.37**).

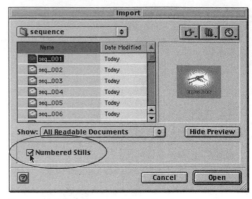

Figure 3.36 In the Import File dialog box, check Numbered Stills, select the first still in the sequence, and click Open.

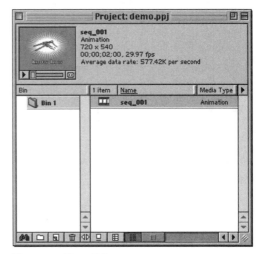

Figure 3.37 The still-image sequence appears as a single clip in the selected bin.

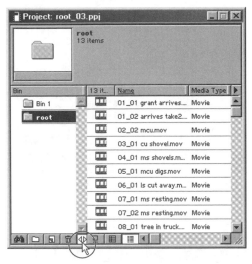

Figure 3.38 Drag the resize bin area button to the left or right...

Figure 3.39 ... to make the bin area wider or narrower.

Customizing the Project Window

This chapter usually depicts the Project window with three visible areas: the clip area, the bin area, and the preview area. You can modify the general appearance of the Project window by concealing the bin or preview areas. You can also resize the bin area to make it narrower or wider (but you can't resize either of the other areas).

When you hide the bin area, only the clips of the selected bin are visible; you'll have to reveal the bins again to look at other clips. Hiding the preview area creates more room in the window vertically and relieves Premiere of the burden of creating a thumbnail image. On the other hand, you'll have to live without the cool little picture and clip information.

To resize the bin area:

◆ Drag the resize bin area button ◫ or the right edge of the bin heading to make the bin area narrower or wider (**Figures 3.38** and **3.39**).

To hide or show the preview or bin areas:

◆ From the Project window menu, choose any of the following (**Figure 3.40**):

Hide Preview Area—conceals the thumbnail preview area; choose Show Preview to reveal it again.

Hide Bin Area—conceals the bin area; choose Show Bin area to reveal it again.

The preview area or bin area is shown or hidden, according to your choice (**Figure 3.41**).

✔ Tip

■ You can open a bin in a separate window by double-clicking the bin icon. But because this tends to clutter the desktop with windows, this book always shows bins within the main Project window.

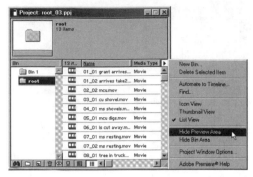

Figure 3.40 Choose to hide the preview area (selected here) or bin area...

Figure 3.41 ...to keep it from appearing as part of the Project window.

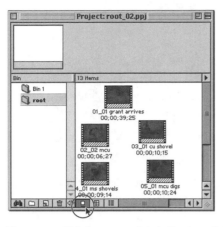

Figure 3.42 Click the appropriate button to switch the Project window to Icon view...

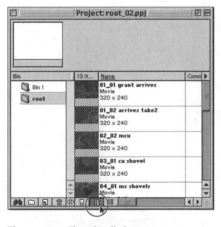

Figure 3.43 ...Thumbnail view...

Figure 3.44 ...or List view.

Working with Project Window Views

The clips in the Project window can be viewed in three ways: icon, thumbnail, or list. Furthermore, each view type has various display options. These choices allow you to customize the window for the task at hand.

To change a Project window view:

At the bottom of the Project window, click the button that corresponds to the view that you want to use:

◆ Icon ▣ (**Figure 3.42**)

◆ Thumbnail ▦ (**Figure 3.43**)

◆ List ▤ (**Figure 3.44**)

WORKING WITH PROJECT WINDOW VIEWS

To choose icon view options:

1. From the Project window menu, choose Project Window Options (**Figure 3.45**). The Project Window Options dialog box appears.

2. Choose Icon View from the pull-down menu (**Figure 3.46**).

   The icon view options appear.

3. Click the radio button for the icon size that you want the window to use (**Figure 3.47**).

4. Check either of the following options:

   Snap to Grid—to make the icons line up with an invisible grid.

   Draw Icons—to make icons visible in the window; uncheck the checkbox to prevent icon display. The clip icon displays the poster frame of the clip. See the section, "To Set the Poster Frame of a Clip," later in this chapter.

5. Click OK to close the Project Window Options dialog box.

✔ Tip

■ When Snap to Grid is off, clips in the icon view can look jumbled or even cover one another. To rearrange the clips neatly in the icon view, make icon view active and then choose Clean Up View from the Project window menu.

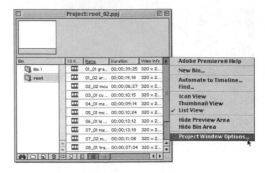

Figure 3.45 Choose Project Window Options from the Project window menu.

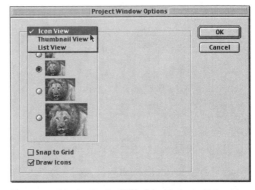

Figure 3.46 In the Project Window Options dialog box, choose Icon View from the pull-down menu.

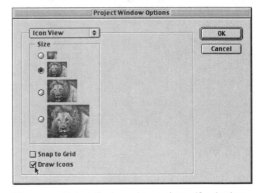

Figure 3.47 Select the icon size, and specify whether you want to draw icons or snap the icons to a grid.

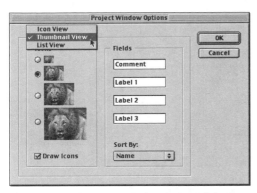

Figure 3.48 In the Project Window Options dialog box, choose Thumbnail View from the pull-down menu.

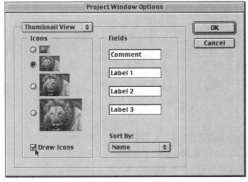

Figure 3.49 Choose an icon size, and specify whether you want Premiere to draw icons in the Project window.

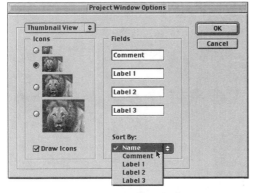

Figure 3.50 Choose a heading by which you want to sort the clips in the Project window. You can enter up to four custom headings.

To choose thumbnail view options:

1. In the Project window menu, choose Project Window Options.

   The Project Window Options dialog box appears.

2. Choose Thumbnail View from the pull-down menu of the Project Window Options dialog box (**Figure 3.48**).

   The thumbnail view options appear (**Figure 3.49**).

3. Click the radio button for the icon size that you want the window to use.

4. Check the Draw Icons checkbox to make icons visible in the window, or uncheck the Draw Icons checkbox to prevent icon display.

5. From the Sort By pull-down menu, choose a heading on which to sort the clips in the window (**Figure 3.50**).

6. To create custom headings, enter names for up to four headings in the Label fields.

7. Click OK to close the Project Window Options dialog box.

WORKING WITH PROJECT WINDOW VIEWS

To choose list view options:

1. In the Project window menu, choose Project Window Options (**Figure 3.51**). The Project Window Options dialog box appears.

2. Choose List View from the pull-down menu (**Figure 3.52**). The list-view options appear.

3. Check the headings for the type of information that you want to view in the list view of the Project window:

   Name—by default, the same as the filename. You can change the name that the clip uses in the project, however.

   Date—the most recent modification date of the source file.

   File Path—the location of the source file on disk.

   Log Comment—if the clip was captured with Premiere, the text in the Comment field.

   Media Type—the kind of file (such as movie or still image).

   Video Info—video attributes, such as the frame size.

   Audio Info—audio attributes, such as the sample rate.

   Video Usage—the number of times that the video track is used in the program.

   Audio Usage—the number of times that the audio track is used in the program.

   Duration—the length of the clip, expressed in the currently selected time display.

   Timecode—the timecode of the first frame, if timecode is present.

   Reel Name—if the clip was captured with Premiere, the name entered in the Reel field.

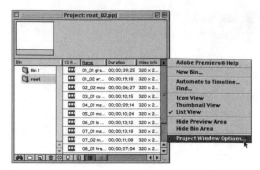

Figure 3.51 From the Project window menu, choose Project Window Options.

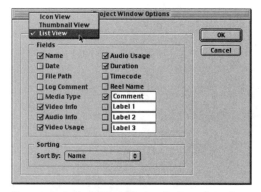

Figure 3.52 In the Project Window Options dialog box, choose List View from the pull-down menu.

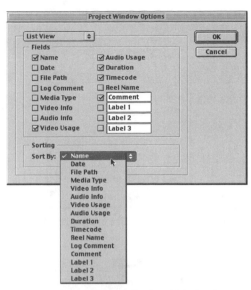

Figure 3.53 Choose the heading by which the clips are sorted from the Sort By pull-down menu.

4. From the Sort By pull-down menu, choose a heading on which to sort the clips in the window (**Figure 3.53**).

You will be able to re-sort clips directly in the list view by clicking a list heading.

5. Click OK to close the Project Window Options dialog box.

To rearrange headings in the list view:

◆ With the list view active, drag a heading in the Project window to the left or right to place it where you want (**Figures 3.54** and **3.55**).

Figure 3.54 Dragging a heading to the left or right...

Figure 3.55 ...changes its relative position in the Project window.

To adjust column width in the list view:

◆ With the list view active, drag the right edge of a heading in the Project window to resize it (**Figures 3.56** and **3.57**).

To sort items in the thumbnail or list view:

◆ With the thumbnail or list view active, do any of the following:

◆ Click a column heading to sort clips by that heading (**Figure 3.58**).

◆ Click the same column heading again to reverse the sort order (**Figure 3.59**).

◆ Open the window options of a Project window (as explained in the section, "To Choose List View Options," or the section, "To Choose Thumbnail View Options," earlier in this chapter), and choose a category from the Sort By pull-down menu to sort items according to that category.

Figure 3.56 Drag the right edge of a heading to resize it.

Figure 3.57 The heading appears narrower or (in this case) wider.

Figure 3.58 In the thumbnail view or list view (shown), click a column heading to sort the clips by that heading.

Figure 3.59 Click the same heading again to reverse the order of the sorted clips.

Figure 3.60 Clicking a bin in the bin area of the Project window reveals its contents in the clip area.

Using the Preview Area of the Project Window

Probably the most noticeable feature of the new Project window is the preview area, which displays a sample image of the selected bin or clip. The preview area also displays the number of clips in a bin or the vital statistics of a clip—its name, file type, image dimensions, and so on.

If the selected clip is a movie file, you can actually play back the clip—with sound—directly in the Project window. In addition, the thumbnail frame used to represent the clip in the icon and thumbnail views is no longer restricted to the first frame of the clip. Now you can set any frame of the clip as the poster frame, the image used to represent the clip in the preview area, the icon view, and the thumbnail view of the Project window. This way, you can choose the most appropriate image to represent the clip.

To display a preview of a bin or clip:

◆ In the Project window, click a bin or clip to select it.

A sample frame and information appear in the preview area of the Project window. Bin information includes the number of files contained by the bin. Clip information can include the clip's name, file type, image size, duration, frame rate, data rate, alpha channel, and so on (**Figure 3.60**).

To play back a movie clip in the preview area:

1. In the Project window, click a movie clip to select it.

   A sample image and information appear in the preview area of the Project window.

2. To play the preview image, *do either of the following:*

   ▲ Below the preview image, click the Play button (**Figure 3.61**).

   or

   ▲ Press the spacebar.

3. Click the play button or press the spacebar again to stop playback.

4. To cue the preview image, drag the slider below the image (**Figure 3.62**).

To set the poster frame for a movie clip:

1. In the Project window, click a movie clip to select it.

   A sample image and information appear in the preview area of the Project window.

2. Below the preview image, drag the slider to cue the preview to the frame you want to set as the poster frame.

3. Below the preview image, click the set poster frame button ▣ (**Figure 3.63**).

   The current frame of the preview becomes the poster frame—the image used to represent the clip in the preview area, the icon view, and the thumbnail view of the Project window (**Figure 3.64**).

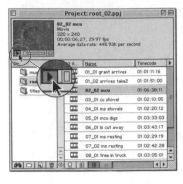

Figure 3.61
You can use playback buttons to watch the preview image of the clip play.

Figure 3.62
You can also drag the slider under the preview image to cue the preview clip to a frame.

Figure 3.63
Cue the clip and click the set poster frame button.

Figure 3.64
When Premiere is set to the icon or thumbnail view, the poster frame represents the clip.

Premiere allows you to manage clips in the project in much the same way that you manage files on your computer's desktop.

To create a bin:

Figure 3.65 Click the create bin button.

1. In the Project window, click the create bin button  (**Figure 3.65**).

   The Create Bin dialog box appears.

2. Enter a name for the bin (**Figure 3.66**).

3. Click OK.

   The new bin appears in the Project window (**Figure 3.67**).

Figure 3.66 In the Create Bin dialog box, enter a name for the new bin, and click OK.

To select and move clips:

1. Click the bin containing the clips you want to view.

2. To select a clip or clips, *do one of the following:*

   ▲ Click a clip.

   ▲ Shift-click several clips.

   ▲ Drag a marquee around two or more clips (**Figure 3.68**).

3. Drag the selected clips to another bin.

Figure 3.67 The new bin appears in the bin area of the Project window.

Figure 3.68 You can click a clip to select it, Shift-click multiple clips, or drag a marquee to select a block of clips (as shown).

ORGANIZING CLIPS IN BINS

To delete a clip from the Project window:

1. In the Project window, select a clip.

2. In the Project window, click the delete button  (**Figure 3.69**) or press [Delete] on your keyboard.

   The clip is removed from the project, but the source file remains on the drive (**Figure 3.70**).

Figure 3.69 Select the clip you want to remove, and click the delete button.

To copy and paste a clip:

1. Select a clip (**Figure 3.71**).

2. Choose Edit > Copy, or press [⌘]-[C] (Mac) or [Ctrl]-[C] (Windows).

3. Select the destination bin.

4. Choose Edit > Paste, or press [⌘]-[V] (Mac) or [Ctrl]-[V] (Windows).

   A duplicate of the clip appears in the selected bin (**Figure 3.72**).

✔ Tip

- Copying and pasting a clip is similar to creating a subclip. However, you usually set in and out points to define the frames contained in a subclip. See the section, "Using Subclips," in Chapter 4.

Figure 3.70 The clip is removed from the project.

Figure 3.71 Select a clip, and press [⌘]-[C] (Mac) or [Ctrl]-[C] (Windows).

Figure 3.72 Select a destination bin, and press [⌘]-[V] (Mac) or [Ctrl]-[V] (Windows) to paste the clip into the current bin.

Figure 3.73 Choose Clip > Set Clip Name Alias, or press ⌘-H (Mac) or Ctrl-H (Windows).

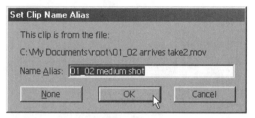

Figure 3.74 In the Set Clip Name Alias dialog box, enter a new name, and click OK to rename the clip.

Figure 3.75 The clip uses a new name in the project, but the source file remains unchanged.

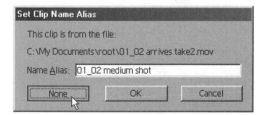

Figure 3.76 Reopen the Set Clip Name Alias dialog box, and click None to restore the original name.

Renaming Clips

After you import a file as a clip, you shouldn't rename the file. Doing so will ruin your project's reference to the file, and Premiere won't be able to locate the file the next time you open the project. Nevertheless, you may still need to identify a clip by another name. Fortunately, you can rename a clip in a project, giving it a *name alias* for the purposes of editing. Renaming the clip doesn't affect the source file's name or interfere with your project's references. You can restore the original name at any time.

To rename a clip:

1. Select a clip.

2. Choose Clip > Set Clip Name Alias, or press ⌘-H (Mac) or Ctrl-H (Windows) (**Figure 3.73**).
   The Set Clip Name Alias dialog box appears.

3. Enter a new name (**Figure 3.74**).

4. Click OK.
   The clip takes another name in the project. The source file on the drive isn't renamed, however (**Figure 3.75**).

To restore the original filename of a renamed clip:

1. Select a renamed clip.

2. Choose Clip > Set Clip Name Alias, or press ⌘-H (Mac) or Ctrl-H (Windows).
   The Set Clip Name Alias dialog box appears.

3. Click None to make the name of the clip match the source-file name (**Figure 3.76**).

RENAMING CLIPS

Finding Clips

Even the most organized editor can lose track of a clip, particularly when the project contains a lot of clips. Here's how to find one from the Project window.

To find a clip:

1. In the Project window, click the find button ![icon].

   The Find dialog box appears. It contains two lines of search criteria (**Figure 3.77**).

2. From the pull-down menu in the top-left corner of the dialog box, choose a category by which to search.

   Find options include the same categories as the Project window's list view.

3. From the next pull-down menu, choose a limiting option.

4. In the search field, enter search content.

5. To narrow the search more, add another search category, limiting option, and search content in the next line.

6. Click Find (**Figure 3.78**).

   If a clip meets your criteria, it is selected in the Project window (**Figure 3.79**). The Find dialog box displays a Find Next button.

7. To search for other clips that meet the search criteria, click Find Next.

   If an additional clip meets your criteria, it is selected in the Project window.

8. Repeat step 7 until you find the clip you're searching for or finish searching.

9. Click Done to close the Find dialog box.

Figure 3.77 Clicking the Find button opens the Find dialog box.

Figure 3.78 Select search criteria and content, and click Find.

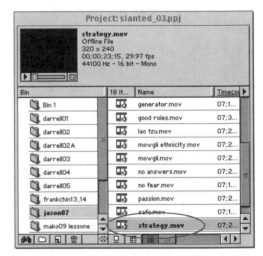

Figure 3.79 The first clip Premiere finds that meets your criteria is selected in the Project window. Click Find Next to search for other items that meet the criteria.

EDITING SOURCE CLIPS

4

You may have heard editing referred to as *cutting*. This is, of course, a reference to film editing, in which you literally cut the work print of the film. In some circles, however, editing is called *joining*, which refers to the process of splicing the film segments together. The term you prefer might say something about your attitude toward editing—emphasizing either the elimination or the union of footage. Literally speaking, of course, editing involves both cutting and joining clips. You select portions of the source footage and arrange them into a sequence, called a *program*.

The tools and techniques you use to accomplish this fundamental task are varied, flexible, and tightly integrated. The following three chapters focus on different areas of the process. Though each chapter tends to emphasize a particular part of the interface, the divisions are really based on the general editing tasks: cutting, joining, and rearranging clips. When you've mastered the material in these chapters, you'll be able to integrate all the techniques smoothly.

You'll begin by learning ways to open and view *clips*: video, audio, and still images. You'll also learn how to control the playback of clips by using the controllers in Premiere's Monitor window. And you'll find out how to mark points of interest in the clip, including the most important in and out points.

The Monitor Window

The Monitor window was probably the most important—and certainly the most visible—of the improvements introduced in Premiere 5. The Monitor window consolidated several of the older version's windows into a single, streamlined window. Premiere 6 refines this essential window by redesigning its controls and expanding its features (**Figure 4.1**).

Depending on your needs or preferences, the Monitor window can appear in three incarnations: dual view, single view, or trim mode. Each view includes controls for playback, for setting editing marks, and for performing edits. All these controls have single-stroke keyboard shortcuts—another time-saving feature that professional editors have come to expect from nonlinear editing tools.

Most of the time, you'll use the Monitor window in *dual view*. In dual view, the left side of the Monitor window is called the *source view*, where you view and set edit

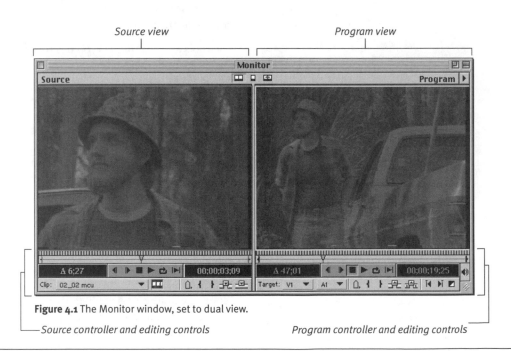

Figure 4.1 The Monitor window, set to dual view.

marks in source clips; the right side is called the *program view*, where you display and set edit marks in the edited program sequence (**Figure 4.2**). Many editors believe that a source/program monitor is the best editing interface. In dual view, the monitor window resembles a traditional videotape-editing suite or even a flatbed film-editing table. But editors don't prefer this layout merely because it's familiar; this type of interface also enables them to see the source and program clips side by side, which helps them make editing decisions. You can even "gang-synch" the views so that the source and program views play in a synched relationship. This feature is invaluable when you need to preview the timing of certain edits.

Though you got a glimpse of the "big picture" in Chapter 1, it's worth reiterating that the

continues on next page

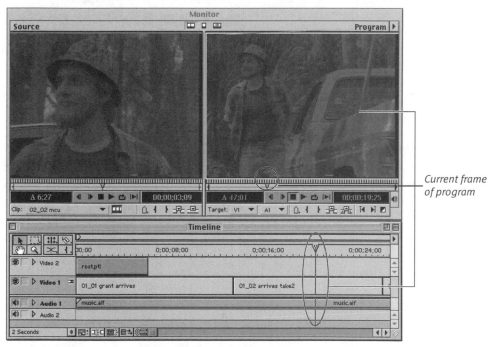

Current frame of program

Figure 4.2 Dual view is also called source/program view: the source clips appear on the left, the program appears on the right.

program side of the Monitor window corresponds with the Timeline window. Both depict the same edited program, although in different ways. The program view shows you how the program will look when you export it as a file or to videotape. The Timeline window graphically represents the clips in the program as bars arranged in tracks in a timeline graph. The video frame displayed in the monitor view corresponds to a vertical line in the Timeline window called the *edit line*. Each window contains its own set of editing tools and controls, with their own special advantages (**Figure 4.3**).

Single view displays only the program view in the Monitor window (**Figure 4.4**). Because the window doesn't include a source side in this view, you must open source clips in separate clip windows when you edit using single view (see "To open a clip in a separate clip window" later in this chapter). As you learned in Chapter 2, choosing the A/B roll editing workspace automatically sets the Monitor window to single view, in addition to setting source clips to open in separate windows. Because of the advantages of dual view, however, this book doesn't recommend using single view for most of your editing.

On the other hand, single view is ideal for editing tasks that don't require viewing source clips, such as audio mixing and effects editing (two other preset workspaces). Single view can also be useful if your computer system supports a second computer monitor or television monitor; you can put the program on a television screen or free up screen space for your other windows.

When it's time to fine-tune the program, the Monitor window conveniently toggles to *trim mode*. Trim mode allows you to make fine adjustments to the clips in the edited program (**Figure 4.5**). You'll find a full explanation of trim mode in Chapter 7.

Figure 4.3 The program view of the Monitor window and the Timeline window depict the same program in different ways.

Figure 4.4 When you set the Monitor window to single view, it displays only the program view. Source clips must be displayed in separate clip windows.

Figure 4.5 Trim mode shows two adjacent clips in the program: the tail of the first clip on the left and the head of the second clip on the right.

Modifying the Monitor Window

As you saw in Chapter 2, you can choose among several preset workspace options to arrange the windows in the way you prefer to work or to optimize them for a particular editing task. You may have noticed that some layouts alter the way the Monitor window looks. However, you can change the way this window looks at any time, not just by changing the workspace.

To change the Monitor window viewing mode:

◆ In the Monitor window, click the icon that corresponds to the view you want to use (**Figure 4.6**):

Dual view— 🖭 includes source view on the left and program view on the right.

Single view— 🔲 includes only program view. Source clips must be opened in separate clip windows.

Trim mode— 🎞 shows two adjacent clips in the timeline: the tail of the first clip on the left side of the Monitor window; and the head of the second clip on the right side. See Chapter 7 for more details.

The Monitor window reflects your choice.

✔ Tips

■ If you insist on using a workspace that more closely resembles older versions of Premiere, choose single view or select the A/B Roll workspace option (see "Selecting an Initial Workspace" in Chapter 2).

■ In some systems, you can drag the Monitor window to a second computer monitor or to a television monitor. Other systems can only mirror (duplicate) your main computer screen on the second screen. An ideal setup sends a full-screen image of the edited program to a television screen while keeping a dual-view Monitor window on the main computer screen. Such a setup may require a camera or deck to send the program video to the Monitor window. DV setups often work this way.

Single view
Dual view   *Trim mode*

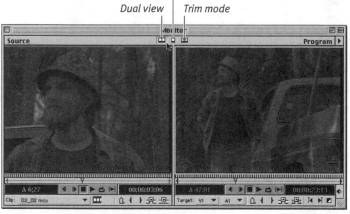

Figure 4.6 In the Monitor window, click the icon that corresponds to the view option you want to use.

MODIFYING THE MONITOR WINDOW

Video Safe Zones

Though the Monitor window displays the entire video frame, television monitors are likely to crop off the outer edges of the image. If your program is destined for full-screen display on a video monitor, you may need to check whether certain parts of the image fall within the video *safe zones*.

In video, the inner 90% of the complete image is considered to be *action-safe*—that is, everything within that area is likely to appear on most television screens. The inner 80% is considered to be *title-safe*. Because you can't afford to let any of the title's content be lost, the title-safe area literally defines a necessary safety margin. The safe-zone guides are for your reference only; they aren't added to the source image and don't appear in the program output. Though it's possible to change the position of the safe-zone guides, 80% and 90% of the image are standard.

To view safe zones:

◆ From the Monitor window's pull-down menu, choose either of the following options (**Figure 4.7**):

Safe Margins for Source Side—Safe-zone guides appear in the source view.

Safe Margins for Program Side—Safe-zone guides appear in the program view.

Safe-zone guides appear in the corresponding view of the Monitor window (**Figure 4.8**). Deselect your option in the pull-down menu to hide the safe-zone guides again.

Figure 4.7 From the Monitor window pull-down menu, choose options to display safe zones in the source and program views.

Figure 4.8 The outer guide indicates the action-safe zone; the inner guide indicates the title-safe zone. Safe-zone guides don't appear in the final output.

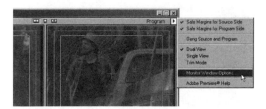

Figure 4.9 Choose Monitor Window Options.

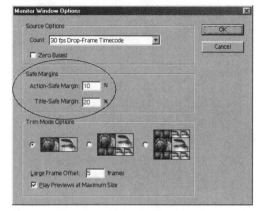

Figure 4.10 Enter values for the Action-Safe Margin and Title-Safe Margin options to change the standard settings.

To set the safe-zone areas:

1. From the Monitor window's pull-down menu, choose Monitor Window Options (**Figure 4.9**).

   The Monitor Window Options dialog box appears.

2. Enter values for the Action-Safe Margin and Title-Safe Margin options (**Figure 4.10**).

3. Click OK to close the dialog box.

   The safe-zone guides reflect the values you entered.

✔ Tip

■ As you might guess, safe zones are particularly useful when you're creating titles or moving images through the screen. See Chapter 12 for more information about titles; see Chapter 14 for more information about motion settings.

VIDEO SAFE ZONES

Viewing Clips

Premiere's intuitive interface makes viewing a clip simple, no matter where it appears in your project.

In a single-track editing workspace, clips are loaded into the source view by default; in an A/B roll editing workspace, clips appear in separate clip windows by default. The following tasks assume that the default is set to opening clips in the source view of the Monitor window (set to dual view). You can change the default at any time, however.

To load a clip in the source view:

Do one of the following:

◆ Double-click a clip in a Project window or the Timeline window.

or

◆ Drag a clip from the Project window into the source view of the Monitor window (**Figure 4.11**).

To load several clips into the source view:

1. In the Project window, select several clips by doing one of the following:
   ▲ [Shift]-click several successive clips.
   ▲ Drag a marquee around a range of clips (**Figure 4.12**).
   ▲ With the program window selected, press ⌘-[A] (Mac) or [Ctrl]-[A] (Windows) to select all the clips in the selected bin.

2. *Do one of the following:*
   ▲ Double-click one of the selected clips.
   or
   ▲ Drag the selected clips to the source view of the Monitor window (**Figure 4.13**).

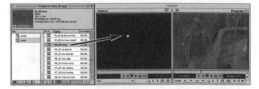

Figure 4.11 Double-click a clip or drag it from the Project window to the source view of the Monitor window, as shown here.

Figure 4.12 Select several clips in the Project window.

Figure 4.13 Double-click one of the selected clips or drag them to the source view of the Monitor window (shown here).

Figure 4.14 Choose the name of a previously viewed clip from the source-view pull-down menu.

The selected clips are loaded into the source view of the Monitor window. The clip listed first in the Project window appears in the source view; the others are accessible through the source-view pull-down menu (see the next task).

To view recently viewed clips with the source-view pull-down menu:

◆ Choose the name of a previously viewed clip from the source-view pull-down menu (**Figure 4.14**).

The selected clip appears in the image area of the source view.

To remove clips from the pull-down menu:

◆ Load a clip into the source view of the Monitor window, and press ⌘-Delete (Mac) or Ctrl-Delete (Windows).

The clip is removed from the source view and from the source-view pull-down menu. The clip remains listed in the Project window.

✔ Tip

■ When you open a movie clip from the Project window, you're opening a master clip. The master clip includes all the frames of the source movie file you imported. Open a master clip before you add it to the program. When you open a clip from the timeline, you're opening a single instance of the master clip. A clip instance includes only the frames you selected before adding the clip to the timeline. Open a clip from the timeline to alter that particular instance. For more information, see "Master Clips and Clip Instances" later in this chapter.

VIEWING CLIPS

Clip Windows

Before Premiere 5, movie clips always appeared in separate clip windows. Now you can choose whether to open clips in the source view or in separate clip windows, and set which method is the default.

Unlike movie clips, still images always open in separate windows (see "Still-Image Clip Windows" later in this chapter). It's also useful to open audio clips in separate windows, to take advantage of a different view of the audio information and use different controls (see "Audio Clip Windows" later in this chapter).

To open a clip in a separate clip window:

◆ Option-double-click a clip in the Project window, source view, or Timeline window.

A separate clip window opens. This window works the same way as in the source view of the Monitor window (**Figure 4.15**).

To make separate clip windows the default:

1. Choose Edit > Preferences > General and Still Image (**Figure 4.16**).

   The General and Still Image panel of the Preferences dialog box opens.

2. Check the Open Movies in Clip Window checkbox (**Figure 4.17**).

3. Click OK.

   This procedure reverses the default settings, so that double-clicking a clip opens it in a separate clip window, and Option-double-clicking a clip opens it in the source view.

Figure 4.15 Option-double-click (Mac) or Alt-double-click (Windows) a clip to view it in a separate clip window.

Figure 4.16 Choose Edit > Preferences > General and Still Image.

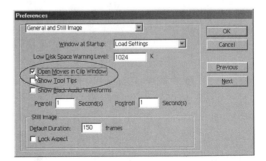

Figure 4.17 In the General and Still Image panel of the Preferences dialog box, check Open Movies in Clip Window.

Figure 4.18 Choose File > Open.

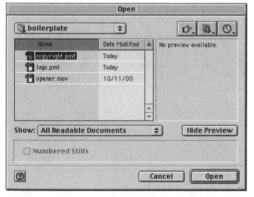

Figure 4.19 In the Open File dialog box, locate the clip that you want to view, and click Open.

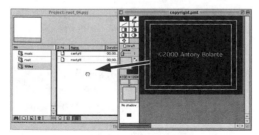

Figure 4.20 To add an open clip to the project, drag it to the Project window.

Opening Clips

You can open a clip that is not currently listed in the Project window and, therefore, not part of the current project. This way, you can look at a clip before you choose to add it to the project.

To open a clip that is not in the project:

1. Choose File > Open (**Figure 4.18**).

    The Open File dialog box appears.

2. Locate the clip that you want to view, and click Open (**Figure 4.19**).

    The clip opens in the source view or clip window, depending on the media type and the preferences you set (see the preceding section, "Clip Windows").

To add an open clip to the project:

Do one of the following:

◆ Drag an open clip to the Project window (**Figure 4.20**).

◆ Drag an open clip to an available track in the timeline.

◆ With the open clip selected, choose Clip > Add Clip to Project (**Figure 4.21**), or press ⌘-Ⓙ (Mac) or Ctrl-Ⓙ (Windows).

Figure 4.21 You can also choose Clip > Add Clip to Project.

OPENING CLIPS

Still-Image Clip Windows

Still-image files always open in a separate clip window. Because these files consist of only one frame, they do not have the same controller as audio or video clips. Instead of choosing an in and out point for still images, you simply set a *duration*—the length of time you want the still image to display in the program. See Chapter 3 for details on setting the still-image default duration.

Figure 4.22 In the still image's clip window, click the Duration button.

To set the duration of a still image:

1. Double-click a still image.

   Still-image clips always open in a separate clip window.

2. In the clip window, click the Duration button (**Figure 4.22**).

   The Clip Duration dialog box appears.

Figure 4.23 Enter a duration in the Clip Duration dialog box.

3. Enter a duration, and click OK (**Figure 4.23**).

   The duration you set appears in the clip information when you select the clip in the Project window and when you add it to the timeline. At any time, you can change the duration of the still-image clip in the Project window or the instance of the clip in the timeline.

✔ Tip

■ You may need to specify the way that Premiere treats the aspect ratio of a still image. See "Importing Still Images" and the sidebar "Aspect Ratios," in Chapter 3 for more information about how Premiere can interpret the dimensions of still images.

Entering Frame Values

Any duration number that you enter in Premiere has a *threshold* of 100. That is, numbers 99 and below are interpreted as frames. Numbers 100 and above are expressed in the units of the selected time display. In a project that uses a timecode display, for example, the number 99 is interpreted as 99 frames, or 3 seconds and 9 frames; the number 100 is interpreted as seconds and frames, or 1 second and 00 frames. When using a film time display numbers over 100 are interpreted as feet and frames. So in a 35mm display, 99 would be 99 frames, or 6 feet and 3 frames; 100 would be 1 foot and 00 frames.

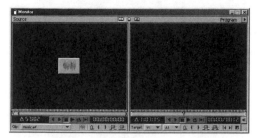

Figure 4.24 In the source view, audio clips display an audio icon.

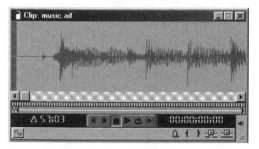

Figure 4.25 An audio-clip window differs from video-clip windows.

Audio Clip Windows

When loaded into the source view of the Monitor window, audio clips work the same way as movie clips. In the source view, audio clips display an audio icon.

When you open an audio clip in a separate clip window, however, it looks and operates slightly differently from the clip window for movies. See the following section, "Using Audio Clip Windows."

To open an audio clip in the source view:

Do one of the following:

◆ Double-click an audio-only clip in the project, or drag it to the source view.

or

◆ Double-click the audio portion of the clip in the audio track of the timeline.

The audio clip opens in the source view (**Figure 4.24**).

To open a separate clip window for audio:

◆ Option-double-click the audio clip in the Project window or in an audio track of the timeline.

The audio clip opens in a separate audio-clip window (**Figure 4.25**).

Using Audio-Clip Windows

The clip window for audio contains several unique features. Audio-clip windows display the audio as a *waveform*—a kind of graph of the audio's power over time. Often, you can identify particular sounds simply by examining the audio waveform. Powerful beats in a song are depicted as spikes in the waveform, for example, and pauses between lines of dialogue appear as lines. In addition, a vertical line indicates the current frame of the audio—the position of the playback head, if you will. You can cue the position of the playback line instantly simply by clicking the waveform area of the audio-clip window. The audio-clip window also displays edit marks; the in point, out point, and markers all appear in the waveform as flagged edit lines. (For more information about editing marks, see "Setting Edit Marks" later in this chapter.)

To change the audio waveform:

◆ Click the waveform button to display a more expanded or condensed view of the waveform (**Figure 4.26**):

⌒ displays the most expanded view of the audio waveform (**Figure 4.27**).

∿ displays a moderately expanded view of the audio waveform.

〰 displays a moderately condensed view of the audio waveform.

▥ displays the most condensed view of the audio waveform (**Figure 4.28**).

The setting doesn't change the audio in any way, just your view of the audio waveform.

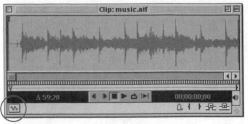

Figure 4.26 The audio-clip window includes a button to toggle the waveform display between views.

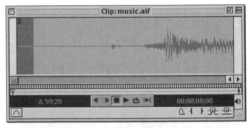

Figure 4.27 The most expanded view of the audio clip shows more detail in the waveform.

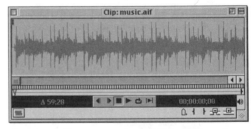

Figure 4.28 The most condensed view of the audio clip shows less detail but more of the waveform.

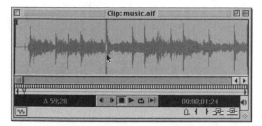

Figure 4.29 You can cue the current time of the audio clip by clicking the waveform area. A vertical line indicates the current time.

Figure 4.30 You can drag the resize box of the audio window to see more of the audio waveform.

To cue the playback line in the audio-clip window:

◆ Click the point in the audio waveform where you want to cue the current time (**Figure 4.29**).

If the audio is currently playing back, the audio instantly begins playing from the point you clicked.

To view more of the audio waveform:

◆ Drag the resize box in the corner of the audio-clip window to increase the size of the window (**Figure 4.30**).

Setting the Time Display

You can see the frame number of the current source clip and program in the time display of their respective views in the Monitor window. You can set which counting method is used in each time display to suit your footage or your output goals.

Though you set the time display as part of the project settings, you can change it at any time. You set the time display of the source view separately. As you learned in Chapter 2 ("Specifying the General Settings"), changing the time display merely changes Premiere's counting method, not the timebase used by the project or the timecode encoded on the source movie file.

To change the count in the source controller:

1. From the Monitor window's pull-down menu, choose Monitor Window Options (**Figure 4.31**).

   The Monitor Window Options dialog box appears (**Figure 4.32**).

2. From the Count pull-down menu, choose the time-measurement method you want to use (**Figure 4.33**):

   24 fps Timecode—standard film.

   25 fps Timecode—PAL video.

   30 fps Drop-Frame Timecode—NTSC video using drop-frame TC, used by standard DV.

   30 fps Non Drop-Frame Timecode—NTSC video using non-drop-frame TC.

   Frames/Samples—video frames and audio samples, useful in audio editing.

   Feet/Frames 16mm—16mm film, which is 40 frames/foot.

   Feet/Frames 35mm—35mm film, which measures 16 frames/foot.

Figure 4.31 From the Monitor window's pull-down menu, choose Monitor Window Options.

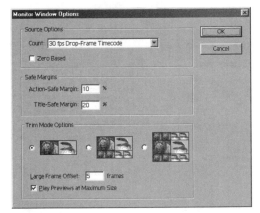

Figure 4.32 The Monitor Window Options dialog box appears.

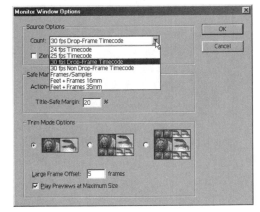

Figure 4.33 From the Count pull-down menu, choose the time-measurement method you want to use.

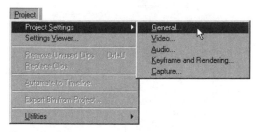

Figure 4.34 Choose Project > Project Settings > General.

Figure 4.35 The General panel of the Project Settings dialog box appears.

Figure 4.36 From the Time Display pull-down menu, choose the time measurement method you want to use.

To change the time-display count in the program view:

1. Choose Project > Project Settings > General (**Figure 4.34**).

   The General panel of the Project Settings dialog box appears (**Figure 4.35**).

2. From the Time Display pull-down menu, choose the time-measurement method you want to use (**Figure 4.36**).

3. Click OK to close the Project Settings dialog box.

   The counting method you chose appears in the time display of the program view of the Monitor window.

✔ Tips

- ⌘-clicking (Mac) or Ctrl-clicking (Windows) either time display toggles through the time measurement options in the order listed in "To change the count in the source controller" earlier in this chapter.

- Setting the source view's time display to Frames/Samples allows you to set audio in points based on audio samples rather than video frames (see "Setting Accurate Audio In Points" later in this chapter).

Playback Controls

Whether you're using a clip window, the source view, or the program view controller, the basic playback controls look and work the same. Most playback controls also have one or more keyboard shortcuts, which are well worth learning (**Figure 4.37**).

Before you use keyboard playback controls, however, make sure that you first select the proper view of the Monitor window. When you select a view, its image frame appears highlighted, and the time display becomes bright green.

Also bear in mind that the program view of the monitor corresponds to the timeline. As you change the current frame in the program view, watch how it affects the edit line in the timeline (and vice versa). The same keyboard playback commands that work for the program view also work when the Timeline window is selected.

To use the playback controls:

◆ Below the image in the source view, program view, or separate source monitor, choose the appropriate playback control:

Play—plays the clip or program until it reaches the last frame.

Stop—stops playback.

Frame advance—moves the current view one frame forward in time (or forward by the timebase division you selected for the time display).

Frame reverse—moves the current view one frame back (or backward by the timebase division you selected for the time display).

Loop selection—repeatedly plays the portion of the clip or program between the selected in and out points until you click Stop.

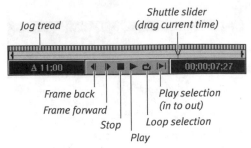

Figure 4.37 Playback controls work the same way in the source view, the program view, and the clip window.

Play selection—plays the portion of the clip or program between the selected in and out point one time.

Jog tread—advances or reverses the clip by small amounts as you drag and release the control. The jog tread is comparable to a jog wheel on a video deck.

Shuttle slider—quickly scans through the clip as you drag the small line. The extreme left side of the slider corresponds to the first frame of the clip; the extreme right side corresponds to the last frame.

For more information about in and out points, see "Setting In and Out Points" later in this chapter.

To use keyboard shortcuts to control playback:

1. Make sure that the appropriate view is active.

2. *Do one of the following:*

▲ To play in reverse, press J.

▲ To stop playback, press K.

▲ To play forward, press L, ~ (tilde).

▲ To increase playback speed, press J or L again.

▲ To toggle play and stop, press the spacebar.

▲ To cue to the first frame, press the ↑.

▲ To cue to the last frame, press the ↓.

▲ To advance one frame, press →.

▲ To reverse one frame, press ←.

▲ To play from the current frame to the out point, ⌘-click (Mac) or Ctrl-click (Windows) the play button.

▲ To play from the in point to the out point with a preroll and postroll (additional frames before and after the selected frames), Option-click (Mac) or Ctrl-click (Windows) the play button.

✔ Tip

■ The J-K-L keyboard combination is worth getting used to. In the next chapter, you'll see how you can use J-K-L along with other keyboard shortcuts for speedy keyboard-based editing. In fact, this keyboard combination has become standard in several popular editing programs. You can think of them as the "home keys" of nonlinear editing.

Cueing Clips Numerically

You can use the time displays to cue the source and program views to a particular frame number, or *absolute time*. Or you can cue to a *relative time*—in other words, add frames to or subtract frames from the current time.

To cue the view to an absolute time:

1. Click the view of the Monitor window that you want to activate.

2. Click the time display for the selected view to highlight the number (**Figure 4.38**).

3. Enter the number of the frame that you want to view, and press [Return] (Mac) or [Enter] (Windows) (**Figure 4.39**).

   As long as the frame number that you entered exists, the view displays that frame (**Figure 4.40**).

Figure 4.38 Click the time display for the selected view to highlight the number.

Figure 4.39 Enter the frame number, and press [Return] (Mac) or [Enter] (Windows).

Figure 4.40 As long as the frame number that you entered exists, the view displays that frame.

Figure 4.41 You can type a relative number to cue the view. Here, the time display is set to cue the current time 60 frames forward.

To cue the view to a relative time:

1. Click either view of the Monitor window to activate it.

2. Click the time display for the selected view to highlight the number.

3. Type a plus (+) or a minus (−) sign and a number (**Figure 4.41**).

   To cue the clip 30 frames after the current frame, for example, type **+30**. To cue the view 60 frames before the current frame, type **−60**.

✔ Tips

- You can highlight individual numbers in the current-time readout and change them to cue the current frame of the view.

- If the time that you enter in the current-time readout does not exist, the view is cued to the nearest available frame— either the first or the last frame of the clip or program.

Master Clips and Clip Instances

Before Premiere 5, whenever you used a clip in the timeline more than once, every use was listed separately in the project. In the current version of Premiere, a clip is listed only once, no matter how many times you use it.

The original clip is called a *master clip*, and each time you use it, you create a new *instance* of the master clip. Clip instances are also referred to as *program clips*. It's useful to understand the distinction between master clips and program clips.

As you know, loading a master clip in the source view makes its name appear in the source-view pull-down menu, and all the frames of the footage are available for playback (**Figure 4.42**). When you load a clip from the timeline, on the other hand, its name appears in the source-view pull-down menu with a number. The number indicates the clip's position in the timeline and reveals that you're viewing a particular instance of the clip (**Figure 4.43**). In the source view, you can play only the frames of an instance which actually appear in the program.

In the source view, you can change the edit marks to shorten a clip instance but not lengthen it. A simple command allows you to load the clip instance's related master clip, however. Alternatively, you can adjust the clip directly in the timeline or by using trim mode. These practical implications will become clearer as you gain more editing experience. For now, you just need to know the basic difference between master clips and individual clip instances.

Although clip instances can be manipulated independently, they still refer to a corresponding master clip, If you delete a master clip, you also delete its instances.

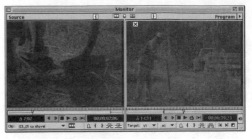

Figure 4.42 A master clip appears in the source view with its original name and full duration.

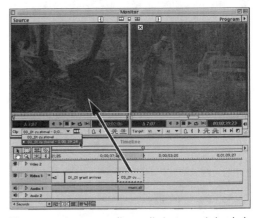

Figure 4.43 A program clip, or clip instance, is loaded from the program in the timeline. Its position in the timeline is added to its name, and its duration reflects its current length in the program.

✔ Tip

■ Because their names can be so similar, clip instances can be difficult to distinguish from one another in the source-view pull-down menu. If you do want to change a clip in the timeline by using source view controls, make sure that you are viewing the correct instance. If you're unsure which one is correct, double-click the instance in the timeline to reload it into the source view.

Setting Edit Marks

Setting edit marks designates the important frames of your clips, as well as those of the program. The following sections focus on setting marks for source clips. In the chapters to follow, you'll apply to the program what you learn here about setting marks.

The most important marks include the in point and out point, which define the portion of a clip that you want to include in the program. You can also set clip markers, which specify other frames of interest.

In Premiere 6, the Monitor window includes a marker button, in addition to the mark in and mark out buttons. The marker-button menu allows you to set, go to, and clear any kind of edit mark. The following tasks emphasize using the controls in the Monitor window to set edit marks.

Using Source Markers

During the editing process, you often need a way to mark important points in time. *Markers* allow you to visibly stamp these points in both individual clips and in the time ruler of the Timeline window (**Figures 4.44** and **4.45**). Markers help you visually identify beats in a song, synchronize video with a sound effect, or note where a title should fade up.

In each clip and in the time ruler, you can add up to 10 numbered markers (0 through 9) and up to 999 unnumbered markers. You can quickly cue the clip or the program directly to a numbered marker or to consecutive markers.

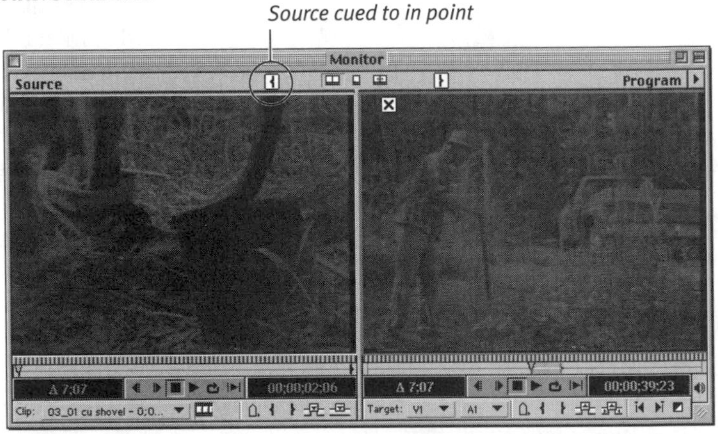

Source cued to in point

Figure 4.44 Clip markers appear above the marked frame in the Monitor window.

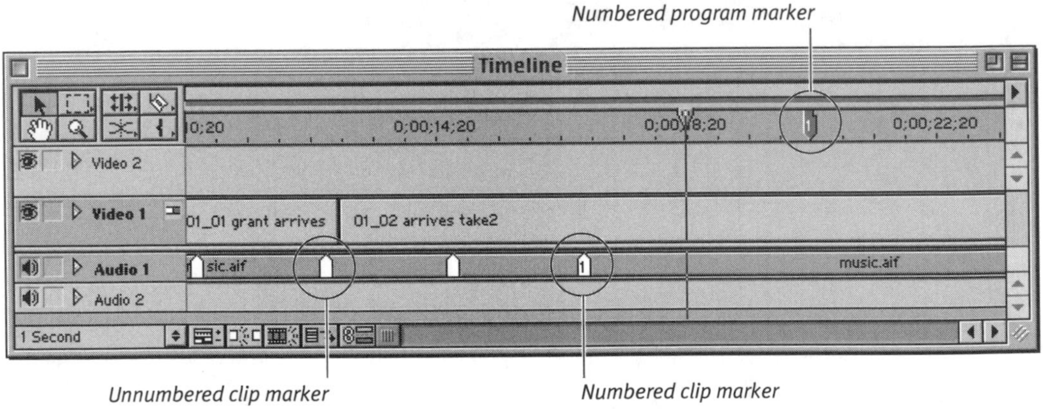

Numbered program marker

Unnumbered clip marker   *Numbered clip marker*

Figure 4.45 In the timeline, clip markers appear within the clip. Program markers appear in the time ruler of the timeline.

Figure 4.46 In the Monitor window, click the marker button.

Figure 4.47 From the Marker menu, choose an unnumbered or numbered marker to mark the current frame.

You can add markers to a clip in the source view or to a clip in the timeline. When you add markers to a master clip, its markers are included with the clip when you add it to the timeline or when you create a subclip (see "Using Subclips" later in this chapter). The markers aren't added to existing subclips or instances of the clip that are already in the timeline. This means that each instance of the clip and each subclip can have a unique set of markers and aren't subject to unintentional changes.

The following sections focus on applying markers to master clips in the source view. Though many of the same techniques can be used for setting markers in the time ruler and for working with program clips, features and techniques unique to those types of markers are discussed in Chapter 6.

To add a marker to a clip in the source view:

1. Open a source clip in the source view or in a clip window.

2. Cue the current frame to the point where you want to add a marker.

3. In the Monitor window, click the marker button (**Figure 4.46**).

   The Marker menu appears.

4. From the Marker menu, choose one of the following options (**Figure 4.47**):

   Mark > Unnumbered—to mark the frame with an unnumbered marker.

   Mark > 0-9—to mark the frame with a marker numbered 0-9.

   continues on next page

This marker appears above the source view whenever the clip is cued to the marked frame (**Figure 4.48**).

To add source markers on the fly:

1. Play a clip in the source view or clip window.

2. Do one of the following:
   - ▲ To add unnumbered markers, press the asterisk key (*) in the number keypad, or press Option-⌘-= (Mac) or Alt-Ctrl-= (Windows).

   or

   - ▲ To add numbered markers, press Option-⌘ (Mac) or Alt-Ctrl (Windows) and a number.

   When you stop playback, the markers appear.

✔ Tips

- ■ Adding a marker to a frame where another marker exists overwrites the first marker. Applying a numbered marker to a different frame eliminates its original position.

- ■ Markers are helpful for marking where lines of dialogue or voiceover begin and end. Try using a numbered marker at the beginning of a line and an unnumbered marker at the end of a line. This technique conserves your limited numbered markers, and makes it easy to identify pauses between lines (which often need to be cut).

- ■ Setting a poster frame actually sets the zero marker for a clip. Therefore, resetting the zero marker also resets the poster frame. For more information about poster frames, see Chapter 3.

- ■ The zero marker/poster frame also has special uses with effects, titles, and the frame-hold command. You may want to conserve the zero marker for these purposes.

Figure 4.48 This marker appears above the source view whenever the clip is cued to the marked frame.

Figure 4.49 Cue the clip to the frame where you want the clip to start, and click the mark in button or press I.

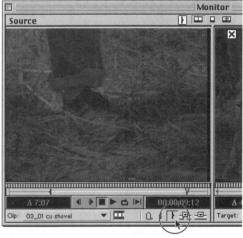

Figure 4.50 Cue the clip to the frame where you want the clip to end, and click the mark out button or press O.

Setting In and Out Points

Setting in points and out points is central to all editing. An *in point* is where you want the clip to start playing, and the *out point* is where you want the clip to stop playing. The length of time between the in and out points is called the *duration*.

When you edit, you can set in and out points for both the source clips and the program. In Premiere, you can accomplish this essential editing task in many ways. Though this section focuses on using the controls in the Monitor window to set in and out points for the source, you will apply the same techniques to setting in and out points for the program. In the chapters to follow, you'll learn many other ways to set and change in and out points.

To mark in and out points in the Monitor window:

1. *Do one of the following:*
   ▲ To mark edit points in the source, open a source clip in the source view or a clip window.

   or

   ▲ To mark edit points in the program, activate the program view or the Timeline window.

2. Cue the clip to the frame where you want the clip to start, and click the mark in button or press ⑴ (**Figure 4.49**). An in-point icon ⏻ appears at the current frame indicator in the shuttle slider part of the playback controls.

3. Cue the clip to the frame where you want the clip to end, and click the mark out button or press ⓞ (**Figure 4.50**).

   continues on next page

An out-point icon ⊞ appears at the current-frame indicator in the shuttle slider section of the playback controls.

4. To change the in or out point, repeat steps 2 and 3, or drag the in- or out-point icon to a new position in the shuttle slider track (**Figure 4.51**).

   The duration display reflects the time between the in and out points (**Figure 4.52**).

5. To preview your selection, click one of the following:

   Loop button— 🔄 to continuously loop playback from the in point to the out point.

   Play Selection button— ⏯ to play from the in point to the out point a single time.

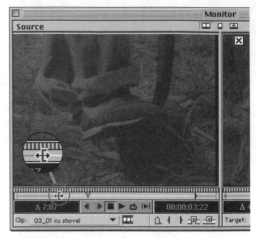

Figure 4.51 You can drag the in- and out-point icons in the shuttle slider section of the view's playback controls.

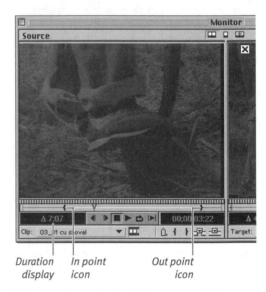

Duration   In point   Out point
display   icon   icon

Figure 4.52 In- and out-point icons appear in the controller, and the duration display reflects the difference between the in and out points.

Figure 4.53 When you change the in or out point of a clip that you opened from the timeline, an Apply button appears above the source view.

✔ Tips

- If the source movie file contains both video and audio, you can set in and out points for video and audio separately. This technique provides one way to create *split edits*, also known as L-cuts. For more information about creating split edits, see Chapter 7.

- When you change the in or out point of a clip that you opened from the timeline, an Apply button appears above the source view (**Figure 4.53**). Click the Apply button to cause the changes that you made to take effect in the timeline. If you do not open a clip in the program, the Apply button does not appear (see "Master Clips and Clip Instances" earlier in this chapter). For more information about editing in the timeline, see Chapter 6.

- Because clips merely refer to media files, the frames of the entire movie file are always available for use.

Cueing to Edit Marks

You can quickly cue the current frame of a Monitor-window view to any edit mark.

To go to edit marks in the source view:

1. Load a source clip into the source view or a clip window.

2. In the source view, click the marker button.

   The Marker menu appears.

3. Choose Clip > Go To, and then choose an option (**Figure 4.54**):

   Next—cues to the marker after the current frame.

   Previous—cues to the marker before to the current frame.

   In—cues to the clip's in point.

   Out—cues to the clip's out point.

   Video In—cues to the video in point when split edit marks are set.

   Video Out—cues to the video in point when split edit marks are set.

   Audio In—cues to the video in point when split edit marks are set.

   Audio Out—cues to the video in point when split edit marks are set.

   0-9—cues to a numbered marker.

   Marks that are in use appear with a bullet (·) next to them.

   When you cue to an edit mark, the corresponding icon appears above the image in the Monitor window (**Figure 4.55**).

To clear edit marks:

1. Load a source clip into the source view or a clip window.

2. In the source view or clip window, click the marker button.

   The Marker menu appears.

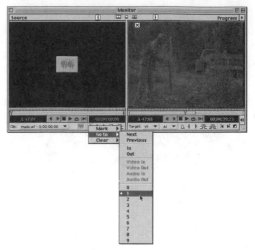

Figure 4.54 In the marker menu, choose Clip > Go To > and choose an option. Markers that are in use appear with a bullet (•) next to them in the list.

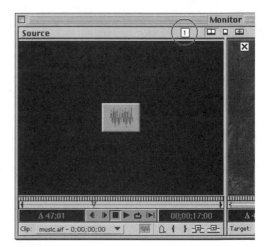

Figure 4.55 When you cue a view to an edit mark, the corresponding icon appears above the image in the view.

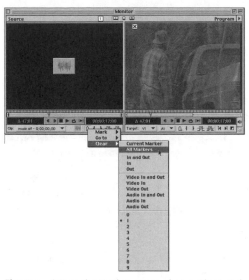

Figure 4.56 From the Marker menu, choose Clear, and then choose an option.

3. Choose Clear and then choose an option (**Figure 4.56**):

Current Marker—removes the marker at the current frame, if any.

All Markers—removes all markers from the clip.

In and Out—resets both the in and out point to the beginning and end of the clip, respectively.

In—resets the clip's in point to the beginning of the clip.

Out—resets the clip's out point to the end of the clip.

Video In and Out—resets the clip's video in and out points to the beginning and end of the clip, respectively.

Video In—clears the video in point when split edit marks are set.

Video Out—clears the video in point when split edit marks are set.

Audio In and Out—resets the clip's audio in and out points to the beginning and end of the clip, respectively.

Audio In—clears the audio in point when split edit marks are set.

Audio Out—clears the audio in point when split edit marks are set.

0-9—cues to a numbered marker.

To clear in and out points by clicking:

Do one of the following:

◆ To delete the in point, (Option)-click (Mac) or (Alt)-click (Windows) the mark in button.

◆ To delete the out point, (Option)-click (Mac) or (Alt)-click (Windows) the mark out button.

Clearing the in point resets its position to the first frame of the complete clip; clearing the out point resets its position to the last frame of the complete clip.

✔ Tip

■ To delete both the in point and the out point, press (G).

Setting Accurate Audio In Points

Setting an in or out point can be compared with cutting film between image frames. Naturally, you can't cut a point in the middle of a frame. In Premiere, frame divisions are set by the timebase of the project, which is based on one of several standard frame rates: 24 fps film, 25 fps PAL video, 29.97 fps NTSC video, or 30 fps video.

Digital audio, however, isn't based on video frame rates, but on audio sample rates. As you recall from Chapter 2, a CD-quality sample rate is 44.1 kHz, or approximately 44,100 samples per second. Therefore, it's possible to cut audio much more finely than video.

In Premiere, you can take advantage of audio's more-precise time divisions by setting audio in points based on samples, rather than frames. Out points, however, are constrained to use the project's timebase divisions.

To set an audio in point based on samples:

1. [Option]-click (Mac) or [Alt]-click (Windows) an audio clip to view it in a separate clip window (**Figure 4.57**).

   Though you can set a sample-based in point by using the source window, using a separate clip window allows you to view its waveform (see "Using Audio-Clip Windows" earlier in this chapter).

2. Choose Window > Window Options > Clip Window Options (**Figure 4.58**). The Clip Window Options dialog box appears (**Figure 4.59**).

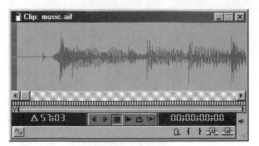

Figure 4.57 Open an audio clip in a clip window.

Figure 4.58 Choose Window > Window Options > Clip Window Options.

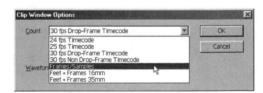

Figure 4.59 The Clip Window Options dialog box appears.

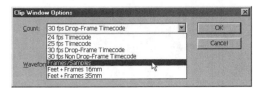

Figure 4.60 In the Clip Window Options dialog box, choose Frames/Samples from the Count pull-down menu.

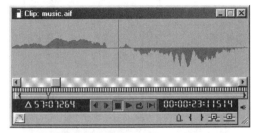

Figure 4.61 The audio-clip window's time display uses frames and samples. You can cue the clip to the sample you want and click the mark in button.

3. From the Count pull-down menu, choose Frames/Samples (**Figure 4.60**), and click OK.

   The time display of the clip window displays frames and audio samples. Clicking the frame-advance button moves the clip forward only one audio sample at a time.

4. Cue the audio to the point where you want the clip to start, and click the mark in button or press ⊙ (**Figure 4.61**).

   The in point is based on audio samples of the clip. The out point must be based on timebase divisions that you set in the project settings.

   You can reset the time display without disturbing the audio in point.

Using Subclips

If you want to name an instance of a clip, or if you want it to be listed separately in the program, you should create a subclip. A *subclip* is created from a portion of a master clip.

Subclips provide you another way to subdivide and organize your source materials. You can create several subclips from a very long master clip, for example, and give each copy a unique name. Without subclips, you would have to search through the lengthy master clip to find the part that you want to use.

Just as master clips refer to media files, subclips refer to the master clip from which the clips were created. If the master clip is deleted, its subclips are also deleted. Otherwise, subclips function exactly like master clips.

In this book and elsewhere, the generic term *clip* refers to both master clips and subclips unless making a distinction between those terms is important.

To create a subclip:

1. Open a master clip in the source view or a separate clip window.

2. Cue the clip to the frame where you want the clip to start, and click the mark in button or press ⏸.

3. Cue the clip to the frame where you want the clip to end, and click the mark out button or press ⏸ (**Figure 4.62**).

   Any markers that you set in the master clip are included in the subclip.

4. Drag the clip from the source view or clip window to the Project window (**Figure 4.63**).

   The Duplicate Clip dialog box opens.

Figure 4.62 Open a master clip, and set edit marks.

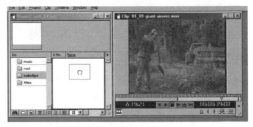

Figure 4.63 Drag the clip from the source view or clip window to the Project window.

Figure 4.64 In the Duplicate Clip dialog box, enter a name for the subclip, and click OK.

Figure 4.65 The subclip appears in the Project window with the name you specified.

5. Enter a name for the subclip, and click OK (**Figure 4.64**).

The subclip appears in the Project window with the name you specified (**Figure 4.65**). The subclip contains only the portion of the master clip you specified by setting in and out points in the master clip.

✔ Tips

■ Copying, pasting, and dragging clips to the timeline creates another instance of the clip, not a subclip. See "Master Clips and Clip Instances" earlier in this chapter.

■ The whole point of creating a subclip is to define a more limited range of frames. If you decide that you need frames that were in its associated master clip, you have to open the master clip.

■ Duplicating or copying and pasting a clip in the project window also creates a subclip. These methods, however, create a subclip that's a complete copy of the master clip rather than a selected portion of the master clip.

■ Subclips are also useful for creating a storyboard edit, as described in Chapter 5.

USING SUBCLIPS

CREATING
A PROGRAM

The last chapter introduced you to the source-footage side of the editing equation. You familiarized yourself with the Monitor window and learned how to use its controls to view footage and set edit marks. In broad terms, you learned how to view and cut the source footage. Now you're ready to arrange the selected portions of the clips into a sequence. This is the program side of the editing equation, in which you join the clips.

Though this chapter includes techniques that use the Timeline window, it concentrates on using the Monitor window to create and view an edited sequence. You may be surprised to find that—with the exception of audio mixing and effects editing—it's possible to do almost all of your editing using the Monitor window alone, without even looking at the timeline. You will look at the Timeline window; of course, but for now, you'll use it mostly to view your edits, not to make them. Eventually, you'll use all the windows as an integrated editing system.

As suggested in Chapter 4, editing techniques are both flexible and tightly integrated. The number of choices can make the process seem more complex than it really is. As you proceed, remember that editing can always be reduced to two simple tasks: defining the part of the clip you want to use and adding it to a particular point in the program.

The basic editing methods covered in this chapter fall into three categories: drag-and-drop editing; editing with the controls in the Monitor window; and a variation of drag-and-drop editing called automated storyboard editing.

Drag-and-Drop vs. Monitor-Window Controls

You add clips to the program in two primary ways. Dragging and dropping is one way; using the Monitor window controls is the other. Each method has its advantages, so knowing both is wise.

Drag-and-drop

The drag-and-drop method takes advantage of the computer's ability to display clips as objects that you can move and place by using the mouse. Most users find this technique to be the most intuitive and reassuringly similar to the way that the Macintosh and Windows systems work (**Figure 5.1**).

Monitor window controls

Although this method is not as intuitive as dragging and dropping clips into the timeline, using the Monitor window controls provides a great degree of flexibility and control. The Monitor window enables you to use a traditional editing technique called three-point editing. You can also perform four-point edits. (For more information on both techniques, see "Editing with the Monitor Window Controls" later in this chapter.) Because the Monitor window's editing controls have single-stroke keyboard shortcuts, using them can be much faster than editing by dragging and dropping (**Figure 5.2**). Most experienced editors favor using the Monitor window controls because of their advantages and consistency with other editing systems.

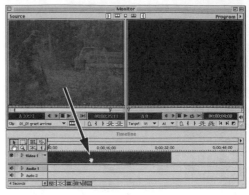

Figure 5.1 The drag-and-drop method of editing is intuitive and straightforward. Here, a clip is dragged from the source view to the Timeline window.

Figure 5.2 Using the editing controls in the Monitor window can give you speed and control. In this example, a typical three-point edit has been performed to insert another clip into the middle of the clip added in Figure 5.1. The insert button is magnified.

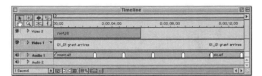

Figure 5.3 In the timeline, each track of video and audio is represented as a separate horizontal row.

Figure 5.4 In the source view, you select the tracks that you want to add by clicking the take video and take audio buttons.

Figure 5.5 For the program, you can choose target tracks from the pull-down menu in the program view of the Monitor window.

Choosing Source and Target Tracks

Video and audio material are often described as discrete tracks of information due to the way that they are physically stored on traditional media, such as magnetic tape. Digital files don't encode video and audio in the same way that tape does, of course. Nevertheless, it's still helpful to think of video and audio as occupying tracks that you can manipulate separately.

In Premiere's timeline, video and audio tracks are represented as separate horizontal rows stacked below a time ruler (**Figure 5.3**). By selecting source and target tracks, you can add video only, audio only, or both video and audio to any combination of tracks in the timeline.

In drag-and-drop editing, you choose the source tracks by clicking the take video and take audio buttons, located below the source view of the Monitor window (as explained in the following section, "To select source tracks") (**Figure 5.4**). You choose the destination, or *target,* tracks by simply dropping the clip into the timeline.

When you edit with the Monitor window controls, however, you must specify both the source and target tracks before you perform an edit. After all, you can choose any of several tracks in the timeline, and Premiere can't make this decision for you. You can choose the video and audio tracks to which a clip will be added from the Target menu below the program view of the Monitor window (explained in "To select target tracks" later in this chapter) (**Figure 5.5**).

continues on next page

By default, both video and audio are selected for the source (if both are available). Below the program view, Video 1 and Audio 1 are selected as the target tracks. For more information about tracks in the timeline, see Chapter 6.

To select source tracks:

Below the source view, *do either of the following:*

◆ To prevent the source video from being added to the timeline, click the take video button so that it appears crossed out. To use the source video, click again to make the take video button appear.

or

◆ To prevent the source audio from being added to the timeline, click the take audio button so that it appears crossed out. To use the source audio, click again to make the take audio button appear (**Figures 5.6** and **5.7**).

If the source clip does not contain a track, the corresponding button will not appear below the source view.

Figure 5.6 Click the take video and take audio buttons to toggle them on and off.

Figure 5.7 When the button appears crossed out, the track will be excluded when you add the clip to the timeline.

Figure 5.8 Choose a video track from the Target pull-down menu in the program view.

Figure 5.9 Choose an audio track from the Target pull-down menu in the program view.

To select target tracks:

Below the program view, *do either of the following:*

◆ From the Target pull-down menu for video, choose the track in the timeline to which you want to add the source video (**Figure 5.8**).

If you don't want to affect the target video track, choose None.

or

◆ From the Target pull-down menu for audio, choose the track in the timeline to which you want to add the source audio (**Figure 5.9**).

If you don't want to affect the target audio track, choose None.

✔ Tip

■ You can also choose a target track by clicking the name of a track in the timeline so that it becomes bold. Clicking the current target track's name deselects it, and it no longer appears bold.

CHOOSING SOURCE AND TARGET TRACKS

125

Drag-and-Drop Editing

Wherever a source clip appears in Premiere, chances are that you can use the mouse to drag it into the timeline.

To add a clip to the timeline from the source view or clip window:

1. Open a clip in the source view of the Monitor window or in a separate clip window (**Figure 5.10**).

2. Set the in point and out point in the source clip.

   You may also want to set numbered or unnumbered markers. See "Setting Editing Marks" in Chapter 4.

3. To set the source tracks, *do either of the following:*

   ▲ To include the source video, set the take video button so that the icon appears. To exclude source video, set the take video button so that the icon is crossed out.

   or

   ▲ To include the source audio, set the take audio button so that the icon appears. To exclude source audio, set the take audio button so that the icon is crossed out. (See "Choosing Source and Target Tracks" earlier in this chapter.)

4. Drag the clip from the source view or clip window to an unused portion of the timeline's video or audio track (**Figure 5.11**).

   Clips containing video or both video and audio must be dragged to an empty video track; clips containing audio only must be dragged to an audio track.

In point   *Source track video only*   *Out point*

Figure 5.10 In the source view or clip window, set an in point, an out point, and select source tracks.

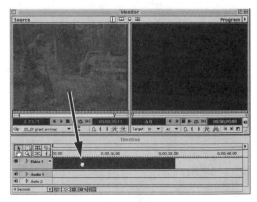

Figure 5.11 Drag the clip to an unoccupied track in the timeline.

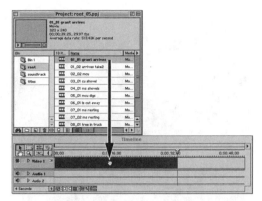

Figure 5.12 Drag a clip from the Project window to an unoccupied track in the timeline.

To add clips to the program from the Project window:

1. Select one or more clips in the Project window.

2. Drag the clip or clips to an unused portion of the timeline's video or audio track (**Figure 5.12**).

   The clip appears in the timeline. If you add more than one clip, the clips appear in the timeline in the sequence in which they are listed in the Project window.

✔ Tip

- If you want to add both video and audio to the program, make sure that you have enough space in both the video and audio tracks of the timeline. If one of the tracks is occupied, you won't be able to drop a linked clip there.

To add a clip between adjacent clips in the timeline:

1. Drag a clip between two clips in the timeline.

   An arrow appears beside the next clip in the timeline (**Figure 5.13**).

2. Release the mouse button.

   The new clip is added to the timeline, and all the following clips shift forward in the timeline to make room for the new clip (**Figure 5.14**).

✔ Tips

- When you add a clip between adjacent clips, the tracks that shift depends on the Shift Tracks option that's selected. See "To specify the Shift Tracks option" later in this chapter.

- With the Project window set to the icon view, you can arrange clips or subclips in storyboard fashion. You may also want to mark in and out points for the clips. You can then select and drag your entire "storyboard" into the timeline to create a program quickly. Premiere 6 includes a dedicated feature for storyboard editing, covered in "Storyboard Editing" later in this chapter.

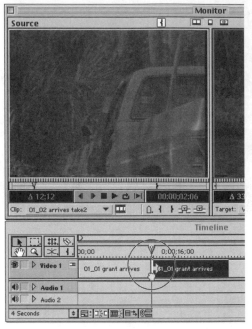

Figure 5.13 Drag a clip between two clips until an arrow appears beside the following clip.

Figure 5.14 The subsequent clips move forward in time to make room for the new clip.

Editing with the Monitor Window Controls

As suggested earlier in this chapter, editing with the Monitor window controls isn't as intuitive as the drag-and-drop method. The Monitor window controls, however, can provide greater flexibility and speed in editing. If you chose Premiere to take advantage of its professional editing tools, you owe it to yourself to learn these controls.

Before you proceed, however, you'll need to understand a few basic concepts:

Three-point and four-point editing— methods to determine where clips begin and end in both the source and the program.

Insert and overlay—methods to determine how a three-point or four-point edit affects the clips in the timeline.

Track options—a setting that determines whether insert edits shift clips in all tracks or only in selected tracks of the program.

Lift and extract—methods of removing frames from the program, comparable to the reverse methods of insert and overlay.

The following sections explain these concepts and then put them into practice. Don't worry—these ideas are as easy to grasp as they are essential. Taking a moment to learn them will be well worth the effort. If you prefer, you can try skipping ahead to the editing tasks and then turning back to see the full explanations.

Three-Point Editing

The *point* in the term *three-point editing* refers to in points and out points. As you know, in points and out points in the clip define where it starts and ends. Similarly, in and out points in the program define where the clip starts and ends in the program.

In drag-and-drop editing, you set the source in and out points in the source view, but the program's in and out points were implied by where you dragged it into the timeline. In the following sections, you mark both the source and program editing points in the Monitor window.

Technically, every edit has four points: source in, source out, program in, and program out. To add a clip to the program, you must define at least three of these four points in the source and program views. If you provide three points, Premiere figures out the fourth.

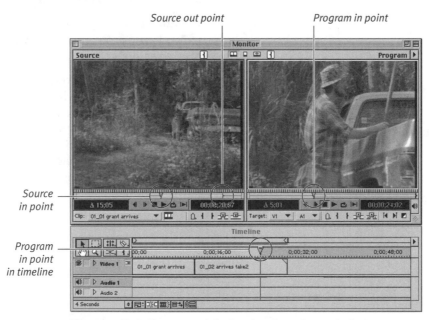

Figure 5.15 Typically, you supply both an in point and out point in the source, but only an in point in the program.

Most often, this means that you mark two in points and one out point. **Figure 5.15** shows a typical edit, in which the source in point and source out point define a portion of the clip, and the program in point defines where it starts in the program. The program out point is implied by the source out point.

Sometimes, however, it is more important to set where the clip ends than to set where it begins. In such a case, you mark two out points and only one in point. In the example shown in (**Figure 5.16**), the editor has determined that the next clip must begin after the last clip in the program (program in) and end at a certain point in the music, at marker #1 (program out). In addition, a particular frame of the clip (source out) must coincide with the program out point. Therefore, the editor doesn't need to mark the source in point, because it is determined by the program in point.

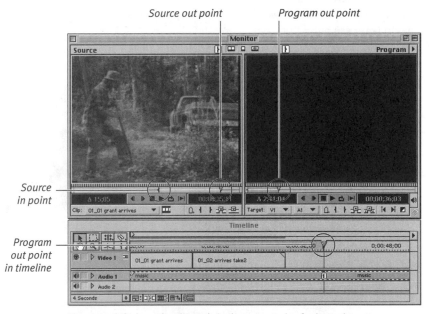

Source out point   *Program out point*

Source in point

Program out point in timeline

Figure 5.16 If where the clip ends in the program is of primary importance, you might specify a program in and out point, but only an out point for the source.

Four-Point Editing

As you have seen, every edit uses four points, but you need to set only three of them. Premiere always figures out the missing variable to balance out the editing equation. Actively marking all four points forces Premiere to balance the equation in another way. If the source duration differs from the program duration, Premiere asks whether you want to shorten the source clip or change the speed of the source clip to fit the program duration.

Typically, you use a four-point edit to change the speed of the source to match a defined area of the program. This technique is frequently called *fit to fill*, because you fit, or change, the duration of the source to fill the duration you specified in the program.

Suppose that you require a two-second cutaway or reaction shot, but your source clip includes only one second of footage. A four-point edit can stretch the one second of source footage to fill two seconds in the program. In the program, the clip plays in slow-motion—in this case, at half normal speed (**Figure 5.17**).

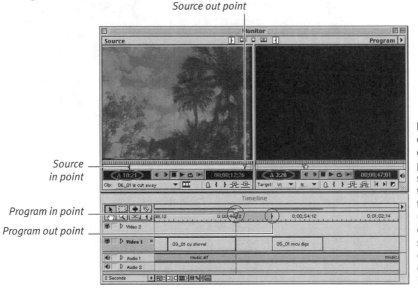

Source out point

Source in point

Program in point

Program out point

Figure 5.17 In this example, the four edit points are pointed out in the source view and timeline. Because the durations (circled) differ, the duration of the source will change to fit the duration defined in the program.

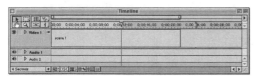

Figure 5.18 Here's what the timeline looks like before the edit. Note that the program in point occurs in the middle of a clip in the timeline. The time ruler and program markers also help you see the results of the edit.

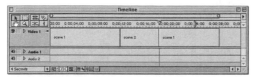

Figure 5.19 After an insert edit, everything after the program in point shifts forward in time to make room for the new clip.

Figure 5.20 Here's the same example in Figure 5.18 after an overlay edit. An overlay edit replaces material in the timeline.

Insert and Overlay

The Monitor window controls include two methods for performing three- and four-point edits: insert and overlay. These methods determine how the new clip affects the clips that are already in the program.

An *insert* edit works much like adding a clip using film, inserting the new clip without removing material that is already in the program reel. When you *insert* a clip, the source clip is added at the designated point in the timeline, and all the subsequent clips are shifted forward in time to make room for the new clip. If the insertion point in the program occurs at a point where clips already occupy the timeline, the clips in the timeline are split, and the portions after the edit are shifted forward in time (**Figures 5.18** and **5.19**). Whether clips are shifted in all tracks or only in selected tracks is determined by the Shift Tracks option, explained in the next section.

An *overlay* edit works like adding a clip using videotape, recording the new clip over any existing material on the master tape. When you *overlay* a clip, the source clip is added at the designated point in the timeline, replacing any clips that were already there (**Figure 5.20**).

Understanding Insert Edits

When you perform an insert edit, clips in the program shift later in time to accommodate the new clip. Several factors determine how the clips shift and which tracks are affected. Your choice of source and target tracks can affect how an insert edit works (see "Choosing Source and Target Tracks" earlier in this chapter). In addition, you can choose to lock or unlock tracks (see "Locking and Unlocking Tracks" in Chapter 6). The primary factor that governs how insert edits work, however, is the shift tracks option. (To learn more about the Timeline window options, see "Customizing the Timeline" in Chapter 6.)

When you set the shift tracks option to shift material in all unlocked tracks, an insert edit causes clips in all tracks of the timeline to move later in time (**Figures 5.21** and **5.22**). Only locked tracks are immune to insert edits (see "Locking and Unlocking Tracks" in Chapter 6). This is usually the best choice, because shifting all the material ensures that you maintain the clips' relative position in time and maintain synch between video and audio.

When you set the shift tracks option to shift material only in target tracks, an insert edit causes clips only in tracks that are designated as target tracks to shift forward in the timeline (**Figure 5.23**). Use this option with caution; used carelessly, it can disrupt the relative positions of clips in different tracks, as well as shift audio and video out of synch.

The shift tracks option also affects how clips shift back in time when you extract a range of frames from the program (see "Lift and Extract" later in this chapter).

Figure 5.21 This is what the clips in the program look like before an insert edit.

Figure 5.22 An insert edit can shift material in all unlocked tracks of the timeline.

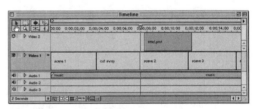

Figure 5.23 Alternatively, an insert edit can shift material in only the designated target tracks.

Figure 5.24 At the bottom of the Timeline window, click the shift tracks option icon to toggle it between shift material in all unlocked tracks...

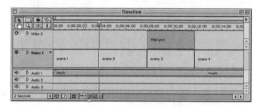

Figure 5.25 ... and shift material only in target tracks.

To specify the shift tracks option:

◆ At the bottom of the timeline window, click the shift tracks button to toggle between the two settings:

Shift material in all unlocked tracks— insert edits cause clips in all unlocked tracks of the timeline to shift later in time (**Figure 5.24**).

Shift material only in target tracks— insert edits cause only clips in target tracks to shift later in time (**Figure 5.25**).

UNDERSTANDING INSERT EDITS

Performing an Edit

Now that you understand the essential concepts behind an edit, it's time to put them into practice.

To perform a three-point edit:

1. View a source clip in the source view of the Monitor window.

2. Specify the tracks you want to use by clicking either of the following buttons:

   Take video—to use the source video in the program.

   Take audio—to use the source audio in the program (**Figure 5.26**).

3. In the program view, choose the target tracks from the corresponding Target pull-down menus (**Figure 5.27**).

   Choose None to exclude the video or audio track from being affected.

Figure 5.26 View a clip in source view, and select the source tracks you want to use.

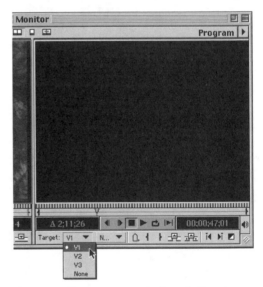

Figure 5.27 Choose target tracks from the Target pull-down menus of the program view.

Figure 5.28 Set at least three in and out points. Here, a source in point, a source out point and a program in point are set.

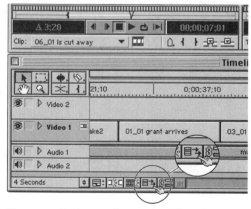

Figure 5.29 For insert edits, set the shift tracks option. Here, shift material in all tracks is selected.

4. Set any combination of three in and out points in the source and program views (**Figure 5.28**).

   Program in and out points appear both in the program-view controller and in the timeline. (See "Setting Edit Marks" in Chapter 4.)

5. To determine how an insert edit affects clips in the timeline, toggle the shift tracks button to display the appropriate icon (**Figure 5.29**):

   to shift material in all unlocked tracks.

   to shift material only in target tracks.

   continues on next page

6. In the source view, click the button for the type of edit you want to perform (**Figure 5.30**):

Insert—to shift subsequent clips in the timeline by the number of frames added to the program.

Overlay—to overwrite, or replace, the frames already in the program with the new frames.

The clip appears in the timeline in the position and tracks you specified (**Figure 5.31**). The edit line in the timeline window (which corresponds to the current frame of the program view) is cued to the end of the clip. The tracks that are affected by insert edits are determined by the shift tracks setting (see "Understanding Insert Edits" earlier in this chapter).

✔ Tip

■ If you do not specify an in or out point in the program view, the current program time (or edit line in the Timeline window) serves as the in point. After an edit, Premiere cues the current program time to the end of the new clip in the program and clears any program in and out points. You can save time by using the program's current time as the in point, especially when you want to assemble clips into a sequence quickly.

To perform a four-point edit:

1. Mark all four edit points in the source and program views (**Figure 5.32**).

2. Select the source tracks by clicking the take video and take audio buttons in the source view.

3. Choose the target tracks from the Target pull-down menus in the program view.

4. Set the shift tracks option.

Figure 5.30 In the source view, click insert or overlay. Here, an overlay edit is being performed.

Figure 5.31 The clip appears in the timeline in the position and tracks you specified.

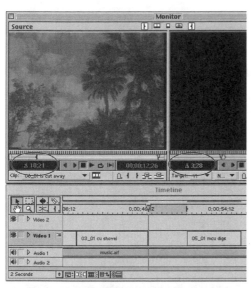

Figure 5.32 In this example, all four edit points are specified. Note the difference in the durations, which are circled.

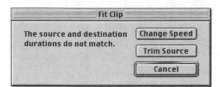

Figure 5.33 If the durations set in the source and program sides of the edit differ, Premiere prompts you to resolve the discrepancy.

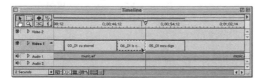

Figure 5.34 Change Speed changes the speed of the source clip so that it matches the duration defined by the program in and out points.

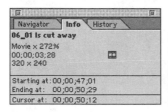

Figure 5.35 You can see the clip's new speed by selecting it and looking at the Info palette.

5. Click the insert or overlay button.

6. If the source duration and program duration differ, Premiere prompts you to choose one of the following options in the Fit Clip dialog box (**Figure 5.33**):

   Change Speed—changes the speed of the source clip to fit the specified duration in the program. Only the speed changes; the in and out points stay the same. In **Figure 5.34**, the source clip has been slowed, making its duration long enough to fit in the range defined by the program in and program out. If the source clip were too long, its speed would increase so that its duration would match the program duration.

   Trim Source—changes the source out point to fit the specified duration in the program. The in point and the speed of the clip are unaffected. (In other words, this option ignores the source out point and works like a three-point edit.)

   Cancel—stops the edit and makes no changes in the program.

   The clip is fit into the specified space in the program, according to your selection (**Figure 5.35**).

✔ Tip

■ You can change the speed of a clip after it's already in the timeline. For more information about using editing techniques in the timeline, see Chapter 6.

Lift and Extract

Just as the source view has two buttons for adding frames to the program, the program view has two buttons for removing frames from the program: lift and extract. You can think of lift and extract as being the opposite of insert and overlay, respectively.

Lift removes the defined range from the timeline, leaving a gap in the timeline.

Extract removes the defined range from the timeline and shifts all the later clips back in the timeline, closing the gap. The Shift Tracks option affects an extract edit in the same way as an insert edit (see "Understanding Insert Edits" earlier in this chapter).

To lift a segment from the program:

1. Set an in and out point in the program view to define the range to be removed from the program.

   You can see the editing marks in both the program view and the Timeline window (**Figure 5.36**).

2. From the Target pull-down menu of the program view, choose the tracks in the program from which the range of frames will be removed (**Figure 5.37**).

   You can also select the tracks by clicking the name of the tracks in the Timeline window.

Figure 5.36 Use the editing controls in the program view of the Monitor window to set program in and out points. The in and out points are circled in the Monitor window and Timeline window.

Figure 5.37 From the Target pull-down menu of the program view, choose the tracks from which the range of frames will be removed.

Figure 5.38 In the program view, click the lift button.

Figure 5.39 The frames between the in and out points in the selected tracks of the program are removed, leaving an empty space.

Figure 5.40 Set an in and out point in the program view to define the range to be removed from the timeline.

Figure 5.41 In the timeline window, set the shift tracks option to shift material in all unlocked tracks.

3. In the program view, click the lift button (**Figure 5.38**).

The frames between the in and out points in the selected tracks of the program are removed, leaving an empty space (**Figure 5.39**).

To extract a program segment from all tracks:

1. Set an in and out point in the program view to define the range to be removed from the timeline (**Figure 5.40**).

2. In the Timeline window, set the shift tracks option to shift material in all unlocked tracks.

The shift tracks button should display the icon (**Figure 5.41**).

continues on next page

3. Click the extract button in the program view (**Figure 5.42**).

The frames between the in and out points are removed, shifting the subsequent clips in all tracks to close the gap (**Figure 5.43**).

✔ Tips

- When using the extract button, it's usually best to set the shift track option to shift all unlocked tracks. Extracting frames from only the target tracks will break the synch between the audio and video of linked clips.

- You know you've lost synch between linked video and audio when red triangles appear at the beginning of the clips in the timeline (**Figure 5.44**). For now, use the Undo command to restore synch. To learn more about linked clips and synch, see Chapter 6.

Figure 5.42 Click the extract button in the program view.

Figure 5.43 The frames between the in and out points are removed, shifting the subsequent clips in all tracks to close the gap.

Figure 5.44 Red triangles appear in the video and audio portions of linked clips when they lose synchronization.

Editing with the Home Keys, or Three-Finger Editing

As any typist will tell you, the basis for touch-typing is learning how to keep your fingers over the home keys. Well, desktop editing programs have developed their own version of home keys: J, K, and L. As you can see in (**Figure 5.45**), keeping one hand on your editing home keys and the other on the mouse is the secret to blazing-fast Monitor window editing. This technique works in other popular editing programs as well. Learning it can produce joy and speed akin to typing 60 words per minute. But if you insist, you can always just use on-screen buttons for the equivalent of hunt-and-peck editing.

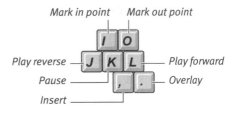

Figure 5.45 You can think of the J-K-L combo as the home keys of nonlinear editing. By using the home keys, you have quick three-finger control of the main playback and editing features.

LIFT AND EXTRACT

Storyboard Editing

Before actually shooting any footage, film-makers usually create a *storyboard*—a series of sketches that depicts each shot in the finished program. By planning each shot in a storyboard, you can save enormous amounts of time, money, and energy in production.

After you have footage in your editing system, you can use a similar storyboarding technique to plan a rough cut and assemble it into a program instantly.

Premiere has long supported an informal version of storyboard editing, allowing you to simply drag and drop multiple clips into the timeline at the same time. In Premiere 6, however, an Automate to Timeline feature adds several convenient options to storyboard editing. In addition, you can now use a specialized Storyboard window to create and save a storyboard.

The following sections explain how to arrange a storyboard in both the Project window and Premiere's new Storyboard window. The sections go on to explain how to use the Automate to Timeline options to assemble either type of storyboard into the program.

Project Window Storyboard Editing

In Chapter 3, you saw how setting the Project window to the icon view allows you to see the clips in a bin as free-floating icon frames rather than a list. Icon view isn't just a nice way to see your clips as large images (which can also be helpful for a partner or client). You can arrange the clip icons into a *story-board*, or a sequence of still images that represent the order that you anticipate for the final program (**Figure 5.46**). When you're happy with your storyboard, Premiere can assemble it into the program automatically for an instant rough cut.

To storyboard-edit from the Project window:

1. Put the clips that you want to use in the same bin of the Project window, and select the bin.

   If you want, you can use clip copies or subclips. For more information about organizing clips in the Project window, see Chapter 3.

2. In the Project window, click the icon view button to set the window to the icon view (**Figure 5.47**).

   Clips in the bin appear as icons. If you want to make more room for the clips, resize the Project window, and hide the bin panel of the Project window.

3. Arrange the clips in the order in which you want them added to the program.

   In the Project window, the sequence of clips proceeds like reading text on a page: from left to right and from top to bottom.

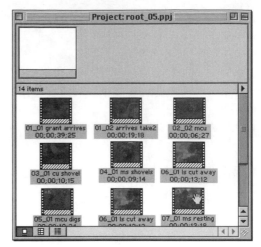

Figure 5.46 You can create a storyboard by using the icon view of the Project window.

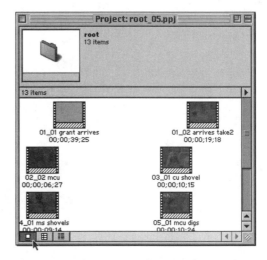

Figure 5.47 In the Project window, click the icon view button to set the window to the icon view.

Figure 5.48
Choose Project ›
Automate
to Timeline.

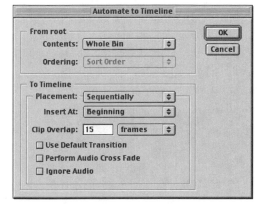

Figure 5.49 In the Automate to Timeline dialog box, specify options to determine how clips are added to the program, and click OK.

4. To select the portion of the clips that you want to use, view them in the source view or clip window, and set in and out points.

   For more information about setting in and out points, see Chapter 4.

5. In the Project window, select the clips you want to include in the timeline.

6. Choose Project > Automate to Timeline (**Figure 5.48**).

   The Automate to Timeline dialog box appears (**Figure 5.49**).

7. Specify options to determine how clips are added to the program, and click OK.

   See "Automate to Timeline Options" later in this chapter. The clips in the Project window appear in the timeline.

Storyboard Window

Though creating a storyboard in the Project window works fine for many situations, Premiere's new Storyboard window provides more full-featured storyboard editing. The Storyboard window provides a spacious, dedicated area to create a storyboard. You can add a descriptive note below each clip in the storyboard. Most important, you can save your storyboard as a file. The storyboard file works much like a program file, referring to the clips that it contains. You can open a storyboard file in the current project or separately.

In addition to adding the clips of the storyboard to the timeline, you can export its contents to video. If you're familiar with previous versions of Premiere, you can see how the Storyboard window acts as a kind of replacement for library and sequence files.

To create a storyboard:

1. Choose New > Storyboard (**Figure 5.50**). An untitled Storyboard window appears (**Figure 5.51**).

2. To add clips to the Storyboard window, *do any of the following:*
   - ▲ Drag a clip from the current Project window to the Storyboard window (**Figure 5.52**).
   - ▲ Double-click an empty area of the Storyboard window to open the Import dialog box.
   - ▲ Choose File > Import to open the Import dialog box.

   In the Storyboard window, clips appear in the order in which they were added.

3. To change the order of clips in the Storyboard window, drag a clip to a new position.

   The clip appears in a new area of the sequence.

Figure 5.50 Choose New > Storyboard.

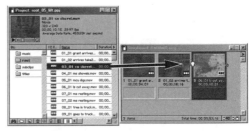

Figure 5.51 An untitled Storyboard window appears.

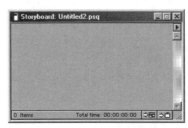

Figure 5.52 You can drag a clip from the current Project window to the Storyboard window.

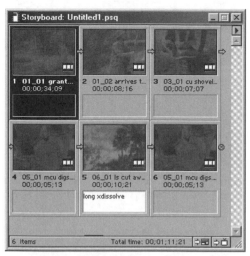

Figure 5.53 To enter a note, double-click the note field below the clip's image.

Figure 5.54 In the Edit Note dialog box, enter a note to caption the clip in the Storyboard window.

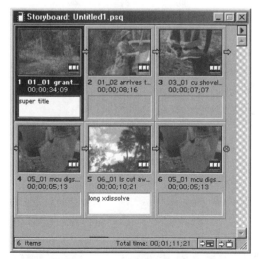

Figure 5.55 The information you enter appears below the clip's image in the Storyboard window.

4. To enter a note for each clip, double-click the note field below the clip's image (**Figure 5.53**).

   The Edit Note dialog box appears.

5. In the Edit Note dialog box, enter a note to caption the clip in the Storyboard window (**Figure 5.54**).

   The information you enter appears below the clip's image in the Storyboard window (**Figure 5.55**).

6. To change the selected portion of the clip, *do either of the following:*

   ▲ Double-click the clip in the storyboard to open it in the source view.

   or

   ▲ Option-double-click (Mac) or Alt-double-click (Windows) the clip in the storyboard to open it in a clip window.

   In the source view or clip window, change the in and out points. The new duration is reflected in the Storyboard window.

7. With the Storyboard window selected, choose File > Save As.

   The Save As dialog box appears.

8. Specify the name and location for the storyboard file, and click OK.

   The storyboard is saved as a separate file.

STORYBOARD WINDOW

To change the icon size in the storyboard:

1. To change the size of the icons in the storyboard, choose Storyboard Window Options from the Storyboard window's pull-down menu (**Figure 5.56**).

   The Storyboard Window Options dialog box appears.

2. Click the radio button next to the icon size you want to use in the storyboard, and click OK (**Figure 5.57**).

   The icons in the storyboard use the icon size you selected.

To storyboard-edit from the Storyboard window:

1. Open the Storyboard window.

2. *Do either of the following:*

   ▲ To assemble only some of the clips in the storyboard in the program, select the clips.

   or

   ▲ To assemble all of the clips in the storyboard, select all the clips or none of them.

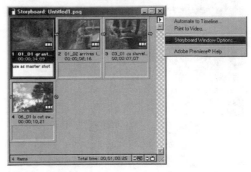

Figure 5.56 Choose Storyboard Window Options from the Storyboard window's pull-down menu.

Figure 5.57 In the Storyboard Window Options dialog box, click the radio button next to the icon size you want to use in the storyboard, and click OK.

STORYBOARD WINDOW

Figure 5.58 In the Storyboard window, click the Automate to Timeline button.

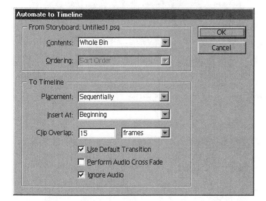

Figure 5.59 In the Automate to Timeline dialog box, specify options for adding the clips in the storyboard to the program, and click OK.

3. In the Storyboard window, click the Automate to Timeline button (**Figure 5.58**).

The Automate to Timeline dialog box appears.

4. Specify options for adding the clips in the storyboard to the program, and click OK (**Figure 5.59**).

The clips in the Program window appear in the timeline. (See "Automate to Timeline Options" later in this chapter.)

✔ Tip

■ Clicking the ⬛ button prints the storyboard to video. For more information about output, see Chapter 15.

Automate to Timeline Options

Whether you use the Project window or the Storyboard window, the options for the Automate to Timeline feature are the same.

To use Automate to Timeline:

1. To open the Automate to Timeline dialog box, *do either of the following:*

   ▲ With a Project window selected, choose Project > Automate to Timeline (**Figure 5.60**).

   or

   ▲ In a Storyboard window, click the Automate to Timeline button (**Figure 5.61**).

   The Automate to Timeline dialog box appears (**Figure 5.62**).

2. Specify which clips are included in the program by choosing an option from the Contents pull-down menu (**Figure 5.63**):

   Whole Bin—assembles all the clips contained in the bin or Storyboard window in the program.

   Selected Clips—assembles only the selected clips in the bin or Storyboard window in the program.

Figure 5.60 With a Project window selected, choose Project › Automate to Timeline.

Figure 5.61 In a Storyboard window, click the Automate to Timeline button.

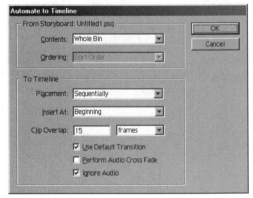

Figure 5.62 The Automate to Timeline dialog box appears.

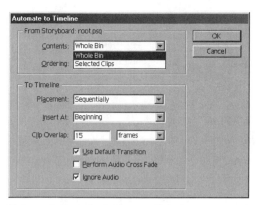

Figure 5.63 From the Contents pull-down menu, choose the clips that are included in the program.

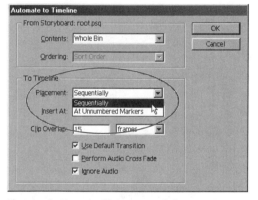

Figure 5.64 From the Placement pull-down menu, choose whether clips will be arranged sequentially or at markers in the timeline.

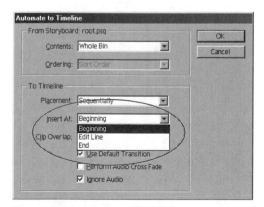

Figure 5.65 From the Insert At pull-down menu, choose where you want to start assembling the clips in the timeline.

3. If available, specify the order in which clips are arranged in the program by making a choice from the Ordering pull-down menu:

   Sort Order—arranges clips in the order in which they are sorted in the Project window.

   Selection Order—arranges clips in the order in which they are selected in the Project window.

4. Specify how the clips are added to the program by making a choice from the Placement pull-down menu (**Figure 5.64**):

   Sequentially—adds the clips in the timeline one after the other.

   At Numbered Markers—adds the clips in the timeline at numbered program markers.

5. Specify where the clips will be assembled in the program by making a choice from the Insert At pull-down menu (**Figure 5.65**):

   Beginning—adds clips starting at the beginning of the program timeline.

   Edit Line—adds clips starting at the edit line in the timeline, which corresponds to the current time of the program.

   End—adds clips starting after the last clip already in the program.

   continues on next page

6. Make a choice from the Clip Overlap pull-down menu to specify the length of transitions between clips and the time unit:

Frames—interprets the value you entered as frames, at the frame rate you set in the project settings.

Seconds—interprets the value you entered as seconds.

If you want only cuts between clips, enter zero (0).

7. Check other checkboxes, as desired:

Use Default Transition—applies the default transition between clips if you specified a positive value for Clip Overlap in step 6.

Perform Audio Cross Fade—performs a cross-fade between audio clips, if you specified a positive value for Clip Overlap in step 6.

Ignore Audio—excludes audio from being added to the program.

8. Click OK.

The clips in the bin or Storyboard window are added to the timeline, according to the options that you specified (**Figure 5.66**).

Figure 5.66 The clips in the bin or the Storyboard window are added to the timeline, according to the options you specified.

Figure 5.67 Cue each view to the frame you want to synchronize; then choose Gang Source and Program from the Monitor window's pull-down menu.

Ganging the Source and Program Views

In some circumstances, you need to preview the relationship between a source clip and the program visually. You may want to preview which frames will be replaced by an overlay edit, for example, before you actually perform the edit.

For these situations, you could calculate durations, or you could simply gang the source and program views. *Ganging* the source and program views puts them into a synchronized relationship, so that playing one plays the other. This way, you can see how the frames of the source view correspond to the program view to help you decide where to set editing marks.

To gang the source and program views:

1. In the Monitor window, cue each view to the frame you want to synchronize.

   Cue the views to the in points you're considering for the next edit, for example.

2. From the pull-down menu, choose Gang Source and Program (**Figure 5.67**).

3. Use the jog tread or shuttle slider in either the source or program view.

   Both views move in synch (**Figure 5.68**).

4. To deactivate the gang feature, click Play in either view.

   Each view moves independently.

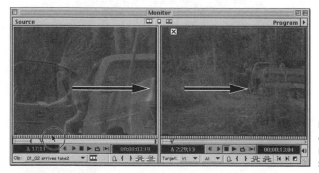

Figure 5.68 Using the jog tread or shuttle slider in either view moves both views in a synchronized relationship.

Creating a Leader

In addition to accepting a wide variety of source files, Premiere provides several useful clips of its own. Some of these clips are useful for creating a standard leader, which typically appears at the beginning of a master edited tape (and, therefore, at the beginning of the timeline). Premiere not only generates standard color bars and a reference audio tone, but also a custom countdown.

The bars and tone are used by video technicians to faithfully reproduce your program's video and audio levels. The visible countdown originally helped a film projectionist know when the program was about to start. It can serve a similar purpose for videotape operators. The standard countdown starts at 8 and ends at 2 (where there is usually a beep, or *2 pop*, to test the sound).

To create bars and tone:

1. In the Project window, select the bin in which you want to store bars and tone.

2. Click the create item button  (**Figure 5.69**).

   The Create dialog box appears (**Figure 5.70**).

3. From the Object Type pull-down menu, choose Bars and Tone (**Figure 5.71**).

Figure 5.69 In the Project window, click the create item button.

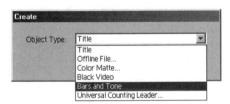

Figure 5.70 The Create dialog box appears.

Figure 5.71 From the Create dialog box's pull-down menu, choose Bars and Tone.

Figure 5.72 A Bars and Tone clip appears in the selected bin of the Project window.

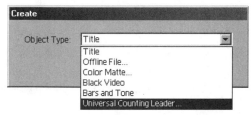

Figure 5.73 From the Create dialog box's pull-down menu, choose Universal Counting Leader, and click OK.

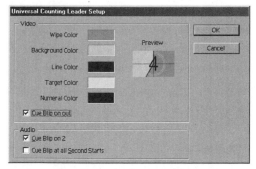

Figure 5.74 In the Universal Counting Leader Setup dialog box, choose options to customize the countdown.

A Bars and Tone clip appears in the selected bin of the Project window (**Figure 5.72**).

To create a countdown:

1. In the Project window, select the bin in which you want to store the bars and tone.

2. Click the create item button. [icon]
   The Create dialog box opens.

3. From the Object Type pull-down menu, choose Universal Counting Leader, and click OK (**Figure 5.73**).
   The Universal Counting Leader Setup dialog box appears (**Figure 5.74**).

4. Specify the following options:
   ▲ To open the Color Picker for each element of the countdown, click the color swatch next to each element.
   ▲ To display a small circle in the last frame of the leader, check the Cue Blip on Out checkbox.
   ▲ To play a beep at the 2-second mark of the countdown, check the Cue Blip on 2 checkbox.
   ▲ To play a beep at the beginning of every second of the countdown leader, check the Cue Blip At All Second Starts checkbox.

continues on next page

5. Click OK to close the dialog box.

A Universal Counting Leader clip appears in the selected bin of the Project window (**Figure 5.75**).

✔ Tips

■ You can also choose black footage from the Create dialog box's pull-down menu.

■ To make a slate (which contains information such as client, producer, and total running time), you can create a title card in Premiere, as explained in Chapter 11.

■ Of the files that you generate by using the New File command, only titles create an actual file on your hard drive. Offline files, color mattes, black video, color bars, and counting leaders exist only as part of your project, not as independent files.

Figure 5.75 A Universal Counting Leader clip appears in the selected bin of the Project window.

CREATING A LEADER

EDITING IN THE TIMELINE

6

As you saw in Chapter 5, the program view of the Monitor window is closely related to the Timeline window. The Timeline window graphically represents the clips of the program arranged in time. The edit line of the timeline directly corresponds to the current time displayed in the program view.

In the timeline, the program looks a lot like edited film. Like film, the timeline lays out the instances of clips before you. Unlike film, however, the timeline allows you to view any segment of the program instantly or to view the entire program. Yet the timeline isn't simply another way to look at or navigate through the program; it's also a way to edit. Editing in the timeline can feel almost as tactile as editing film but can be far more flexible and efficient than using razors and tape. You can select, move, rearrange, trim, cut, copy, and paste clips in the timeline. To help you find your way through longer programs, you can use the timeline's companion, the Navigator window.

Along with the rest of the interface, the timeline underwent a real overhaul in Premiere 5. Premiere 6 has made additional refinements. As you saw back in Chapter 2, A/B roll and single-track layouts are more clearly distinguished. Several controls are more conveniently located along the bottom of the Timeline window. Also, the program markers in the timeline include enhanced features.

Understanding the Timeline and the Editing Workspace

As you saw in Chapter 2, the initial appearance of the timeline reflects the editing model you prefer: A/B roll or single-track editing.

In the A/B roll layout, transitions (such as dissolves and wipes) are represented in three tracks of the timeline: an A track, a B track, and a transitions track. In a single-track editing workspace, you apply transition clips in a single track. What would appear as overlapping frames in the A/B view are not visible in a single track.

You'll notice that this chapter typically shows the timeline in single-track view. All the techniques covered in this chapter apply to both workspaces, however. Just bear in mind that the A/B roll layout splits the Video 1 track into two video tracks, plus a transition track. So when a tool or technique affects a track of the timeline, the A and B tracks are treated separately. Transitions in the transitions track can be moved like clips but can't be edited in the same way. For more information about transitions, see Chapter 8.

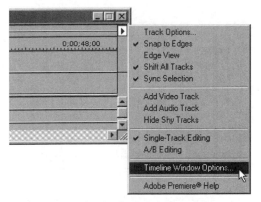

Figure 6.1 From the Timeline window's pull-down menu, choose Timeline Window Options.

Figure 6.2 In the Timeline Window Options dialog box, click the radio button next to the icon size and track format you want to use.

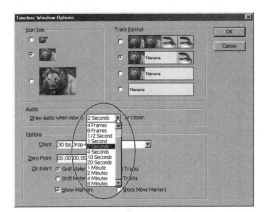

Figure 6.3 In the Audio section of the dialog box, choose the time unit at which audio waveforms are displayed in an expanded audio track.

Customizing the Timeline

You can customize the Timeline window's appearance to fit your needs or simply your tastes.

To change the icon size and track format:

1. From the Timeline window's pull-down menu, choose Timeline Window Options (**Figure 6.1**).

   The Timeline Window Options dialog box appears.

2. Click the radio button next to the icon size that you want to use (**Figure 6.2**).

   Choose among small, medium, and large icons for clips in video tracks.

3. Select the radio button next to the track format that you want to use:

   Icon view—displays an icon for each time unit of the current time scale of the timeline.

   Heads and tails view—displays an icon for the first and last time units of a clip, with the name of the file between them (if the length of the clip allows).

   Heads view—displays an icon for the first time unit of the clip, followed by the file name (if the length of the clip allows).

   Name only view—displays only the name and no icons for clips in video tracks.

4. In the Audio section of the dialog box, choose the time unit at which audio waveforms are displayed in an expanded audio track (**Figure 6.3**).

   Audio waveforms do not appear at time units greater than the unit you specify.

5. Click OK to close the Timeline Window Options dialog box and apply the changes.

✔ Tip

■ To maximize both screen space and performance, display only the information that you need. Large icons, detailed track formats, and waveforms not only use up valuable screen space, but also take longer to display. Excessive detail can result in an overcrowded screen and slow scrolling in the timeline.

To change the track heading width:

◆ In the timeline, position the pointer over the border between the track headings and time ruler until the pointer becomes a resize icon ⟨↔⟩ and drag (**Figure 6.4**). Dragging to the right widens the track heading column; dragging to the left makes the column narrower.

To change the ratio of video and audio tracks displayed:

1. Drag the split-window bar, located on the right side of the timeline, between the video and audio tracks (**Figure 6.5**).

   The pointer changes to a resize icon ⟨⤢⟩ when you're in the correct place.

2. Drag down to reveal more video tracks or up to reveal more audio tracks.

   This procedure is helpful when a program has more tracks than the timeline can display.

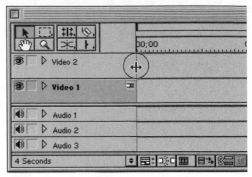

Figure 6.4 Position the pointer at the edge of the track heading column so that it becomes the resize tool. Drag to the left or right to resize the column.

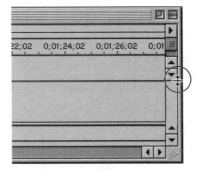

Figure 6.5 Drag the split-window bar, located on the right side of the timeline, between the video and audio tracks.

Figure 6.6 From the Timeline window's pull-down menu, choose Timeline Window Options.

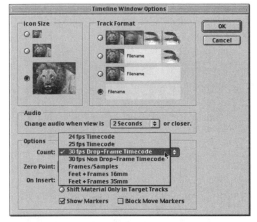

Figure 6.7 In the Timeline Window Options dialog box, choose a time count from the Count pull-down menu.

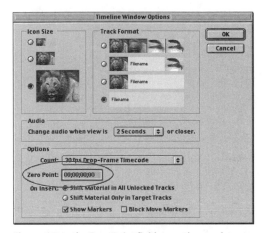

Figure 6.8 In the Zero Point field, type the number at which you want the timeline to start.

Customizing the Time Ruler

As you learned in Chapter 2, frames can be counted in several ways. The time ruler at the top of the timeline can display any of these time measurements. By default, the timeline starts at zero, but you can set it to start at any number.

To change the time count in the timeline:

1. From the Timeline window's pull-down menu, choose Timeline Window Options (**Figure 6.6**).

   The Timeline Window Options dialog box appears.

2. From the Count pull-down menu, choose a time count (**Figure 6.7**).

To change the zero point:

1. From the Timeline window's pull-down menu, choose Timeline Window Options.

   The Timeline Window Options dialog box appears.

2. In the Zero Point field, type the number at which you want the timeline to start (**Figure 6.8**).

✔ Tip

■ An edited master tape typically contains information at the head of the tape, before the program starts. A common practice is to start the tape at 00:58:00:00. The program itself always begins at 01:00:00:00, which gives you 2 minutes from the beginning of the tape to the program start. The 2 minutes usually include 30 seconds of black, 1 minute of bars and tone, a 10-second slate, 10 more seconds of black, an 8-second countdown, and 2 seconds of black.

CUSTOMIZING THE TIME RULER

Adding, Deleting, and Naming Tracks

By default, the timeline opens with two video tracks and three audio tracks. Although this number is adequate for many projects, Premiere permits you to have as many as 99 video and 99 audio tracks in the timeline. What's more, you can name all those tracks, so it's much easier to discern the sound-effects track from the music and dialogue tracks, for example.

To add tracks:

1. At the bottom of the Timeline window, click the track options button (**Figure 6.9**)

   The Track Options dialog box appears.

2. Click the Add button (**Figure 6.10**).

   The Add Tracks dialog box appears.

3. Enter the number of video tracks and audio tracks that you want to add (**Figure 6.11**).

4. Click OK to close the Add Tracks dialog box.

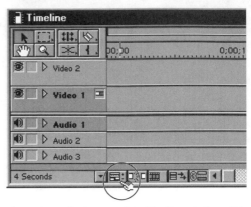

Figure 6.9 At the bottom of the Timeline window, click the track options button.

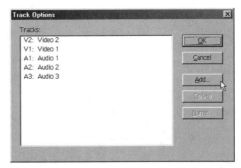

Figure 6.10 In the Track Options dialog box, click the Add button.

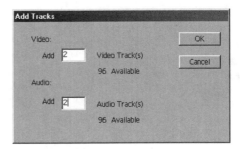

Figure 6.11 In the Add Tracks dialog box, enter the number of video tracks and audio tracks that you want to add.

Figure 6.12 Additional tracks appear in the timeline.

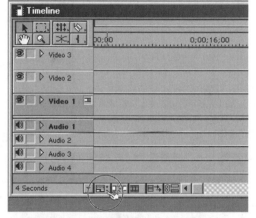

Figure 6.13 At the bottom of the Timeline window, click the track options button.

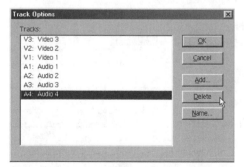

Figure 6.14 In the Track Options dialog box, select the name of the track that you want to delete, and click Delete.

5. Click OK to exit the Track Options dialog box.

Additional tracks appear in the timeline (**Figure 6.12**).

To delete tracks:

1. At the bottom of the Timeline window, click the track options button (**Figure 6.13**).

The Track Options dialog box appears.

2. Select the name of the track that you want to delete (**Figure 6.14**).

You can delete only video track 2 and higher; you can delete only audio track 4 and higher.

3. Click the Delete button to delete the track.

The track is removed from the list.

4. Click OK to exit the dialog box.

The specified tracks are deleted from the timeline, and other tracks are renumbered (**Figure 6.15**).

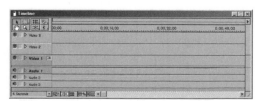

Figure 6.15 The specified tracks are deleted from the timeline, and other tracks are renumbered.

To name tracks:

1. At the bottom of the Timeline window, click the track options button 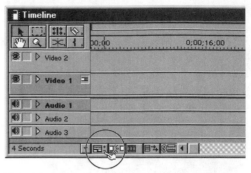 (**Figure 6.16**).

   The Track Options dialog box appears.

2. *Do one of the following:*

   ▲ Click the name of a track and then click the Name button.

   or

   ▲ Double-click the name of the track (**Figure 6.17**).

   The Name Track dialog box appears.

3. Enter a name for the track (**Figure 6.18**).

4. Click OK.

   The name of the track in the timeline displays the name you entered (**Figure 6.19**).

✔ Tip

■ You can add a single video or audio track quickly by choosing Timeline > Add Video Track or Timeline > Add Audio Track.

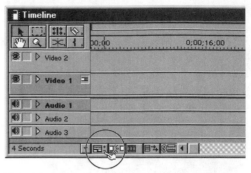

Figure 6.16 At the bottom of the Timeline window, click the track options button.

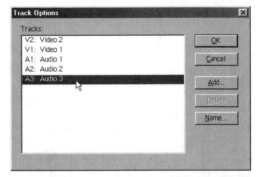

Figure 6.17 In the Track Options dialog box, double-click the name of the track.

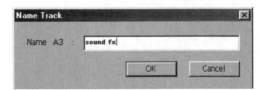

Figure 6.18 In the Name Track dialog box, enter a name for the track.

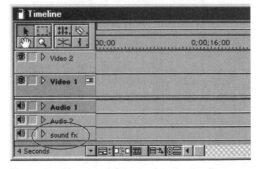

Figure 6.19 The name of the track in the timeline displays the name you entered.

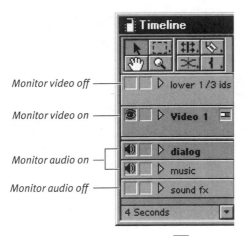

Monitor video off

Monitor video on

Monitor audio on

Monitor audio off

Figure 6.20 Tracks with the eye icon are visible during playback, and tracks with the speaker icon can be heard.

Monitoring Tracks

When used as a noun, the term *monitor* can refer to a video screen or audio speaker. It is also used as a verb, meaning to see or hear, as in "to monitor the video and audio." In Premiere, you can monitor any combination of the tracks in the timeline. Only monitored tracks are included during playback and when you preview or export the program. Though you usually monitor all the tracks, at times you may want to monitor only certain tracks. You may want to hear the dialogue track without the music and effects tracks, for example.

To monitor tracks:

In the Timeline window, *do any of the following:*

◆ Click next to the name of a video track to hide or reveal the eye icon.

◆ Click next to the name of a video track to hide or reveal the speaker icon.

When a monitor icon is visible, you can see or hear the clips contained in the corresponding track; when a monitor icon is hidden, clips in the track are excluded from playback (**Figure 6.20**).

✔ Tips

■ Isolating a single audio monitor can be especially helpful when you are synching sound effects to video. (On an audio mixer, this procedure would be called *soloing* the track.) The other sound tracks often prevent you from hearing whether a sound effect is synched properly.

■ The Audio Mixer window includes switches for monitoring audio tracks during mixing. For more information about mixing audio, see Chapter 10.

■ Option-click (Mac) or Alt-click (Windows) next to the track name in the timeline to reveal or hide all the speaker icons or all the eye icons.

■ A white monitor icon indicates that the track is shy. See "Using Shy Tracks" later in this chapter.

MONITORING TRACKS

Locking and Unlocking Tracks

Locking a track protects the clips in the track from accidental changes. You can't move or modify the clips that are in the locked track. Clips in locked tracks don't shift in time after an insert edit is performed. Also, you can't add clips to a locked track; the track's name appears dimmed in the Target menu. If you place the pointer or other tool on the locked track, it appears with a lock icon to indicate its locked status (**Figure 6.21**).

Although you can't alter the clips in a locked track, you can still monitor those clips, and the track is included when you preview or export the program.

To lock and unlock tracks:

◆ Click next to the track name to display or hide the lock icon (**Figure 6.22**).

   This icon indicates that the corresponding track is locked and can't be modified. No icon indicates that the track is unlocked.

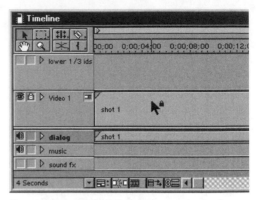

Figure 6.21 If you place the pointer or other tool on a locked track, a lock icon appears.

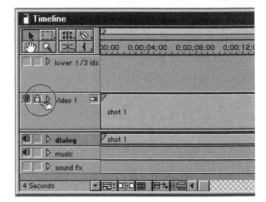

Figure 6.22 Click to make the lock icon appear, locking the track. Click again to make the icon disappear, unlocking the track.

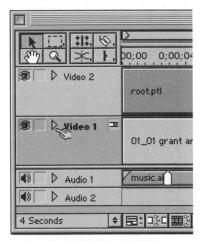

Figure 6.23 Clicking the triangle toggles a track from collapsed to expanded view. A collapsed track is leaner and hides additional information.

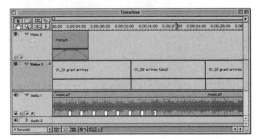

Figure 6.24 Expanded tracks reveal additional information about the clips in the tracks.

Expanding and Collapsing Tracks

You can expand and collapse tracks in the timeline, using the same rotating triangle you're familiar with from other programs or even from the Macintosh system interface. Expanding a track reveals additional information and controls for the clips in the track. When you don't need these features, collapse the track to reduce screen clutter and decrease the time it takes to redraw the windows.

Expanding an audio track reveals fade and pan controls, as well as an audio waveform. (See Chapter 10 for more information about these features.) Expanding the Video 1 track reveals an area for keyframing effects (see Chapter 11). In addition to effects, expanding higher video tracks reveals fade controls for superimposing the clips (see Chapter 12).

To expand or collapse tracks:

◆ Click the triangle next to the track name to expand or collapse a track (**Figures 6.23** and **6.24**).

Depending on the type of track, expanding a track reveals different types of information and controls.

✔ Tip

■ Premiere 6 displays the Video 1 track in a slightly different way than Premiere 5 did. In Premiere 6, you choose between single-track and A/B roll editing by selecting a workspace, not by expanding the Video 1 track. The split track button, however, does allow you to view a single-track editing workspace in an A/B format, albeit for viewing purposes only. See Chapter 2 for more about selecting an initial workspace.

Using Shy Tracks

When your project includes numerous tracks, conserving screen space can become an issue. When you don't need to view the clips in a track all the time, you can mark the track as *shy*. You can hide shy tracks quickly when you don't need them and show them again when you're ready to work with them again. Whether they are hidden or visible, shy tracks are still included during playback and when you preview or output the program.

To mark tracks as shy:

◆ ⌘-click (Mac) or Ctrl-click (Windows) a video-monitor icon 🎥 or audio-monitor icon 🔊 to toggle the track setting between shy and not shy.

The monitor icons are white 🎥 🔊 when the tracks are marked as shy (**Figure 6.25**).

To hide and show shy tracks:

◆ Choose an option from the Timeline window's pull-down menu (**Figure 6.26**):

Hide Shy Tracks—conceals shy tracks in the Timeline window.

Show Shy Tracks—makes shy tracks visible in the Timeline window.

According to your selection, shy tracks are revealed or concealed (**Figure 6.27**).

✔ Tip

■ If you're concentrating on video editing, mark most or all of the audio tracks as shy. Hide them until you need to view them again. If you're focusing on adjusting audio levels, mark the video layers as shy, and hide those layers.

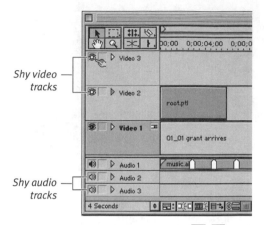

Shy video tracks

Shy audio tracks

Figure 6.25 The monitor icons are white 🎥 🔊 when the tracks are marked as shy.

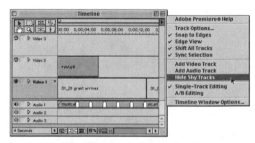

Figure 6.26 From the Timeline window's pull-down menu, choose to show or (shown here) hide tracks.

Figure 6.27 The shy tracks are hidden from view but will still be included in the program view and in output.

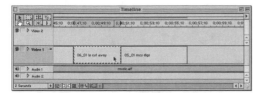

Figure 6.28 Double-click a clip in the timeline to open it.

Figure 6.29 Change the edit marks, and click the Apply button.

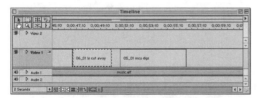

Figure 6.30 The changes take effect in the timeline.

Opening a Clip in the Timeline

As you learned in Chapter 4, changing a master clip does not affect any instances of that clip that are already in the timeline. If you want to view a program clip, you can still open it in the source view or a clip window, and you can change any of its editing marks by using the controller.

To open and change a clip in the timeline:

1. Open a program clip (or clip instance) by doing either of the following:

   ▲ Double-click a clip in the timeline to view it in the source view (**Figure 6.28**).

   ▲ [Option]-double-click (Mac) or [Alt]-double-click (Windows) a clip in the timeline to view it in a clip window.

   The clip opens in the source view or clip window.

2. In the source view or clip window, make changes in the in point, the out point, or marked frames.

   (To review these techniques, see Chapter 4.) The Apply button appears above the image in the source view or clip window.

3. Click the Apply button to make the changes take effect in the clip in the timeline (**Figures 6.29** and **6.30**).

OPENING A CLIP IN THE TIMELINE

Getting Around the Timeline

You can navigate the program in the timeline in several ways. You can zoom in, zoom out, and scroll through the timeline. You can also use the new Navigator palette to find your way.

To view part of the program in more detail:

Do any of the following:

◆ From the Time Unit pull-down menu, choose a smaller time increment (**Figures 6.31** and **6.32**).

◆ In the Navigator palette, drag the time unit slider to the right (**Figure 6.33**), or click the magnify icon ▲.

◆ In the toolbox of the Timeline window, select the zoom tool and then click the part of the timeline that you want to see in more detail.

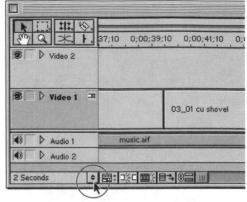

Figure 6.31 There are several ways to view the timeline in more detail. One way is to click the Time Unit display...

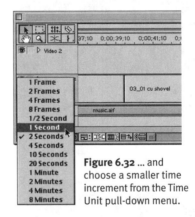

Figure 6.32 ... and choose a smaller time increment from the Time Unit pull-down menu.

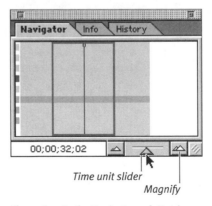

Time unit slider

Magnify

Figure 6.33 In the Navigator palette, drag the time unit slider to the right.

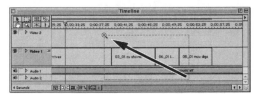

Figure 6.34 Create a marquee with the zoom tool.

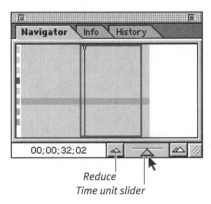

Reduce
Time unit slider

Figure 6.35 In the Navigator palette, drag the time unit slider or click the reduce icon.

Figure 6.36 Option-click (Mac) or Alt-click (Windows) with the zoom tool to view more of the program.

◆ In the toolbox of the Timeline window, select the zoom tool and then drag a marquee around the area of the timeline that you want to see in detail (**Figure 6.34**).

To view more of the program in the timeline:

Do one of the following:

◆ From the Time Unit pull-down menu, choose a larger time increment.

◆ In the Navigator palette, drag the time unit slider to the left or click the reduce icon ⬛ (**Figure 6.35**).

◆ In the toolbox, select the zoom tool and then (Option)-click (Mac) or (Alt)-click (Windows) the part of the timeline that you want to center in the wider view (**Figure 6.36**).

When you press (Option) or (Alt), the zoom tool icon appears with a minus sign, to indicate that it will zoom out.

✔ Tips

■ To zoom out quickly to view the entire program in the timeline, press the back-slash key (\).

■ To select the zoom tool quickly, press (Z).

GETTING AROUND THE TIMELINE

To scroll through the timeline:

Do one of the following:

◆ At the bottom of the Timeline window, click either the left or right scroll arrow to move across a close view of the program gradually.

◆ Drag the scroll box right or left to view a different part of the program.

◆ Click the scroll bar to the right or left of the scroll handle to shift the view one width of the timeline (**Figure 6.37**).

◆ In the toolbox, select the hand tool and then drag the program to the right or left (**Figure 6.38**).

◆ In the Navigator palette, drag the view box to the right or left to show another part of the timeline (**Figure 6.39**).

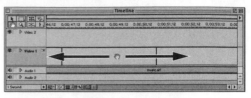

Figure 6.38 Drag in the program with the hand tool to scroll through the timeline gradually.

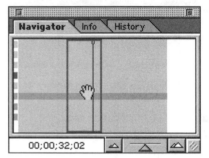

Figure 6.39 In the Navigator palette, drag the view box to the right or left to scroll through longer programs easily.

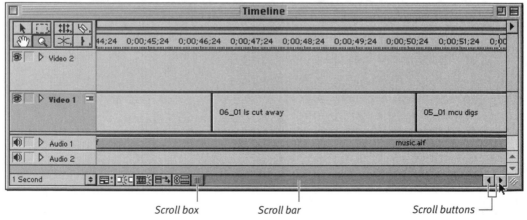

Scroll box   Scroll bar   Scroll buttons

Figure 6.37 There are several ways to scroll through the program in the timeline. In the Timeline window, use the standard scroll bar.

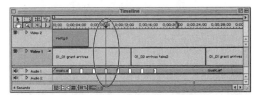

Figure 6.40 Click the time ruler to move the edit line to that point in the timeline. In this figure, the edit line appears at the fourth unnumbered marker in the music clip.

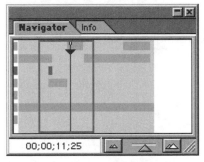

Figure 6.41 In the Navigator palette, hold down the Shift key while you drag in the Navigator's miniature timeline.

Figure 6.42 In the Navigator palette, highlight the time-code readout and then enter a new time code.

Playing the Program in the Timeline

In Chapter 4, you learned to use playback controls in the Monitor window to cue the current frame of the program. In the time-line, the current frame of the program is indicated by the *edit line*, a small triangular indicator with a vertical line extending from it. In addition to using the playback controls in the Monitor window, you can change the current time of the program by moving the edit line directly.

To cue the edit line:

Do one of the following:

◆ Click the time ruler to move the edit line to that point in the timeline (**Figure 6.40**).

◆ In the Navigator palette, hold down the Shift key while you drag in the Navigator's miniature timeline (**Figure 6.41**).

◆ In the Navigator palette, highlight the time-code readout and then enter a new time code (**Figure 6.42**).

◆ Use the playback controls in the program view (or a keyboard shortcut) to cue the current program frame. (See "Using Playback Controls" in Chapter 4.)

To cue to the next or previous edit:

◆ In the program view of the Monitor window, click either of the following (**Figure 6.43**):

Previous edit button— [◄|] cues the edit line to the previous edit in a selected track.

Next edit button— [|►] cues the edit line to the next edit in a selected track.

An *edit* is the point between two clips, or the point directly before or after a clip in a selected track. Cueing the edit line by clicking the previous edit and next edit button makes it easy to insert a clip before, after, or between clips in the timeline.

✔ Tip

■ Remember what you learned in Chapter 4: you can also use the playback controls in the program view to cue the edit line to an absolute or relative time position, or an in point, out point, or program marker. See "Playback Controls" in Chapter 4 for more details.

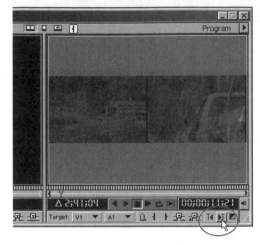

Figure 6.43 Click the previous edit and next edit buttons to cue the current time from one cut to another.

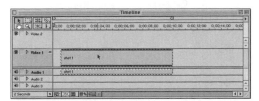

Figure 6.44 Simply click a clip to select it. Clicking a linked clip selects both the video and audio portions of the clip.

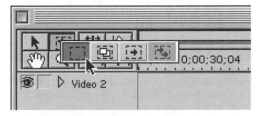

Figure 6.45 Select the range-select tool.

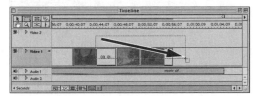

Figure 6.46 With the range-select tool, drag a marquee around clips to select them.

✔ Tip

■ Each method of selecting clips treats linked clips differently. Clicking or Shift-clicking with the selection tool selects either or both tracks of a linked clip, depending on the synch mode. The range select tool disregards the synch mode setting and selects only the clips that you click or draw a marquee around.

Selecting Clips in the Timeline

Not surprisingly, whenever you want to manipulate or affect a program clip in any way, you have to select it first.

To select clips in the timeline:

◆ Click a clip in the timeline.

When a clip is selected, its border has an animated highlight (sometimes described as "crawling ants") (**Figure 6.44**).

When synch mode is set to linked, clicking a linked clip selects both the video and audio tracks. See "Using Linked Clips" later in this chapter.

To select multiple clips in the timeline by clicking:

◆ Hold down the Shift key as you click multiple clips in the timeline.

Multiple clips are selected.

To select multiple clips in the timeline with the range select tool:

1. In the toolbox, select the range-select tool ⬚ (**Figure 6.45**).

2. Drag a marquee around the clips that you want to select (**Figure 6.46**).

Clips within the marquee are selected.

3. To add to the selection, press Shift as you click or drag a marquee around unselected clips with the range-select tool.

4. To subtract clips from the selection, Shift-click a selected clip with the range select tool.

Only the clips clicked or within the marquee are selected, regardless of the sync mode setting. (See "Using Linked Clips" later in this chapter.)

Deleting Clips and Gaps from the Timeline

If you can select a clip, deleting it is a simple matter. The same is true of gaps between clips.

To delete clips from the timeline:

1. Select one or more clips in the timeline.

2. Press (Delete).

   The selected clips are removed from the timeline.

To delete a gap between clips:

1. Select a gap in the timeline (**Figure 6.47**).

2. (Control)-click (Mac) or right-click (Windows) the gap in the timeline.

   A contextual menu appears.

3. Choose Ripple Delete (**Figure 6.48**).

   The subsequent clips shift back in the timeline to close the gap (**Figure 6.49**).

✔ Tip

■ Delete and Ripple Delete are great for removing entire clips or gaps. The Lift and Extract commands can remove portions of clips and remove frames from several clips and tracks. See "Lift and Extract" in Chapter 5.

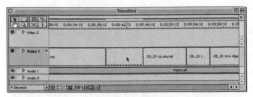

Figure 6.47 Select a gap in the timeline.

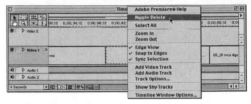

Figure 6.48 (Control)-click (Mac) or right-click (Windows) the gap in the timeline, and choose Ripple Delete from the contextual menu.

Figure 6.49 The subsequent clips shift back in the timeline to close the gap.

Figure 6.50 Select one or more clips in the timeline, and choose Clip > Enable Clip on Timeline.

Figure 6.51 Unchecking the option disables the selected clips, which appear in the timeline with a pattern of backslashes (sloping down to the right).

Enabling and Disabling Clips

Disabling a clip in the timeline prevents it from appearing during playback and when you preview or export the program. Disabling a clip is useful if you want to keep the clip in the program but want to exclude it temporarily. You might want to disable a single audio clip to hear what the program sounds like without it, for example. You can still move and make other changes in a disabled clip.

To disable or enable a clip:

1. Select one or more clips in the timeline.

2. Choose Clip > Enable Clip on Timeline (**Figure 6.50**).

   A check indicates that the clip is enabled. No check indicates that the clip is disabled. Disabled clips appear in the timeline with a hatch pattern of backslashes over them (**Figure 6.51**). Notice that backslashes on a disabled clip slope down to the right.

ENABLING AND DISABLING CLIPS

Locking and Unlocking Clips

Locking a clip protects it from any unintentional changes. You can't move or modify locked clips. Locked clips appear in the timeline with a hatch pattern of slashes over them. Notice that slashes on a locked clip slope down to the left. Although you can't alter locked clips, you can monitor them, and they're still included when you preview or export the program.

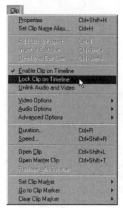

Figure 6.52 Select one or more clips in the timeline, and choose Clip › Lock Clip on Timeline.

To lock and unlock a clip:

1. Select one or more clips in the timeline.

2. Choose Clip > Lock Clip on Timeline (**Figure 6.52**).

   A check indicates that the clip is locked. No check indicates that the clip is unlocked. Locked clips appear in the timeline with a hatch pattern of slashes (**Figure 6.53**).

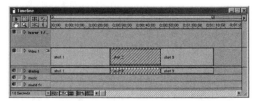

Figure 6.53 Checking the option locks the selected clips, which appear with a pattern of slashes (that slope down to the left).

✔ Tips

- You can also disable and lock clips via a contextual menu.

- You can lock an entire track to protect it from unintentional changes (explained in "Locking and Unlocking Tracks" earlier in this chapter).

LOCKING AND UNLOCKING CLIPS

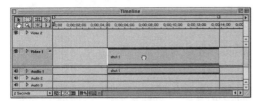

Figure 6.54 When you move a linked clip in the timeline, the video and audio portions of the clip move together.

Using Linked Clips

When a clip contains both video and audio material, it is known as a *linked clip*. When you move a linked clip in the timeline, the video and audio portions of the clip move together (**Figure 6.54**). Similarly, when you change the edit marks of a linked clip, the video and audio tracks both change—unless you deliberately treat them separately.

The link helps you keep the video and audio synchronized. Even if your video and audio were recorded separately (as in a film shoot), you can create an artificial link, or *soft link*, between video and audio. If you've ever edited film and magnetic tape, you know how convenient linked clips are.

Nevertheless, it's still possible to lose synch between the tracks of a linked clip. Fortunately, Premiere alerts you to the loss of synch by tagging the affected clips in the timeline. Premiere even tells you exactly how much the clips are out of synch and provides easy ways to restore it.

Although the link is usually an advantage, Premiere permits you to override the link, if necessary. You can even break the link, if you want.

To perform the tasks described in this chapter, you need to understand how linked clips behave in the timeline. In later chapters, you learn to tackle more advanced tasks related to synch and links.

USING LINKED CLIPS

Setting the Synch Option

The synch option controls whether one track or both tracks of a linked clip are affected when you select or edit a clip in the timeline. When the synch option is on, linked clips retain their link between video and audio. Selecting either the video or audio portion of linked clips selects both tracks. In Chapter 7, you'll see how changing the in or out point of a linked clip changes the point in both the video and audio portion of the clip. Setting the synch mode to on helps keep the synched relationship between the video and audio.

On the other hand, it's often useful to treat the video and audio portions of a linked clip independently. You may want to remove only the video or audio from the timeline. Or you may want to create a *split edit*, or *L-cut*, by setting different in or out points for the video than for the audio of a linked clip. (For more information about split edits, see Chapter 7.) Switching synch mode back on restores the link between the video and audio portions of a linked clip.

To set synch mode:

◆ At the bottom of the Timeline window, click the synch option button to toggle between the two settings:

Synch mode on 8⊟ —retains the link between the video and audio portions of linked clips (**Figure 6.55**).

Synch mode off ⊟ —temporarily ignores the link between the video and audio portions of linked clips (**Figure 6.56**).

✔ Tip

■ Synch mode effectively replaces the link override tool from previous versions of Premiere.

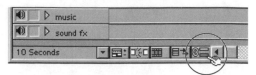

Figure 6.55 Setting synch mode on respects the link between the video and audio portions of linked clips.

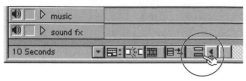

Figure 6.56 Turning synch mode off allows you to treat each track of a linked clip independently.

Figure 6.57 You can drag a clip to any available area of the timeline or between clips. When synch mode is on, the audio and video portions of a clip move together.

Figure 6.58 When synch mode is off, you can move the video and audio parts of a linked clip separately. In this figure, the video has been moved to the Video 1B track without moving its associated audio.

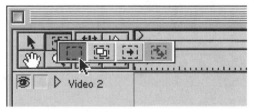

Figure 6.59 In the toolbox of the Timeline window, select the range-select tool.

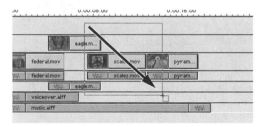

Figure 6.60 With the range-select tool, drag a marquee around the clips to select them.

Moving Clips in the Timeline

You can manipulate clips directly in the timeline to shift and rearrange them. You can move individual clips, multiple clips, or entire tracks.

To move a clip in the timeline:

◆ Drag selected clips to an unused part of the timeline.

When synch mode is on, both portions of linked clips move together (**Figure 6.57**); when synch mode is off, the video and audio portions of linked clips move independently (**Figure 6.58**).

To move a range of clips in the timeline:

1. In the toolbox of the Timeline window, select the range select tool (**Figure 6.59**).

2. Drag a marquee around the clips that you want to select (**Figure 6.60**).

continues on next page

MOVING CLIPS IN THE TIMELINE

3. Drag the selection to an unused part of the timeline.

When you drag the selection, the tool changes to the move icon 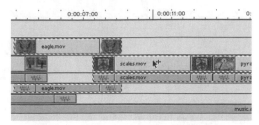 (**Figure 6.61**).

To move all the clips in a track:

1. In the toolbox of the Timeline window, choose the track tool ![track tool icon] (**Figure 6.62**).

2. Click a clip in the timeline.

All the clips in the track from that clip forward are selected (**Figure 6.63**).

3. Drag the selected clips to shift their position in the timeline (**Figure 6.64**).

✔ Tip

■ Be careful: The track tool ignores any links between audio and video. Whenever you use the track tool, it's easy to lose synch between video and audio. (See "Using Linked Clips" earlier in this chapter.)

Figure 6.61 When you drag the selection, the tool changes to the move icon.

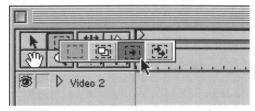

Figure 6.62 In the toolbox of the Timeline window, choose the track tool.

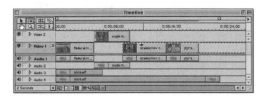

Figure 6.63 With the track tool, select a clip to select it and all subsequent clips in that track.

Figure 6.64 Drag the selection to shift it in the timeline.

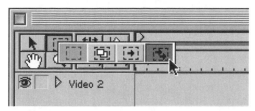

Figure 6.65 In the toolbox of the Timeline window, choose the multitrack tool.

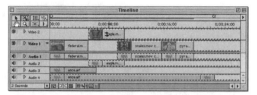

Figure 6.66 With the multitrack tool, select a clip to select it and all subsequent clips in all tracks.

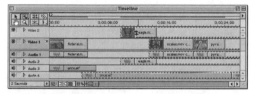

Figure 6.67 Drag the selection to shift it in the timeline.

To move all the clips in multiple tracks:

1. In the toolbox of the Timeline window, choose the multitrack tool (**Figure 6.65**).

2. Click a clip in the timeline.

   All the clips in all tracks from that clip forward are selected (**Figure 6.66**).

3. Drag the selected clips to shift their position in the timeline (**Figure 6.67**).

✔ Tip

■ As usual, you can add to or subtract from your selection by Shift-clicking the timeline. When you use the track tool, add another track to your selection by Shift-clicking a clip in another track. Deselect a track by Shift-clicking it. Your selection can also start at different points in different tracks.

MOVING CLIPS IN THE TIMELINE

Using Snap to Edges

When you move clips in the timeline, you usually want to align them precisely. In a sequence of clips in a single track, alignment usually isn't a problem: you can easily drag clips to butt up against one another. At times, however, aligning clips isn't as straightforward. You may want a title in video track 2 to start right after the clip in track 1 ends, for example. When you are placing a sound effect, you may want to align a marker in a video clip with a marker in an audio clip. Or you may want to move a clip to exactly where you placed the edit line.

When you create transitions in an A/B workspace, the proper alignment of clips is critical. Unless you zoom in for a very close view of the program or continually consult the Info window, precise placement of clips in the timeline can be difficult (**Figures 6.68** and **6.69**).

The timeline provides an easy way to align clips, through a feature called *snap to edges*. When snap to edges is activated, clips behave as though they're magnetized; they tend to snap to the edge of another clip, to a marker, and to the edit line. Snap to edges also works when you're trimming clips in the timeline (covered in Chapter 7). When snap to edges is off, the clips move smoothly past one another as you drag them in the timeline. Because snap to edges is so convenient, you'll probably leave it on most of the time.

To toggle snap to edges on and off:

◆ At the bottom of the Timeline window, click the snap to edges button to toggle it on and off.

   The ⬚ icon indicates that snap to edges is on (**Figure 6.70**); the ⬚ icon indicates that snap to edges is off (**Figure 6.71**).

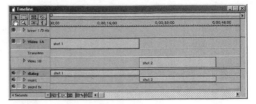

Figure 6.68 These two clips look aligned with one another when the timeline is zoomed out…

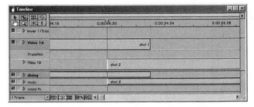

Figure 6.69 …but a closer looks reveals that they actually overlap.

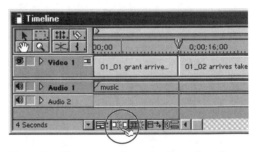

Figure 6.70 Set snap to edges on to have clips align as you move them.

Figure 6.71 Setting snap to edges off allows you to move clips freely but makes it harder to align them.

Figure 6.72 Position the pointer over the marker until the pointer turns blue.

Figure 6.73 When snap to edges is on, you can drag the clip by the marker to align the marker to clip edges, the edit line, or other markers.

To use snap to edges:

1. At the bottom of the Timeline window, click the snap to edges button to toggle it on.

   The ▢▢▢ icon indicates that snap to edges is on.

2. Do one of the following:

   ▲ Drag a clip in the timeline close to the edge of another clip, a marker, or the edit line.

   ▲ Position the selection tool (the standard pointer) over a marker within a clip in the timeline until the pointer turns blue (**Figure 6.72**).

   As you drag the clip or the marker, it snaps to the edges of other clips, other markers, and the edit line (**Figure 6.73**).

✔ Tips

■ When snap to edges is on, it's easy to use clip markers to cut video to the beat of music or to synch sound effects to video.

■ Occasionally, several edges are so close together that snap to edges makes it difficult to place the clip properly. In these infrequent cases, you should zoom into the timeline so that competing edges appear farther apart. Alternatively, of course, you can turn off snap to edges and disable its magnetic effect.

USING SNAP TO EDGES

Splitting Clips

Sometimes, you need to cut a clip in the timeline into two or more pieces. You may want to apply an effect to one part of a shot but not to another, for example. When you split a clip, each piece becomes an independent program clip, or clip instance. When you split a linked clip, both the video and audio tracks are split.

To split a clip with the razor:

1. In the toolbox of the Timeline window, select the razor tool 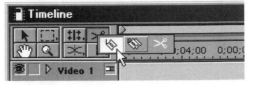 (**Figure 6.74**).

2. Click a clip in the timeline at the point where you want to split it (**Figure 6.75**).

   The clip is split into two individual clips at that point (**Figure 6.76**).

To split clips in multiple tracks:

1. In the toolbox of the Timeline window, select the multirazor tool  (**Figure 6.77**).

2. Click the point in the timeline where you want to split the clips in all tracks (**Figure 6.78**).

Figure 6.74 In the toolbox of the Timeline window, select the razor tool.

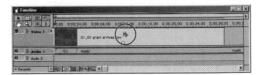

Figure 6.75 Click a clip in the timeline at the point where you want to split it.

Figure 6.76 The clip is split into two individual clips.

Figure 6.77 In the toolbox of the Timeline window, select the multirazor tool.

Figure 6.78 Click the point in the timeline where you want to split the clips in all tracks.

Figure 6.79 All unlocked clips in all unlocked tracks are split at the same point in the timeline.

Figure 6.80 Position the edit line at the point where you want to split the clip.

Figure 6.81 Choose Timeline > Razor at Edit Line.

Figure 6.82 All unlocked clips in all unlocked tracks are split at the same point in the timeline.

All unlocked clips in all unlocked tracks are split at the same point in the timeline (**Figure 6.79**).

✔ Tip

■ You can turn the razor tool into the multirazor tool by pressing Option (Mac) or Alt (Windows).

To split clips at the edit line:

1. Position the edit line at the point where you want to split the clip (**Figure 6.80**).

2. Choose Timeline > Razor at Edit Line (**Figure 6.81**).

   All unlocked clips in all unlocked tracks are split at the same point in the timeline (**Figure 6.82**).

Match-Frame Edits

Splitting a clip creates a cut that is visible in the timeline but invisible during playback. This kind of cut is called a *match-frame edit*. In traditional tape-based editing, match-frame edits are essential to A/B roll editing. In Premiere, match-frame edits can be useful if you want to add an effect or speed change to one part of a shot but not another. Because the viewer can't detect a match-frame edit, the effect appears to be seamless.

Cutting, Copying, and Pasting Clips

As you would expect of any computer program, Adobe Premiere uses copy and paste functions. You might be pleasantly surprised by Premiere's powerful paste commands. In this section, you learn how to copy and paste the contents of a clip. Later chapters discuss how you can use the same command to copy the settings used by one clip and paste them into another clip.

To use the Paste to Fit command:

1. Select a clip in the timeline, or load it into the source view or a clip window (**Figure 6.83**).

   You can set in and out points, if you want.

2. Choose one of the following:

   Edit > Copy—to copy the selected clip and leave it in the timeline.

   Edit > Cut—to copy the selected clip and remove it from the timeline.

3. Select an empty segment in a track of the timeline (**Figure 6.84**).

4. Choose Edit > Paste to Fit (**Figure 6.85**). The Fit Clip dialog box appears.

5. Choose an option (**Figure 6.86**):

   Change Speed—changes the speed of the source clip to fit the specified duration in the program. Only the speed changes; the in and out points stay the same. If the source clip is pasted into a longer gap, the clip's speed is decreased, making its duration long enough to fit in the range defined by the program in and out points. If the source clip is longer than the gap, its speed increases, so that its duration matches the program duration.

Figure 6.83 Select a clip in the timeline, and choose [Cmd]-C (Mac) or [Ctrl]-C (Windows) to copy it.

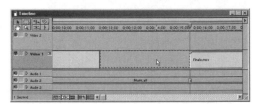

Figure 6.84 Select an empty segment in a track of the timeline.

Figure 6.85 Choose Edit > Paste to Fit.

Figure 6.86 Choose an option in the Fit Clip dialog box.

Figure 6.87 Premiere fits the clip into the specified space in the program, according to your selection.

Figure 6.88 Select a clip in the timeline, and choose [Cmd]-C (Mac) or [Ctrl]-C (Windows) to copy it.

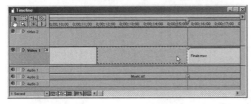

Figure 6.89 Select an empty segment in a track of the timeline.

Trim Source—changes the source out point to fit the specified duration in the program. The in point and the speed of the clip are unaffected. (In other words, this option ignores the source out point and works like a three-point edit.)

Cancel—stops the edit and makes no changes in the program.

Premiere fits the clip into the specified space in the program, according to your selection (**Figure 6.87**).

To use the Paste Attributes command:

1. Click a clip in the timeline to select it (**Figure 6.88**).

2. Choose one of the following:

 Edit > Copy—to leave the clip in the timeline.

 Edit > Cut—to remove the clip from its current position.

3. Select an empty segment in a track of the timeline (**Figure 6.89**).

continues on next page

CUTTING, COPYING, AND PASTING CLIPS

4. Choose Edit > Paste Attributes (**Figure 6.90**).

The Paste Attributes dialog box appears (**Figure 6.91**).

5. Click the Content radio button.

6. Choose an option from the pull-down menu (**Figure 6.92**).

Animations dynamically illustrate the effect of each option, as follows:

Normal—works the same as an ordinary paste.

Move Source Out Point—works the same as Paste to Fit by changing the source out point to fit into the space in the timeline.

Move Destination In Point—changes the next clip's in point to accommodate the pasted clip.

Move Source In Point—changes the source clip's in point to fit the clip into the space in the timeline. The source out point remains unchanged.

Move Destination Out Point—changes the out point of the preceding clip to accommodate the pasted clip.

Change Speed—changes the speed of the clip to fit it into the space in the timeline. The source in and out points remain unchanged.

Shift Linked Tracks—shifts the following clips and their linked tracks forward in time to accommodate the pasted clip.

Shift All Tracks—shifts the following clips in all tracks forward in time to accommodate the pasted clip.

7. Click Paste.

The clip contents are pasted into the timeline, according to the option you specified.

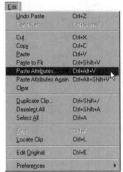

Figure 6.90 Choose Edit > Paste Attributes.

Figure 6.91 The Paste Attributes dialog box appears.

Figure 6.92 In the Paste Attributes dialog box, click the Content radio button and choose an option from the pull-down menu.

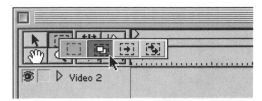

Figure 6.93 In the toolbox of the Timeline window, select the block-select tool.

Figure 6.94 Drag to select the part of the program that you want to block-copy.

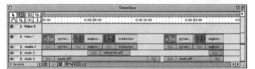

Figure 6.95 (Option)-drag (Mac) or (Alt)-drag (Windows) the selection to an empty part of the timeline to copy the entire range of clips.

To block-copy a range of the program:

1. In the toolbox of the Timeline window, select the block-select tool ⬚ (**Figure 6.93**).

2. Drag to select the part of the program that you want to block-copy (**Figure 6.94**).

3. (Option)-drag (Mac) or (Alt)-drag (Windows) the selection to an empty part of the timeline.

 The block-copy function copies the selected area in all tracks; you can't limit the effect to certain tracks (**Figure 6.95**).

✔ Tip

■ If you don't hold down Option or Alt when you drag with the block-select tool, you create a virtual clip instead of block-copying the selection. For more information about virtual clips, see Chapter 8.

Changing the Speed of a Clip

When a clip is in the timeline, you can change its speed to make it play either faster or more slowly. Changing the speed of a clip directly affects its duration. The source in and out points remain intact, however.

In Premiere, you can change the speed of a clip by choosing a menu command or by dragging directly in the timeline.

To change the speed of a clip by using the Speed command:

1. In the timeline, select a clip (**Figure 6.96**).

2. Choose Clip > Speed (**Figure 6.97**). The Clip Speed dialog box appears.

3. Choose either of the following options (**Figure 6.98**):

   New Rate—to enter a speed for the clip, expressed in a percentage of the normal speed. A value less than 100% increases the clip's speed; a value greater than 100% decreases the clip's speed.

   New Duration—to enter a total duration for the clip. Durations shorter than the original increase the clip's speed; durations longer than the original decrease the clip's speed.

4. Click OK to close the Clip Speed dialog box. In the timeline, the clip's speed—and, therefore, its duration—change according to the values you specified (**Figure 6.99**). The source in and out points are not changed, only the speed of the clip.

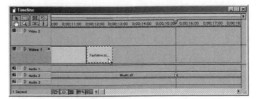

Figure 6.96 Select a clip in the timeline.

Figure 6.97 Choose Clip > Speed.

Figure 6.98 In the Clip Speed dialog box, enter either a new rate or a new duration.

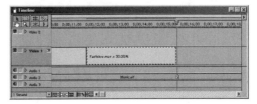

Figure 6.99 In the timeline, the clip's speed changes.

Figure 6.100 In the toolbox of the Timeline window, select the stretch tool.

Figure 6.101 Position the stretch tool at the edge of a clip in the timeline.

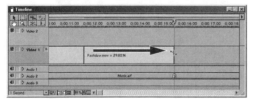

Figure 6.102 Dragging with the stretch tool changes a clip's speed, not its in or out points.

To change the speed of a clip by using the stretch tool:

1. In the toolbox of the Timeline window, select the stretch tool ![stretch tool icon] (**Figure 6.100**).

2. Position the stretch tool at the edge of a clip in the timeline, and drag the edge (**Figures 6.101** and **6.102**).

   Dragging the edge to shorten the clip increases its speed; dragging the clip to lengthen it decreases its speed. The source in and out point frames are not changed, only the speed of the clip.

✔ Tip

- The quality of a slow-motion effect is limited by your source material. When shooting film, you can create a slow-motion effect in the camera by *overcranking*. Overcranking sets the frame rate higher than the film's standard frame rate. Because the film has captured a greater number of unique frames, the slow-motion image appears to be very smooth and crisp. Video cameras, on the other hand, can't increase their frame rate. Creating a slow-motion effect in a program such as Premiere creates additional frames by repeating the existing frames. Compared with overcranking the camera, this kind of slow motion doesn't look nearly as smooth.

CHANGING THE SPEED OF A CLIP

193

Using Program Markers

Just as clip markers can help you identify important frames in the source clips, program markers can specify important points in the timeline.

In most respects, program markers work exactly the same way as clip markers. Although you use set, delete, and cue to program markers from the marker pull-down menu on the program side of the Monitor window, the controls are identical to those on the source side. And of course, program markers appear in the time ruler, rather than in clips. Apart from these minor differences, the methods you learned in Chapter 4 can be applied to program markers, and won't be repeated here. However, program markers have a few unique features that merit a separate explanation. First of all, program markers can include a text message. Though this comment appears in the program view whenever you're cued to the marker (or a specified duration after the marker), it's for your reference only, and doesn't appear in playback or export.

In addition, program markers can contain a Web link or chapter link. When a marker containing a link is reached during playback, a Web link automatically opens a Web page in your browser; a chapter link cues a QuickTime movie or DVD to a specified chapter.

To add a comment to a program marker:

1. In the time ruler of the Timeline window, double-click a program marker (**Figure 6.103**).

   A dialog box for the marker appears.

Figure 6.103 In the time ruler, double-click a program marker.

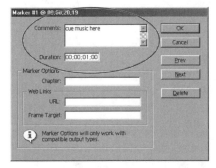

Figure 6.104 A dialog box for the marker appears. In the dialog box, enter a comment and a duration for the comment to appear in the program view.

Figure 6.105 When the current time is cued to the time range of the marker's comment, the comment appears in the program view.

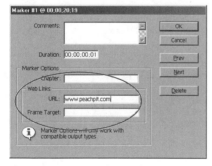

Figure 6.106 In the time ruler, double-click a program marker.

Figure 6.107 To set a chapter link, enter the name of the chapter in the Chapter field. To set a Web link, enter a URL, and if you want, a filename for the Frame Target.

2. In the Marker dialog box, enter information in the following fields (**Figure 6.104**):

   Comment—enter a text message that will appear in the program view of the Monitor window.

   Duration—enter the amount of time the comment will appear, beginning at the marked time in the program.

3. Click OK to close the Marker dialog box.

   In the time ruler, the program marker appears blue, and a line extending from the marker indicates the comment duration you specified. When the current time is cued to the time range of the comment, the comment appears in the program view of the Monitor window (**Figure 6.105**).

To add a Web or chapter link to a program marker:

1. Double-click a program marker (**Figure 6.106**).

   A dialog box for the marker appears.

2. In the Marker dialog box, do one of the following:

   ▲ To set a chapter link, enter the name of the chapter in the Chapter field (**Figure 6.107**).

   ▲ To set a Web link, enter the Web address in the URL field.

   ▲ To activate a particular frame of the site in a Web link, enter the filename of the frame in the Frame Target field.

3. Click OK to close the Marker dialog box.

Block Moving Program Markers

Ordinarily, shifting clips down the timeline won't affect the position of program markers—they stick to where you set them on the time ruler. However, you can set program markers to shift when you perform edits that cause the clips in the program to shift their position. This way, the program markers will maintain their relationship with the clips in the program.

To block move markers on insert edits:

1. Choose Windows > Window Options > Timeline Window Options (**Figure 6.108**). The Timeline Window Options dialog box appears.

2. In the Timeline Window Options dialog box, check Block Move Markers (**Figure 6.109**).

3. Click OK to close the dialog box.

   When edits shift clips in the timeline, program markers automatically shift to maintain their relationship with the clips.

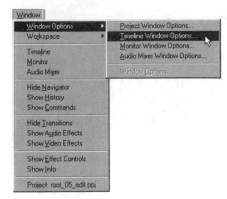

Figure 6.108 Choose Windows > Window Options > Timeline Window Options.

Figure 6.109 In the Timeline Window Options dialog box, check Block Move Markers.

REFINING
THE PROGRAM

After you assemble a rough cut, you can refine it by making adjustments to the in and out points of the clips in the program—a process known as *trimming*. Although you already know several ways to trim clips in the program, the techniques in this chapter will expand your repertoire.

You'll learn to use various editing tools to make fine adjustments to clips directly in the timeline. You'll also learn how you can make subtle adjustments to the in and out points of clips in the program by switching the Monitor window to trim mode (also known as the trim view).

This chapter also covers techniques that deal with the link between video and audio. You'll learn how to create split edits, or L-cuts, by trimming linked video and audio separately. You also learn how to create—and break—a link between video and audio. In addition, you learn how to detect when audio and video are out of synch and how to correct the problem.

Choosing a Trimming Method

Making an adjustment to a clip's in point or out point—particularly a small adjustment—is called *trimming*. You can trim a clip by manipulating it directly in the timeline or by working on it in trim mode in the Monitor window. Although you can use either method to perform some editing tasks, each has its unique features.

Trimming in the timeline relies on using the mouse to move the edges of a program's clips, thereby changing their in or out points (**Figure 7.1**). By selecting various tools, you can perform specialized trimming tasks, known as ripple edits, rolling edits, or simple trimming. You can also slip or slide clips—something that you can't accomplish in trim mode. (See the section, "Making Slip and Slide Edits," later in this chapter.) Like all timeline editing, trimming in the timeline is graphically clear and intuitive. The precision of the edit, however, depends partly on the detail of your view of the timeline. Also, this kind of trimming doesn't permit you to preview the changes before you make them final.

When you activate trim mode, the Monitor window switches to an editing mode designed for trimming clips in the program (**Figure 7.2**). Like trimming in the timeline, trimming in trim mode lets you perform ripple edits and rolling edits. Although using trim mode is not as intuitive as editing directly in the timeline, trim mode always gives you precise control. Trim mode also provides a large view of the edit as you make adjustments and allows you to preview the changes.

The following sections explain trimming techniques used in the timeline first and then cover trim mode.

Figure 7.1 Trimming in the timeline relies on using the mouse to move the edges of a program's clips, thereby changing their in or out points. In this example, a rolling edit is being performed to change the current cut point between two clips in the timeline.

Figure 7.2 When you activate trim mode, the Monitor window switches to an editing mode designed for trimming clips in the program.

✔ Tips

- Extending the length of a clip is often referred to as *trimming out* the in or out point; reducing the clip's duration is called *trimming in*.

- You can't extend an in point or an out point beyond the limits of the master clip, of course. If Premiere doesn't let you trim any farther, you're probably out of source material.

- In most of the examples to follow, the timeline's synch mode is on. When synch mode is off, the trimming tools (Trim, Ripple Edit, Rolling Edit, Slip, and Slide) are outlined in white. See "Using Links" later in this chapter.

Figure 7.3 Turn edge viewing on to see the edge in the program view as you trim.

Figure 7.4 Turn edge viewing off to prevent the program view from displaying the trimmed edge.

Using Edge Viewing

The left edge of a clip in the timeline is the in point, or *head*; the right edge is the out point, or *tail*. In the sections to follow, you'll learn to use various tools to trim a clip's edges directly in the timeline. Though the positions of the edges give you an idea of where a clip starts and ends in the timeline, they can't show you what the frame actually looks like. To see the edge frames in the program view as you trim, activate edge viewing. If you don't need to see the edge frame as you trim, turn edge viewing off to spare Premiere the work of updating the program view.

To view edges:

◆ At the bottom of the timeline, click the edge view button to toggle edge viewing on and off:

Edge View On ![icon] —to view the edge (in or out point) in the program view of the Monitor window as you trim it (**Figure 7.3**).

Edge View Off ![icon] —to disable the display of the edge frame as you trim (**Figure 7.4**).

Trimming Clips in the Timeline

You don't need to choose a special tool to trim clips directly in the timeline. The default tool, the selection tool, automatically switches to a trim tool when you position it at a clip edge in the timeline. The trim tools' icons have changed since the last version of Premiere; they now more clearly indicate whether you're preparing to trim an in point or an out point. However, you will select special tools from the toolbox to perform specialized editing tasks, such as ripple, rolling, slip, and slide edits. These techniques are covered in later sections.

To trim a clip in the timeline:

1. Using the selection tool ► *do either of the following:*

   ▲ To trim the in point, position the pointer on the left edge of a clip in the timeline.

   The pointer becomes the trim in tool ⊞.

   or

   ▲ To trim the out point, position the pointer on the right edge of a clip in the timeline.

   The pointer becomes the trim out tool ⊞ (**Figure 7.5**).

2. Drag the trim tool to the left or right to change the clip's in or out point (**Figure 7.6**).

   If edge viewing is active, you can view the edge frame in the program view (see "To view edges" earlier in this chapter).

   When you release the mouse button, the clip's in or out point changes (**Figure 7.7**). When no more source footage remains, you won't be able to trim the edge out any farther, and the clip's edge displays a folded corner.

Figure 7.5 When you position the pointer at the left edge of a clip, the pointer becomes the trim in tool; at the right edge, the pointer becomes the trim out tool.

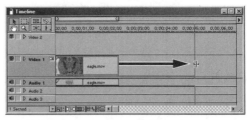

Figure 7.6 Drag the trim tool to the left or right to change the clip's in or out point.

Figure 7.7 When you release the mouse button, the clip's in or out point changes. When the edge has been trimmed out so that no more source footage remains, the edge of the clip displays a folded corner.

✔ Tip

■ If Snap to Edges is active, edges snap to other edges, markers, or the edit line as you trim. This setting is often advantageous, but if it prevents you from trimming to the frame you want, turn off Snap to Edges. (See "Using Snap to Edges" in Chapter 6.)

The Timeline Toolbox

Most tasks in this book assume that the selection tool ▶ is active. When you choose other editing tools from the Timeline window's toolbox, remember to switch back to the selection tool. Otherwise, you may spend time wondering why a particular technique isn't working.

Also, you should understand that not all the tools are visible at the same time. A tiny triangle next to a tool indicates that clicking and holding the mouse-button down reveals a hidden, extended palette of related tools (**Figures 7.8** and **7.9**).

Each tool button has a single-stroke keyboard shortcut. For tools grouped in a hidden tool palette, press the shortcut key repeatedly to cycle through all the tools in the group (**Figure 7.10** and **7.11**).

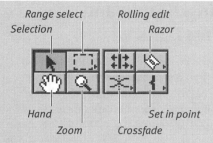

Figure 7.10 These are the tools in the timeline's toolbox.

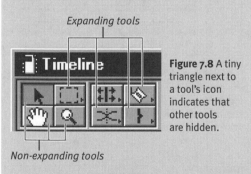

Figure 7.8 A tiny triangle next to a tool's icon indicates that other tools are hidden.

Figure 7.9 Clicking and holding the tool reveals an extended palette of tools.

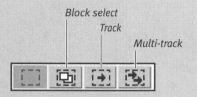

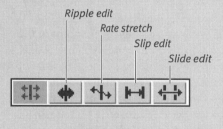

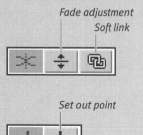

Figure 7.11 Other tools can be found by expanding the palette.

Making Ripple and Rolling Edits

When two clips are side by side in a track in the timeline, you can perform a ripple or rolling edit. You can make ripple or rolling edits by using tools in the Timeline window or by using trim mode.

In a *ripple edit*, you change the duration of one clip but do not affect the duration of the adjacent clips. After you ripple-edit the edge of the clip, all the adjacent clips shift in the timeline to compensate for the change, in a ripple effect. Therefore, the total length of the program changes (**Figures 7.12** and **7.13**). In Premiere 6, you can ripple-edit in and out points in the timeline and in trim mode. (Previous versions didn't permit you to ripple-edit an in point in the timeline.)

In a *rolling edit*, you change the out point of one clip while you change the in point of the adjacent clip. In other words, you make one clip shorter while you make the adjacent clip longer. One clip rolls out while the other rolls in. Therefore, the total length of the program remains the same (**Figure 7.14**). You can perform rolling edits in the timeline and in trim mode.

To perform a ripple edit in the timeline:

1. In the toolbox of the Timeline window, select the ripple edit tool ⬌ (**Figure 7.15**).

   If the ripple edit tool is hidden, click and hold the tool that is visible in the appropriate location in the toolbox (the rolling edit, rate stretch, slip, or slide tool) to reveal an expanded menu.

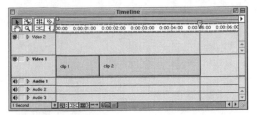

Figure 7.12 Note the duration and positions of the clips before the edit.

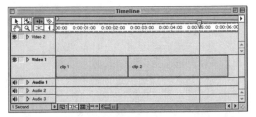

Figure 7.13 After a ripple edit, subsequent clips shift forward in time, maintaining their in and out points.

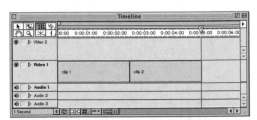

Figure 7.14 After a rolling edit, one clip becomes shorter while its adjacent clip becomes longer. Therefore, subsequent clips don't shift in the timeline.

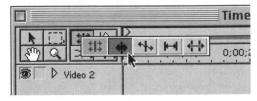

Figure 7.15 Select the ripple edit tool.

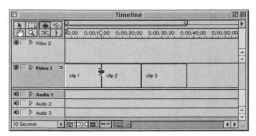

Figure 7.16 Position the ripple edit tool at the in point or out point of a clip in the timeline. Here, the out point will be changed.

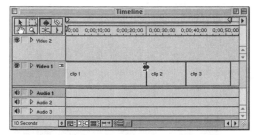

Figure 7.17 With the ripple edit tool, drag the clip's edge to shorten or lengthen it. Here, the out point is trimmed out, or extended. Subsequent clips shift back in time to accommodate the trimmed clip.

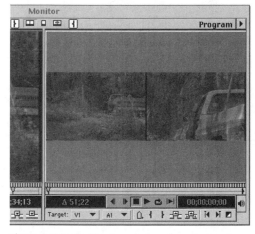

Figure 7.18 In the Monitor window, the program view shows a split view when you are performing ripple and rolling edits.

2. *Do either of the following:*

▲ To ripple-edit an out point, position the mouse over the right edge (out point) of the first of two adjacent clips in the timeline.

The pointer becomes the ripple edit out tool (**Figure 7.16**).

or

▲ To ripple-edit an in point, position the mouse over the left edge (in point) of the second of two adjacent clips in the timeline.

The pointer becomes the ripple edit in tool (**Figure 7.17**).

3. Drag to the left or right to trim the clip's edge.

The subsequent unlocked clips shift in the timeline to compensate for the edit (**Figure 7.18**).

✔ **Tips**

■ All unlocked clips shift after a ripple edit. If you don't want a clip to move in the timeline, lock the clip. See "Locking and Unlocking Clips" in Chapter 6.

■ Premiere 6 uses new icons for ripple edits in the timeline.

To perform a rolling edit in the timeline:

1. In the toolbox, select the rolling edit tool ‡|‡ (**Figure 7.19**).

   If the rolling edit tool is hidden, click and hold the tool that is visible in the appropriate location in the toolbox (the ripple edit, rate stretch, slip, or slide tool) to reveal an expanded menu.

2. Position the pointer between the two adjacent clips that you want to change.

   The pointer becomes the rolling edit tool (**Figure 7.20**).

3. Drag to the left or right to trim the out point of the first clip and the in point of the second clip by the same number of frames (**Figure 7.21**).

   If edge viewing is active, you can see the edge frames in the Monitor window as you trim.

✔ Tip

- You can use a rolling edit to adjust the point at which you split a clip with the razor. If you weren't precise when you split the clip, simply use the rolling edit tool to move the cut point to the left or right.

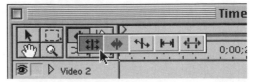

Figure 7.19 Select the rolling edit tool.

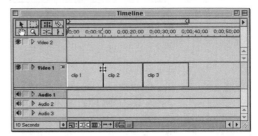

Figure 7.20 Position the mouse between two clips so that the rolling edit tool appears.

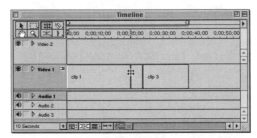

Figure 7.21 Drag to change the out point of the first clip and the in point of the second clip by the same amount.

MAKING RIPPLE AND ROLLING EDITS

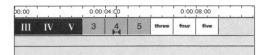

Figure 7.22 Notice how the frames of the clip in the center look before a slip edit. This figure uses numbers to represent image frames to illustrate the effect.

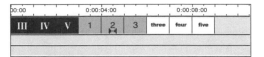

Figure 7.23 Dragging the center clip with the slip edit tool changes its in and out points simultaneously, to maintain its duration.

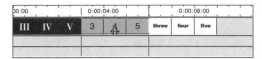

Figure 7.24 Notice how these three clips look before a slide edit. Again, numbers represent image frames to make the effect clear.

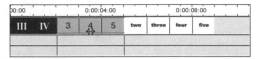

Figure 7.25 A slide edit retains the in and out point of the center clip while changing the out point of the preceding clip and the in point of the following clip.

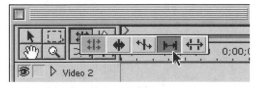

Figure 7.26 Select the slip tool.

Making Slip and Slide Edits

When you have three clips side by side in the timeline, you can perform specialized editing techniques called slip edits and slide edits. Slip and slide edits are unique to timeline editing.

In a *slip edit*, you change both the in point and the out point of a clip at the same time without altering the adjacent clips. It's as if you're viewing part of the clip through a space between the two other clips; when you slip the center clip back and forth, you get to see a different part (**Figures 7.22** and **7.23**).

In a *slide edit*, the duration of the clip remains the same as you shift it in the timeline. When you drag, or slide, the clip to the left, the preceding clip gets shorter as the following clip gets longer. When you slide the clip to the right, the preceding clip gets longer as the following clip gets shorter (**Figures 7.24** and **7.25**).

To slip a clip:

1. In the toolbox, select the slip edit tool (**Figure 7.26**).

2. Position the pointer on a clip that is between two other clips in a track of the timeline.

   The mouse pointer changes to the slip edit icon.

   continues on next page

3. Drag left or right to change the clip's in and out points without changing the clip's duration or position in the timeline (**Figure 7.27**).

   The Monitor window displays the frames at the edit points of the slip edit, as well as the number of frames by which you are shifting the clip (**Figure 7.28**).

To slide a clip:

1. In the toolbox, select the slide edit tool (**Figure 7.29**).

2. Position the pointer on a clip that is between two other clips in the timeline.

   The pointer changes to the slide edit icon .

3. Drag right or left to shift the clip in the timeline (**Figure 7.30**).

   The Monitor window displays the frames at the edit points of the slide edit, as well as the number of frames by which you are shifting the clip (**Figure 7.31**).

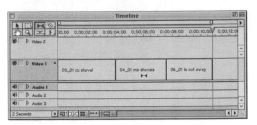

Figure 7.27 Drag a clip positioned between clips to perform the slip edit.

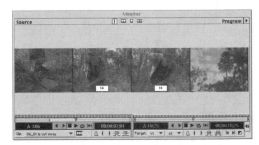

Figure 7.28 The Monitor window displays the frames at the edit points. A numerical display shows the number of frames by which the center clip is shifted.

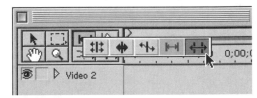

Figure 7.29 Select the slide tool.

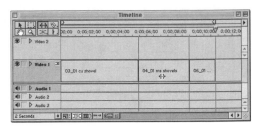

Figure 7.30 Drag a clip positioned between clips to perform a slide edit.

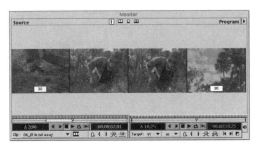

Figure 7.31 The Monitor window displays the frames at the edit points. A numerical display shows the number of frames trimmed from the out point of the first clip and the in point of the last clip.

Figure 7.32 In trim mode, the Monitor window shows two adjacent clips in the timeline.

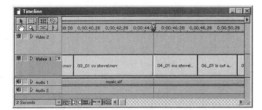

Figure 7.33 Position the current frame on or near the cut you want to trim.

Figure 7.34 At the top of the Monitor window, click the trim mode button.

Figure 7.35 The Monitor window switches to trim mode.

Using Trim Mode

In Chapter 4, you saw that the Monitor window toggles to single view or dual view for editing. When you're ready to fine-tune edits in the program, you can switch the Monitor window to trim mode. In trim mode, the Monitor window shows two adjacent clips in the timeline (**Figure 7.32**). The out point of the first clip appears on the left; the in point of the second clip appears on the right. An array of controls allows you to perform ripple and rolling edits.

Though you can perform ripple and rolling edits in the timeline, trim mode has several unique advantages. In trim mode, you can view both sides of the edit in a large window and trim them with numerical precision. Unlike trimming in the timeline, trimming in trim mode allows the clips to occupy different tracks. Also, you can preview your changes in trim mode before you finalize them.

In the following tasks, trim mode appears in its default setting. To change the appearance of trim mode, see "Customizing Trim Mode" later in this chapter.

To activate trim mode:

1. Position the current frame on or near the cut you want to trim (**Figure 7.33**).

2. To activate trim mode, *do either of the following:*

   ▲ At the top of the Monitor window, click the trim mode button (**Figure 7.34**).

   or

   ▲ Press ⌘-T (Mac) or Ctrl-T (Windows).

   The Monitor window switches to trim mode (**Figure 7.35**). The way that this view appears on your screen depends on how you set the trim-mode options, which are explained in "To customize trim mode" later in this chapter.

To deactivate trim mode:

Do either of the following:

◆ At the top of the Monitor window, click the dual view icon ▦ or the single view icon ▣.

or

◆ In the Timeline window, click the time ruler to return the Monitor window to the previous editing view.

To find the cut you want to trim:

Do either of the following:

◆ In the Timeline window, position the edit line (the program's current time) on or before the cut you want to trim, and activate trim mode.

  If the edit line isn't positioned on a cut point, trim mode cues to the next cut in the timeline.

or

◆ In trim mode, click the previous edit button or the next edit button (**Figure 7.36**).

  If you alter an edit in trim mode, the changes are finalized by cueing to another cut point.

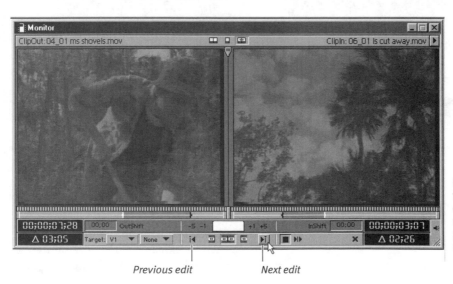

Previous edit   Next edit

Figure 7.36 To trim a different cut in trim mode, click the previous edit or next edit button.

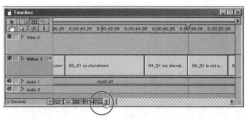

Figure 7.37 Set synch mode by clicking the synch mode button at the bottom of the Timeline window. Here, synch mode is on, so that linked clips retain their link as they are trimmed.

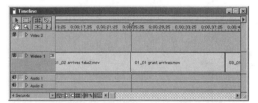

Figure 7.38 Cue the current program frame on or near the edit, and activate trim mode by pressing ⌘-T (Mac) or Ctrl-T (Windows).

Figure 7.39 In trim mode, specify the target tracks that you want to affect. Here, Video 1 is selected.

Editing in Trim Mode

After you activate trim mode and choose a cut to adjust, you can perform ripple and rolling edits, and switch between the two freely. Preparing for either type of edit involves the same steps.

To prepare to edit in trim mode:

1. At the bottom of the Timeline window, toggle synch mode on or off:

   ⊟ —to trim both tracks of linked clips, regardless of the target track (**Figure 7.37**).

   ⊟ —to trim only clips in selected tracks, and override the link between the audio and video tracks of linked clips. Turn synch mode off to create a split edit (see "Creating Split Edits" later in this chapter).

2. Cue the current time on or near the cut you want to adjust (**Figure 7.38**).

3. In the Monitor window, click the trim mode button ⊞ , or press ⌘-T (Mac) or Ctrl-T (Windows).

   The Monitor window switches to trim mode.

4. From the Target video and audio pull-down menus, choose the tracks that you want to affect (**Figure 7.39**).

   The examples to follow trim both the video and audio of linked clips. For details on trimming video and audio separately, see "Creating Split Edits" later in this chapter.

209

To perform a ripple edit in trim mode:

1. In trim mode, *do either of the following:*

   ▲ To trim the out point of the first clip, click the image on the left, or click the set focus left button (**Figure 7.40**).

   or

   ▲ To trim the in point of the second clip, click the image on the right or click the set focus right button.

   The active image appears with a white border, the controls below the active side of the trim view are highlighted, and the time display becomes green.

2. To trim frames in the active view, *do any of the following:*

   ▲ Click -1 to trim one frame to the left (earlier in time).

   ▲ Click -5 to trim several frames to the left (earlier in time).

   ▲ Click +1 to trim one frame to the right (later in time).

   ▲ Click +5 to trim several frames to the right (later in time).

   ▲ In the OutShift field or InShift field, type a positive number to add frames to the selected view, or type a negative number to subtract frames from the selected view; then press Return (Mac) or Enter (Windows).

   ▲ Drag the jog track control below the selected view.

   ▲ Drag the out-point icon in the left view or the in-point icon in the right view.

   As you trim frames, the number of trimmed frames appears in the OutShift field and InShift field. Trimming to the left subtracts from an out point or adds to an in point. Trimming to the right adds to an out point or subtracts from an in point (**Figure 7.41**). You can see the effects in the timeline.

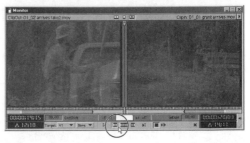

Figure 7.40 Choose the clip that you want to trim by clicking the view or its corresponding button. Here, the set focus left button is selected to trim the out point of the first clip.

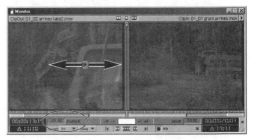

Figure 7.41 Use the trim buttons, or drag the jog track or edit mark to trim the selected clip. You can also enter a number of frames in the OutShift or InShift fields. Here, the out point has been trimmed out by one second.

✔ Tips

■ By default, the multi-frame trim buttons +5 and -5 trim 5 frames. However, you can change this amount. See "Customizing Trim Mode," later in this chapter.

■ In trim mode, you can switch between trimming the left and right clips simply by clicking the view that you want to trim.

Figure 7.42 Click the set focus both button, or click between the two views.

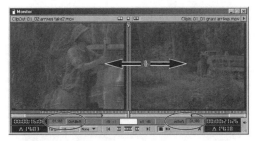

Figure 7.43 To perform a rolling edit, you can use the trimming controls, or position the mouse between the two views so that the rolling edit tool appears. Drag to the left to trim the edit to the left; drag to the right to trim the edit to the right.

Figure 7.44 By performing a rolling edit, you can move the edit point to the left or to the right.

✔ **Tip**

■ In trim mode, you can switch between ripple and rolling edits before you apply the edit.

To perform a rolling edit in trim mode:

1. In trim mode, *do either of the following* to activate both views:
   ▲ Click the set focus both button [icon] (**Figure 7.42**).
   or
   ▲ Click between the two views.

   The image in both views appears selected, and both time displays appear green.

2. To trim frames in both views, *do any of the following:*
   ▲ Click **-1** to trim one frame to the left.
   ▲ Click **-5** to trim several frames to the left.
   ▲ Click **+1** to trim one frame to the right.
   ▲ Click **+5** to trim several frames to the right.
   ▲ Using the numeric keypad, type a positive number to move the edit forward in time, or type a negative number to move the edit back in the timeline; then press (Return) (Mac) or (Enter) (Windows).
   ▲ Drag the jog track control below the selected view to trim.
   ▲ Place the pointer between the two views, so that the pointer becomes the rolling edit tool, and drag left or right to trim.
   ▲ Drag the out-point icon in the left view or the in-point icon in the right view.

   As you trim frames, the number of trimmed frames appears next to the OutShift display and InShift display. A rolling edit moves both the InShift and OutShift by the same amounts (**Figure 7.43**). Trimming to the left moves the cut earlier in time; trimming to the right moves the cut later in time. You can see your changes in the timeline (**Figure 7.44**).

Previewing and Applying Trim Mode Edits

After you've made your adjustments in trim mode, you can play them back—complete with audio—before you finalize your changes. After you take a look at your handiwork, you can confirm the changes and trim the next cut, apply the changes and exit trim mode, or cancel the changes and start over.

To preview the edit in trim mode:

◆ To review your changes, *do any of the following:*

▲ Click the preview button  (**Figure 7.45**).

▲ Press the spacebar.

▲ Press ⎣L⎦.

The Monitor window shows a single image and plays the edit from three seconds before the cut to three seconds after the cut (**Figure 7.46**). For details on maximizing the size of the previews, see "Customizing Trim Mode" later in this chapter.

To apply the trimmed edit and trim other edits:

In trim mode, *click either of the following buttons:*

◆ **Next edit** —to trim the next edit in a selected track of the timeline (**Figure 7.47**).

or

◆ **Previous edit** —to trim the previous cut in a selected track of the timeline.

The current frame of the program (edit line) is cued to the next or previous cut, which is displayed in the trim view. Trim the cut as usual.

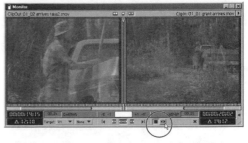

Figure 7.45 To preview the trimmed edit, click the preview button, or press the spacebar or ⎣L⎦.

Figure 7.46 When you are previewing the edit, trim mode shows a single image and plays the program from three seconds before the edit to three seconds after the edit.

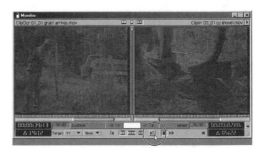

Figure 7.47 To apply the changes and trim another cut, click the next edit or previous edit button.

Figure 7.48 Click the single view or dual view button to return the Monitor window to that view. Or press ⌘-T (Mac) or Ctrl-T (Windows) to exit trim mode and return to the previous editing view.

To apply the trimmed edit and exit trim mode:

In trim mode, *do any of the following:*

◆ At the top of the Monitor window, click the dual view or single view (**Figure 7.48**).

The Monitor window switches to the view you selected.

◆ Press ⌘-T (Mac) or Ctrl-T (Windows).

The Monitor window switches back to the previous view (whether dual or single).

◆ In the Timeline window, click the time ruler.

The Monitor window returns to the previous view (whether dual or single view).

To cancel the edit in trim mode:

◆ In trim mode, click the cancel edit button ✕.

Any changes that you made to in and out points are reset to zero. You can resume making adjustments or exit trim mode.

PREVIEWING AND APPLYING TRIM MODE EDITS

Customizing Trim Mode

In the preceding examples, trim mode appears is in its default appearance. However, you can customize its look and function. You can display additional frames before and after the edit, specify the number of frames trimmed by the multiple-frame trim button, and set large images for previews.

To customize trim mode:

1. From the Monitor window's pull-down menu, choose Monitor Window Options (**Figure 7.49**).

   The Monitor Window Options dialog box opens.

2. In the Trim Mode Options section of the dialog box, choose one of the following display options (**Figure 7.50**):

   ▲ The first option displays the out frame of the left clip and the in frame of the right clip.

   ▲ The second option displays large edge frames as well as the frames before and after the edge frames.

   ▲ The third option displays large edge frames as well as the first and fifth frames before and after the edge frames.

3. For Large Frame Offset, enter the number of frames that are trimmed when you use the multiple-frame trim buttons.

   By default, these buttons trim five frames at a time.

4. To make trimming previews appear at the largest size that fits in the Monitor window, check Play Previews at Maximum Size.

   Deselect this option to make trimming previews play at the program frame size that you set in the program settings.

5. Click OK to close the dialog box.

   Trim mode reflects the settings that you specified (**Figure 7.51**).

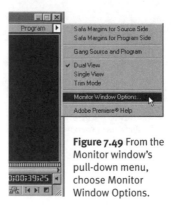

Figure 7.49 From the Monitor window's pull-down menu, choose Monitor Window Options.

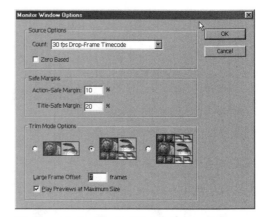

Figure 7.50 In the Monitor Window Options dialog box, choose a default display for trim view. Also, specify the number of frames trimmed by the multiple-frame trimming buttons and whether to view previews at maximum size.

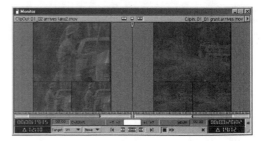

Figure 7.51 Trim mode reflects the settings that you specified. Here, trim mode shows the edge frames as well as the first and fifth frames before and after the edge frames.

Working with Links

As you learned in earlier chapters, a linked clip contains both video and audio. Though the video and audio portions of the clip appear in different tracks of the timeline, a link between the two portions of the clip helps maintain their synchronized relationship. As long as synch mode is set to linked, both tracks of linked clips move together and are trimmed by the same amount. (See "Using Linked Clips" in Chapter 6.)

At times, however, you want to manipulate the two parts of a linked clip separately. You might want to employ a traditional editing technique called the split edit or L-cut. Sometimes, you want to break the link altogether, so that the video and audio can be manipulated independently. Or you may want to create a link between audio and video clips that weren't captured together. In film production, for example, the image and sound are recorded separately. After they are digitized, you can create a link to synchronize the two elements in the timeline.

The following sections describe how to manipulate linked clips in the timeline.

Creating Split Edits

In a *split edit*, or *L-cut*, the video and audio have different in points or out points. A dialogue scene serves as a good example. First, you see and hear a person talking, in synch. Then you hear a person's voice but see the person to whom that person is talking. In this case, the video out point occurs earlier than the audio out point. In the timeline, the video and audio would form an L—hence, the name *L-cut*. Split edits are a great way to make your edits feel much smoother. Watch a movie closely, and you'll find that split edits far outnumber *straight cuts*, in which the video and audio share the same in point.

By now, you know numerous ways to create a split edit. The following tasks outline a few ways you might create a split edit from a straight cut in the timeline.

To split edit clips in the timeline:

1. At the bottom of the Timeline window, set synch mode off, to ignore the link between linked clips' video and audio.

   The ![synch] icon indicates that synch mode is off (**Figure 7.52**).

2. In the toolbox of the Timeline window, select the rolling edit tool ![tool] (**Figure 7.53**).

3. Position the rolling edit tool between two clips in the timeline in either the video or audio track.

   The pointer becomes an outlined version of the rolling edit tool ![tool] (**Figure 7.54**).

4. Drag to perform a rolling edit in the audio without editing the corresponding video, or vice versa.

   The in and out points in the video track differ from those in the audio track (**Figure 7.55**).

Figure 7.52 Click the synch mode button to turn synch mode off.

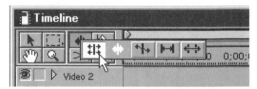

Figure 7.53 Choose the rolling edit tool.

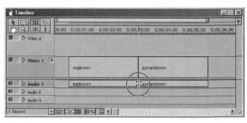

Figure 7.54 Position the rolling edit tool between two clips. Here, the rolling edit will be performed for the audio clips only.

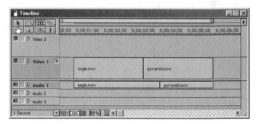

Figure 7.55 Drag to trim one track of the clips independently of the others. Here, the audio of the first clip is extended, or trimmed out, while the audio portion of the second clip is trimmed in. As a result, both clips have a split edit.

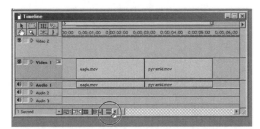

Figure 7.56 At the bottom of the Timeline window, toggle synch mode off.

Figure 7.57 Cue the current time on or near the cut you want to adjust, and press ⌘-T (Mac) or Ctrl-T (Windows).

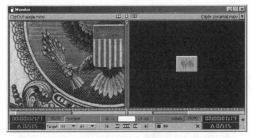

Figure 7.58 The Monitor window switches to trim mode.

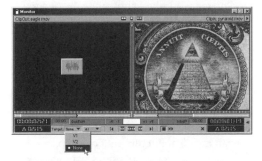

Figure 7.59 In trim mode, specify the target tracks you want to affect. Here, only Audio 1 is selected; for video, None is selected.

5. At the bottom of the Timeline window, click the synch mode button to turn it back on.

The ⊞ icon indicates that synch mode is on. The link between the video and audio of linked clips is restored. This way, Premiere will warn you if you later lose synch (see "Keeping Synch" later in this chapter).

✔ Tip

■ Whenever synch mode is off, the trimming tools appear with a white outline. The white outline reminds you that synch mode is off and that trimming affects the video and audio portion of linked clips separately.

To split edit clips in trim mode:

1. At the bottom of the Timeline window, toggle synch mode off.

The ⊟ icon indicates that synch mode is off (**Figure 7.56**).

2. Cue the current time on or near the cut you want to adjust (**Figure 7.57**).

3. In the Monitor window, click the trim mode button ⊞, or press ⌘-T (Mac) or Ctrl-T (Windows).

The Monitor window switches to trim mode (**Figure 7.58**).

4. In trim mode, specify the tracks you want to affect by making choices from the Target video and audio pull-down menus (**Figure 7.59**).

The examples to follow trim both the video and audio of linked clips. For details on trimming video and audio separately, see "Creating Split Edits" earlier in this chapter.

continues on next page

CREATING SPLIT EDITS

5. In trim mode, *do either of the following* to activate both views:

 ▲ Click the set focus both button (**Figure 7.60**).

 or

 ▲ Click between the two views.

The image in both views appear selected, and both time displays appear green.

6. To trim frames in both views, *do any of the following:*

 ▲ Click **-1** to trim one frame to the left.

 ▲ Click **-5** to trim several frames to the left.

 ▲ Click **+1** to trim one frame to the right.

 ▲ Click **+5** to trim several frames to the right

 ▲ Using the numeric keypad, type a positive number to move the edit forward in time, or type a negative number to move the edit back in the timeline; then press (Return) (Mac) or (Enter) (Windows).

 ▲ Drag the jog track control below the selected view to trim.

 ▲ Place the pointer between the two views, so that the pointer becomes the rolling edit tool, and drag left or right to trim.

 ▲ Drag the out point icon in the left view, or the in point icon in the right view.

As you trim frames, the number of trimmed frames appears next to the OutShift display and InShift display. Because synch mode is off, only the selected track is trimmed, creating a split edit (**Figure 7.61**).

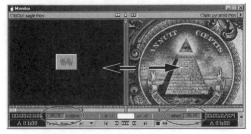

Figure 7.60 Click the set focus both button, or click between the two views.

Figure 7.61 When you perform a rolling edit for the audio track only (with synch mode off), you create a split edit.

✔ Tips

 ■ Unless you're sure you know what you're doing, don't use a ripple edit to create a split edit. Because ripple edits cause clips to shift, only the selected tracks will shift, causing linked clips to lose synch.

 ■ Portions of linked clips typically occupy corresponding tracks—video track 1 and audio track 1, for example, or video track 2 and audio track 2. When synch mode is set to unlinked, you can move the video or audio portion of a linked clip to another track.

 ■ By shifting audio to separate tracks, you can create split edits that overlap, or cross-fade. For more information about this technique, see "Cross-Fading Audio Linked to Video" in Chapter 10.

Figure 7.62 Choose Clip › Unlink Audio and Video.

Breaking and Creating Links

You can break or create links in the timeline. When you do so, however, you affect only the instances of the clips in the timeline: the links of the master clips and their associated files on the drive remain unaffected.

To break a link:

1. In the timeline, select the video portion of a linked clip.

   Both video and audio tracks of the linked clip appear selected.

2. Choose Clip > Unlink Audio and Video (**Figure 7.62**).

   The video and audio portions unlink, becoming two independent clips. An unnumbered marker appears in the middle of each of the resulting video and audio clips. You can keep each clip synchronized with the other by aligning these markers (**Figure 7.63**).

Figure 7.63 The video and audio portions unlink, becoming two independent clips with markers that you can use to synchronize the clips.

To create a soft link:

1. In the toolbox of the Timeline window, select the soft link tool ⬚ (**Figure 7.64**).

2. Click a video clip and then click an audio clip (or vice versa).

   When you position the pointer on the second clip, the soft link tool appears (**Figure 7.65**). After you click the second clip, the clips are linked in the timeline, but the master clips and their associated files on the drive remain separate.

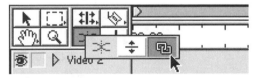

Figure 7.64 In the toolbox of the Timeline window, select the soft link tool.

✔ Tip

■ Soft links are great for synching film footage with audio. Just mark the frame in the video where the slate (clapper board) closes, mark the sound of the slate mark in the audio, align the marks, and soft-link the clips.

Figure 7.65 Click either the video or audio clip. When you position the pointer over the clip's partner, the soft link tool appears. Click to link the clips in the timeline.

Keeping Synch

During the course of editing, you may inadvertently lose synch between linked video and audio. Fortunately, Premiere alerts you when linked clips are out of synch, and it provides a simple way to correct the problem.

To detect a loss of synch:

◆ A red triangle appears at the left edge of linked video and audio that are out of synch (**Figure 7.66**).

To restore synch:

1. Click the red out-of-synch triangle, and hold down the mouse button.

2. Drag to highlight the number next to the red triangle (**Figure 7.67**), and release the mouse button.

   If there is available space in the track, the clip shifts in the timeline to resynchronize with the linked portion (**Figure 7.68**). Otherwise, you'll have to create space in the track before resynching the clips.

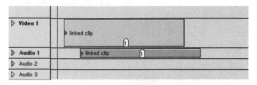

Figure 7.66 A red triangle appears at the left edge of linked video and audio that are out of synch.

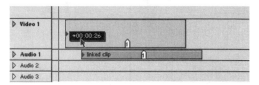

Figure 7.67 Drag to highlight the number next to the red triangle.

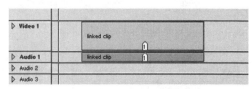

Figure 7.68 When you release the mouse button, the clips shift in the timeline to resynchronize (provided that there's room in the timeline).

Synching Up

If clicking the out-of-synch indicator isn't a practical way to resynchronize the clips, you can use many other techniques to solve the problem:

◆ Move a clip manually with the synch mode off.

◆ Use the track tool ⟦⟧ to shift all the clips in a track back into synch.

◆ Open the source clip and edit it into the program again.

✔ Tip

■ Prevention is the best medicine. Avoid loss of synch by locking clips or tracks that shouldn't be moved, using the track tool cautiously, creating a soft link between clips that require a synchronized relationship, and using markers as synch marks that you can use to check alignment visually.

KEEPING SYNCH

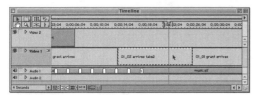

Figure 7.69 Select a clip in the timeline.

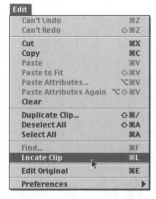

Figure 7.70 Choose Edit > Locate Clip.

Figure 7.71 The program clip's associated master clip appears highlighted in a bin.

Finding Master Clips

As you edit in the timeline, you may want to reexamine a clip to see the footage beyond the current in and out points. The master clip may contain another take of the shot or other footage you'd like to see, for example. But as you know, trimming the clip in the timeline would disturb your current edit, and double-clicking the clip in question would allow you to view the clip instance only in the source view, not the master clip. Fortunately, you can view the master clip associated with a program clip quickly and easily, without having to search through your project bins.

To find a master clip from the timeline:

1. Select a clip in the timeline (**Figure 7.69**).

2. Choose Edit > Locate Clip (**Figure 7.70**).

   The program clip's associated master clip appears highlighted in a bin (**Figure 7.71**).

To view a master clip from the timeline:

1. Select a clip in the timeline (**Figure 7.72**).

2. Choose Clip > Open Master Clip (**Figure 7.73**).

   The program clip's associated master clip appears in the source view. The in and out points of the master clip match the portion used in the program, but all the source footage is available to play back (**Figure 7.74**). Changing the edit marks in the master clip does not change the clip in the program. You can, of course, set new edit marks in the master clip and add it to the program, using any of the editing techniques you have learned so far.

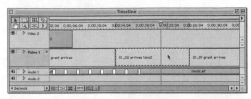

Figure 7.72 Select a clip in the timeline. If you double-click the clip, it sets in and out points around the clip in the program, which can be handy. (Double-clicking also loads the program clip in the source view, but you'll go on to load the master clip.)

Figure 7.73 Choose Clip > Open Master Clip.

Figure 7.74 The program clip's associated master clip appears in the source view.

Figure 7.75 Cue the program to the frame for which you want to find the match frame.

Figure 7.76 When you press ⊤, the match frame appears in the source view.

Finding the Match Frame

Experienced editors may wonder whether Premiere has a *match-frame* feature. A match-frame feature not only opens a program clip's associated master clip, but also cues the source edit line to the identical frame in the program. In other words, by cueing the edit line in the program, you can find the matching frame in the appropriate master clip.

To find a program clip's master frame:

1. Cue the program to the frame for which you want to find a match frame (**Figure 7.75**).

2. Press ⊤.

   The master clip appears in the source view (**Figure 7.76**) and is cued to the match frame.

✔ Tip

- After you find the match frame, you can keep the master clip and the program in a synched relationship by ganging them together. See "Ganging the Source and Program Views," in Chapter 5.

FINDING THE MATCH FRAME

TRANSITIONS

Figure 8.1 Although the cut is the most basic transition, the term *transition* usually refers to a more gradual change from one clip to another.

A *transition* is the way one clip visually replaces the next. Although the cut is the most basic transition, the term *transition* usually refers to a more gradual change from one clip to another (**Figure 8.1**). Adobe Premiere ships with 75 customizable transitions, including an array of dissolves, wipes, and special effects.

Available transitions are listed in a new, improved Transitions palette. In Premiere 6, the Transitions palette organizes the available transitions into categorized folders. This arrangement makes it easy to sift through all the transitions to locate the one you need. Like all palettes, the Transitions palette can be grouped or docked with other palettes, and it can be customized to display just the information you need.

You can save and load custom sets of transitions. You can also specify a default transition, which can be applied at the click of a button.

Ordinarily, you use a transition in the traditional manner: to change completely from one shot to the next. But you can also customize transitions to achieve effects that aren't, strictly speaking, transitions. In addition, you can layer transitions to create complex effects by using a feature called virtual clips.

Using the Transitions Palette

The Transitions palette lists 75 customizable transitions. You can customize the palette to display more or less information about the transitions and to temporarily hide the transitions that you don't need. You can also save and load custom sets of transitions.

To open the Transitions palette:

Do either of the following:

◆ Choose Window > Show Transitions.

 or

◆ In a grouped palette, click the Transitions palette's tab.

 The Transitions palette appears as the active palette (**Figure 8.2**).

To animate transition icons:

◆ From the Transitions palette's pull-down menu, choose Animate (**Figure 8.3**).

 When Animate is checked, the transition icons dynamically illustrate how each transition works. In the animated icon, "A" represents the first clip, and "B" represents the second clip in a transition.

Figure 8.2 Click the Transitions tab in a grouped palette to make the Transitions palette appear in front of the other palettes.

Figure 8.3 Choose Animate from the Transitions palette's pull-down menu.

Figure 8.4 Click the triangle next to a folder to expand or collapse it. Here, the Dissolve folder is expanded to reveal its contents.

Figure 8.5 Choose Expand All Folders to reveal the contents of all the folders in a palette; choose Collapse All Folders to show only folders.

Figure 8.6 In this figure, all folders are expanded.

Expanding and Collapsing Palette Folders

In Premiere 6, items in the Transitions, Video, and Audio palettes are organized in categorized folders. Folders turn a long list of 75 transitions into a shorter, more manageable list of 12 expandable folders.

To expand and collapse folders:

◆ In the Transitions, Video, or Audio palettes, click the triangle next to a folder (**Figure 8.4**).

To expand or collapse all folders:

◆ From the Transitions, Video, or Audio palettes' pull-down menus, choose either of the following:

Expand All Folders—expands all folders in the palette so that you can see individual items (**Figure 8.5**).

Collapse All Folders—collapses all folders in the palette, so individual items are hidden.

All folders in the palette are expanded or collapsed, according to your choice (**Figure 8.6**).

Hiding and Showing Items in a Palette

Just as you can make tracks in the timeline shy, you can specify which items in a palette you'd like to be able to conceal quickly. Though the palette doesn't use the term *shy*, hiding items in the Transitions, Video, or Audio palette works a lot like hiding shy tracks in the timeline.

To specify items in a palette to hide:

1. In the Transitions, Video, or Audio palettes, select a folder or item contained in a folder (**Figure 8.7**).

   Select only items whose names are not in italics. Italics indicate that the item is already marked as hidden.

2. In the palette's pull-down menu, choose Hide Selected (**Figure 8.8**).

   The selected item is marked as hidden. When Show Hidden is checked, hidden items appear in italics: when Show Hidden is unchecked, hidden items do not appear in the palette.

To hide and show items in a palette:

◆ From the Transitions, Video, or Audio palettes' pull-down menus, choose Show Hidden to check or uncheck it (**Figure 8.9**).

   When Show Hidden is checked, hidden items appear in italics: when Show Hidden is unchecked, hidden items do not appear in the palette (**Figure 8.10**).

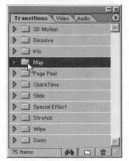

Figure 8.7 Select a folder or item in the palette.

Figure 8.8 From the palette's pull-down menu, choose Hide Selected.

Figure 8.9 To hide the specified items, uncheck Show Hidden.

Figure 8.10 When Show Hidden is unchecked, the specified items don't appear in the palette.

Figure 8.11 To show hidden items, check Show Hidden. Notice the italics on the Map folder; it's still officially hidden but appears in the list anyway.

Figure 8.12 Hidden items appear in italics. Select an item that appears in italics, and choose Show Selected from the pull-down menu.

Figure 8.13 The item no longer appears in italics and is no longer hidden.

To specify items to show in a palette:

1. From the palette's pull-down menu, check Show Hidden.

   Items marked as hidden appear in the palette in italics (**Figure 8.11**).

2. Select an item in italics.

3. From the palette's pull-down menu, choose Show Selected (**Figure 8.12**).

   The item no longer appears in italics. It always appears listed in the palette (and cannot be hidden) (**Figure 8.13**).

HIDING AND SHOWING ITEMS IN A PALETTE

Creating, Deleting, and Renaming Palette Folders

If you're not satisfied with the logic of the preset folder categories, you can rename, delete, or create entirely new folders that abide by your own idiosyncratic thinking.

To create a folder:

1. In the Transitions, Video, or Audio palettes, click the new folder button ▭ (**Figure 8.14**).

   The New Folder dialog box appears.

2. Enter the name for the folder, and click OK (**Figure 8.15**).

   The folder appears in the palette (**Figure 8.16**).

To delete or rename a folder:

1. In the Transitions, Video, or Audio palettes, select a folder.

2. In the palette, click the delete button 🗑 (**Figure 8.17**).

   The folder and its contents are removed from the palette (**Figure 8.18**).

Figure 8.14 Click the new folder button.

Figure 8.15 In the New Folder dialog box, enter the name for the folder, and click OK.

Figure 8.16 The folder appears in the palette.

Figure 8.17 Select the folder you want to delete, and click the delete button.

Figure 8.18 The folder and its contents are removed from the palette.

Figure 8.19 Dragging a folder or item up or down in the list...

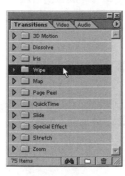

Figure 8.20 ...repositions it in the palette.

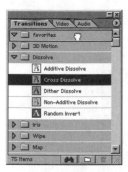

Figure 8.21 You can also drag an item from one expanded folder...

Figure 8.22 ...and drop it into another folder.

To organize items in folders:

In the Transitions, Video, or Audio palettes, *do any of the following:*

◆ To move a folder to a new position in the list, drag it up or down in the list (**Figures 8.19** and **8.20**).

◆ To move an item to a new position within a folder, drag it up or down in the list.

◆ To move an item from one folder into another, drag the item from one expanded folder to another folder (expanded or collapsed) (**Figures 8.21** and **8.22**).

A highlighted border indicates the item's new position as you drag it. When you release the mouse button, the item appears in the new position.

To find an item in a palette:

1. In the Transitions, Video, or Audio palettes, click the find button  (**Figure 8.23**).

   A Find dialog box appears. The name of the dialog box corresponds to the active palette.

2. In the dialog box, *do either of the following:*

   ▲ To find matching items only in expanded folders, leave Expand Folders unchecked.

   or

   ▲ To find matching items in any folder and expand the folder, check Expand Folders (**Figure 8.24**).

3. Enter the name of the item you're looking for, and click Find.

   If a matching item exists, it appears selected in the palette (**Figure 8.25**). If several items match your search criteria, a Find Again button appears in the dialog box.

4. Click either of the following:

   Find Again—finds additional items, if available.

   Done—closes the Find dialog box.

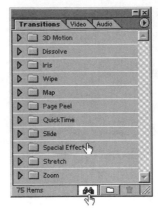

Figure 8.23 Click the Find button.

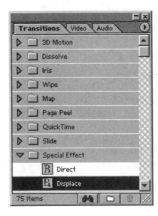

Figure 8.24 In the Find dialog box, check Expand Folders to locate the item in any folder. Enter the name of the item you're looking for, and click Find.

Figure 8.25 If a matching item exists, it appears selected in an expanded folder.

FINDING ITEMS IN PALETTE FOLDERS

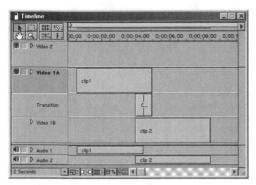

Figure 8.26 Transitions in an A/B roll workspace illustrate a transition more clearly.

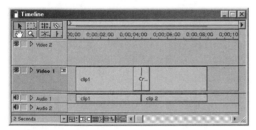

Figure 8.27 The same transition in a single-track workspace doesn't show all the frames involved in the transition.

A/B Roll vs. Single-Track Transitions

From the beginning of this book, you learned that transitions are displayed differently, depending on whether you set the workspace to A/B roll editing or single-track editing. In this chapter, you finally see the difference in action. You can achieve the same results by using either layout, but each requires a different approach.

When you set the workspace to A/B roll, the Video 1 track is split into an A track and B track. Transitions appear in the transition track, which runs between the A and B tracks. This layout emulates a traditional A/B roll editing suite. In A/B roll editing, transitions are accomplished by playing two source tapes (A and B) at the same time and transitioning between the two with a switcher. The tracks of the expanded view correspond to this editing model.

The A/B roll workspace tends to be easier than the single-track workspace to understand visually (**Figure 8.26**). The tracks do take up more screen space, however, and require you to assemble clips in alternating A and B tracks, in checkerboard fashion.

When the workspace is set to single-track editing, clips and transitions are applied to a single track. What appear to be overlapping frames in the expanded view are not visible in the collapsed view. Because the frames that are being used to create the transition are not visible in the timeline, it can be harder to understand how to define a transition, how to plan for it, and how to adjust it. This workspace consumes less window space, however, and allows you to avoid alternating tracks, but it takes some getting used to (**Figure 8.27**).

continues on next page

The single-track workspace, however, includes a track mode button ![track mode button], which allows you to view and adjust transitions in A/B-roll fashion (**Figure 8.28**).

By learning both methods thoroughly, you'll not only become more adept at Premiere, but also master the two methods used by other nonlinear editing programs.

✔ Tip

■ Premiere's User Guide refers to the track mode button as the ganged tracks icon. But as you learned in Chapter 7, the term *gang* refers to putting the source and program views in a synched relationship. In fact, both the term and technique are used in film editing. When referring to viewing the single-track video track in A/B roll style, however, the term *gang* seems to be both less appropriate and more confusing. For this reason, I'll refer to the button as the *track mode button*, which toggles between a *single-track* and *split-track* view. Thanks for your indulgence.

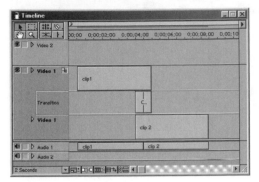

Figure 8.28 You can set the track mode to show the single track in A/B roll style.

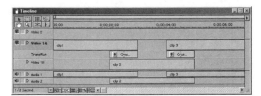

Figure 8.29 Premiere almost always sets the track direction and alignment of a transition correctly. You can see that the track-selector button shows an arrow pointing from the first clip down to the second, and another pointing from the second clip to the third.

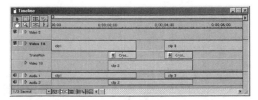

Figure 8.30 Incorrect track direction makes the transition look wrong when you preview it. In this example, the transition arrows are reversed.

Using A/B Roll Transitions

In an A/B Roll editing layout, clips in the A and B tracks overlap, and a transition is positioned between the overlapping areas. When you add a transition, Premiere automatically sizes it to the overlapping area and transitions properly between one clip and the next. If you adjust the duration of the transition, Premiere automatically trims the corresponding clip to compensate for the change and to ensure that the transition will work properly.

Even though Premiere usually makes these adjustments automatically, you may have to adjust a transition manually at times. You should understand two basic concepts about the proper arrangement of a typical transition: track direction and clip alignment. As the old saw says, you should understand the rules before you attempt to break them creatively.

Track direction—To work properly, a transition must be set to switch from the first clip to the second clip. If the first clip is in track A, the transition must be set to switch from A to B, and vice versa. Transitions set in the opposite direction won't look correct during playback. A track-selector button indicates how the transition is set. This button is visible on the transition in the timeline (if the view is large enough) (**Figures 8.29** and **8.30**) and in the transition settings. (See "Modifying Transition Settings" later in this chapter.)

Alignment—Ideally, the transitions should be aligned with the edges of the clips used in the transitions. Premiere attempts to align transitions automatically, but it's still possible to misalign them. Transitions that aren't aligned properly may not look correct during playback, particularly if the clip in track A is out of alignment. A clip in track A supercedes a clip in track B if no transition is provided

continues on next page

between them. Therefore, if a clip in track A extends beyond the edge of a transition, you see an unwanted cut to A during playback (**Figure 8.31**). Conversely, if a transition extends beyond the overlap, the empty track appears as an unwanted black image during the transition. Go ahead and deliberately misalign a transition to see the result.

✔ Tip

■ Turn on Snap to Edges to help you align transitions and clips, as explained in Chapter 6.

To add a transition to the expanded track:

1. Arrange clips in track A and B so that part (or all) of the clips overlap in the timeline.

   The amount by which the clips overlap determines the duration of the transition.

2. Drag a transition from the Transitions palette to the transition track, between the overlapping clips (**Figure 8.32**).

   Premiere sets the alignment and direction of the transition automatically (**Figure 8.33**). A red line appears above the transition in the time ruler, indicating that you must preview the transition to view it.

3. To preview the transition, make sure the work area bar is over the transition; then press [Return] (Mac) or [Enter] (Windows).

   See Chapter 9 for a full explanation of previewing transitions.

✔ Tip

■ To trim a transition without affecting a clip, hold down the [⌘] (Mac) or [Ctrl] (Windows) key as you trim.

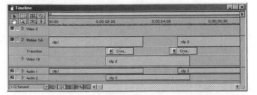

Figure 8.31 Incorrect alignment can also ruin a transition. In this example, neither transition will blend smoothly from one clip to the next.

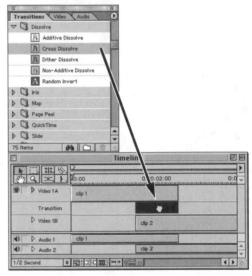

Figure 8.32 Arrange clips in the A and B tracks so that they overlap, then drag a transition from the Transitions palette to the Transition track.

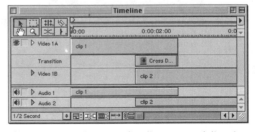

Figure 8.33 Premiere sets the alignment and direction of the transition automatically.

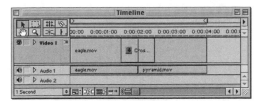

Figure 8.34 In the single-track layout, you can view the Video 1 track as a single track...

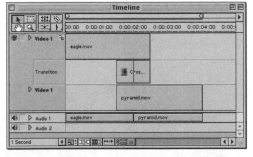

Figure 8.35 ... or you can use the track mode button to view the Video 1 track in split-track mode, which resembles an A/B roll workspace. You can adjust transitions in either single-track or split-track mode.

Single-Track Transitions

In essence, a transition in a single track works the same as it does in an A/B roll layout, except that the frames that are used in the transition are hidden from view (**Figure 8.34**). You can reveal these hidden frames by clicking the track mode button , which lets you view the transition in A/B roll style without actually switching to an A/B roll workspace (**Figure 8.35**).

Without overlapping the clips in advance, you add a transition to adjacent clips in a single track. Each clip, however, must have enough footage beyond the current edit points to create overlapping frames, even though they won't be visible in a single track. In other words, the first clip must have frames available after the current out point; and the second clip must have more frames before the current in point. When you add a transition, Premiere uses these "hidden" frames to create the transition.

If you want to reveal these hidden frames, you can use the track mode button to toggle the single Video 1 track to resemble an A/B roll layout—let's call it *split-track mode*. In split-track mode, you can see that Premiere takes care of the transition's track direction and alignment automatically. In single-track mode, however, you should be aware of two other concepts: duration and position.

Duration—In single-track editing, the initial duration of the transition is the same as the default transition's duration. You can trim the duration of the transition the same way as you change the duration of clips. (For information on setting the duration of the default transition, see "Using a Default Transition" later in this chapter.)

continues on next page

Position—Because you don't see the overlapping frames in a single track, it's less clear
which frames are actually involved in the
transition. Although the duration determines
how many frames are used in the transition,
the position of the transition relative to the
cut determines which frames are involved.
Like duration, the initial position of the transition is set by the default transition. There
are three possibilities: center of cut, start of
cut, and end of cut.

Center of Cut—centers the transition over
the cut so that an equal number of hidden
frames on both sides of the edit are used to
create the transition. A one-second transition centered on the cut would use 15 frames
of footage before the in point of the first clip
and 15 frames after the out point of footage
of the second clip (in a 30-fps project)
(**Figure 8.36**).

Start of Cut—starts the transition at the
cut, so that the hidden frames of the first clip
are combined with the frames of the second
clip that were visible before the transition
was applied. Using the same example as
before, the transition would use zero frames
of the footage before the in point of the second clip and 30 frames of footage after the
first clip's out point (**Figure 8.37**).

End of Cut—ends the transition at the cut,
so that the hidden frames of the second clip
are combined with the frames of the first clip
that were visible before you added the transition. Using the same example as above, the
transition would use 30 frames of the footage
before the second clip's in point and zero
frames of the footage after the out point of
the first clip (**Figure 8.38**).

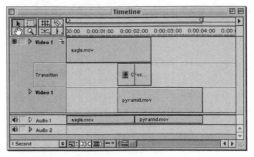

Figure 8.36 It's easier to see how position works if
you translate it into what it would look like in an
A/B roll-style view. In this example, a one-second
(30-frame) transition is centered on the cut.

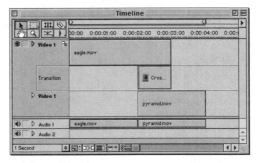

igure 8.37 Here, the same 30-frame transition starts
at the cut. The transition includes hidden frames of
the first clip, after the out point you set.

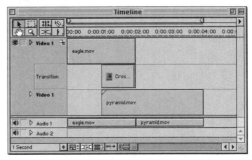

Figure 8.38 In this example, the 30-frame transition
ends at the cut. The transition includes the hidden
frames of the second clip before the in point you set.

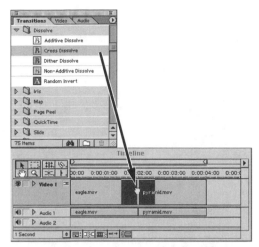

Figure 8.39 In the single-track workspace, drag a transition to the cut between two clips in the Video 1 track.

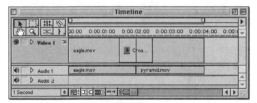

Figure 8.40 The transition appears at the cut between the clips and uses the default position and duration.

Though the initial position is determined by the default setting, you can adjust the position manually afterward. In this case, you might create a custom position, using an unequal number of hidden frames on either side of the cut. If there's a shortage of hidden frames to create the transition, Premiere prompts you to resolve the problem by changing the duration or position of the transition (see "Fixing Transitions" later in this chapter).

To add a transition in a single-track workspace:

1. In the single-track workspace, drag a transition to the cut between two clips in the Video 1 track (**Figure 8.39**).

   The transition appears at the cut between the clips and uses the default position and duration (**Figure 8.40**). A red line appears above the transition in the time ruler, indicating that you must preview the transition to view it.

2. Press Return (Mac) or Enter (Windows) to preview the transition.

   See Chapter 9 for a full explanation of previewing transitions.

To add a transition in a split-view single-track workspace:

1. With the timeline set to single-track editing, click the track mode button to set the Video 1 track to split view.

   The 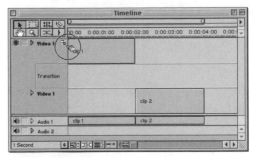, and the Video 1 track appears as two tracks with a transition track (**Figure 8.41**).

2. Drag a transition from the Transitions palette to the transition track at the cut between clips (**Figure 8.42**).

   The transition appears in the transition track at the cut between the clips and uses the default position and duration (**Figure 8.43**). If the clips don't already appear in different tracks, one clip shifts to the B track. The edges of the clips extend to align them with the edges of the transition. (The audio portions of linked clips are not extended.) A red line appears above the transition in the time ruler, indicating that you must preview the transition to view it.

3. Press [Return] (Mac) or [Enter] (Windows) to preview the transition.

   See Chapter 9 for a full explanation of previewing transitions.

✔ Tip

- The clips must have enough source material beyond the current edit points to accommodate the transition. See "To fix a transition" in the following section.

Figure 8.41 Click the track mode button to split the Video 1 track.

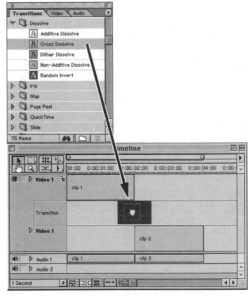

Figure 8.42 Drag a transition from the Transitions palette to the transition track at the cut between clips.

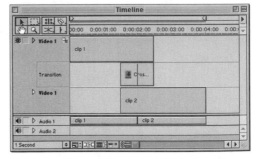

Figure 8.43 The transition appears in the transition track at the cut between the clips and uses the default position and duration.

SINGLE-TRACK TRANSITIONS

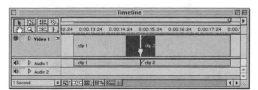

Figure 8.44 Adding a centered-on-cut transition between these clips won't work, because there's not enough hidden footage beyond the cut point. In this case, the folded corner at the edge of the second clip makes it clear that no additional footage is available for a transition.

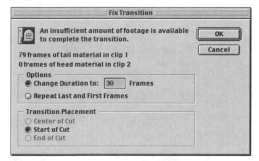

Figure 8.45 The Fix Transition dialog box appears. In this example, one solution would be to have the transition start at the cut—which would use the hidden footage from clip 1 and not require any hidden footage from clip 2.

Fixing Transitions

Adding a transition to a cut in a single track presumes that there's enough hidden footage to create the transition. If there's not enough footage, Premiere prompts you to change the duration or position of the transition. Premiere can also create extra frames by repeating existing frames, though this option may look strange.

To fix a transition:

1. Add a transition between clips in a single-track layout.

   If the clips do not have enough footage beyond the current edit points for the transition, the Fix Transition dialog box appears. The dialog box displays the number of frames currently available to create the transition (**Figures 8.44** and **8.45**).

2. In the Options section, select a radio button:

   Change Duration To—allows you to shorten the transition's duration.

   Repeat Last and First Frames—repeats frames to supply enough additional frames to meet the duration of the transition.

3. In the Transition Placement section, choose an option:

   Center of Cut—uses the same number of hidden frames after the first clip and before the second clip.

   Start of Cut—uses the hidden frames after the out point of the first clip.

   End of Cut—uses the hidden frames before the in point of the second clip.

4. Click OK to close the dialog box and apply your changes.

   The transition appears in the timeline.

Adjusting a Single-Track Transition

Even if you're good at anticipating how a single-track transition will look, chances are that you'll need to make small adjustments. You can adjust the transition in either track mode, though it's usually easier to make small changes when you set track mode to display a split Video 1 track.

To adjust a single-track transition:

1. Click the track mode button to view the Video 1 track in split-track mode.

   The ⊞ icon indicates that the single track is in split-track mode.

2. For the transition you want to adjust, *do any of the following:*

   ▲ To change the position of the transition without changing its duration, drag the transition to the right or left (**Figures 8.46** and **8.47**).

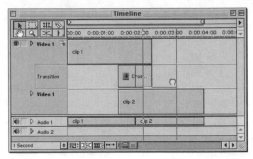

Figure 8.46 To change the position of the transition without changing its duration, drag the transition to the right or left.

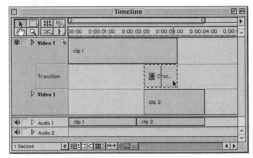

Figure 8.47 After the transition is moved, Premiere trims the corresponding edges of the clips accordingly.

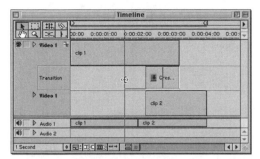

Figure 8.48 To change the duration of the transition, drag the edge of the transition. In this example, synch mode is turned off so that the video can be trimmed unrestricted by the audio.

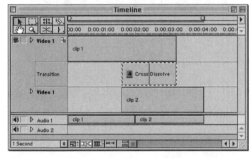

Figure 8.49 After you trim the transition, Premiere trims the corresponding edges of the clips accordingly.

▲ To change the duration of the transition by changing its starting point, drag the left edge of the transition or the in point of the second clip (**Figures 8.48** and **8.49**).

▲ To change the duration of the transition by changing where it ends, drag the right edge of the transition or the out point of the first clip.

Premiere trims the corresponding edges of the transition or clip to keep the edges aligned.

Using a Default Transition

If you frequently use a transition, you can set it as the default transition to apply it quickly, without going to the Transitions palette. The default transition also defines the initial duration of transitions added in the single-track workspace.

To specify the default transition and duration:

1. In the Transitions palette, choose the transition that you want to set as the default.

2. From the Transitions palette's pull-down menu, choose Set Selected as Default (**Figure 8.50**).

   The Default Effect dialog box appears.

3. Enter a duration, in frames, for the default transition (**Figure 8.51**).

4. From the Effect Alignment pull-down menu, choose an alignment (**Figure 8.52**):

   Center at Cut—uses the same number of hidden frames after the out point of the first clip and before the in point of the second clip.

   Start at Cut—uses the hidden frames after the out point of the first clip.

   End at Cut—uses the hidden frames before the in point of the second clip.

5. Click OK to set the default transition and close the dialog box.

   When you apply the default transition, it reflects the settings you specified.

To use the default transition:

1. Position the edit line where two clips meet or overlap (**Figure 8.53**).

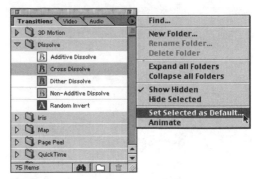

Figure 8.50 Select a transition, and choose Set Selected as Default.

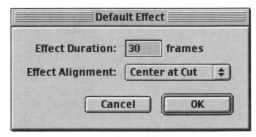

Figure 8.51 In the Default Effect dialog box, enter a duration.

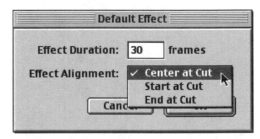

Figure 8.52 Select an alignment option, and click OK. These settings apply not only to the default transition, but also to any transition applied in a single-track workspace.

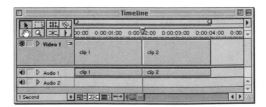

Figure 8.53 Position the edit line where two clips meet or overlap.

Figure 8.54
Below the program view, click the default transition button, or press ⌘-D (Mac) or Ctrl-D (Windows).

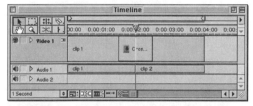

Figure 8.55 The transition appears at the cut and uses the default position and duration.

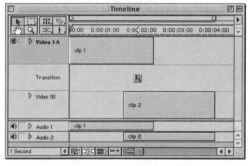

Figure 8.56 In an A/B roll workspace, ⌘-Option-Shift-click (Mac) or Ctrl-Alt-Shift-click (Windows) the transition track between two overlapping clips to apply the default transition.

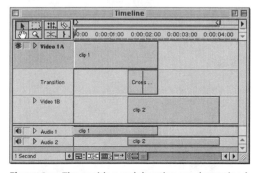

Figure 8.57 The position and duration are determined by the overlap.

2. *Do either of the following:*

▲ Click the default transition button [img] in the Monitor window (**Figure 8.54**).

In a single-track workspace, the transition appears at the cut and uses the default position and duration (**Figure 8.55**).

or

▲ In the A/B roll workspace, ⌘-Option-Shift-click (Mac) or Ctrl-Alt-Shift-click (Windows) the transition track between two overlapping clips (**Figures 8.56** and **8.57**).

If not enough trimmed frames are available for Premiere to create the transition, a warning appears, and you must adjust the clips before you can proceed.

✔ Tip

■ The default duration can be applied automatically to a sequence created with the Automate to Timeline feature (explained in Chapter 5).

Modifying Transition Settings

Each transition has several customizable settings that affect the way it looks during playback. The specific settings depend on the particular transition. The transitions have settings' dialog boxes that can show a sample of the transition, in which A represents the first clip and B represents the second; or the dialog boxes can show representative frames from the program.

To change a transition's default settings:

1. In the Transitions palette, double-click a transition.

   The settings dialog box specific to the transition appears. The available settings depend on the particular transition.

2. Adjust the settings, and click OK.

   The transition uses the settings you specified whenever you apply it between clips in the timeline.

To change settings for a single instance of a transition:

1. Double-click a transition in the timeline (**Figure 8.58**).

   The settings dialog box appears. The available settings depend on the particular transition (**Figure 8.59**).

2. Adjust the settings, and click OK.

   Only this particular instance of the transition uses the settings you specified.

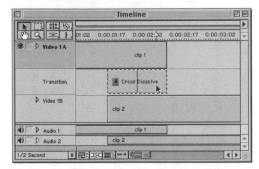

Figure 8.58 Double-click a transition to make its settings dialog box appear. You can open settings for the master transition in the Transitions palette, or for a particular instance of the transition in the program.

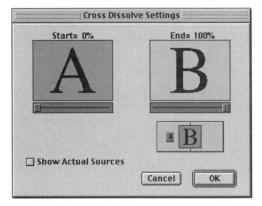

Figure 8.59 A transition settings dialog box appears. The available settings depend on the particular transition.

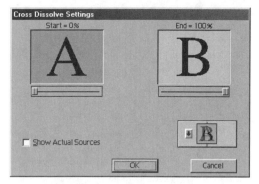

Figure 8.60 A and B icons represent clips in the transition.

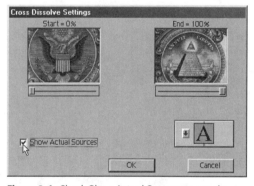

Figure 8.61 Check Show Actual Sources to see the poster frames of the actual clips involved in the transition.

Adjusting Transition Settings

Each transition has its own set of customizable settings. The available options depend on the transition you're modifying. By modifying these settings, you can effectively expand your list of 75 transitions into an even greater selection. You can, for example, set the wipe transition to wipe in any of eight directions; you can make it hard-edged or soft-edged; you can add a border of any color or thickness. You can even set a static wipe, so that it works as a split-screen effect.

To adjust the start and end of the transition:

In the settings dialog box for the transition, *do any of the following:*

◆ To show the starting and ending frames of the clips in the transition, check Show Actual Sources (**Figures 8.60** and **8.61**).

continues on next page

◆ To define the initial and final appearances of the transition, drag the start and end sliders (**Figures 8.62** and **8.63**).

A standard transition starts at 0 and ends at 100. Hold down the Shift key to set both sliders to the same value and move them together.

✔ Tips

■ You can use the sliders to get a preview of the transition, but make sure that you reset the transition to the position you want before you close the dialog box.

■ You can't keyframe a transition; you can only set a start and end state. In an A/B roll workspace, however, you can arrange a sequence of transitions to achieve effects you couldn't get with just one transition (**Figure 8.64**).

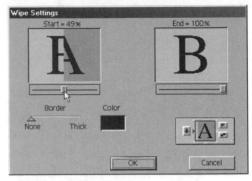

Figure 8.62 Drag the start and end sliders to define the initial and final appearance of the transition. A standard transition goes from 0 (showing only shot A) to 100 (showing only shot B).

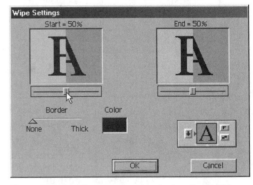

Figure 8.63 In this example, the start and end sliders are both set to 50. Therefore, the transition is static, showing a mix of the A and B shots for the duration of the transition.

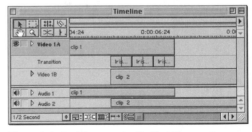

Figure 8.64 In this example, the first iris round transition's start and end points are set at 0 and 50, respectively; the second is set to 50 and 50; the last is set to 50 and zero. Therefore, the first transition opens the iris, the second one holds the iris in place, and the third one closes it completely.

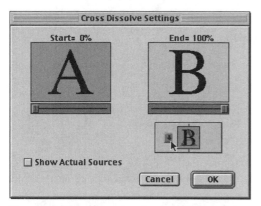

Figure 8.65 The arrow points down to switch from video track A to track B.

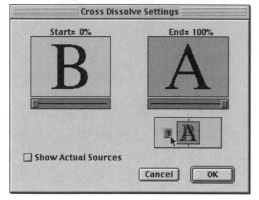

Figure 8.66 The arrow points up to switch from video track B to track A.

To adjust the track direction for the transition:

◆ In the settings dialog box for the transition, click the track selector button 🔽 to determine which clip starts the transition.

The button toggles between up and down. The arrow points down to switch from video track A to track B (**Figure 8.65**); it points up to switch from B to A (**Figure 8.66**).

To set the transition orientation and direction:

In the settings dialog box for the transition, *do any of the following:*

- To make the transition play forward or backward, click the forward/reverse button.

    An F plays the transition forward (**Figure 8.67**); an R plays the transition in reverse (**Figure 8.68**).

- Click the small arrows, or edge selector, around the transition thumbnail to select the orientation of the transition (**Figures 8.69** and **8.70**).

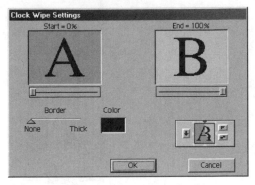

Figure 8.67 Toggle the button to F to play the transition forward.

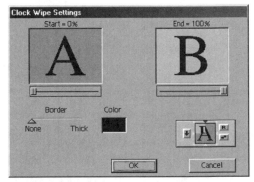

Figure 8.68 Toggle the button to R to play the transition in reverse.

Figure 8.69 Click the small arrows, or edge selector, around the transition thumbnail to select the orientation of the transition. Here, the wipe is set to wipe from the top-right corner.

Figure 8.70 You can set the wipe to wipe from the right side by clicking the appropriate edge selector.

Figure 8.71 The anti-aliasing button toggles through three settings: low, high (shown here), and off.

Figure 8.72 When anti-aliasing is set to off, the curved edge of the iris wipe looks like this.

Figure 8.73 When anti-aliasing is set to high, the curved edge of the iris wipe looks like this.

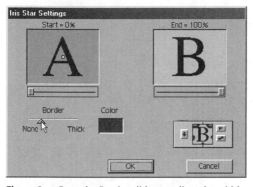

Figure 8.74 Drag the Border slider to adjust the width of a transition's optional border. Click the color swatch to open the color picker and choose a color for the border.

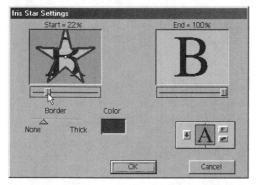

Figure 8.75 The edge of the transition uses the border you specified.

To set the edge-smoothing option:

◆ In the settings dialog box for the transition, click the anti-aliasing button to smooth the edge or border of a transition.

Clicking this button cycles through the options Low (smoother) , High (smoothest) , and Off (rough)  (**Figures 8.71**, **8.72**, and **8.73**).

To set border color and thickness:

In the settings dialog box for the transition, *do any of the following* (**Figure 8.74**):

◆ Drag the Border slider to adjust the width of a transition's optional border.

◆ Click the color swatch to select a color for the border by using the color picker.

The edge of the transition uses the border you specified (**Figure 8.75**).

✔ Tip

■ If the Start slider is set to 0, you won't see the border in the thumbnail of the transition. To see the border, set the Start slider to a higher number (such as 50) as you adjust the border. Make sure to set the border back to 0 before you close the dialog box.

ADJUSTING TRANSITION SETTINGS

To set the center-point origin of the transition:

◆ In the settings dialog box for the transition, drag the handle in the Start or End image to set the center point of the transition (**Figure 8.76**).

The handle represents the center of an iris transition, for example (**Figure 8.77**).

To set custom settings:

◆ In the settings dialog box for the transition, click the Custom button to define settings specific to that transition (**Figure 8.78**).

You can define the number of slashes in the slash slide transition, for example (**Figure 8.79**).

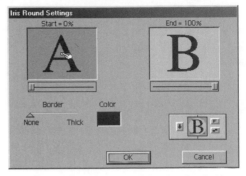

Figure 8.76 Drag the handle in the thumbnail view to set the center point of the transition.

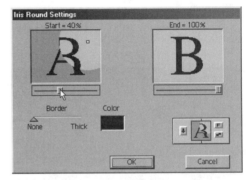

Figure 8.77 In this example, the center point, or origin, of the transition has been moved to one side of the image.

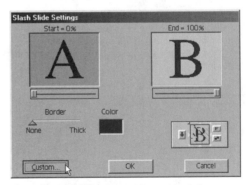

Figure 8.78 Click the Custom button to define settings specific to that transition.

Figure 8.79 The Custom button opens a dialog box to specify the number of slices in the Slash Slide transition.

ADJUSTING TRANSITION SETTINGS

Creating Special Transitions

Most transitions included with Premiere operate along the same lines and use similar settings. A few transitions, however, work a little differently from the rest. Because these transitions can't all be covered in the limited scope of this book, the following list describes the ones to which you should give special attention:

Channel map—to manipulate the red, green, blue, and alpha channels of the image.

Luminance map—to manipulate the luminance values of the image.

Displace—to shift pixels in an image based on the luminance values of a clip or other image.

Gradient wipe and **image mask**—to transition between clips using a separate image as a matte or mask. These transitions are explained in detail in the Adobe Premiere 6 User Guide.

Motion—to transition to another clip by using a preset or saved custom motion setting (see Chapter 14).

QuickTime—to use QuickTime's built-in effects to achieve a variety of transitions with minimal computer processing. The Adobe Premiere 6 User Guide explains how to use QuickTime transitions in detail.

✔ Tip

- Transitions Factory has been eliminated in Premiere 6.

Using Virtual Clips

A *virtual clip* is a clip that refers to a range of clips in the timeline. Although the virtual clip is created from multiple clips, transitions, and effects in multiple tracks, it is represented as a single clip. You can edit, reuse, and apply effects to a virtual clip as you would to any other clip.

By allowing you to represent complex sequences as a single clip, virtual clips can benefit you in several ways. You can repeat complex sequences easily, for example, and apply different settings to each instance. Or you can update all the instances of the virtual clip at the same time by adjusting the sequence to which it refers.

In addition, you can use virtual clips to layer transitions. Ordinarily, you can create a transition between only two clips at a time. If you create a virtual clip from those two clips, however, you can use the virtual clip in another transition, thereby layering the effect. For that matter, you can create virtual clips from other virtual clips. Premiere allows you to nest as many as 64 levels of virtual clips (**Figure 8.80**).

Because the clips that you use to create a virtual clip are almost like another program in the timeline, you should keep them separate from your main program. Set aside space at the beginning or end of the timeline for the clips that you'll use to create virtual clips. Make sure that you do not include this material when you output your final program.

Figure 8.80 This effect was created by a series of circle wipes and nested virtual clips.

Figure 8.81
Select the block select tool.

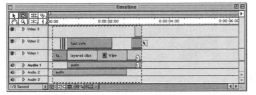

Figure 8.82 Drag to select the part of the timeline that you want to include in the virtual clip.

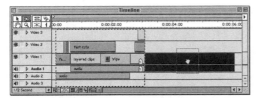

Figure 8.83 Position the tool inside the selected area, and drag to an available space in the timeline.

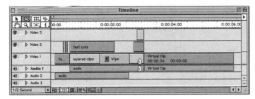

Figure 8.84 The selected portion of the program appears as a single virtual clip.

To create a virtual clip:

1. In the Tools palette, select the block select tool 🖸. (**Figure 8.81**).

2. Drag to select the part of the timeline that you want to include in the virtual clip (**Figure 8.82**).

3. Position the block select tool inside the selected area.
   The virtual clip tool 🖾 appears.

4. Drag the block to an available space in the timeline (**Figure 8.83**).
   The selected portion of the program appears as a single virtual clip (**Figure 8.84**).

✔ Tips

- After you create a virtual clip, lock the clips from which it was created. This procedure protects them (and the related virtual clip) from accidental changes (see Chapter 6).

- Double-clicking a virtual clip cues the edit line to the virtual clip's source clips.

PREVIEWING TRANSITIONS AND EFFECTS

As you know, playing back your edited program is easy: just hit the program view's play button and enjoy. This works great as long as your program consists of simple cuts. But you may have noticed that transitions and other effects don't play back so readily. Instead, the program view displays an X in the corner of the image, ignoring transitions, filters, motion settings, or superimposed clips (**Figure 9.1**).

continues on next page

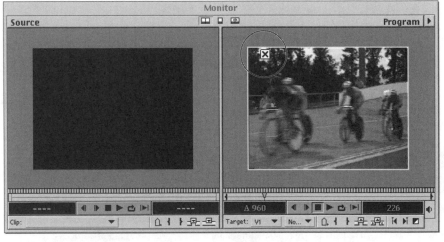

Figure 9.1
The program view displays an X in the corner of the image if the effect has not been previewed.

257

In a cuts-only sequence, the source video and audio undergoes relatively little processing; it's pretty much ready to play. Transitions and other effects, on the other hand, must be generated, or *rendered*, by processing the footage. In the Timeline window, a red line above the time ruler indicates the areas that require processing (**Figure 9.2**). Rendering these portions of the program for playback is known as *previewing*.

The necessity of rendering effects has always been considered the Achilles' heel of non-linear editing systems. Though various NLEs share similar features, processing speed has always distinguished the higher-end, higher-priced systems. As you learned in Chapter 1, hardware components can accelerate the rendering process, allowing you to preview certain effects right away, in "real time." Matrox and Pinnacle offer Premiere systems with real-time effects.

Even without hardware acceleration, however, rendering times shouldn't unduly hinder most types of work. Technical developments—like ever-increasing processing power and the DV format—make processing even high-quality video much faster than in the past.

In this relatively short chapter, you'll learn the different preview methods, as well as how to manage files related to them.

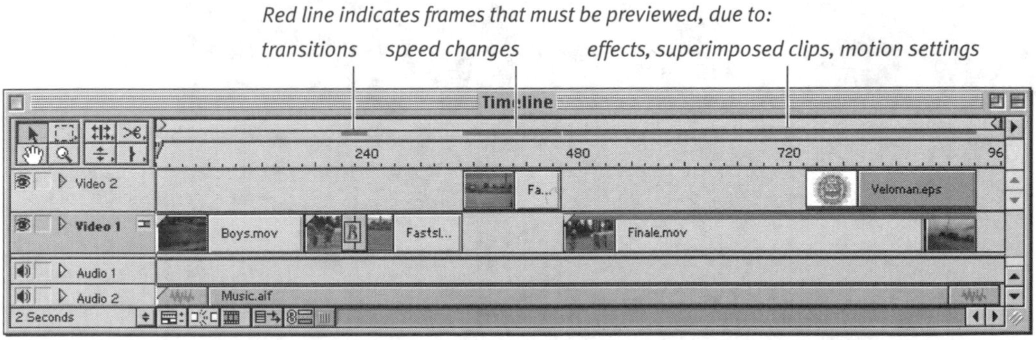

PREVIEWING TRANSITIONS AND EFFECTS

Red line indicates frames that must be previewed, due to:
transitions   speed changes   effects, superimposed clips, motion settings

Figure 9.2 In the Timeline window, a red line above the time ruler indicates the areas that require processing.

Previewing Methods

Because previews are a result of processing video and audio, they can take time. The amount of time it takes to render a preview depends upon the complexity of the effect, the size of the source files, and the speed of your computer. Your project settings—frame size, audio quality, frame rate, and so on—also influence the processing time.

Premiere offers several different previewing methods. Each method represents a different compromise between seeing the effect right away and seeing it at full playback speed:

Scrubbing the Edit Line previews effects right away, but only as you manually drag the edit line, not at the project's frame rate

Preview to Disk previews effects at the project's frame rate by rendering effects to disk, as preview files. After an effect is previewed, it plays back in real time until you change the effect or delete the preview file.

Preview to RAM previews effects by rendering them to RAM rather than by creating preview files on disk. This method works quickly, but is limited by the amount of available RAM.

Preview to Screen previews effects as quickly as possible, depending upon their number and complexity, the image size and resolution, and the computer's processing speed. This method does not create preview files.

The first method, scrubbing the edit line, allows you to instantly preview the frame at the edit line. The other methods all preview a span of the project, which you can define with a control called the work area bar. The following sections explain each preview method in more detail.

Previewing by Scrubbing

You can see an effect right away by scrubbing, or dragging in the time ruler. *Scrubbing* is a term borrowed from tape-based audio and video editing. It refers to slowly rolling the tape over the tape heads. As a previewing method, scrubbing the edit line allows you to watch an effect right away, but not at full playback speed, and without audio.

To preview by scrubbing the time ruler:

◆ Option-drag (Mac) or Alt-drag (Windows) the edit line in the time ruler (**Figure 9.3**).

The top of the edit line changes from a triangle to a down arrow. The program, including effects, is visible in the program view. Audio does not play while you scrub.

✔ Tip

■ Shift-Option-drag (Mac) or Shift-Alt-drag (Windows) the edit line to view only the alpha channel mask.

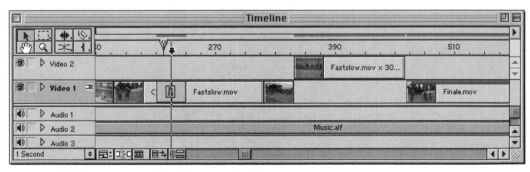

Figure 9.3 Option-drag (Mac) or Alt-drag (Windows) the edit line to preview effects as you scrub.

Previewing the Work Area

The other previewing methods—previewing to disk, to screen, and to RAM—all preview a specified segment of the project, called the *work area*. You can define the work area with, appropriately, the *work area bar*. The work area bar is the yellow bar located in a thin band (the *work area track*) near the top of the Timeline window (**Figure 9.4**). The clips in the timeline located under the bar are included in previews. You can also export the work area, as explained in Chapter 15.

This section explains how to set the work area bar and preview the part of the program it includes. Later sections explain how to specify one of the three methods used to create a preview of the work area: preview to disk, to RAM, and to screen.

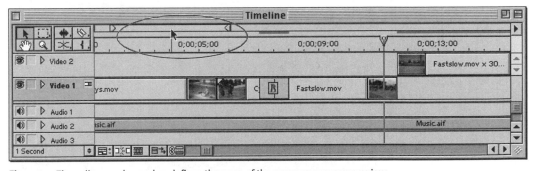

Figure 9.4 The yellow work area bar defines the span of the program you can preview.

To set the work area:

1. To set the work area bar over the part of the program that you want to preview, *do any of the following:*

   ▲ To move the work area bar without resizing it, click and hold on the center of the bar to grab it and then drag the bar over another part of the program (**Figure 9.5**).

   ▲ To resize the work area bar, drag either end to shorten or lengthen it (**Figure 9.6**).

   ▲ To size the work area bar over a contiguous series of clips, (Option)-click (Mac) or (Alt)-click (Windows) the work area track over any of the clips in the series.

   ▲ To set the work area bar to the width of the Timeline window, double-click in the work area track.

2. *Do either of the following:*

   ▲ Choose Timeline > Preview.

   or

   ▲ Press (Return) (Mac) or (Enter) (Windows).

   A window appears, predicting the approximate processing time, based on the current operation (**Figure 9.7**). When processing is complete, the audio and video under the work area bar plays back in the program view of the Monitor window.

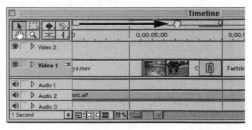

Figure 9.5 Drag the work area bar over the area that you want to preview.

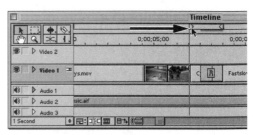

Figure 9.6 Drag the edges of the work area bar to resize it.

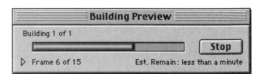

Figure 9.7 Premiere estimates the time required to process the effects.

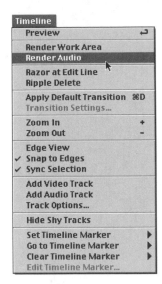

Figure 9.8
Choose Timeline ›
Render Audio.

To preview audio only:

1. Set the work area bar over the audio that you want to preview (see the preceding section).

2. Choose Timeline > Render Audio (**Figure 9.8**).

   A window appears, predicting the approximate processing time. When processing is complete, the audio plays back.

✔ Tips

- After you preview to disk or to RAM, a blue or green line appears in the timeline over the previewed area of the program, indicating that it can be played back in real time (**Figure 9.9**). See the section, "Using Preview Files," later in this chapter.

- To create a preview without automatically playing back the area under the work area bar, choose Timeline > Render Work Area.

- In earlier versions of Premiere, in and out point buttons in the old preview window would set the work area. Both that feature and the preview window are long gone.

Green or blue = preview file   Red = no preview

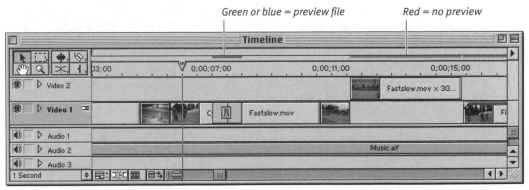

Figure 9.9 The blue or green line indicates that effects have been previewed and can be played back in real time.

PREVIEWING THE WORK AREA

Previewing to Disk

By default, a new project is set to preview to disk. By rendering to disk, you can see effects most accurately at the project's frame rate (assuming your disk and system supports the project settings you selected, such as frame rate, frame size, etc.). Along with scrubbing, this is probably the most common preview method, and is generally considered to be the standard.

Of course, this also means you must have ample disk space for the files generated by previews. Like all the files associated with your project, you must specify where to save preview files, understand how they are referenced, and learn how to manage them.

Previewing to RAM

Premiere 5.1 introduced the ability to use the RAM in your computer to preview effects. Because frames aren't written to and played back from disk, previewing to RAM can get quicker results.

On the down side, previews are limited to the amount of RAM you can allocate to Premiere. And because old previews are purged from RAM to make room for new ones, you may end up previewing areas more than once. If the processing demands are too high, frames may be dropped during playback. If not enough RAM is available to process the preview, Premiere displays the message, "Previewing from Disk," and uses that method instead. For these reasons, you may want to set the project settings for a relatively small frame size and frame rate to get the most from your RAM previews.

Project Settings and Previews

The previous section explained how to change the type of preview method in the Project Settings dialog box. Back in Chapter 2, you learned to set several other options that help determine how Premiere previews your project. Now that you've acquired more experience, it may be a good idea to revisit the Project Settings dialog box to review these options.

Choose Project > Settings > Keyframe and Rendering and review the rendering options that affect your previews. Also choose Project > Settings > Audio to review options that affect your audio previews.

PREVIEWING TO DISK AND RAM

Figure 9.10 Choose Project › Project Settings › Keyframe and Rendering.

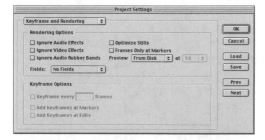

Figure 9.11 The Keyframe and Rendering panel of the Project Settings dialog box appears.

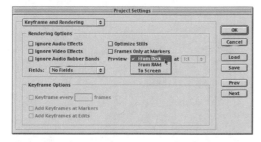

Figure 9.12 Choose a preview method from the pull-down menu.

Figure 9.13 Choose a resolution from the Preview At pull-down menu.

Previewing to Screen

Like a RAM preview, the Preview to Screen option can be one of the faster preview methods, as long as you don't mind the preview playing at less than the project frame rate. However, previewing to screen is not limited by the amount of RAM you have. But because it renders frames as quickly as possible, its results are greatly influenced by the amount and complexity of effects, the image size and resolution, and the speed of your system.

To select a preview method:

1. Choose Project > Project Settings > Keyframe and Rendering (**Figure 9.10**).

   The Keyframe and Rendering panel of the Project Settings dialog box appears (**Figure 9.11**).

2. In the Preview pull-down menu, choose a preview method (**Figure 9.12**):

   From Disk renders preview files to disk, as preview files.

   From RAM renders previews to RAM.

   To Screen renders previews on the fly.

3. In the Preview At pull-down menu, choose a resolution (**Figure 9.13**):

   1:1 previews at the project's full resolution.

   1:2 previews at one half the project's resolution.

   1:4 previews at one fourth the project's resolution.

   This option is available for previewing to RAM and to screen only.

4. Click OK to close the Project Settings dialog box.

Using Preview Files

When you preview to disk (the default method), Premiere automatically renders the effect as a *preview file*. By default, preview files are stored in a Preview Files folder, located in the same location as the associated project file. The preview files are organized into folders, according to the project to which they belong (**Figure 9.14**). You can determine the location of the Preview Files folder manually by specifying a *scratch disk*, the disk Premiere uses to store temporary files.

Once you render a preview file for a portion of the program, you can continue to play back those effects in real time, without re-rendering a preview. If your project settings match your eventual output settings, Premiere can utilize the preview files to reduce the processing time of export.

However, any changes you make to previewed areas make the current preview files obsolete, and you'll have to render another preview to see the changes. But Premiere maintains previews if editing merely shifts the clips in the timeline. And when you alter only part of the previewed area, the unchanged portion retains its associated preview files.

Colored bars in the timeline indicate the status of previews:

Red indicates previewing is required to see effects under the line.

Blue indicates a preview has been rendered for the area below the line.

Green indicates all effects below the line have been rendered and will play back in real time.

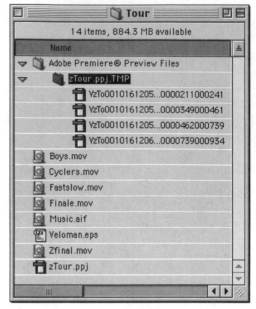

Figure 9.14 By default, a folder of each project's preview files is stored in the same location as the project file.

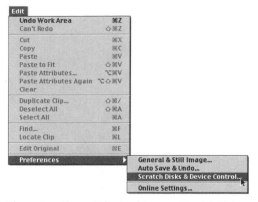

Figure 9.15 Choose Edit > Preferences > Scratch Disks and Device Control.

Figure 9.16 The Scratch Disks and Device Control panel lets you choose scratch disks for captured movies, and video and audio previews.

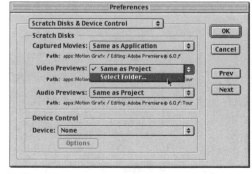

Figure 9.17 Choose a scratch disk from the pull-down menu.

To choose a scratch disk for preview files:

1. Choose Edit > Preferences > Scratch Disks and Device Control (**Figure 9.15**).

   The Scratch Disks and Device Control panel of the Preferences dialog box appears (**Figure 9.16**).

2. From the Video Previews and Audio Previews pull-down menus, choose a disk on which store the preview files (**Figure 9.17**):

   Same As Project File—stores preview files in the same folder as the current project.

   Select Folder—allows you to select a folder in which to store the preview files folder.

3. Click OK to close the Preferences dialog box.

✔ Tip

■ Because this disk will play back audio and/or video files, it should be a relatively large, fast disk. If you have several volumes, put the Premiere application, media files, and preview files on separate volumes.

USING PREVIEW FILES

267

To delete preview files:

1. Select the clips in the timeline with pre-viewed transitions or effects (**Figure 9.18**).

   Above the time ruler, a blue or green line indicates areas that have been previewed.

2. Press ⌘-Delete (Mac) or Ctrl-Backspace (Windows).

   The blue or green indicators disappear, replaced by a red line that indicates areas of the project that have no preview files.

✔ Tip

■ Deleting a preview file in this way actually disassociates the project from the preview file. In other words, the project no longer references the preview file. The file itself, however, is not deleted from the preview file folder, and still consumes storage space. You can delete actual preview files from the hard drive, but it can be difficult to discern the ones still referenced by your project from the obsolete preview files.

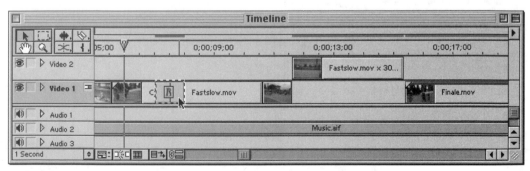

Figure 9.18 Select the clips in the timeline with previewed transitions or effects and press ⌘-Delete (Mac) or Ctrl-Backspace (Windows) to delete them.

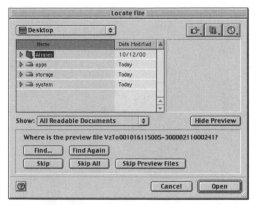

Figure 9.19 When you open a project with missing preview files, a Locate File dialog box opens. You can either locate and select the files, or skip them.

Projects and Preview Files

When you save your project, any preview files that you created are associated with the project. When you open the project again, Premiere attempts to locate the preview files. If the preview files are present, you can still view the previewed portions of your program. If the preview files have been deleted or moved from your drive since you saved the project, Premiere will be unable to locate them. In this case, Premiere prompts you the same way it does when source files are missing (see Chapter 2). You must either confirm that the preview files are in a new location, or eliminate references to the file. In either case, you can still open the project. Of course, any previews that are still missing cannot be played back, and you may need to preview those sections of the program again.

To open a project with missing preview files:

1. Open a Premiere project (see Chapter 2).

    If preview files are missing, a Locate File dialog box opens (**Figure 9.19**).

2. To find the file, *do one of the following*:

    ▲ Allow Premiere to locate and select the missing preview file automatically.

    ▲ Navigate to the missing preview file and select it.

    ▲ Click Find to open a Find File dialog box to search for the file.

    Premiere often finds the right file, but not always. Always compare the name of the missing file with the one you select to make sure they match.

    continues on next page

PROJECTS AND PREVIEW FILES

3. Choose one of the following options in the Locate File dialog box:

Select (Mac) or **OK** (Windows)— to replace the missing file with the selected file.

Skip—to disassociate the missing file from the project.

Skip All—to disassociate all missing files from the project without being prompted for confirmation. Select this option with caution.

Skip Preview Files—to disassociate only the missing preview files from the project without being prompted for confirmation. Select this if you know that none of the missing preview files are available.

After you specify the status of missing preview files, the project opens.

4. To save the file with the current file references, choose File > Save.

✔ Tip

■ The same Locate File dialog box opens if any source files are missing, not just preview files. If you deleted the preview files, you can choose Skip Preview Files. Do not choose Skip All. Skip All could skip missing source files, not just preview files, and could cause your project to remove references to files that you need. If this happens, don't panic. Just close the project without saving it, open it again, and take care to make the correct choices.

10

Mixing Audio

Whether you use all 99 possible audio tracks or only two, you will probably need to make subtle adjustments to them to achieve the best overall effect. This process, known as *audio mixing*, can be accomplished by manipulating audio clips in the timeline or by employing the new Audio Mixer window.

If you thought the last version of Premiere expanded its audio features, you'll be that much more impressed with the improvements you'll find in Premiere 6. In addition to the real-time Audio Mixer window, Premiere 6 includes an extensive list of audio effects from After Effects. In the timeline, audio pan and fade controls are easier to see and select, and you can toggle the waveform display on and off. And though you could keyframe effects in the last version of Premiere, now keyframes are visible in the timeline.

You'll be happy to know that you can hear the results of audio mixing right away, in real time. Although multiple layers of audio or audio effects must be previewed to be heard (see Chapter 9), previewing audio doesn't take nearly as long as previewing video effects.

In addition, Premiere provides a wide range of audio effects you can use to correct or enhance audio—a process called *audio sweetening*.

Viewing Audio Information

In Premiere 6, expanded audio tracks display information a little differently than in previous versions. Whereas Premiere 5.x displayed audio fade and pan controls at the same time, relying on colors to differentiate them, Premiere 6 uses buttons to toggle between displaying fade and pan controls. The expanded audio track also allows you to show and hide audio waveform displays. If you're using audio effects, you can switch from showing the fade or pan controls to showing keyframe markers, which you use to change an audio effect over time.

To show controls in an audio track:

1. If necessary, expand an audio track by clicking the triangle next to the name of the track (**Figure 10.1**).

   The track expands.

2. In the audio track, click one of the following buttons (**Figure 10.2**):

   ▲ To view pan controls, click the blue pan control button ▣ .

   ▲ To view fade controls, click the red fade control button ▣ .

   ▲ To view keyframes for audio effects, click the keyframes button ◈ .

   Selecting one of these buttons switches the other two off.

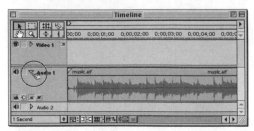

Figure 10.1 Expand the audio track by clicking the triangle next to the name of the track.

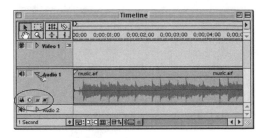

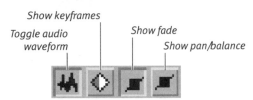

Figure 10.2 To view keyframes, pan controls, or fade controls, click the corresponding button in the expanded audio track.

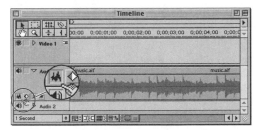

Figure 10.3 Select the waveform button so that the audio clip displays a waveform.

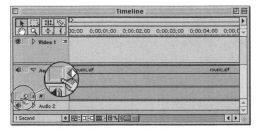

Figure 10.4 Deselect the waveform button to conceal the waveform.

To view waveforms:

1. If necessary, expand an audio track by clicking the triangle next to the name of the track.

   The track expands.

2. In the audio track, click the waveform button to toggle a visual representation of the audio on and off.

   When the button is selected, a waveform is visible (**Figure 10.3**); when the button is deselected, no waveform appears (**Figure 10.4**).

✔ Tip

- Waveforms appear only when the timeline is viewed at (or closer than) the time unit you set in the Timeline Window Options dialog box.

Logarithmic Fades and Enhanced Rate Conversion

Remember the enhanced rate conversion and logarithmic audio fade options in the audio settings, discussed in Chapter 2?

When Premiere processes audio, it first converts, or *resamples*, the audio to the sample rate that you specified in the project settings. Enhanced Rate Conversion determines the level of quality used in converting to a higher sample rate (*upsampling*) or to a lower sample rate (*downsampling*). Set Enhanced Rate Conversion to Off for faster processing but lower quality, Better for medium speed and quality, or Best for maximum quality but slower processing.

When you choose Logarithmic Audio Fade, Premiere processes gain levels according to a logarithmic scale; when the option is unselected, Premiere processes gain changes by using a linear curve. Conventional volume controls also use a logarithmic scale, which emulates the way that the human ear perceives audio gain increases and decreases. Logarithmic fades sound more natural but require more processing time.

Adjusting a Clip's Overall Gain

You can adjust the overall volume, or *gain level*, of a clip in the timeline by using a menu command.

To adjust the overall gain:

1. Select an audio clip in the timeline (**Figure 10.5**).

2. Choose Clip > Audio Options > Audio Gain (**Figure 10.6**).

    The Audio Gain dialog box appears.

3. To adjust the gain, *do either of the following* (**Figure 10.7**):

    ▲ Enter a value for the gain.

    A value of more than 100 amplifies the audio; a value of less than 100 *attenuates* the audio, making it quieter.

    or

    ▲ Click Smart Gain to have Premiere calculate a gain value automatically.

    Smart Gain *normalizes* the audio, attempting to boost the volume where it's too quiet and limit it where it's too loud.

4. Click OK.

    The audio clip's overall gain is adjusted by the amount you specified.

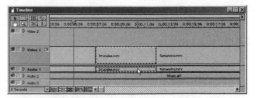

Figure 10.5 Select an audio clip in the timeline.

Figure 10.6 Choose Clip > Audio Options > Audio Gain.

Figure 10.7 In the Audio Gain dialog box, enter a value to adjust the gain manually, or choose Smart Gain to have Premiere normalize the gain automatically.

✔ Tip

■ The Compressor/Expander audio effect gives you more control of audio gain.

Controlling Audio Quality

You must maintain audio quality at every step of the production process: recording, digitizing, processing, and export. At each step, your goal is to capture and maintain a strong audio signal without distorting it. At the same time, you want to minimize noise: any extraneous sounds, including electronic hum and hiss. Audio engineers like to call achieving these goals maintaining a good signal-to-noise ratio; you might think of it as keeping the sound loud and clear.

If you use good recording and digitizing techniques, preserving audio quality in the editing and export process will be much easier.

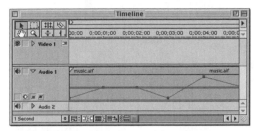

Figure 10.8 In the timeline, you adjust panning and fading by using "rubber-band" controls.

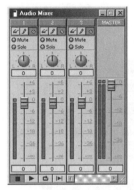

Figure 10.9 In the Audio Mixer window, you adjust panning and fading by using controls similar to those of a traditional mixing board.

Percentages versus dB

In previous versions of Premiere, audio levels were measured strictly in terms of percentages. Though this was meaningful in relative terms, it didn't correspond to conventional sound measurements.

Fortunately, Premiere can now display levels in terms of decibels, or dB. A decibel is the standard measure of acoustical power used by audio professionals everywhere. To double the volume, increase the level +6dB.

Technically speaking, a decibel is one-tenth of a bel, which measures the ratio of two audio power levels—usually, an audio signal and a reference (such as the threshold of hearing). And yes, it's bel as in Alexander Graham Bell, the telephone guy.

Fading and Panning

Audio mixing consists of two primary tasks: fading and panning. *Fading* audio adjusts its gain level, or volume. Fading up audio increases its volume; fading down decreases it. Fading helps you match the audio levels of different clips, as you would with dialogue. Or you can create audio transitions or effects, such as making a car sound more and more distant.

Panning affects how a clip's audio is distributed between the left and right audio speaker. Panning audio can imply an apparent position for a sound.

Starting with Premiere 6, you can mix audio by using either the timeline controls or the audio mixer. In the timeline, you can manipulate lines that represent fade and pan levels. The line is sometimes referred to as a "rubber-band," and manipulating it is called "rubber-banding" (**Figure 10.8**). Adjusting the slope of the lines affects the clip's volume and distribution. This method is precise and visually clear. On the other hand, it doesn't provide simultaneous audio playback.

The Audio Mixer window resembles a traditional audio mixing board (**Figure 10.9**). It controls fading and panning in real time, using more conventional-looking fader controls and pan knobs. This method favors simultaneous audio response to precise graphical control.

Another important distinction between the two methods is the context in which they're used. The timeline controls are clip-oriented, whereas the audio mixer is track-oriented. In other words, you manipulate the fade and pan lines for each clip in the program in the timeline; you use the audio mixer to mix entire tracks of the program. You can switch between methods at will, depending on your preferences and the task at hand.

Using Audio Pan and Fade Controls

When you expand the audio tracks, the fade and pan controls are revealed. Clicking the red fade button displays a red line, or fade control (**Figure 10.10**); clicking the blue pan button toggles to the blue line, or pan control (**Figure 10.11**). You can fade and pan the audio by altering the position and slope of these lines. You do this by adding a control point, or handle, to the line and dragging it to a new position. The line slopes up or down to represent the fade and pan. Every clip has a handle at its beginning and end, but you can add an unlimited number of handles in between for precise control of the audio.

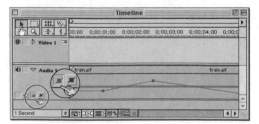

Figure 10.10 Clicking the red fade button reveals the red fade control.

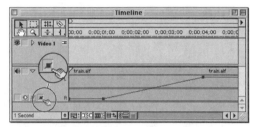

Figure 10.11 Clicking the blue pan button reveals the blue pan control.

Fading

The red line, or fade control, controls the level of the audio clip. By default, the line appears in the middle of the clip, at the normal gain level of 100. You can drag a handle anywhere from 0 (silence), at the bottom of the clip, to 200 (twice the volume), at the top of the clip (**Figure 10.12**).

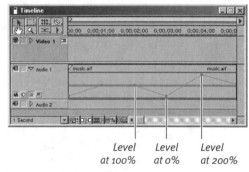

Level at 100%   Level at 0%   Level at 200%

Figure 10.12 Volume levels are measured vertically in the expanded audio clip—from 0% at the bottom to 200% at the top.

Subtractive Mixing

When you adjust audio levels, follow the principle of subtractive mixing. In *subtractive mixing*, you favor reducing (subtracting) gain levels over increasing them. First, establish a strong, representative audio level for the program (such as the standard level for dialog). Then, if necessary, decrease the gain of a clip in relation to others. Increasing a level in relation to other clips often leads to successive increases. Adding gain increases not only the signal (the sounds you want), but also the noise (the sounds you don't want, such as buzz and hiss), and can introduce distortion.

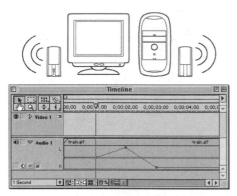

Figure 10.13 At the current time (indicated by the edit line), this audio clip's pan control is centered, and plays equally from both speakers.

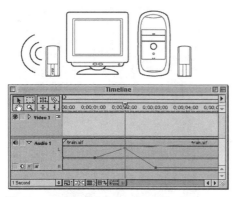

Figure 10.14 When the pan control line is positioned at the top of the expanded clip, the audio is distributed to the left speaker.

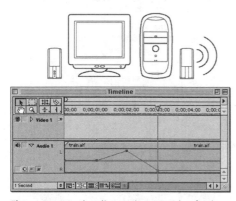

Figure 10.15 As the clip continues to play (and the edit line moves to the right) the pan control line slopes to the bottom of the clip, distributing the audio to the right speaker.

Panning and Balancing

The blue line, or *pan control*, controls how a monophonic (mono) audio of a clip is distributed between left and right stereo speakers. Changing the distribution is called *panning*. Redistributing the audio channels of a stereophonic (stereo) clip works the same way, but the process is called *balancing*. Because the processes for panning and balancing audio are so similar, the following sections use the term *pan* to refer to both pan and balance (unless otherwise noted).

By default, the pan control appears in the middle of the clip, indicating that the pan is centered—in other words, equally distributed between the two speakers. Dragging a control handle to the top pans the audio to the left speaker; dragging it to the bottom pans the audio to the right speaker. An expanded audio track displays a blue L and R to remind you how the line corresponds to the speakers (**Figures 10.13**, **10.14**, and **10.15**.)

✔ Tips

- You can use the Paste Custom command to copy and paste pan and fade adjustments from one clip to another.

- As it refers to panning audio, the term *balanced* means centering the audio track to play back equally in both speakers. You should be aware that the term *balanced* can also refer to a type of audio cable and connector.

USING AUDIO PAN AND FADE CONTROLS

Fading

The fade control gives you precise control of the audio levels, enabling you to adjust levels in increments as small as 1%. Starting with Premiere 6, you can also view your adjustments in terms of decibels (dB), not just percentages.

To create and use a fade handle:

1. Position the pointer on the red fade line where you want to create a fade handle.

   The pointer changes to a white finger icon with red +/– 🖐 to indicate that you are about to add a fade handle (**Figure 10.16**).

2. Click to create a fade handle.

   A handle (red dot) appears on the fade line.

3. Drag the fade handle up or down to change the level of the audio at that point or side to side to change the handle's position (**Figure 10.17**).

To delete a fade handle:

Drag a fade handle all the way outside the audio track, and release the mouse button. The fade handle disappears (**Figure 10.18**).

✔ Tip

■ Activate the Info palette before you use the fade handle. As you drag a handle, you can see the current level value update in the Info palette (**Figure 10.19**).

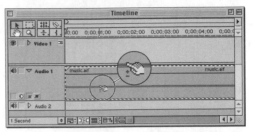

Figure 10.16 The pointer changes to a white finger icon to indicate that you are about to add a fade handle.

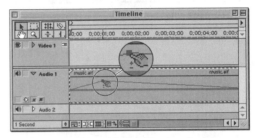

Figure 10.17 Click to add a handle, then drag the handle to the desired position.

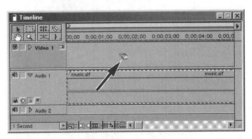

Figure 10.18 Dragging a handle all the way outside the audio track removes it from the line.

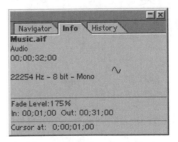

Figure 10.19 The Info palette displays updated information about a fade handle as you drag it.

FADING

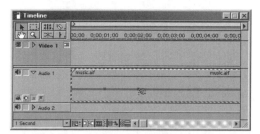

Figure 10.20 The pointer changes to a gray finger icon to indicate that you are about to move a fade handle.

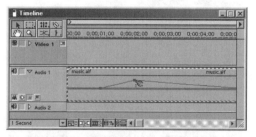

Figure 10.21 Drag the handle up or down to change the level; drag to the left or right to change the handle's position in time.

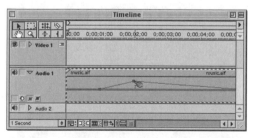

Figure 10.22 The pointer changes to a gray finger icon to indicate that you are about to move a fade handle.

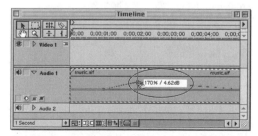

Figure 10.23 (Shift)-dragging the handle up or down adjusts the level in increments of 1%. A display shows the level in percentages and in dB.

To move a fade handle:

1. Position the pointer on a red fade handle.

   The pointer changes to a gray finger icon with red +/– to indicate that you are about to move a fade handle (**Figure 10.20**). If the finger is white, you are about to create a new handle.

2. Drag the fade handle up or down to change the level of the audio at that point or side to side to change the handle's position in time (**Figure 10.21**).

To fade in increments of 1%:

1. Position the pointer on the fade handle you want to adjust.

   The pointer changes to a gray finger icon with red +/– to indicate that you are about to move a fade handle (**Figure 10.22**).

2. (Shift)-drag the handle up or down.

   A numeric display appears, indicating the current fade level in percentages and dB. As long as you hold down the (Shift) key, you can drag beyond the top or bottom of the audio track, allowing you to adjust the level in increments of 1% (**Figure 10.23**).

FADING

279

Using Other Handle Adjustment Tools

Other tools can help you make adjustments to a handle. Though they're explained here, along with other fade controls, these tools also work with the fade line and even the video fade line (explained in Chapter 13).

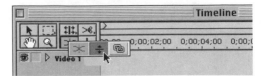

Figure 10.24 Select the fade adjustment tool.

To move two handles simultaneously:

1. In the Timeline window, select the fade adjustment tool ![icon] (**Figure 10.24**).

2. Position the fade adjustment tool between the two handles you want to adjust.

3. Drag up or down to move both handles, shifting the level between the two (**Figure 10.25**).

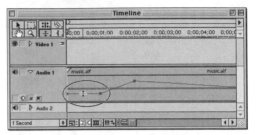

Figure 10.25 Drag with the fade adjustment tool to move two handles at the same time.

To create two adjacent handles:

1. In the Timeline window, select the scissors tool ![icon] (**Figure 10.26**).

   The scissors tool is grouped with the razor and multi-razor tools. If the scissors tool is hidden, press and hold one of the other tools in the group to make a fly-out tool palette appear, and then select the scissors tool. Or, with the Timeline window active, press ⓒ repeatedly, until the scissors tool appears.

2. Click the fade or pan control where no handles are present.

   Two adjacent handles appear, although they may be too close together for you to see both clearly (**Figure 10.27**).

3. In the Timeline window, select another tool (such as the selection tool).

4. Adjust the handles as needed (**Figure 10.28**).

Figure 10.26 Select the scissors tool.

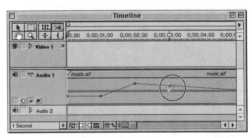

Figure 10.27 Clicking with the scissors tool creates two adjacent handles on the line.

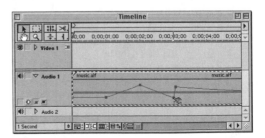

Figure 10.28 Adjust the handles as needed.

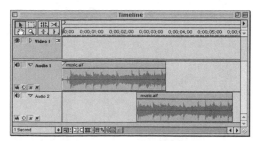

Figure 10.29 Overlap two audio clips in time, and display the red fade line.

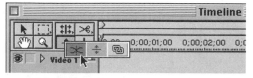

Figure 10.30 Select the cross-fade tool.

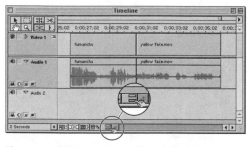

Figure 10.31 Click one audio clip and then the overlapping audio clip. Clicking the second clip creates a standard cross-fade automatically.

Creating Cross-Fades

A *cross-fade* occurs when one audio clip fades out (grows silent) while another audio clip fades in (becomes audible). You can manipulate fade handles manually to create a cross-fade, or you can use Premiere's cross-fade tool to create simple cross-fades quickly. Incidentally, this technique also works with the video fade line.

To use the cross-fade tool:

1. Overlap two audio clips in time, and display the red fade line (**Figure 10.29**).

2. In the Timeline window, select the cross-fade tool (**Figure 10.30**).

3. Click one audio clip.

4. Click the other audio clip.

   When you position the pointer over the second clip, the cross-fade tool appears. When you click, Premiere creates a standard cross-fade (**Figure 10.31**).

Cross-Fading Audio Linked to Video

Because a cross-fade requires two audio clips to overlap, audio linked to video initially seems to present a problem: The linked video prevents you from dragging the audio clip to another track to overlap the audio (**Figure 10.32**).

If you apply what you learned in Chapter 7, however, you can overcome this problem easily by turning off synch mode to create the split edit. This technique permits you to move and trim the audio independently. When you reactivate synch mode, you also restore the link between the video and audio, which helps you keep them in synch later. Although split edits are discussed in Chapter 7, the topics are worth reviewing in the context of audio mixing.

To cross-fade audio linked to video:

1. In the Timeline window, deactivate synch mode (**Figure 10.33**).

   When synch mode is active, the synch mode button displays a link icon ; click it to deactivate it so that the icon displays no link .

2. Drag one audio clip to another track.

   Do not shift the clip in time (horizontally); if you do, the clip loses synch with the linked video.

3. Trim the edges of one or both of the audio clips so that they overlap (**Figure 10.34**).

Figure 10.32 Linked audio and video can prevent you from extending the audio to create an audio cross-fade.

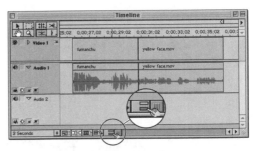

Figure 10.33 Deactivate synch mode.

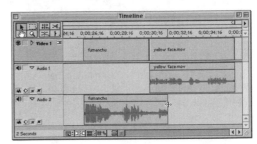

Figure 10.34 With synch mode deactivated, you can move one of the audio clips to another track and extend it so that it overlaps the other audio clip.

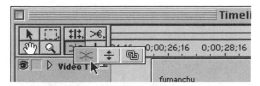

Figure 10.35 Select the cross-fade tool.

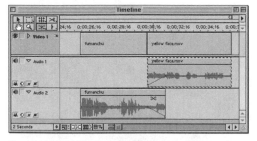

Figure 10.36 Using the cross-fade tool, click one audio clip and then the other to create a standard audio cross-fade.

4. Select the cross-fade tool 🔀 (**Figure 10.35**).

5. Click one audio clip and then the other.

When you position the pointer on the second clip, the cross-fade tool appears. When you click, Premiere creates a standard cross-fade (**Figure 10.36**).

CROSS-FADING AUDIO LINKED TO VIDEO

Panning and Balancing

Redistributing monophonic audio between stereo speakers is called *panning*. Redistributing stereophonic audio between two speakers is called *balancing*. Premiere gives you the same control of panning and balancing that you have of fading. You can pan or balance audio over time and adjust it in increments of 1%.

This section covers the basics of panning audio. Except for the cross-fade tool, the tools available for fading audio—the fade adjustment and scissors tools—work exactly the same way for the pan/balance control.

To pan an audio clip:

1. Expand the audio track, and click the blue pan button to display the pan control (**Figure 10.37**).

2. Position the pointer on the blue pan line where you want to create a pan handle.

   The pointer changes to a white finger icon with small blue arrows 🖐 to indicate that you are about to add a pan handle (**Figure 10.38**).

3. Click to create a pan handle.

   A handle (blue dot) appears on the pan line.

4. Drag the pan handle up to pan the audio to the left; drag it down to pan it to the right (**Figure 10.39**).

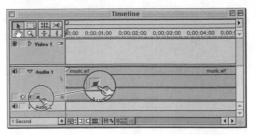

Figure 10.37 Expand the audio track, and click the blue pan button to display the pan control.

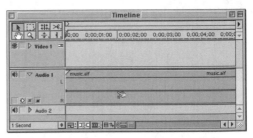

Figure 10.38 The pointer changes to a white finger icon to indicate that you are about to add a pan handle.

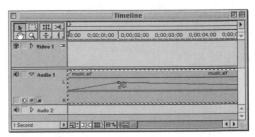

Figure 10.39 Drag the pan handle up to pan the audio to the left; drag it down to pan it to the right.

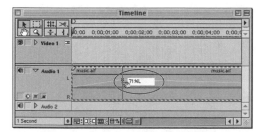

Figure 10.40 ⌘Shift-drag the pan handle to make adjustments in increments of 1%.

To pan in increments of 1%:

1. Expand the audio track, and click the blue pan button to display the pan control.

2. Position the pointer on the pan handle you want to adjust.

   The pointer changes to a gray finger icon with small blue arrows 🖑 to indicate that you are about to move a pan handle.

3. ⌘Shift-drag the handle up or down (**Figure 10.40**).

   A numeric display indicates the current pan level. Pan center is at 0%. As long as you hold down the ⌘Shift key, you can drag beyond the top or bottom of the audio track. You can adjust the pan in increments of 1%.

Using Stereo Audio Clips

Unlike some audio editing programs, Premiere places stereo clips in a single audio track in the timeline. Nevertheless, several commands allow you to manipulate each channel of a stereo track separately. Using these commands, you can duplicate, mute, and swap the left or right stereo channels of an audio clip.

Duplicating one channel of a stereo clip copies it to the other channel. Making both channels the same effectively creates a monophonic clip and makes a pan control appear. This can be useful for clips that have information on a single channel.

Muting a channel eliminates it, leaving only the other channel audible.

Swapping channels exchanges the right and left channels, reversing their stereo placement.

To modify one channel of a stereo clip:

1. In the timeline, select a stereo audio clip, and reveal its pan control (**Figure 10.41**).

2. *Do one of the following* (**Figure 10.42**):

   ▲ To duplicate the left channel, choose Clip > Audio Options > Duplicate Left.

   ▲ To duplicate the right channel, choose Clip > Audio Options > Duplicate Right.

   ▲ To mute the left channel, choose Clip > Audio Options > Mute Left.

   ▲ To mute the right channel, choose Clip > Audio Options > Mute Right.

   ▲ To swap the channels, choose Clip > Audio Options > Swap Channels.

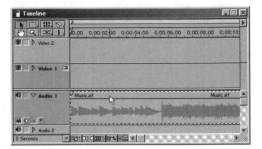

Figure 10.41 In the timeline, select a stereo audio clip, and reveal its pan control.

Figure 10.42 Choose Clip > Audio > and then choose an option, depending on whether you want to duplicate, mute or swap channels.

Figure 10.43 Choose Clip > Audio Options > Normal.

To restore a stereo track to its original state:

1. In the timeline, select a stereo audio clip, and reveal its pan control.

2. Choose Clip > Audio Options > Normal (**Figure 10.43**).

   The duplicate, mute, and swap settings are removed, and the stereo clip is restored to its original state.

✔ Tips

- Make sure your audio cabling is correct. It's surprisingly common for the left and right channels to be reversed.

- In stereo equipment, the left channel is synonymous with audio channel 1 and a white connector. The right channel is synonymous with audio channel 2 and a red connector.

- You can use the Pan, Fill Right, or Fill Left audio effects to pan audio, but you won't see their effects in the pan line of the audio track.

Using the Audio Mixer

The audio mixer resembles a conventional mixing board in both form and function (**Figure 10.44**). Just as each channel of a mixing board contains controls to adjust and monitor each audio source, each channel in the audio mixer corresponds to a track in the program. Unlike its physical counterpart, however, the audio mixer adds channels for each track you add to the program. Faders (or fade controls) control the audio levels, expressed in decibels (dB). Alternatively, you can enter a numeric value for the level.

Similarly, you can pan audio by using the audio mixer's pan knobs or by entering a numerical value. You can also *group* channels, making it possible to control more than one channel simultaneously.

You make these adjustments in each track as the video and audio play back. As you do, Premiere creates handles in the corresponding fade and pan lines in the timeline. If you're not satisfied, you can redo your adjustments or use the techniques covered in the previous sections to fine-tune the handles directly in the timeline.

To help you evaluate the levels, a VU (volume unit) meter graphically represents the levels of each channel, as well as the overall combined, or *master,* level. An indicator light at the top of the VU meter warns you if your levels are too high and *clipping* (causing distortion).

Each channel of the audio mixer also contains standard buttons for selectively monitoring (listening to) each track. You can monitor all the channels, mute a channel to stop monitoring it, or solo a channel to monitor it without the others.

Each channel also includes three automation buttons that allow you to store, recall, or ignore your mixing settings.

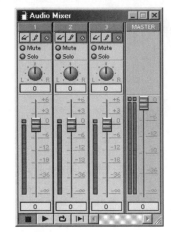

Figure 10.44 The Audio Mixer window resembles a conventional mixing board.

Figure 10.45 Choose Window > Workspace > Audio.

Setting the Workspace for Audio Mixing

As a rule, you mix a project's audio only after you're satisfied with the editing (a stage sometimes referred to as *picture lock*). For this reason, the standard editing workspace isn't ideally suited for audio editing. The source view of the Monitor window, for example, isn't useful when you mix the audio tracks of the program. By using a simple command, you can optimize the arrangement of windows for audio mixing.

To set the workspace for audio mixing:

◆ Choose Window > Workspace > Audio (**Figure 10.45**).

The arrangement of windows is optimized for audio mixing (**Figure 10.46**).

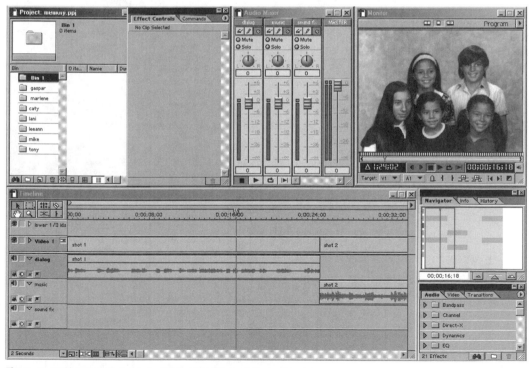

Figure 10.46 The arrangement of windows is optimized for audio mixing.

Customizing the Audio Mixer

By default, the Audio Mixer window displays both mixing channels and the master, or *output*, channel. You can hide either the mixer channels or the output channel.

To hide and show input or output channels:

1. Control-click (Mac) or right-click (Windows) the title bar of the audio mixer.

   A contextual menu appears.

2. From the contexual menu, choose Audio Mixer Window Options (**Figure 10.47**).

   The Audio Mixer Window Options dialog box opens.

3. Choose one of the following options (**Figure 10.48**):

   Audio Tracks and Master Fader—displays both the mixer channels and the master fade control.

   Audio Tracks Only—displays the mixer channels without the master fade control.

   Master Fader Only—displays only the master fade control.

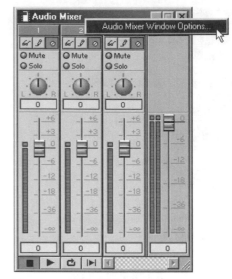

Figure 10.47 In the Audio Mixer's contextual menu, choose Audio Mixer Window Options.

Figure 10.48 In the Audio Mixer Window Options dialog box, select the channels that you want to be visible in the Audio Mixer window.

Figure 10.49 Clicking a channel's Mute button excludes the corresponding audio track from playing back.

Figure 10.50 Clicking a channel's Solo button allows you to hear the corresponding track exclusively.

Clipping indicator   *Clipping indicator*

Figure 10.51 When a sound is too loud, the clip indicator light becomes illuminated.

Monitoring Channels in the Audio Mixer

Though mixing audio is about making all the tracks sound good together, one way to do this is to listen to them separately. Buttons at the top of each channel allow you to control which one you listen to, or *monitor*. If you don't want to monitor a track, use the Mute button. Conversely, use the Solo button to monitor that track without the others. Monitor buttons don't affect the levels—just whether you hear the audio during the mixing process.

To mute a track:

◆ In the audio mixer, click the Mute button for the track you want to exclude from playback (**Figure 10.49**).

   Deselect the Mute button to include the track's audio in playback.

To solo a track:

◆ In the audio mixer, click the Solo button for the track you want to hear exclusively (**Figure 10.50**).

   Deselect the button to include the audio of other tracks in playback.

Reading the VU Meters

As you monitor the audio, watch the levels in the VU meters. Your speaker volume can provide only a relative, changeable indication of levels. You can rely on the VU meters for a more objective measure. The loudest sounds should reach their highest levels, or *peak*, near the top of the meters, at 0 dB. If a sound is too loud to be accurately reproduced, it *clips* and will sound distorted. When clipping occurs, the indicator light above a VU meter becomes illuminated (**Figure 10.51**). Click the lights to turn them off. Readjust the levels to avoid clipping.

Using Automation Write Options

Using the audio mixer to create fades and pan handles in the audio track is also known as the *automation write* process. How the automation write function works depends on options you set in the Audio Mixer Window Options dialog box.

These settings specify whether you want to enable controls for fading, panning, or both. Other options determine how the fade and pan controls operate as you create fade and pan handles. (Though the dialog box offers an explanation of these options, the instructions in the following sections describe each choice in less technical terms.)

To set the automation write options:

1. (Control)-click (Mac) or right-click (Windows) the title bar of the audio mixer.

   The audio mixer's contextual menu appears.

2. From the contextual menu, choose Audio Mixer Window Options (**Figure 10.52**).

   The Audio Mixer Window Options dialog box appears.

3. To specify how fade and pan controls operate, select one of the following radio buttons (**Figure 10.53**):

   Touch—releasing the mouse button automatically returns the fade/pan control to 0.

   Latch—releasing the mouse button leaves the fade/pan control at the current position. When playback is stopped and restarted, the fade/pan control resumes from 0.

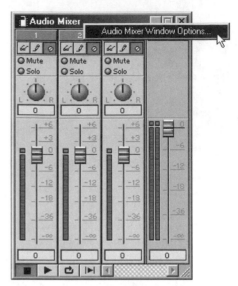

Figure 10.52 From the Audio Mixer window's contextual menu, choose Audio Mixer Window Options.

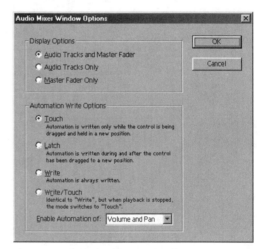

Figure 10.53 In the Audio Mixer Window Options dialog box, specify how you want the Audio Mixer window's automation write feature to operate.

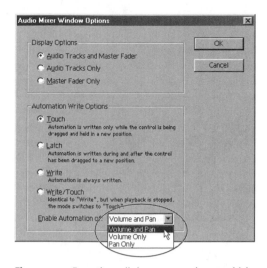

Figure 10.54 From the pull-down menu, choose which controls you want to enable for automation.

Write—releasing the mouse button leaves the fade/pan control at the current position. When playback is stopped and restarted, the fade/pan resumes from the current position.

Write/Touch—functions like Write mode during playback; after playback is stopped, it functions like Touch mode.

4. From the Enable Automation Of pull-down menu, choose an option (**Figure 10.54**):

Volume and Pan—enables both fade and pan automation for selected channels.

Volume Only—enables only the fade automation for selected channels.

Pan Only—enables only the pan automation for selected channels.

5. Click OK to close the dialog box.

Ganging Fade Controls

Usually, you adjust the level of each track in separate passes. Sometimes, however, you want to adjust two or more tracks simultaneously. You can do this by *ganging* fade controls—assigning them to a group. Ganged fade controls appear with the same color coding and move together as you make adjustments.

To group channel fade controls:

1. In the audio mixer, ⸢Control⸣-click (Mac) or right-click (Windows) a fade control, to open the contextual menu.

2. From the menu, select a group for the fade control (**Figure 10.55**).

3. Repeat steps 1 and 2 for fade controls in other channels.

   Fade controls in the same group appear with the same color code and move as a group (**Figures 10.56** and **10.57**).

To ungroup fade controls:

◆ ⸢Control⸣-click (Mac) or right-click (Windows) the grouped fade controls, and choose No Gang (**Figure 10.58**).

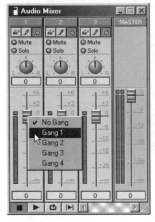

Figure 10.55 From the fade control's contextual menu, choose a Gang option.

Figure 10.56 To gang fade controls, choose the same Gang option for other fade controls.

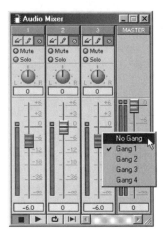

Figure 10.58 Choose No Gang to allow the fade control to move independently.

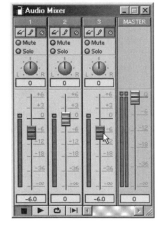

Figure 10.57 Ganged fade controls share a color code and move together.

Mixing and Playing in the Audio Mixer

Using the audio mixer is comparable to using a traditional mixing console that can automate adjustments. In other words, the audio mixer records your adjustments in real time. Afterward, you can set the audio mixer window to read, or play back, the adjustments you made.

To adjust an audio track, you set its corresponding channel in the Audio Mixer window to *automation write* mode. To hear the adjustments you made, set the channel to *automation read* mode. To leave a track untouched, choose neither option for the channel in the Audio Mixer window.

Because your computer's mouse allows you to adjust only one thing at a time (and because doing so is a more efficient strategy), you should make adjustments to a single track and then adjust the other tracks in separate passes. The Audio Mixer window's automation modes and other controls make it easy to make careful adjustments in multiple passes. You can, of course, set some channels to automation write and others to automation read.

While the Audio Mixer window is open, you can hear adjustments only for channels in automation read mode. When you finish mixing, close the Audio Mixer window; all your adjustments to the fade and pan controls play back normally.

To prepare to mix with the Audio Mixer window:

1. In the Timeline window, expand the audio tracks you want to mix, and view the fade or pan controls.

2. If necessary, set options in the Audio Mixer Window Options dialog box (explained in the preceding section).

3. In the Audio Mixer window, choose the monitoring options for each channel.

4. Click the Automation Write button for the tracks you want to adjust (**Figure 10.59**).

5. To group tracks, Control-click (Mac) or right-click (Windows) a fade control and then choose a group from the contextual menu (**Figure 10.60**).

   Fade controls assigned to the same group move in tandem. For more information about grouping fade controls, see the section "Ganging Fade Controls."

6. To define the area of the program you want to mix, set an in point and out point in the program.

To mix audio in the Audio Mixer window:

1. In the timeline or program view, cue the current frame to the point of the program where you want to begin mixing (**Figure 10.61**).

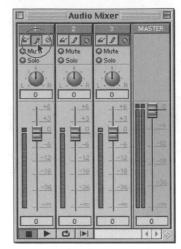

Figure 10.59 Click the Automation Write button for the tracks you want to adjust.

Figure 10.60 To group tracks, Control-click (Mac) or right-click (Windows) a fade control, and choose additional channels.

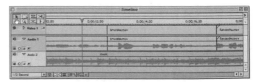

Figure 10.61 Cue the edit line to the point of the program where you want to begin mixing.

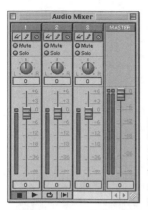

Figure 10.62 Use one of the playback controls to playback the video and audio. You can also press the spacebar to start and stop playback.

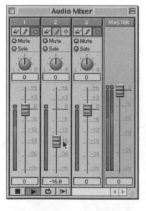

Figure 10.63 During playback, you can fade a channel by dragging a fade control or by entering a number in the field below the fade control.

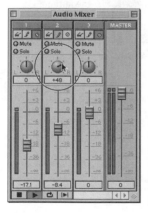

Figure 10.64 To pan an active channel, you can drag the pan knob, or enter a numeric value in the field under the pan knob.

2. In the Audio Mixer window, click one of the following buttons to play the program (**Figure 10.62**):

Play ▶ —plays the program from the edit line.

Loop ↻ —loops playback from the program's in point to the program's out point.

In to Out ▶| —plays the program from the program's in point to the program's out point.

You can also press the spacebar instead of clicking the play button.

3. To fade an active channel, *do either of the following* (**Figure 10.63**):

▲ Drag its fade control.

or

▲ Enter a numeric value in the field under its fade control, in dB.

4. To pan an active channel, *do either of the following* (**Figure 10.64**):

▲ Use the mouse to turn its pan knob.

or

▲ Enter a numeric value in the field below its pan knob.

continues on next page

MIXING AND PLAYING IN THE AUDIO MIXER

5. To stop mixing, click the stop button ▪️ or press the spacebar.

In the Timeline window, your adjustments appear as handles in the fade and pan controls of the audio tracks (**Figure 10.65**).

6. To redo your adjustments or to mix other parts of the program, repeat steps 1 through 5.

✔ Tip

■ When you finish a mixing task, make sure to set the automation option buttons to the settings you want. Your adjustments won't be recorded if the automation mode is off; conversely, leaving it set to write mode can overwrite settings by mistake.

To play back audio mixer automation:

1. In the timeline or the program view, cue the current frame to the point of the program where you want to begin playing back (**Figure 10.66**).

2. In the Audio Mixer window, select the monitoring options for each channel.

3. Click the automation read button 🖉 for the tracks that have adjustments you want to hear (**Figure 10.67**).

4. In the Audio Mixer window, click one of the following buttons to play the program:

Play ▶️ — plays the program from the edit line.

Loop 🔁 — loops playback from the program's in point to the program's out point.

In to Out ⏭️ — plays the program from the program's in point to the program's out point.

You can also press the spacebar instead of clicking the play button. The tracks set to automation read mode include fade and pan adjustments when played back.

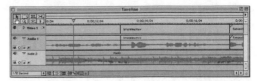

Figure 10.65 In the Timeline window, your adjustments appear as handles in the fade and pan controls of the audio tracks.

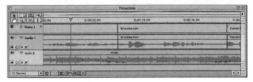

Figure 10.66 Cue the current frame to the point of the program where you want to begin playing back.

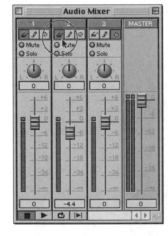

Figure 10.67 Click the automation read button for the channels with adjustments you want to play back.

MIXING AND PLAYING IN THE AUDIO MIXER

Audio Effects

Audio effects or filters not only filter out unwanted sounds, but also enhance or alter audio and create special effects. You can apply multiple effects to the same clip, and you can change their behavior over time. You can even apply the same effect to a single clip more than once, using different settings each time.

In Premiere 6, using effects has been redesigned to more closely resemble the workings of Premiere's software sibling, After Effects. In fact, Premiere outright borrows actual After Effects audio plug-ins and should support any third-party audio plug-ins made for After Effects as well.

Like other effects, the audio effects are located in Premiere's Plug-Ins folder. You can also add filters offered by other manufacturers. Because you apply audio effects the same way that you add video effects, a more detailed discussion of the process is reserved for the next chapter.

Audio Effects

These are the audio effects included with Premiere, listed in the Audio palette by category:

- **Bandpass** removes specified frequencies, and includes Highpass, Lowpass, and Notch/Hum.

- **Channel** manipulates the left and right channels of a stereo audio clip. This category includes Auto Pan, Fill Right, Fill Left, Pan, and Swap Left and Right.

- **Dynamics** alters the dynamic range of the audio, and includes Boost, Compressor/Expander, and Noise Gate.

- **EQ** emphasizes or deemphasizes specified frequencies. Bass & Treble, Equalize, and Parametric Equalize are filters in the EQ category.

- **Effect** manipulates the delay, phase, and modulation to create special audio effects, and includes Chorus, Flanger, and Multi-Effect.

- **Reverb & Delay** repeats, delays, and decays sound to create musical effects or to imply physical space. It includes Echo, Multitap Delay, and Reverb.

Audio Processing

Now that you are familiar with the ways in which you can adjust audio, you should know how Premiere processes it. Knowing the order in which Premiere processes audio can influence the way that you plan your adjustments (or troubleshoot problems). Premiere processes audio in the following order:

1. The audio settings you selected (Chapter 2), regardless of the clips' original audio settings.

2. Audio filters.

3. Pan and fade adjustments.

4. Adjustments resulting from the Clip > Audio Options > Gain command.

ADDING EFFECTS

Figure 11.1
These images are just a few simple examples of the more obvious video effects. You can also apply effects to achieve more subtle results and to manipulate audio (which can't be illustrated here).

Just as a cinematographer adds filters to the lens of a camera to enhance or alter the image, you can add digital filters to clips in the timeline. Though Premiere 6 has discarded the term *filter* in favor of the broader term *effects*, the principle is the same. Premiere ships with dozens of customizable video and audio effects, which you can apply to clips in any number or combination. You can use effects to subtly correct a clip or dramatically stylize it (**Figure 11.1**).

Like the clip itself, Premiere effects are dynamic—that is, most can change settings and intensity over time. Starting with Premiere 5, you could animate an effect over time by using keyframes, specifying precise values for the various properties of an effect at different points in time. Premiere 6 greatly enhances the keyframing feature. Now you can view and alter keyframes directly in the clips of the timeline. In addition, Premiere 6 includes an Effect Controls palette, which provides efficient and convenient control of effects. Incidentally, these new keyframing features make Premiere 6 much more consistent with Adobe's other animation software packages, such as After Effects and Live Motion.

continues on next page

As with all effects, you must preview a clip to see its effects in real time (see Chapter 9). Depending on their number and complexity, effects can add considerable processing time to previewing or exporting a final movie.

Effects are stored in Premiere's Plug-Ins folder. Adobe and other manufacturers offer other filters that are designed for, or compatible with, Premiere. In fact, many of Premiere 6's effects are transplanted from After Effects. You can add compatible plug-in filters by dragging them to the Plug-Ins folder when Premiere is not running. When Premiere starts, the names of the filters are displayed in the splash screen as they load. Rather than attempt to provide detailed information about each effect, this chapter explains how to use any effect. You'll learn everything you need to know to experiment with effects on your own.

After Effects Plug-Ins

Premiere 6 includes 96 video effects and 20 audio effects. Many of the available effects have been brought over from Adobe's highly regarded animation/compositing/effects program, After Effects. You can distinguish the effects native to Premiere from those transplanted from After Effects by their icons in the Video effects palette:

—native Premiere effect

—After Effects plug-in effect

Only those After Effects plug-ins included with Premiere 6 are guaranteed to work within Premiere.

Premiere Effects from After Effects

- Brightness & Contrast
- Channel Mixer
- Posterize
- Directional Blur
- Fast Blur
- Gaussian Blur
- Invert
- Mirror
- Polar Coordinates
- Color Balance (HLS)
- Median
- Tint
- Basic 3D
- Bevel Alpha
- Bevel Edges
- Drop Shadow
- Transform
- Sharpen
- Color Emboss
- Emboss
- Find Edges
- Mosaic
- Noise
- Strobe Light
- Texturize
- Echo
- Posterize Time
- Broadcast Colors
- Reduce Interlace Flicker

Figure 11.2 From the Video palette's pull-down menu, choose Show Hidden.

Figure 11.3
The Obsolete effects folder appears in italics.

Obsolete Effects

Not surprisingly, Premiere 6's enhanced package of effects renders many of the older ones obsolete. Some effects have been replaced with newer versions of the same name; similar but superior effects have replaced others. Premiere 6 still supports obsolete effects, however, just in case you need to open a project created in Premiere 5.x. By default, obsolete video effects are contained in a folder named Obsolete and are set to be hidden in the Video palette.

To reveal obsolete video effects:

◆ From the Video palette's pull-down menu, choose Show Hidden (**Figure 11.2**).

Items specified as hidden (or shy, if you prefer) appear in italics (**Figure 11.3**). By default, obsolete video effects are stored in a folder named Obsolete.

✔ Tip

■ You can view, find, and organize folders and effects in the Video and Audio palettes in the same way as you would transitions in the Transitions palette. To review these techniques, see Chapter 8.

Premiere's Obsolete Effects

◆ Backwards [video] (obsolete)
◆ Better Gaussian Blur (obsolete)
◆ Blur (obsolete)
◆ Blur More (obsolete)
◆ Brightness & Contrast (obsolete)
◆ Emboss (obsolete)
◆ Find Edges (obsolete)
◆ Gaussian Blur (obsolete)
◆ Hue & Saturation (obsolete)
◆ Image Pan (obsolete)
◆ Invert (obsolete)

◆ Median (obsolete)
◆ Mirror (obsolete)
◆ Mosaic (obsolete)
◆ Polar (obsolete)
◆ Posterize (obsolete)
◆ Posterize Time (obsolete)
◆ Sharpen (obsolete)
◆ Sharpen More (obsolete)
◆ Strobe (obsolete)
◆ Tint (obsolete)
◆ Video Noise (obsolete)

OBSOLETE EFFECTS

Using the Effects Workspace

As pointed out in the workflow outline back in Chapter 1, you typically do your effects work late in the editing process. Typically, you're already satisfied with the editing. So if you're not viewing source clips, why use the typical editing workspace? Instead, optimize the workspace for effects editing. The preset Effects workspace displays a single program view in the Monitor window, which conveniently leaves enough extra space to accommodate the Effect Controls palette.

To set the workspace for effects editing:

◆ Choose > Window > Workspace > Effects (**Figure 11.4**).

The arrangement of windows and palettes is optimized for effects editing (**Figure 11.5**).

✔ Tip

■ You can improve the Effects workspace by resizing the Project window to be narrower. This way, you can shift the Monitor window to the left and widen the Effect Controls palette. A wider Effect Controls palette not only allows you to see the full names of the effect controls, but also makes the value sliders wider and, therefore, more precise.

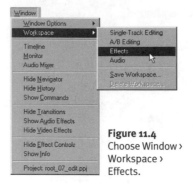

Figure 11.4
Choose Window >
Workspace >
Effects.

Figure 11.5 The arrangement of windows and palettes is optimized for effects editing.

Effect Settings
dialog box

Effect Controls
palette

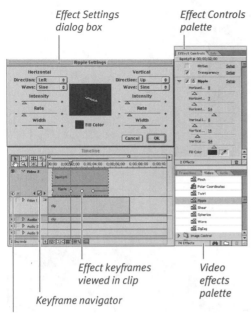

Effect keyframes
viewed in clip

Video
effects
palette

Keyframe navigator

Display keyframe icon

Figure 11.6 In Premiere 6, you can animate effects by using the new Effect Controls palette and controls in the timeline.

Applying Static and Animated Effects

Adding an effect to a clip is nearly self-explanatory: you simply drag an effect from the Video or Audio palette directly to a clip in the timeline. If the effect has adjustable settings—and most effects do—specify values for the effect's various properties by using the Effect Controls palette or the effect's settings dialog box.

When you add an effect to a clip, it's applied to the entire duration of the clip in the timeline. If you don't want to alter the whole clip, you can move the first and last keyframes of the effect (see "Modifying Effect Keyframes" later in this chapter) or split the clip (using the razor tool, for example) and apply the effect to only one instance.

You can also animate most effects over time. By specifying different values to the effect's properties at different points in time—a process known as *keyframing*—the effect can change in character or intensity as the clip plays. To animate an effect, you'll not only need to view the Effect Controls palette, but also the keyframe controls in the timeline: keyframe icons and the keyframe navigator. (**Figure 11.6**).

In the following sections, you'll first learn how to apply a static effect—an effect that uses a single set of property values for the duration of the clip. When you know how to apply effects and use the Effect Controls palette, you'll go on to learn how to animate an effect. In the process, you'll learn how to view and manipulate keyframes in the clips in the timeline.

Using the Effect Controls Palette

Premiere 6 introduces a new palette that furnishes you with a much more efficient and convenient way to control your effects. Appropriately, this palette is called the Effect Controls palette. You'll need to view the Effect Controls palette to adjust static or animated effects.

To open the Effect Controls palette:

◆ *Do either of the following:*

Choose Window > Show Effect Controls (**Figure 11.7**).

or

In a grouped palette, click the Effect Controls tab.

The Effect Controls palette appears.

When a clip containing effects is selected in the timeline, the Effect Controls palette lists the effects in the order in which they have been applied to the clip (**Figure 11.8**). The Effect Controls palette also gives you access to the clip's transparency settings and motion settings (see Chapters 13 and 14, respectively).

Figure 11.7 Choose Window > Show Effect Controls.

Figure 11.8 When a clip containing effects is selected in the timeline, the Effect Controls palette lists the effects in the order in which they have been applied to the clip.

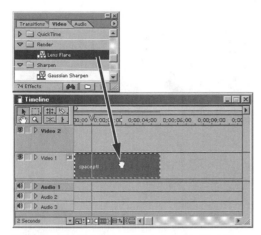

Figure 11.9 To add a video effect, drag an effect from the Video palette to a video clip in the timeline (or from the Audio palette to an audio clip).

Figure 11.10 If a settings dialog box appears automatically, specify values for the effect's properties, and click OK. The Lens Flare effect, for example, immediately opens a settings dialog box when you apply it.

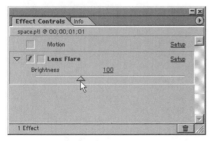

Figure 11.11 You can also use the controls in the Effect Controls palette to set the effect's property values. The palette contains all the controls for some effects, though other effects also use a separate dialog box, which you can access by clicking Setup.

Adding an Effect

This task summarizes the basic process of adding an effect to a clip. You'll discover that each effect has a unique set of parameters, or properties, that you can customize. Specific instructions for setting values for effects using the Effect Controls palette are covered in the next section, "Adjusting Effects Settings."

To add an effect to a clip in the timeline:

1. *Do either of the following:*
   ▲ To add a video effect, drag an effect from the Video palette to a video clip in the timeline (**Figure 11.9**).

   or

   ▲ To add an audio effect, drag an effect from the Audio palette to an audio clip in the timeline.

2. To adjust the effect's settings, *do any of the following* (depending on the particular effect):
   ▲ If a settings dialog box appears automatically, specify values for the effect's properties, and click OK (**Figure 11.10**).
   ▲ In the Effect Controls palette, use the controls below the name of the effect to set its values (**Figure 11.11**).
   ▲ In the Effect Controls palette, click Setup next to the name of the effect to open a settings dialog box.

A settings dialog box particular to the effect appears. Specify values for each of the effect's properties, and click OK.

continues on next page

ADDING AN EFFECT

3. To animate the clip, specify keyframes as described in "Using Effect Keyframes" later in this chapter.

4. To add more effects to the clip, repeat steps 1–3.

Each effect you add appears in the Effect Controls palette (whenever the clip is selected). The order in which the effects are added determines the final effect. See "Using Multiple Effects" later in this chapter.

5. To preview the effect, make sure the work-area bar is positioned over the appropriate range of the timeline, and press (Return).

The effect renders and plays back in the program view (**Figure 11.12**). For a detailed explanation of previewing transitions and effects, see Chapter 9.

✔ Tip

■ You can preview some effects in the effect's settings dialog box. The zoom tool, hand tool, and collapse button work just as they do for the transparency settings, as explained in Chapter 13.

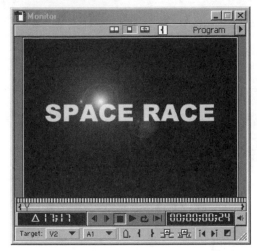

Figure 11.12 Preview the effect to see (or hear it) in real time. In this example, the lens flare effect has been applied to a title (also created in Premiere).

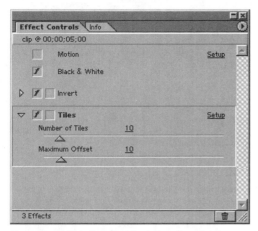

Figure 11.13 Click the triangle next to the effect's name to expand and collapse its controls. Black & White contains no adjustable controls; Invert is collapsed to conceal its property controls; Tiles is expanded.

Adjusting Effect Settings

Though a few effects don't contain customizable properties (Black & White, for example), most have properties with values you can set. Depending on the effect, you can set these property values in the Effect Controls palette, a separate settings dialog box, or both.

As explained in the preceding section, some effects open a settings dialog box as soon as you apply them to a clip; others require you to open a settings dialog box. The following tasks focus on a few of the most common controls. But with more than 100 video and audio effects at your disposal, you'll undoubtedly need to explore the possibilities on your own.

As you adjust an effect, you can see the results in the program view of the Monitor window. This preview image works only while you're making the adjustment, however. To see the effect play back in real time or even slowly, preview the effect by using the methods you learned in Chapter 9.

To expand and collapse effect controls:

◆ In the Effect Controls palette, click the triangle next to the effect's name to expand and collapse its controls, if available (**Figure 11.13**).

ADJUSTING EFFECT SETTINGS

To adjust settings in the Effect Controls palette:

1. Make sure that the Effect Controls palette is visible, and select a clip in the timeline containing an effect.

   To adjust a video effect, click the video portion of a linked clip; to adjust an audio effect, click the audio portion. The name of the effect is selected in the Effect Controls palette.

2. Below the name of the effect in the Effect Controls palette, use any of the following controls to adjust its settings:

   Slider—drag the slider to the left to decrease the value of the property; drag to the right to increase the value (**Figure 11.14**).

   Underlined value—click to open a dialog box and enter a numeric value (**Figure 11.15**).

   Pull-down menu—choose among a set of effect options (**Figure 11.16**).

   Color swatch—click to open a Color Picker dialog box, in which you can select a color for an effect value.

   Eyedropper—select the eyedropper tool to pick a color from a sample frame (**Figure 11.17**).

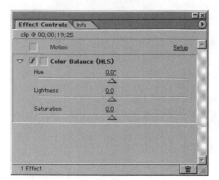

Figure 11.14 The Color Balance effect contains only sliders to control hue, saturation, and lightness.

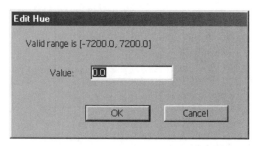

Figure 11.15 Clicking the underlined value display opens a dialog box in which you can enter numeric values.

Figure 11.16 The invert effect includes a pull-down menu for choosing a channel option.

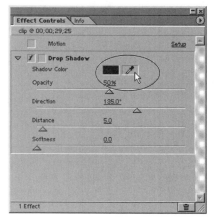

Figure 11.17 The drop shadow effect contains a color swatch and eyedropper tool for selecting colors.

ADJUSTING EFFECT SETTINGS

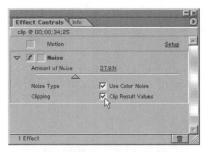

Figure 11.18 The noise effect has options you can select by using checkboxes.

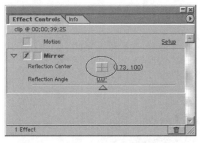

Figure 11.19 The mirror effect uses a center-point value to define the plane, or center of reflection. Click the center point button; then click the image in the program view.

Figure 11.20 The effect uses the center point you specified.

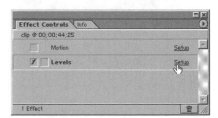

Figure 11.21 The levels effect has controls that you can access only by clicking the Setup button.

Checkbox—check options you want to activate for the effect (**Figure 11.18**).

Center point button—click the button ; then click the image to set the center, origin, or pivot point of an effect (**Figures 11.19** and **11.20**). You can also click the coordinates to enter x and y values in a dialog box.

Setup button—click to open a separate Settings dialog box for the effect (**Figures 11.21** and **11.22**).

The settings you specify are applied to the clip. If you are using keyframes, the new value either creates a keyframe or resets the value of the current keyframe. See "Keyframing Effects" later in this chapter.

✔ Tip

■ When you are setting values at keyframes, the keyframing process must be active, and the edit line must be set to a keyframe. See "Keyframing Effects" later in this chapter.

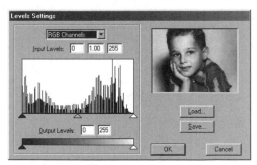

Figure 11.22 Clicking Setup opens the Levels Settings dialog box, which has controls that are too complex to fit into the Effect Controls palette.

Removing and Disabling Effects

The Effect Controls palette also permits you to remove an effect or merely disable it temporarily. Disabling an effect leaves it applied to the clip with its settings intact, but it excludes it from previews and export. Disabling a clip is useful when you want to compare how the clip looks with and without the effect. It's also handy if you're already satisfied with the effect but don't want to slow previews.

To remove an effect:

1. In the Timeline window, select a clip containing effects.

   A thin blue line at the top of the clip indicates that it contains effects. When the clip is selected, its effects are listed in the Effect Controls palette.

2. In the Effect Controls palette, select the name of the effect you want to remove.

   The name of the effect appears in bold.

3. Click the delete button (**Figure 11.23**).

   Premiere prompts you to confirm whether you want to delete the effect.

4. In the warning dialog box, click OK to confirm your choice.

   The effect is removed from the list, and the clip no longer contains the effect (**Figure 11.24**).

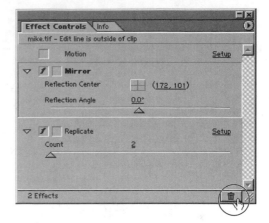

Figure 11.23 In the Timeline window, select the clip containing the effect. In the Effect Controls palette, select the name of the effect and then click the delete button.

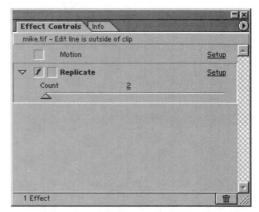

Figure 11.24 The effect is removed from the list, and the clip no longer contains the effect.

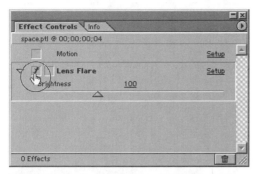

Figure 11.25 To disable an effect, click the Enable Effect icon to toggle it off.

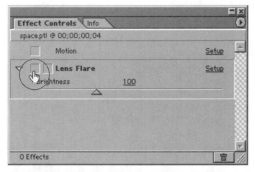

Figure 11.26 When the icon is gone, the effect is disabled and won't appear in previews or output.

To disable an effect:

1. In the Timeline window, select a clip containing effects.

   A thin blue line at the top of the clip indicates that it contains effects. When the clip is selected, its effects are listed in the Effect Controls palette.

2. In the Effect Controls palette, click the enable effect icon 🏱 in the box next to the name of the effect to toggle the icon off (**Figure 11.25**).

   The icon disappears (**Figure 11.26**). The effect is disabled when the icon is toggled off; the effect is enabled when the icon is toggled on.

REMOVING AND DISABLING EFFECTS

Using Multiple Effects

You can add any number of effects to a clip. You can layer different effects onto a single clip or apply the same effect multiple times, specifying different settings each time.

When a clip has more than one effect, Premiere applies the effects in the order in which they appear in the list, from top to bottom. When you need to alter an effect—such as to remove it or adjust its keyframes—make sure you have the correct one selected.

To select the current effect in the Effect Controls palette:

1. Make sure that the Effect Controls palette is visible, and select a clip in the timeline.

2. In the Effect Controls palette, click the name of the effect you want to adjust.

   The name of the effect appears in bold (**Figure 11.27**). The name of the effect appears in the clip in the timeline if its track is expanded.

To select the current effect in the timeline:

1. If necessary, expand the track containing the clip with the effects by clicking the triangle next to the track name.

2. In a clip in the timeline that contains more than one effect, click the pull-down-menu button (**Figure 11.28**).

   The pull-down menu displays the name of the effects applied to the clip. If you can't see the pull-down menu, zoom into the timeline to make the clip appear larger.

3. From the pull-down menu, choose the name of the effect you want to adjust (**Figure 11.29**).

   The name of the effect appears in the expanded area of the clip. In the Effect Controls palette, the effect's name appears in bold.

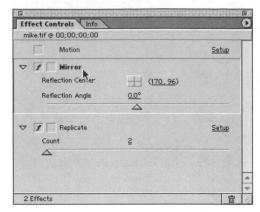

Figure 11.27 In the Effect Controls palette, click the name of the effect you want to adjust or remove. The name of the selected effect appears in bold.

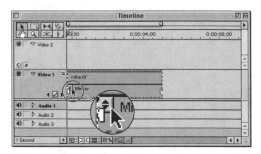

Figure 11.28 A clip that contains more than one effect displays a tiny pull-down menu when the track is expanded.

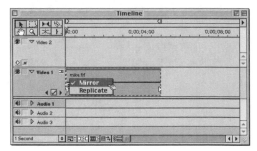

Figure 11.29 From the pull-down menu, choose the name of the effect you want to use. The selected effect's keyframes appear in the clip.

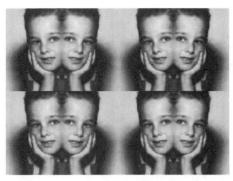

Figure 11.30 The mirror effect followed by the replicate effect results in this image.

Figure 11.31 Reversing the order of the effects results in this image.

Ordering Effects

Because each filter adds to the effect of the preceding one, the order of the filters determines the cumulative effect. Changing the order of filters can change the final appearance of the clip (**Figures 11.30** and **11.31**).

To change the order of effects:

◆ In the Effect Controls palette, drag an effect up or down in the list to change its position in the list (**Figure 11.32**).

The effect name appears in the new position (**Figure 11.33**). You can't drag an effect above the Motion or Transparency sections of the Effect Controls palette; they are separate from effects.

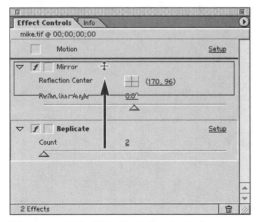

Figure 11.32 In the Effect Controls palette, drag an effect up or down in the list to change its position in the list.

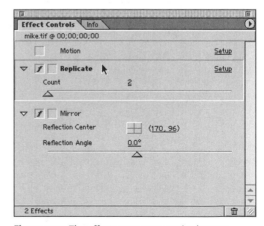

Figure 11.33 The effect name appears in the new position. Replicate is now above Mirror.

Video Effects and Image Size

Some effects—such as Pointillize, Crystallize, and Image Pan—use settings expressed in pixels. The pixel settings of these filters remain constant, even if you change the size of the video image. Therefore, the apparent effects of these filters change according to the image size of the output (**Figures 11.34** and **11.35**). So-called "size-relative" effects can mislead you if you preview these filters at a different image size than the final output or if you use smaller source clips as proxies for larger clips. To get a more accurate representation of the effect, preview it at your output size.

✔ Tip

■ You can use Image Pan to simulate a motion-control camera panning over parts of a clip's image. You often see this effect in documentaries that use still images. Because the image pan effect's settings are expressed in pixels, however, the effects are relative to the size of the clip. If you apply Image Pan to a smaller proxy clip, you have to reset the filter when you replace the proxy with a larger source clip.

Figure 11.34 A clip with the crystallize effect set to 10 looks like this when the image is previewed at 320x240.

Figure 11.35 When the clip is previewed at 640x480, the same effect looks like this. The effect settings are the same, but the crystals now appear half the size relative to the clip.

Animating Effects

As you have seen, most effects include various attributes, or properties, that you can customize. You control the final result of the effect by setting values for these properties. So far, you've set a single set of values to achieve a static effect. An animated effect results from varying its properties over time. In Premiere and other programs, you define and control these changes by using keyframes.

A *keyframe* defines the property values for an effect at a specific point in time. When you create at least two keyframes with different values, Premiere calculates the values for every frame between the keyframes, using a linear progression. Each effect you apply to a clip can contain any number of keyframes, independent of the keyframes contained by other effects.

Keyframes

Keyframe is a term borrowed from traditional animation. In a traditional animation studio, a senior animator might draw only the keyframes—what the character looks like at key moments in the animation. The junior animators then draw the rest of the frames, or *in-betweens*. The same principle applies to computer animations: if you supply the keyframes, the computer program determines the in-between frames. When you think about it, every handle on an audio fade line is like a keyframe. You define the gain-level values at particular points in time, and Premiere interpolates all the values in between, in a linear progression. The fade handles are the keyframes; the lines connecting them are the interpolated values. When you apply a motion setting to a clip, you use keyframes to animate its position on the screen (Chapter 14). By adding keyframes to an effect, you can define the values of an effect at different points in the clip, thereby animating its intensity or other characteristics over time.

Viewing Keyframes

When you create an effect keyframe, it creates a visible icon in the clip in the timeline. You can view the effect keyframes of a clip by expanding its video track and—if the track isn't the Video 1 track—choosing the Display Keyframe icon in the expanded track.

When the applied effect isn't animated, the effect uses a single set of property values throughout the clip. These static keyframes appear as rectangles in the expanded clip. You can move them, but you can't assign different values to each one (**Figure 11.36**).

When the effect is animated, keyframes appear as diamonds. Every clip has a keyframe at its beginning and end; these cannot be deleted. The first keyframe is shaded on the left; the last is shaded on the right; other keyframes aren't shaded (**Figure 11.37**).

When keyframes are visible, selecting a clip containing one or more effects reveals a keyframe navigator. The keyframe navigator appears below the track name in the timeline (**Figure 11.38**). As its name implies, the keyframe navigator includes controls to cue the current time to each keyframe of the selected effect in the clip. The keyframe navigator also has a checkbox that not only indicates when the current time is cued to a keyframe, but also allows you to add or delete a keyframe at the current time. Using the keyframe navigator is explained in the next section, "Keyframing Effects."

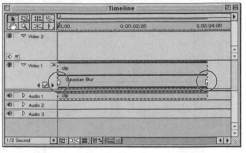

Figure 11.36 Unlike keyframes that create animation, these static keyframes must have the same values, though they can be moved in time. In this example, you can see half of each square icon because the keyframes are located at the edges of the clip.

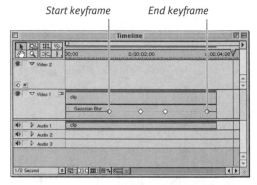

Figure 11.37 When an effect is animated, keyframes appear as diamonds. The first keyframe is shaded on the left; the last keyframe is shaded on the right; other keyframes aren't shaded. This example uses four keyframes.

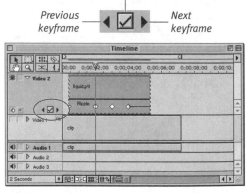

Figure 11.38 When keyframes are visible, selecting a clip containing one or more effects reveals a keyframe navigator.

Show keyframe button

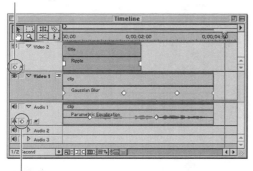

Show keyframe button

Figure 11.39 Expanding a track reveals information that is otherwise hidden, including effect keyframes. For audio tracks, and for video track 2 and higher, you must also select the keyframe button.

To view keyframes in the timeline:

1. In the Timeline window, click the triangle next to a track name.

   The track expands to reveal additional information in the clips in the track.

2. Depending on the track, click the show keyframe button to view effect keyframes instead of other clip information (**Figure 11.39**):

   Audio—click the show keyframe icon.

   Video 2 and higher—click the show keyframe icon.

   Video 1—do nothing; Video 1 track shows only effect keyframes.

   Effect keyframes appear in the clips of the track in place of other controls, such as fade and pan.

Keyframing Effects

After you activate the keyframing process, keyframing involves nothing more than repeating the same two-step procedure: setting the current frame of the clip and then setting the effect's property values for that frame. The specific steps are outlined in the following tasks.

To prepare to animate an effect:

1. In the Timeline window, expand the track containing the clip with the effect you want to animate by clicking the triangle next to the track's name.

   The expanded track reveals additional information about the clips.

2. To reveal keyframes in the audio or superimpose tracks, select the track's show keyframe icon.

   Effect keyframes appear instead of other clip information, such as pan and fade controls.

3. To make sure that the Effect Controls palette is visible, *do either of the following:*

   ▲ Choose Window > Show Effect Controls (**Figure 11.40**).

   or

   ▲ In a grouped palette, click the Effect Controls tab (**Figure 11.41**).

   The Effect Controls palette appears, displaying the effects contained in the currently selected clip.

Figure 11.40 Choose Window > Show Effect Controls.

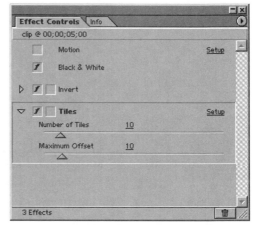

Figure 11.41 Click the palette's tab to bring it to the forefront of a window that contains more than one palette.

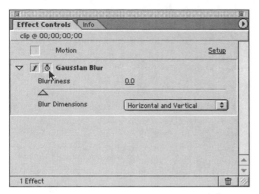

Figure 11.42 Click the box to the left of the effect's name so that the time-vary, or stopwatch, icon appears.

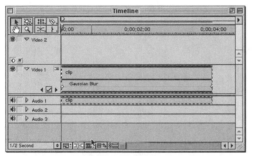

Figure 11.43 In the timeline, the clip containing the effect displays diamond starting and ending keyframe icons, and a keyframe navigator appears below the track name.

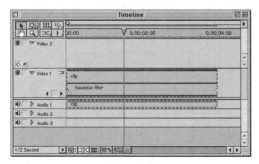

Figure 11.44 To create a new keyframe, position the edit line where no keyframes exist.

To animate an effect using keyframes:

1. Select the clip in the timeline that contains the effect you want to animate.

   In the clip, the first and last effect keyframes appear as rectangles. The effects applied to the clip appear in the Effect Controls palette.

2. In the Effect Controls palette, click the box to the left of the effect's name so that the time-vary, or stopwatch, icon appears (**Figure 11.42**).

   The stopwatch icon ⏱ appears, activating the keyframing process. In the timeline, the clip containing the effect displays diamond starting and ending keyframe icons, and a keyframe navigator appears below the track name (**Figure 11.43**).

3. Position the edit line at the point in the clip at which you want to set keyframe values:

   ▲ To create a new keyframe, position the edit line where no keyframes exist; in the keyframe navigator, no check appears (**Figure 11.44**).

   Watch the current frame of the clip in the program view of the Monitor window.

   continues on next page

4. To set a keyframe, *do either of the following:*

▲ To set a keyframe using a new value, set the value by using controls in the Effect Controls palette (**Figure 11.45**).

or

▲ To set a keyframe without changing the value at that frame, check the box in the keyframe navigator (**Figure 11.46**).

The value of a keyframe created by checking the box in the keyframe navigator is based on the previously interpolated value for that frame.

5. To create additional keyframes, repeat steps 3 and 4.

6. To see the effect animate, position the work-area bar over the clip, and press Return (Mac) or Enter (Windows).

For a complete explanation of previewing effects, see Chapter 9.

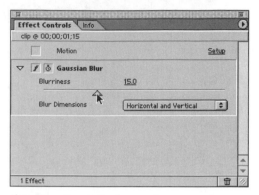

Figure 11.45 To set a keyframe using a new value, set the value by using controls in the Effect Controls palette.

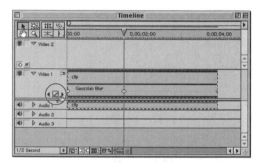

Figure 11.46 To set a keyframe without changing the value at that frame, check the box in the keyframe navigator. No matter how you create a keyframe, a diamond appears in the clip.

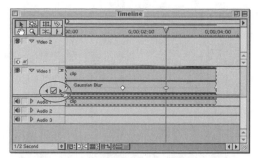

Figure 11.47 Use the keyframe-navigator buttons to cue the edit line to the next or previous keyframe in the selected clip. When the edit line is on a keyframe, a check appears between the cue buttons.

Modifying Effect Keyframes

After you set keyframes, you can adjust their values or their position in time. You must cue the edit line to a keyframe before you can adjust it.

To cue to keyframes:

1. Select a clip containing effects, and position the edit line somewhere in the clip.

   If the clip contains effect keyframes, a keyframe navigator appears next to the track name.

2. In the keyframe navigator, click either of the following (**Figure 11.47**):

   ▶—cues the edit line to the next keyframe in the selected clip.

   ◀—cues the edit line to the previous keyframe in the selected clip.

   When the edit line is cued to a keyframe, a check appears in the keyframe navigator. Adjusting an effect's settings when cued to a keyframe adjusts the settings at the keyframe.

To modify values at a keyframe:

1. To cue the edit line to a keyframe, *do either of the following*:

   ▲ In the keyframe navigator, click the previous keyframe or next keyframe button.

   or

   ▲ Click the keyframe in the clip.

   The edit line is cued to the keyframe, and the keyframe navigator displays a check.

2. Change the property values for the effect at the current keyframe by using the controls in the Effect Controls palette (**Figure 11.48**).

   See "Adjusting Effect Settings" earlier in this chapter. The current keyframe uses the property values you specify.

To move a keyframe in time:

◆ In a clip containing an effect, drag a keyframe to the left or right to change its position in time (**Figure 11.49**).

   The edit line stays cued to the keyframe. You can view the current frame in the program view of the Monitor window.

✔ Tip

■ Though you can't delete the start and end keyframes, you can move them. The frames of the clip before the start keyframe and after the end keyframe will appear with no effect applied. It's as though you applied the effect to only one part of the clip.

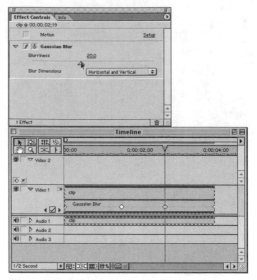

Figure 11.48 With the edit line cued to a keyframe, change its settings by using the controls in the Effect Controls palette.

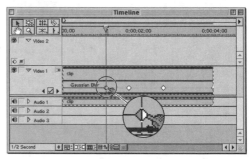

Figure 11.49 To move the keyframe's position in time, drag it to the left or right.

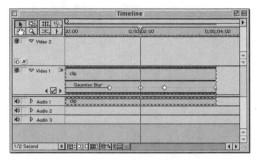

Figure 11.50 Cue the edit line to a keyframe.

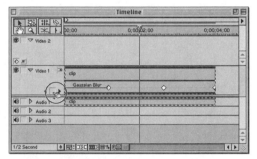

Figure 11.51 In the keyframe navigator, click the checkbox to remove the check and the keyframe.

Removing Keyframes

You can remove a single keyframe from an effect or remove the animation altogether. When you remove the animation, the effect's keyframes disappear, and the effect uses a single set of property values taken from the first keyframe.

To delete a keyframe:

1. To cue the edit line to a keyframe, *do either of the following*:

   ▲ In the keyframe navigator, click the previous keyframe or next keyframe button.

   or

   ▲ Click the keyframe in the clip.

   The edit line is cued to the keyframe, and the keyframe navigator displays a check in the box (**Figure 11.50**).

2. In the keyframe navigator, click the checkbox to remove the check and the keyframe (**Figure 11.51**).

   The keyframe is removed, and the effect's property values are reinterpolated based on the existing keyframes.

To remove animation:

1. Select a clip containing an animated effect (**Figure 11.52**).

2. In the Effect Controls palette, click the time-vary (stopwatch) icon to deactivate it (**Figure 11.53**).

   The icon appears deactivated, and the effect is set to the values used by the first keyframe (**Figure 11.54**).

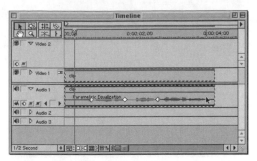

Figure 11.52 Select a clip containing an animated effect.

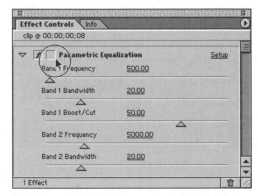

Figure 11.53 In the Effect Controls palette, click the time-vary (stopwatch) icon to deactivate it.

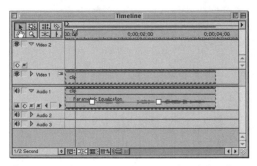

Figure 11.54 The animation is removed, and the clip uses a single set of values based on the first keyframe.

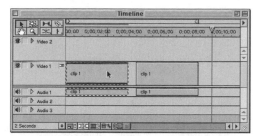

Figure 11.55 Select a clip containing effects (or fade, transparency, or motion settings), and press ⌘-Ⓒ (Mac) or Ctrl-Ⓒ (Windows).

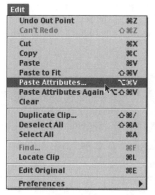

Figure 11.56 Select the clip to which you want to paste the copied effects, and choose Edit > Paste Attributes.

Copying and Pasting Effects

If you spend a lot of time tweaking an effect, you might flinch at the prospect of doing it all over again for another clip or, worse, a lot of clips. Fortunately, you can duplicate even a complex effect by copying it from one clip and pasting it to another. The Paste Attributes command works not only for effects, but also for any combination of fade controls, transparency settings, and motion settings.

To copy effects from one clip to another:

1. In the timeline, select a clip containing the effects you want to copy (**Figure 11.55**).

   You can also copy any combination of its fade control keyframes, transparency settings, and motion settings.

2. Choose Edit > Copy or press ⌘-Ⓒ (Mac) or Ctrl-Ⓒ (Windows).

3. Select the clip to which you want to paste the copied effects.

4. Choose Edit > Paste Attributes (**Figure 11.56**).

   The Paste Attributes dialog box appears.

   continues on next page

5. Select the Settings radio button, and check the attributes of the copied clip you want to paste to the selected clip (**Figure 11.57**).

Check Filters to paste effects to the selected clip.

6. Click OK to close the dialog box and paste the attributes.

The selected clip contains the pasted attributes. The clip displays a thin blue line, indicating that it contains effects (**Figure 11.58**).

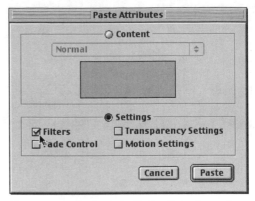

Figure 11.57 In the Paste Attributes dialog box, select the Settings radio button, and check the attributes of the copied clip you want to paste to the selected clip.

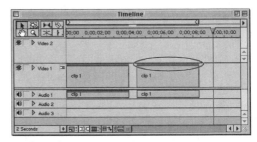

Figure 11.58 The clip displays a thin blue line, indicating that it contains effects.

12

CREATING TITLES

Although Premiere accepts files created with other applications, it also has its own powerful tool, the title window, for creating text and graphics. In the title window, you can create graphics that include straight lines, shapes, or text in any font available on your computer. You can easily manipulate the color, transparency, and arrangement of these objects; apply a drop shadow; or include an alpha channel so that you can superimpose the title over other clips. If you need to change any element, you can simply reopen the title, edit it, and save the new version.

Though Premiere has evolved considerably since earlier versions, the title window has required few changes. In fact, the title window hasn't changed at all since version 5, which introduced a feature to create title rolls and crawls. If you haven't used Premiere since version 4, you'll be happy to find that you no longer need to use motion settings or filters to create these common effects.

Admittedly, Premiere's title window may not offer the extensive control of a dedicated graphics program such as Adobe Illustrator, but it does share one important characteristic with its more full-featured siblings. Like Illustrator, Premiere creates object-oriented, or vector-based, graphics. This means objects can be scaled to any output size without an apparent loss of quality.

Unlike some of the other images you create within Premiere, such as color mattes or a counting leader, titles are independent files, which you save separately from your project. As you can with other source files, you can open more than one title window at a time, and you can import the same titles into any project. After you import them and add them to the Timeline, titles can be edited just like any other clips.

The Title Window and Menus

Whenever you create or change a title clip, it opens in a title window. This window includes a drawing area and a set of tools for creating and editing text and graphics (**Figure 12.1**). When the title window is active, a Title menu appears in the menu bar (**Figure 12.2**). Like the other windows, the title window has options that you can access through the Windows menu or a contextual menu.

Figure 12.2 When a title window is active, a Title menu appears in the menu bar.

Figure 12.1 The title window includes a drawing area and its own set of tools for creating and editing text and graphics.

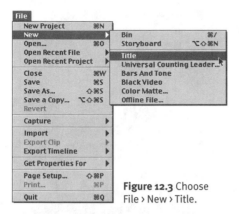

Figure 12.3 Choose File > New > Title.

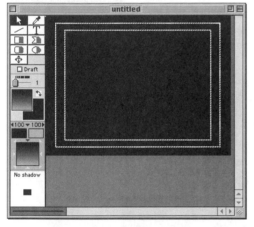

Figure 12.4 An untitled title window appears.

Figure 12.5 Click the new item button.

Creating a New Title

You can create a new title by choosing a menu command or by clicking the Create Item button in the Project window. Don't forget that although you generate titles within Premiere, you save them as independent files, separate from your project file.

To create a new title with a menu command:

◆ Choose File > New > Title (**Figure 12.3**).

An untitled title window appears (**Figure 12.4**).

To create a new title with the Create Item button:

1. In the Project window, click the new item button 🔲 (**Figure 12.5**).

The Create dialog box opens.

2. In the Create dialog box, choose Title from the pull-down menu (**Figure 12.6**).

3. Click OK.

An untitled title window appears (**Figure 12.4**).

Figure 12.6 In the Create dialog box, choose Title from the pull-down menu.

To save a new title:

1. Select an open title window (**Figure 12.7**).

2. Choose File > Save As (**Figure 12.8**).
   The Save File As dialog box appears (**Figure 12.9**).

3. Specify a location and name for the title, and click Save.
   The title appears in the current bin of the Project window.

✔ Tip

■ If you make changes to a title and save it, you won't be prompted for a name and location; the new version is saved over the old version. To save different versions, choose File > Save As.

Figure 12.7 Select an open title window.

Figure 12.8 Choose File > Save As.

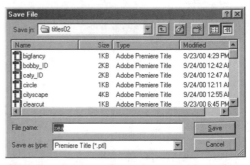

Figure 12.9 In the Save File As dialog box, specify a name and location for the title file, and click Save.

Figure 12.10 Select an open title window, and choose Clip > Add Clip to Project...

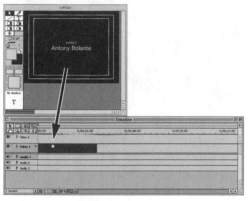

Figure 12.11 ... or drag the title window to an empty area of a video track in the timeline.

Adding Titles to a Project

When you create and save a new title while a project is open, Premiere adds the title to the current bin automatically. Otherwise, you have to add titles actively to the current project. In other words, just because a title window is open doesn't mean that it's part of the current project. Like other independent source files, titles aren't part of the project unless they are listed in the Project window.

To add the title to the current project:

Do one of the following:

◆ Select an open title window, and choose Clip > Add Clip to Project (**Figure 12.10**).

◆ Select an open title window, and press ⌘-J (Mac) or Ctrl-J (Windows).

◆ Drag the title window to the Project or Timeline window (**Figure 12.11**).

◆ Choose File > Import > File, and select the title file to import it.

The initial duration of the title is determined by the default still-image duration (see "To Set the Default Duration of Still Images" in Chapter 4).

✔ Tips

■ When you drag a title to a bin, a project, or the timeline, ⌘-drag to avoid selecting any of the objects contained in the title accidentally.

■ Keep your project and source files organized. On the hard drive, keep titles stored in a separate folder; in the Premiere project, keep titles in their own bin.

ADDING TITLES TO A PROJECT

333

Modifying Titles

When you want to change the content of a title in any way, you can simply open and resave it. You could also modify a title to save several titles that have a similar design, such as an onscreen identification. Unlike other clips, reopening a title always opens a title window, never the source view of the Monitor window.

Be aware that the changes you make to a title are changes to a source file, not just a single instance of the title in the project. Whatever changes you save appear in every instance of the title in the project and timeline. If another project uses the same title, it also reflects the changes.

To modify and save a title:

1. *Do either of the following:*
   - ▲ To open a title that's already in the project, double-click the title in the Project or Timeline window (**Figure 12.12**).

   or

   - ▲ To open a title that's not part of the current project, choose File > Open, select the title, and click Open.

   The title window appears (**Figure 12.13**).

2. Make changes to the objects in the title window (**Figure 12.14**).

3. *Do either of the following:*
   - ▲ To save the title with the changes, choose File > Save.

   or

   - ▲ To save another version of the title as a separate file, choose File > Save As.

   If you choose File > Save As, the Save File As dialog box appears. In the Save File As dialog box, specify a name and location for the title file, and click OK.

4. If necessary, add the title to the project.

Figure 12.12 To open a title, double-click it in the Project window, or double-click any instance of it in the Timeline window.

Figure 12.13 The title opens in a title window.

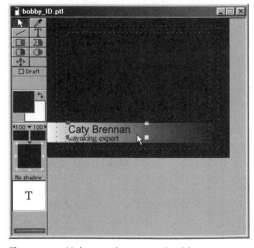

Figure 12.14 Make any changes to the title.

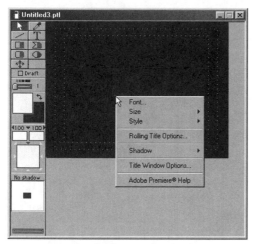

Figure 12.15 Control-click (Mac) or right-click (Windows) the title window to open a contextual menu. This menu provides quick access to many commands, including the title window options.

Title Window Options

Because they are tucked away in the Window menu, the title window options can be easy to overlook. Nevertheless, they control several important attributes of a title. The title window options control the size and aspect ratio of the title's drawing space, the video safe zones and colors, the background color, and whether the background will be opaque or transparent. The following sections explain the title window options and how to set them.

✔ Tip

- The following sections explain how to access the title window options from the menu bar. You might prefer to use a contextual menu to access these options and other title-related commands. Control-click (Mac) or right-click (Windows) the title window to open the contextual menu (**Figure 12.15**).

Drawing Space and Aspect Ratio

The drawing space determines the pixel dimensions of the title clip. When you add the title to the program, Premiere automatically scales it to fit the screen dimensions you set for the video settings (see "Specifying Video Settings" in Chapter 2).

The drawing area of the title window and the size of the program's video don't necessarily need to match, however. Objects that you create in the title window are vector-based, so Premiere can scale a title to the output size without making the edges look jagged (**Figures 12.16** and **12.17**).

Although scaling a title up to a larger size doesn't adversely affect its resolution, scaling a title to a different aspect ratio does distort it (**Figures 12.18** and **12.19**).

In addition to matching the image aspect ratio of the video—4:3 for standard video—titles should match the pixel aspect ratio of the video format. The title window options include a pull-down menu to ensure that the aspect ratio of the title matches the standard you're using. (For more information about screen size and pixel aspect ratios, see Chapter 2. For additional technical grounding, see Chapter 18.)

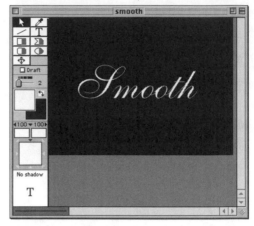

Figure 12.16 Because title objects are vector-based, creating a title at 320 x 240 ...

Figure 12.17 ... looks just as good after Premiere scales it to output size, 640 x 480.

Figure 12.18 Discrepancies in aspect ratios can result in distortion. This title uses DV's standard pixel size, but not the proper pixel aspect ratio ...

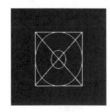

Figure 12.19 ... and the title appears distorted when scaled to the project's frame aspect ratio and pixel aspect ratio.

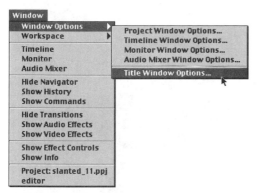

Figure 12.20 Choose Window > Window Options > Title Window Options.

Figure 12.21 Enter the pixel dimensions for the title's drawing space.

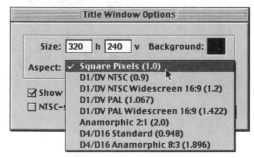

Figure 12.22 Choose the appropriate pixel aspect ratio from the Aspect pull-down menu.

To set the drawing space size and aspect ratio for a title:

1. With a title window active, choose Window > Window Options > Title Window Options (**Figure 12.20**). The Title Window Options dialog box appears.

2. Type the horizontal (h) and vertical (v) dimensions of the title window, expressed in pixels (**Figure 12.21**).

3. To ensure that the title clip doesn't become distorted when added to the program, choose the pixel aspect ratio that matches your project (see "Specifying Video Settings" in Chapter 2) from the Aspect pull-down menu (**Figure 12.22**). Premiere recalculates the horizontal and vertical values according to the pixel aspect ratio you selected.

4. Click OK to close the Title Window Options dialog box.

✔ Tips

- You may be wondering: "If title objects are vector-based and scalable, why should I worry about pixels at all?" You should because when a title is scaled to the display size, it's *rasterized*—converted to a bitmapped, pixel-based image. Premiere needs to know what standard to use when rasterizing the image.

- Effects (Chapter 11) and motion settings (Chapter 14) manipulate the rasterized title. This means that scaling up a title with an effect or motion setting can reveal pixel-based artifacts, such as aliasing and blockiness.

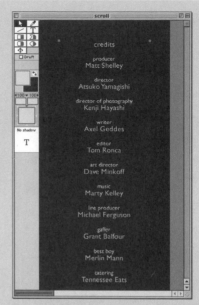

Figure 12.23 Before Premiere 5, you could make a title roll by creating a tall title ...

Thinking Outside the Box: Making Titles Tall or Wide

To avoid distorted titles, you typically set the image aspect ratio of your titles to match that of the video program (usually 4:3). However, titles with other aspect ratios—very tall or wide titles—can be used in conjunction with Image Pan to create some useful effects.

If you used Premiere before version 5, you may remember that you can create title rolls by typing the screen credits in a drawing area many times taller than the video output screen (**Figure 12.23**). Applying the image pan effect allowed you to move the visible area of the video down the length of the title, removing distortion and rolling the title up the screen (**Figure 12.24**).

Even though the title window now includes features that create title rolls and crawls, this old technique can still be put to good use. You can, for example, use the title window's graphic-creation tools to create a wide background and then use the image pan effect to pan across it to create a simple animation (**Figure 12.25**).

When you use this technique, you should still set the title's pixel aspect ratio to match that of your program.

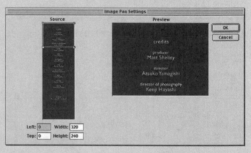

Figure 12.24 ... and applying the image pan effect to pan down the title.

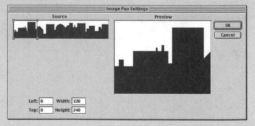

Figure 12.25 The same technique can be applied to other purposes. Here, Image Pan is used with a wide title (on the left) to create a moving backdrop image of a cityscape (on the right).

Figure 12.26 Just as you can display action-safe and title-safe zones in the Monitor window ...

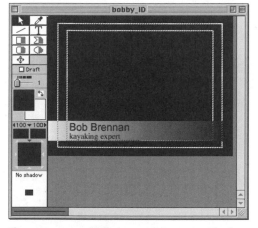

Figure 12.27 ... you can also use safe-zone guides in the title window.

Creating Titles for Television

As you recall from Chapter 3, standard television monitors overscan the image, cropping off the outer edges. For this reason, the Monitor window can display NTSC *safe zones*: reference marks indicating the areas of the screen that are considered to be action-safe and title-safe (**Figure 12.26**). It's only logical that the title window also display guides to help you keep the titles you create within the title-safe zone (**Figure 12.27**).

The difference between how computers and television monitors display color is another important factor to consider when creating titles for television. A color that looks great on your computer screen may not be NTSC-safe and will appear "noisy" or "bleed" on television. Fortunately, Premiere can adjust the colors of titles destined for television automatically.

To set title window safe-zones and safe-colors options:

1. With a title window active, choose Window > Window Options > Title Window Options.

   The Title Window Options dialog box appears.

2. Check either of the following checkboxes (**Figure 12.28**):

   Show Safe Titles—display NTSC title-safe and action-safe guides.

   NTSC-Safe Colors—automatically shift the colors of the title that are outside NTSC color space into the NTSC color space when the title is rendered.

3. Click OK to close the Title Window Options dialog box.

✔ Tips

- For more information on NTSC safe zones, safe colors, and other technical considerations for video, consult Chapter 18.

- Clips other than titles can contain colors that are not NTSC-safe. The NTSC Safe Colors effect ensures that the video levels conform to broadcast specifications. For more about effects, see Chapter 11.

Figure 12.28 Choose whether to display safe zones and whether to automatically correct colors that are not NTSC-safe.

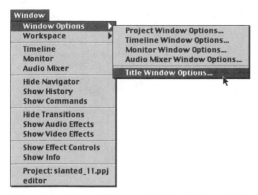

Figure 12.29 Choose Window > Window Options > Title Window Options.

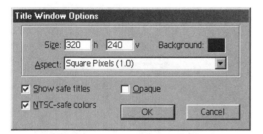

Figure 12.30 Click the color swatch to open the color picker and choose a background color.

Figure 12.31 Choose a background color from the color picker.

Background Color

You can set the background of a title to any color. But because the control is tucked away in the title window options, many new users end up clicking frantically at the various color swatches that appear in the title window itself. Now you know better.

If you plan to make the background transparent, refer to the following section, "Background Opacity," and take a look at "Superimposing Clips" in Chapter 13.

To set the background color for a title:

1. With a title window active, choose Window > Window Options > Title Window Options (**Figure 12.29**).
   The Title Window Options dialog box appears.

2. Click the color swatch rectangle (**Figure 12.30**).
   The Color Picker window appears.

3. In the color picker, choose a color for the title's background (**Figure 12.31**).

4. Click OK to close the color picker.
   You return to the Title Window Options dialog box.

5. Click OK to close the Title Window Options dialog box.

✔ Tips

- When the title window is active, you can press W to quickly change to a white background or B to change to a black background.

- The background color is always a flat, solid color. If you need a gradient for the title's background, create a filled rectangle to cover the background instead. You can apply a gradient to the rectangle. See the sections on creating graphic objects and gradients later in this chapter.

Background Opacity

The remaining title window option allows you to specify whether you want the title to have an opaque background color or whether you want to assign a transparency value, or *alpha channel*, to the background. As you will learn in Chapter 13, you can use the alpha channel to make the background transparent and superimpose the title over another clip.

To set the background opacity for a title:

1. With a title window active, choose Window > Window Options > Title Window Options (**Figure 12.32**).

    The Title Window Options dialog box appears.

2. *Do either of the following* (**Figure 12.33**):

    ▲ To make the background color opaque, check the Opaque checkbox.

    or

    ▲ To enable the background as an alpha channel, leave the Opaque checkbox unchecked.

3. Click OK to close the Title Window Options dialog box.

    The Opacity setting isn't apparent in the title window itself. Unchecking the Opacity checkbox simply assigns a transparency value—or alpha channel— to the background. The background appears transparent in the program view only after an alpha channel key type has been applied to the title. For more information, see "Alpha Channel Key Types" in Chapter 13.

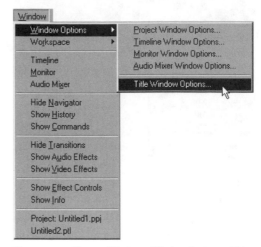

Figure 12.32 Choose Window › Window Options › Title Window Options.

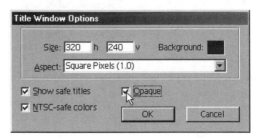

Figure 12.33 Check the Opaque checkbox to use an opaque background color; leave the box unchecked if you are going to superimpose the title over another clip (explained in Chapter 13).

✔ Tip

■ If you intend to make the background color transparent (by unchecking the Opaque checkbox), set the background color to black or white. This setting makes it easier to superimpose titles later. See "Black and White Alpha Matte Keys" in Chapter 13.

Figure 12.34 Choose Clip > Mark > 0 in the frame you want to use as the background in the title window.

Figure 12.35 Drag from the image area of the clip to the drawing space of the title window.

Figure 12.36 When you release the mouse button, the frame of the clip marked zero appears in the background of the title window.

Background Clips

If you plan to superimpose a title over another clip, you can use a representative frame from the clip as the background in the title window. The background frame gives you an idea of how the title will look when you superimpose it over the actual clip in the Timeline. This way, you can design the title more confidently, adjusting the colors and placement of elements so that it works well with the clip in the background.

The background frame itself isn't saved as part of the title; it's merely a helpful reference, which you can use or remove at any time.

You can designate the frame of the video clip you want to use as a background by setting the zero marker on that frame. Otherwise, the first frame of the clip serves as the background frame.

To use a background clip:

1. Open the title window that you plan to superimpose over a clip.

2. Open the clip that you plan to use as the background.

3. Cue the clip to the frame you want to use as a background frame in a title window.

4. Choose Clip > Mark > 0 to set the frame as the background frame (**Figure 12.34**).

5. Drag the frame of the clip into an open title window (**Figure 12.35**).

6. When the border of the drawing area highlights, release the mouse button.

   The frame marked zero appears in the background of the title as a reference (**Figure 12.36**).

To remove a background clip:

◆ With a title window that uses a background clip active, choose Title > Remove Background Clip (**Figure 12.37**).

The background clip disappears from the title window, revealing the current background color.

✔ Tips

■ To change the background frame, simply move the zero marker to a different frame of the clip.

■ Use the title window's eyedropper tool 🖉 to load colors from the background clip into the foreground or shadow color. See the section "Other Ways to Choose Colors" later in this chapter.

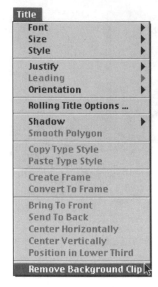

Figure 12.37 With a title window that uses a background clip active, choose Title > Remove Background Clip.

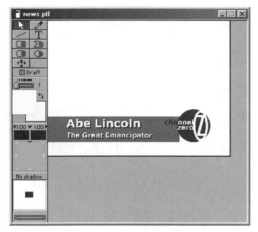

Figure 12.38 Check the Draft checkbox to display objects faster, but at lower quality ...

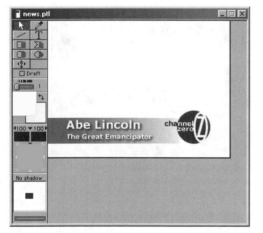

Figure 12.39 ... or leave Draft unchecked to view objects at full quality.

✔ Tip

■ If your titles fail to display semitransparent objects, smooth antialiased edges, or soft drop shadows, don't panic and start messing with your system. You might just be working in draft mode.

Objects and Attributes

The following sections explain how to create text and graphic objects. Each object you create can have its own set of properties, or attributes—such as color, opacity, line weight, and font. In the following sections, the attributes unique to each kind of object—text and graphics—are addressed first. Later sections deal with attributes that are relevant to both text and graphics.

You can set most attributes before or after you create an object. If you want to change the attributes of an object, make sure it's selected. A bounding box with selection handles appears around a selected object. If you want to set the attributes first without affecting existing objects, make sure no objects are selected.

Draft Mode

By default, the title window displays objects at full quality, also known as *preview mode*. If the title window displays and updates objects slowly, however, you can work in draft mode. *Draft mode* displays text and graphic objects faster but at lower quality. In draft mode, the title window doesn't display smooth edges, soft drop shadows, or transparency. Draft mode affects only the display of the title window, not the final output.

To use draft mode to increase display speed:

◆ Check the Draft checkbox in the tools area of the title window to display objects in draft mode (**Figure 12.38**).

Uncheck the Draft checkbox to display the objects at full quality, known as preview mode (**Figure 12.39**).

Text Objects

You can create text objects containing any font available on your computer, including PostScript and TrueType fonts. The font must be loaded and available on the computer whenever you open the title window.

Attributes unique to text objects include font, size, style, justification, and orientation. You can also precisely control the spaces between characters (called *kerning*) and between lines of text (called *leading*).

To create a text object:

1. Select the type tool T (**Figure 12.40**).

2. Click anywhere in the drawing space to position the top-left corner of the text object.

   A blinking insertion point appears, indicating that you are in text-editing mode and able to type text.

3. Type the text you want to use (**Figure 12.41**).

4. When you finish typing, click an empty area of the title window to exit text-editing mode.

   The text object is selected and uses the current attributes, such as font, style, size, and color. You can change these attributes at any time (**Figure 12.42**).

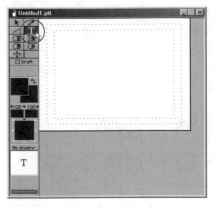

Figure 12.40 Select the type tool.

Figure 12.41 When the insertion point appears, type the text you want.

Figure 12.42 Click an empty area of the title window to exit text-editing mode. The text object appears selected.

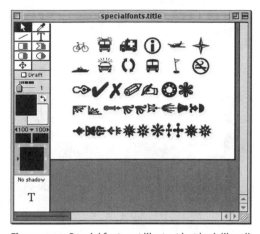

Figure 12.43 Special fonts act like text but look like all sorts of complex shapes and symbols.

✔ Tips

- Not all fonts look like letters. By loading special fonts—often called symbols, ornaments, and dingbats—you can create useful graphic elements easily. You use these fonts just like other fonts, and you don't have to draw a thing (**Figure 12.43**).

- If you have more fonts than you care to have appear in the Font menu, you should turn to a font-management utility, such as Suitcase (by 5th Generation Systems, Inc.) or Master Juggler.

- A more complete discussion of fonts and typesetting could fill books—and has. A great place to start learning more about fonts is *How to Boss Your Fonts Around*, by Robin Williams (Peachpit Press). Ms. Williams has written several other great titles about fonts, typesetting, and design.

TEXT OBJECTS

Selecting Text

You can set most text attributes before you create a text object. But if you want to edit text that is already in the title window (or modify its other attributes), you must first select all or part of the text.

To select text for editing:

1. To select text, *do any of the following:*
   ▲ Using the selection tool, click the text object to select the entire text object (**Figure 12.44**).
   ▲ Using the selection tool, double-click the text object to quickly switch to the type tool and set an insertion point (**Figure 12.45**).
   ▲ Using the type tool T, click the text object to position the insertion point in the text.
   ▲ Using the type tool, drag to select a range of text (**Figure 12.46**).

2. Type to change the selected text, or insert text at the insertion point. You can also change other attributes of selected text, such as font, size, and color. See the section "Font, Style and Size" later in this chapter.

3. When you finish making changes to the text, click an empty area of the title window to exit text-editing mode.

✔ Tip

■ You can use the left and right arrow keys to move the insertion point.

Figure 12.44 You can click the text object to select the entire text object ...

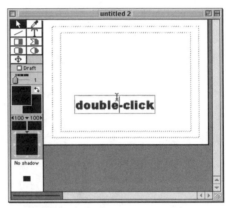

Figure 12.45 ... double-click to switch to the text tool and set an insertion point ...

Figure 12.46 ... or drag with the type tool to select a range of text.

Figure 12.47 Select text so that its bounding box appears.

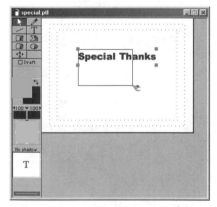

Figure 12.48 Drag a handle to resize the bounding box.

Figure 12.49 The text reflows to fit the resized bounding box.

The Text Bounding Box

When you select an entire text object, its bounding box appears. The *bounding box* consists of four corner handles; it indicates the confines in which text can appear. The right side of the bounding box works like the right margin in a word processing program; it causes what is known as a *soft return*, forcing the text to create a new line. For this reason, it's often necessary to resize the bounding box to accommodate the text it contains—after you add text or increase the font size, for example.

To resize the text bounding box:

1. Click a text object to select it.

   Four corner handles appear, representing the bounding box for the text (**Figure 12.47**).

2. Drag any of the handles to change the size of the text object's bounding box (**Figure 12.48**).

   The text in the box reflows to accommodate the size of the bounding box (**Figure 12.49**).

✔ Tip

■ Resizing the bounding box reflows only lines of text created by soft returns. *Hard returns*—new lines created by pressing (Return) (Mac) or (Enter) (Windows)—are not affected by resizing the bounding box.

Stretching Text

The following section, "Font, Style, and Size," explains how to use common menu commands to change the size of text by discrete point size increments. You can also resize text by dragging. Stretching permits you to resize the horizontal and vertical aspects of the text by different amounts, but you won't be able to reverse or flip text.

To stretch type:

1. Select a text object.

   Four corner handles appear, representing the bounding box for the text (**Figure 12.50**).

2. **Option**-drag (Mac) or **Alt**-drag (Windows) any of the handles to stretch the vertical and horizontal scale of the text object.

   The cursor becomes the stretch tool ⊹ as you drag (**Figure 12.51**). When you release the mouse button, the text appears with different horizontal and vertical scaling (**Figure 12.52**).

✔ Tips

- Though the title window's tools are extensive, you can't use them to reverse, flip, tilt, skew, or rotate objects, or make them follow a curved path. You can expand your possibilities, however, by using titles in conjunction with motion settings (Chapter 14) and effects (Chapter 11). For more complete control, you may need to turn to one of Adobe's other image-editing and animation tools, such as Illustrator, Photoshop, or After Effects.

- Premiere 4.1.2 included a text animation feature. Search as you might, you won't find it in Premiere 5 or 6. Though this feature was a great way to scale text over time, you can achieve similar results with some extra planning and the motion settings feature (Chapter 14).

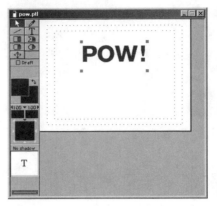

Figure 12.50 Select the text object you want to stretch.

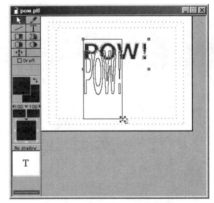

Figure 12.51 **Option**-drag (Mac) or **Alt**-drag (Windows) a handle to stretch the text.

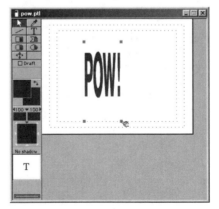

Figure 12.52 When you release the mouse button, the text appears with different proportions—in this case, much taller and narrower than before.

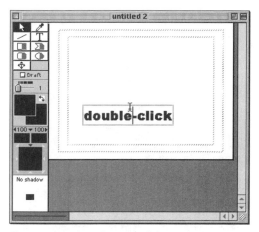

Figure 12.53 Select all or part of the text in a text object, or select multiple text objects.

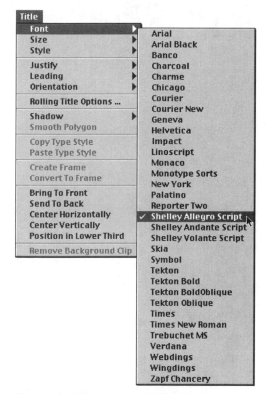

Figure 12.54 With all or part of the text selected, choose a new font from the Title > Font submenu.

Font, Style, and Size

You can modify a text object's font, style and point size in much the same way that you would in other graphics and word processing programs.

To set font, style, and size:

1. *Do either of the following:*
   ▲ Select all or part of the text in a single object (**Figure 12.53**).

   or

   ▲ Select more than one text object.

2. Choose any of the following:

   Title > Font—select a font for any selected text and any new text (**Figure 12.54**).

   continues on next page

Title > Size—select a point size for any selected text and any new text (**Figure 12.55**).

Title > Style—check any styles you want to apply to selected text and any new text (**Figure 12.56**).

The selected text acquires the attributes you specified (**Figure 12.57**).

3. Click an empty area of the title window to deselect the text.

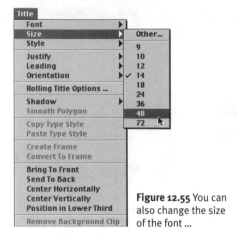

Figure 12.55 You can also change the size of the font ...

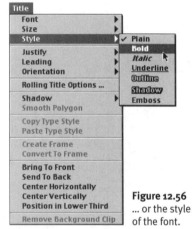

Figure 12.56 ... or the style of the font.

Figure 12.57 The selected text acquires the attributes you specified.

FONT, STYLE, AND SIZE

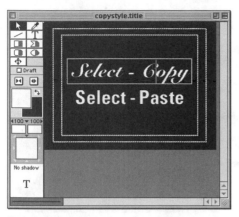

Figure 12.58 Place the insertion point in the text that has the attributes you want to copy.

Figure 12.59 Choose Title > Copy Type Style.

Copying Text Attributes

Premiere's title window also allows you to copy the attributes from one range of text or text object to another. This feature can be useful for matching a text style quickly, without revisiting many menu commands.

To copy attributes from one range of text to another:

1. Double-click a text object to enter text-editing mode, and place the insertion point in the text that has the attributes you want to copy (**Figure 12.58**).

   See the section "Selecting Text" earlier in this chapter.

2. Choose Title > Copy Type Style (**Figure 12.59**).

   continues on next page

3. Select the characters of the text to which you want to copy the attributes (**Figure 12.60**).

4. Choose Title > Paste Type Style.

Attributes (font, size, color, etc.) are copied to the selected text (**Figure 12.61**).

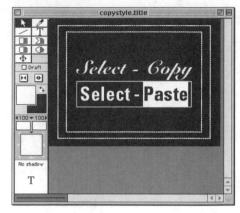

Figure 12.60 Select the range of text to which you want to paste the style.

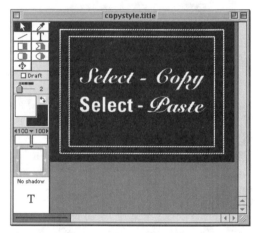

Figure 12.61 The text takes on the attributes of the text you copied earlier.

Figure 12.62 Position the insertion point in the line of text you want to justify.

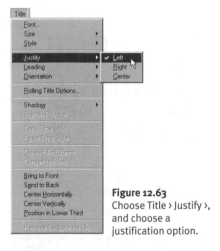

Figure 12.63
Choose Title > Justify >, and choose a justification option.

Figure 12.64 All three lines of text are centered horizontally but justified differently: left, center, and right.

Justifying Text

As in many graphics and text-editing programs, the text you create in Premiere's title window can be justified left, center, or right. Note that the text is justified within its bounding box, not within the title window itself. For more information about positioning an object in respect to the drawing area, see the section "Moving Objects" later in this chapter.

To justify text in the text object's bounding box:

1. Position the insertion point in the line of text you want to justify (**Figure 12.62**).

2. Choose one of the following (**Figure 12.63**):

   Title > Justify > Left—to position the line of text flush left in the bounding box.

   Title > Justify > Right—to position the line of text flush right in the bounding box.

   Title > Justify > Center—to center the text horizontally in the bounding box.

   The selected text object is justified within its bounding box (**Figure 12.64**).

Orienting Text

Ordinarily, text flows horizontally within its bounding box (from left to right). You can orient the text vertically, so that it flows from the top of the bounding box to the bottom. Without vertical orientation, you would have to create vertical lines of text letter by letter. This feature is particularly useful for Chinese or Japanese characters, which are frequently presented vertically, from right to left.

To change text orientation:

1. Select a text object.

2. Choose either of the following (**Figure 12.65**):

   Title > Orientation > Horizontal— to orient the text horizontally from left to right.

   Title > Orientation > Vertical— to orient the text vertically from top to bottom, right to left.

   The selected text aligns according to your choice (**Figure 12.66**).

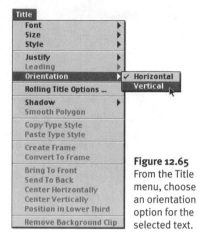

Figure 12.65
From the Title menu, choose an orientation option for the selected text.

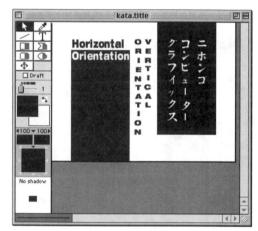

Figure 12.66 This title contains English text and Japanese characters oriented vertically.

Figure 12.67 In text-editing mode, kerning buttons appear in the title window's tool area, below the Draft checkbox.

Figure 12.68 Click the decrease kerning button to reduce the space between selected letters ...

Figure 12.69 ... or click the increase kerning button to increase the space between selected letters.

Kerning

Kerning is a typesetting term that describes the adjustment of space between two letters. The title window's kerning buttons allow you to adjust the spaces between two letters or a range of letters.

To adjust kerning:

1. *Do either of the following:*
   ▲ Select a range of characters in the text.
   or
   ▲ Position the insertion point between characters in a text object.

   Kerning buttons appear below the Draft checkbox (**Figure 12.67**).

2. *Do either of the following:*
   ▲ Click the decrease kerning button ◨ to move letters closer together (**Figure 12.68**).
   or
   ▲ Click the increase kerning button ◧ to move letters farther apart (**Figure 12.69**).

3. Click an empty area of the title window to exit text-editing mode.

✔ Tip

■ You can use easy keyboard shortcuts to kern text. Press Option-← (Mac) or Alt-← (Windows) to decrease kerning; press Option-→ (Mac) or Alt-→ (Windows) to increase kerning.

Leading

Leading (which rhymes with *wedding*) is a typesetting term that describes the space between lines of text. If a single title object contains more than one line of text, you can adjust the space between the lines.

To adjust leading:

1. Select a text object containing more than one line of text.

2. Choose one of the following (**Figure 12.70**):

    Title > Leading > More Leading— increases the space between lines (**Figure 12.71**).

    Title > Leading > Less Leading— decreases the space between lines (**Figure 12.72**).

    Title > Leading > Reset Leading— restores the default leading for the font.

✔ Tip

■ Unfortunately, Premiere has no buttons for adjusting leading, but you can use keyboard shortcuts. Press (Option)-(↓) (Mac) or (Alt)-(↓) (Windows) to increase leading; press (Option)-(↑) (Mac) or (Alt)-(↑) (Windows) to decrease leading.

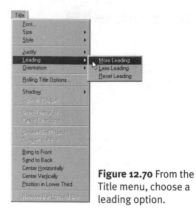

Figure 12.70 From the Title menu, choose a leading option.

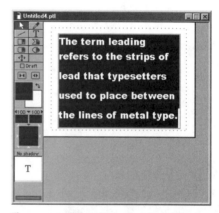

Figure 12.71 Choose Title > Leading > More Leading to increase the space between selected lines of text.

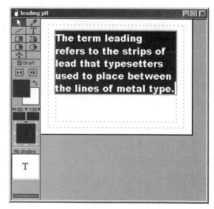

Figure 12.72 Choose Title > Leading > Less Leading to decrease the space between selected lines of text.

LEADING

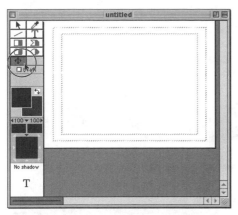

Figure 12.73 Select the rolling title tool.

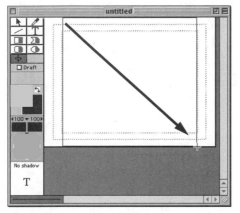

Figure 12.74 Drag in the drawing space to define the boundaries for the rolling or crawling text.

Figure 12.75 Type the text for the roll or crawl.

Rolls and Crawls

In a title *roll*, text appears to move from beyond the bottom of the screen to beyond the top of thc screen. Title rolls are frequently used in a final credit sequence or to present lengthy text on-screen.

A title *crawl* moves across the screen horizontally, typically from right to left. A news bulletin is a classic example of a title crawl. Sometimes, very large crawling type is used for a dramatic opening title (remember "*Rocky*"?).

Previous versions of Premiere required you to use motion settings or the image pan effect to create rolls or crawls. Now those features are built into the title window. Bear in mind, however, that you can roll or crawl only text, not graphic objects.

To create a text roll or crawl:

1. Select the rolling title tool ⟨Ṯ⟩ (**Figure 12.73**).

2. Drag in the drawing space to specify the area of the rolling text objcct (**Figure 12.74**).

   For a standard title roll, make the bounding box align with the top and bottom of the drawing space (not the title-safe zone). You can drag the bottom-right corner to resize the object at any time.

   For a standard crawl, make the bounding box align with the left and right edges of the drawing space and with the bottom of the title-safe zone.

3. Type the text for the roll or crawl (**Figure 12.75**).

   Press ⟨Return⟩ to create a new line or extra space for a roll; press the spacebar to create extra space for a crawl. Scroll bars allow you to scroll through the text that is visible within the bounding box.

   continues on next page

4. Click an empty area of the title window to exit text-editing mode.

The rolling or crawling title object appears selected. The size of the text object restricts how much of the text you can view at any time.

To preview rolls and crawls:

◆ Drag the slider in the bottom-left corner of the title window (**Figure 12.76**).

All rolling and crawling text objects play back as you drag. You cannot preview special timings by dragging the slider, however.

If the title uses a frame of a clip as a background, the clip containing the frame is used as the duration of the roll or crawl, and it plays back as you drag the slider.

✔ Tips

■ Previewing a roll or crawl in the title window gives you only an approximation of how it will look in the program. To see the final effect, add the title to the program and then preview it, using the methods explained in Chapter 8.

■ You can create more than one rolling or crawling text object in the same title window. You wouldn't do this for conventional credit rolls or crawls, but it could create an interesting effect. To control the timing of the rolls separately, however, you would have to create multiple text objects and layer them, as explained in Chapter 13.

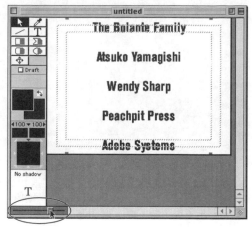

Figure 12.76 In the bottom left of the title window, drag the slider to preview the roll or crawl.

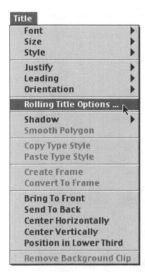

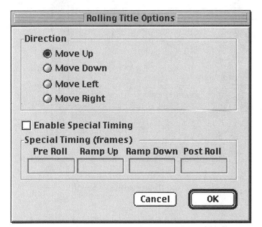

Figure 12.77 Select a rolling or crawling text object and then choose Title > Rolling Title Options.

Figure 12.78 In the Rolling Title Options dialog box, choose a direction for the roll or crawl, and specify any special timings you want to use.

Controlling Rolls and Crawls

By default, rolling text moves up the screen; crawling text moves to the left. Roll options allow you to roll or crawl a title in the opposite direction.

In addition, the roll options provide special timings, which allow you to more precisely control the motion of the title roll or crawl. Use special timings to make the text pause at the beginning and end of the roll. Special timings can also soften the beginning and ending of a roll or crawl, making it get up to speed and come to a halt more gradually.

To use special timings options:

1. Select a rolling or crawling text object.

2. Choose Title > Rolling Title Options (**Figure 12.77**).

   The Rolling Title Options dialog box appears (**Figure 12.78**).

3. In the Direction section of the dialog box, choose a direction for the type to move.

4. To gain more control of the motion, check the Enable Special Timings checkbox, and enter values for any of the following options:

   Pre Roll—the number of frames in which you want the text to appear motionless after the title's in point.

   Ramp Up—the number of frames the title will use to accelerate to full speed.

   Ramp Down—the number of frames the title will use to decelerate to a full stop.

   Post Roll—the number of frames in which you want the text to appear motionless until the title's out point.

5. Click OK to close the Rolling Title Options dialog box.

CONTROLLING ROLLS AND CRAWLS

Graphic Objects

The title window includes tools for creating graphic objects: straight lines, rectangles, ellipses, and polygons. You can create shapes that are framed (outlines only) or filled. You can control the thickness of lines and framed objects and specify whether polygons have sharp or rounded corners. As usual, you can change an object's position, shape, color, and other attributes at any time.

To create a straight line:

1. Select the line tool ✐ (**Figure 12.79**).

2. *Do either of the following:*
   ▲ Drag in the drawing space to draw a line of any angle or length (**Figure 12.80**).

   or

   ▲ [Shift]-drag to constrain the angle of the line to 45-degree increments.

To create a rectangle, round-cornered rectangle, or ellipse:

1. *Do either of the following:*
   ▲ Click the left side of a shape tool to create a framed shape.

   or

   ▲ Click the right side of the shape tool to create a filled shape (**Figure 12.81**).

Figure 12.79 Select the line tool.

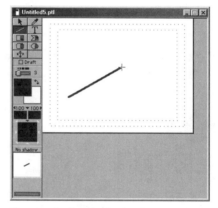

Figure 12.80 Drag in the drawing area to draw a straight line of any angle or length.

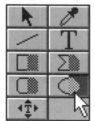

Figure 12.81 Click the left side of one of the shape tools to draw a framed shape, or click the right side to create a filled shape. Here, the filled oval tool is selected. Double-clicking a tool turns its background black and prevents Premiere from reverting to the selection tool automatically.

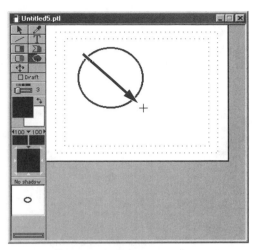

Figure 12.82 Drag in the drawing area to draw the shape from one corner to the opposite corner.

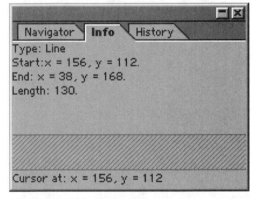

Figure 12.83 The Info palette displays exact information about the objects in the title window.

2. *Do either of the following:*

▲ Drag in the drawing area to draw the shape (**Figure 12.82**).

or

▲ [Shift]-drag to constrain the dimensions to perfect circles, squares, or squares with rounded corners.

Dragging draws the shape from one corner to the opposite corner.

✔ Tips

■ After you use a tool, the currently selected tool automatically reverts to the selection tool. To keep the same tool selected for multiple uses, double-click the tool so that its background turns black instead of the normal gray.

■ Check the Info palette to see information on the exact size and position of the objects you create in the title window (**Figure 12.83**).

■ Unlike some graphics programs, holding down the [Option] (Mac) or [Alt] (Windows) key while you draw has no effect. Specifically, it doesn't allow you to draw the shape from the center.

To create a polygon:

1. *Do either of the following:*

   ▲ Click the left side of the polygon tool to create a framed polygon.

   or

   ▲ Click the right side of the polygon tool ∑▓ to create a filled polygon.

2. Position the polygon tool in the drawing area, and click to create the first corner point of the shape.

   A line segment connects the corner point to the polygon tool.

3. Position the polygon tool, and click to set the next corner point.

4. Repeat steps 2 and 3 until you are ready to set the last corner point.

5. *Do either of the following:*

   ▲ Click the first corner point to close the shape (**Figure 12.84**).

   A dot appears next to the polygon tool to indicate that it is positioned over the first point.

   or

   ▲ Double-click to place the last point and create an open framed shape (**Figure 12.85**).

   You cannot leave a filled polygon open.

Figure 12.84 Click to create corner points on the polygon, and click the last point to close the shape.

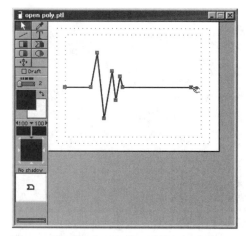

Figure 12.85 If you're creating a framed polygon, you can double-click the last point to leave the shape open. You can use the polygon tool to make a line on a graph.

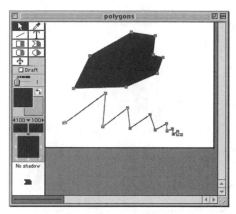

Figure 12.86 Select one or more polygon objects. They can be open or closed shapes.

Figure 12.87 Choose Title > Smooth Polygon.

To smooth a polygon:

1. Select a polygon object (**Figure 12.86**).

2. Choose Title > Smooth Polygon (**Figure 12.87**).

   The selected polygons toggle from sharp corners to smoothed corners (**Figure 12.88**).

✔ Tip

■ The title tool doesn't include Bézier control handles or a full-featured pen tool. Make those shapes in Illustrator, and import them into Premiere.

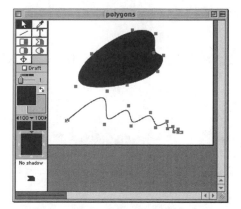

Figure 12.88 The sharp corners are smoothed.

To reshape a graphic object:

1. With the selection tool, click a shape to select it.

2. Position the mouse pointer over the shape's handle until the finger pointer 🖑 appears.

3. Drag the handle to resize the object, reposition a corner of a polygon, or move one end of a line (**Figure 12.89**).

   Release the mouse button to modify the shape (**Figure 12.90**).

✔ Tips

- ⎡Shift⎤-drag to constrain the dimensions of a shape or the angle of a line.

- You can select and move the corner points of a polygon, even if you have selected smooth corners.

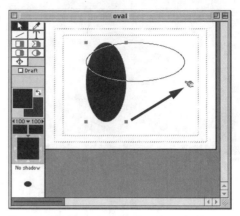

Figure 12.89 Drag a handle of a selected object ...

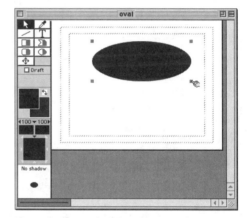

Figure 12.90 ... and release the mouse button to change its shape.

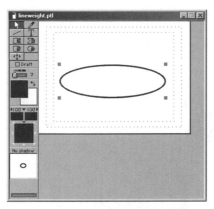

Figure 12.91 Select a line or framed object.

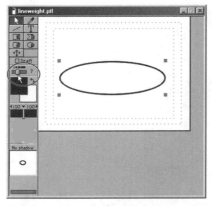

Figure 12.92 Drag the line-weight slider to set the thickness of the line or framed object.

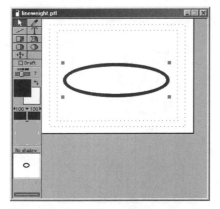

Figure 12.93 The thickness of the selected object reflects the line-weight value you selected.

Line Weight

You can change the *line weight*, or thickness, of lines and framed objects.

To change the line weight of a line or framed object:

1. Select a line or framed object (**Figure 12.91**).

   The line-weight slider appears below the Draft checkbox.

2. Drag the line-weight slider to change the selected line weight (**Figure 12.92**).

   The thickness of the line or framed object changes according to your adjustments (**Figure 12.93**).

Using Filled and Framed Objects

Unlike the objects you create in Adobe Illustrator, which can be both filled and stroked, the objects you create in Premiere must be either filled or framed. Commands allow you convert a framed object to a filled object (and vice versa), however, or to create a framed version of a filled object (and vice versa).

To change a framed object to a filled object, or vice versa:

1. Select a framed or filled object (**Figure 12.94**).

2. Choose either of the following (**Figure 12.95**):

   ▲ Title > Convert to Filled

   ▲ Title > Convert to Framed

   The selected object changes, according to your choice (**Figure 12.96**).

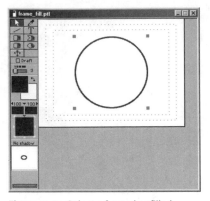

Figure 12.94 Select a framed or filled shape. Here, a framed shape is selected.

Figure 12.95 Depending on the object you selected, choose Title > Convert to Filled (shown) or Title > Convert to Framed.

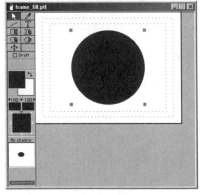

Figure 12.96 In this case, the framed object changes to a filled object with the same dimensions.

Figure 12.97 Choose Title > Create Framed Object to create a framed duplicate of a filled object. Choose Title > Create Filled Object to do the reverse.

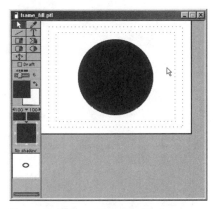

Figure 12.98 Here, a framed object was created from the filled object shown in Figure 12.97. The color of the framed object has been changed to distinguish it from its filled counterpart.

To duplicate a framed object as a filled object, or vice versa:

1. Select a framed or filled object.

2. Choose either of the following (**Figure 12.97**):

   Title > Create Framed Object—to create a framed copy of a filled object.

   Title > Create Filled Object—to create a filled copy of a framed object.

   The new copy appears in the same position as the original, higher in the stacking order.

3. Move or change the attributes of the new copy to distinguish it from the original (**Figure 12.98**).

   If you don't see the framed object, it's probably hidden behind the filled object. Change the stacking order by choosing Title > Bring to Front. See the section "Stacking Order."

✔ Tip

- You can create a framed object from a filled object (or vice versa) to simulate a single object that's stroked and filled. Though Premiere doesn't include a Group command, you can select both objects and move them together. See the following section, "Selecting Objects."

USING FILLED AND FRAMED OBJECTS

Selecting Objects

Although selecting and moving objects in
Premiere is both intuitive and consistent
with the methods you use in most graphics
programs, a few techniques may not be
so obvious.

To select objects:

Do any of the following:

▲ Click an object to select it.

▲ Shift-click to select additional objects
   and to deselect them.

▲ Choose Edit > Select All to select all
   the objects in the title window.

▲ Press period (.) to select the next
   object higher in the stacking order.

▲ Press comma (,) to select the next
   object lower in the stacking order.

Selected objects always display small
gray handles or a bounding box.
(**Figure 12.99**).

✔ Tips

■ You can't draw a marquee or lasso several
   items to select them, or use the Shift key in
   conjunction with the keyboard shortcut to
   select several items at the same time.

■ You can use standard copy and paste
   functions on any object in the title window. Select the object, and choose ⌘-C
   (Mac) or Ctrl-C (Windows) to copy it.
   Deselect the object, and choose ⌘-V
   (Mac) or Ctrl-V (Windows) to paste a
   copy of it in the drawing space.

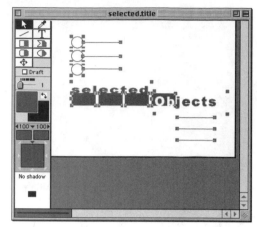

Figure 12.99 Selected objects display the handles of
their bounding box.

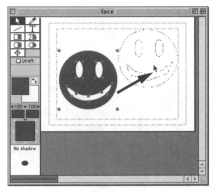

Figure 12.100 Simply select the objects you want to move and drag them with the mouse (shown here). Or you can use the arrow keys to nudge the selected objects.

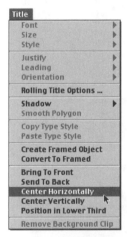

Figure 12.101 Choose a positioning option for the selected objects.

Moving Objects

You can move selected objects by dragging them with the mouse or by pressing the arrow keys. Premiere can also center objects automatically or align objects with the bottom of the title-safe zone.

To move objects:

1. Select the objects that you want to move.

2. *Do any of the following:*
   ▲ To move the selected objects with the mouse, drag them to a new position in the drawing area (**Figure 12.100**).
   ▲ To nudge the selected objects one pixel at a time, press an arrow key.
   ▲ To nudge the selected objects five pixels at a time, hold down the (Shift) key as you press an arrow key.

To position objects automatically:

1. Select the objects that you want to align.

2. Choose one of the following (**Figure 12.101**):
   ▲ Title > Center Horizontally
   ▲ Title > Center Vertically
   ▲ Title > Position in Lower Third

   The selected title repositions according to your choice (**Figure 12.102**).

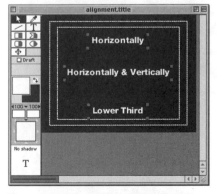

Figure 12.102 These three objects illustrate your positioning options. All of them are centered horizontally.

✔ Tips

- Identification titles (like the ones you see in news broadcasts, sports programs, or documentaries) are usually positioned in the bottom third of the screen, aligned with the bottom of the title-safe zone (**Figure 12.103**). Such superimposed ID titles are referred to simply as *lower thirds*. Subtitles also appear in the lower-third position.

Figure 12.103 Titles that identify the person onscreen are usually positioned in the lower third, aligned with the bottom of the title-safe area.

Subtitling Tips

Programs that include audio in foreign languages require *subtitles*—onscreen text translations—to be understood by wider audiences. Though an online suite with a character generator (or CG) and switcher may be the best way to add subtitles to longer programs, you can get the job done in Premiere. Here are a few things to keep in mind:

- ◆ Use a simple, legible font. Avoid scripts or novelty fonts. Avoid small fonts or fonts with thin lines or serifs.
- ◆ Respect the title-safe zones.
- ◆ Don't present too many words at one time. Try to use only one line of text.
- ◆ Use a drop shadow, or place the text against a semitransparent box to set the text apart from the background image.
- ◆ Don't create the subtitle cards with the title window if you can more easily convert the transcription from a text-editing program to still-image frames. Make sure that the frames match the pixel dimensions of the final video program.

Figure 12.104 Select the object you want to move in the stacking order.

Figure 12.105 Choosing the appropriate option from the Title menu ...

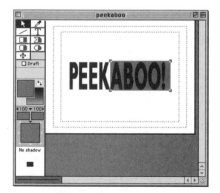

Figure 12.106 ... changes the selected object's relative position in the stacking order. In this case, the rectangle is sent to the back of the stacking order and appears behind the text.

Stacking Order

In addition to controlling the position of objects, you can control how they are layered. Initially the most recently created object appears in front of the others, but you can change the stacking order at any time.

To change the stacking order:

1. Select the object you want to re-order (**Figure 12.104**).

2. Choose either of the following (**Figure 12.105**):

   Title > Bring to Front—brings an object to the foreground, higher in the stacking order.

   Title > Send to Back—sends an object to the background, lower in the stacking order (**Figure 12.106**).

Drop Shadows

You can add a drop shadow to both graphic and text objects. This effect can set an object apart from the background or impart a sense of depth. A shadow can have any color, opacity, or gradient, independent of the object with which it's associated.

To add a shadow:

1. Select the objects to which you want to apply a shadow.

2. Drag the shadow offset control to set the shadow's angle and distance from the object (**Figure 12.107**).

   The numbers in the shadow offset control indicate the shadow's distance from the selected object, in horizontal and vertical pixels. The sample figure represents how the shadow looks for the selected object.

To remove a shadow:

1. Select an object with a shadow.

2. Drag the shadow offset control outside or to the center of the control area until it displays the message *No shadow* (**Figure 12.108**).

   The selected object's shadow is removed (**Figure 12.109**).

Figure 12.107 Drag the shadow offset control to set the shadow's angle and distance. The shadow in the control represents the actual shadow.

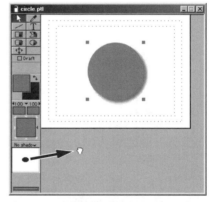

Figure 12.108 Drag outside the shadow offset control to remove the shadow, so that it displays the message No Shadow.

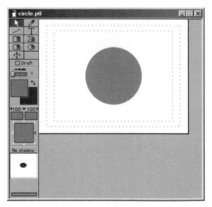

Figure 12.109 The selected object's shadow disappears.

DROP SHADOWS

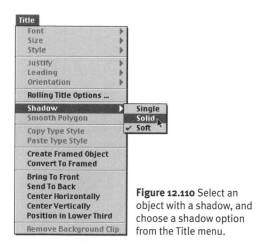

Figure 12.110 Select an object with a shadow, and choose a shadow option from the Title menu.

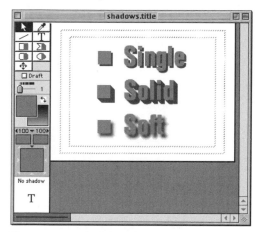

Figure 12.111 Each of these three objects uses a different type of drop shadow. Otherwise, their drop shadows all have the same color, opacity, angle, and distance from the object.

To choose a shadow type:

1. Select an object that has a shadow.

2. Choose Title > Shadow, and then choose a type of shadow (**Figure 12.110**):

   Single—creates a simple drop shadow.

   Solid—creates a shadow connected to the object, simulating extruded, three-dimensional text.

   Soft—creates a soft-edged drop shadow.

   The shadow of the selected object reflects your choice (**Figure 12.111**).

✔ Tip

- By default, the shadow color is set to black at 50 percent opacity—a common setting. But shadows don't have to be black or semitransparent. Why not create a black title over a black background with a white shadow?

Color

By using the two large, overlapping color swatches in the title window, you can control the color of an object and the color of its shadow independently. Use the left swatch to choose the color of the object; use the right swatch to choose the color of the shadow. Note that the selected swatch appears in front of the other. As you'll learn in the following sections, selecting the object or shadow color swatch also lets you control opacity and gradient levels.

To set object and shadow color:

1. *Do either of the following:*
   - ▲ Select an entire object.
   or
   - ▲ Select a range of text.

2. To select the color swatch of the color you want to change, *do either of the following:*
   - ▲ To select the object color, click the object color swatch (the left swatch) or press Ⓒ.
   or
   - ▲ To select the shadow color, click the shadow color swatch (the right swatch) or press Ⓧ.

   The selected color swatch appears in front of the other (**Figure 12.112**).

3. Click the selected color swatch to open the Color Picker window.

4. Choose a color (**Figure 12.113**).

5. Click OK to close the color picker and apply the change.

Figure 12.112 Select either the object or shadow color swatch so that it appears in front. Click the selected swatch to open the color picker.

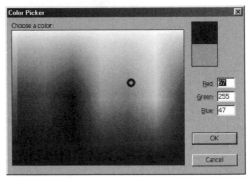

Figure 12.113 Choose a color from the Color Picker window, and click OK to close the window.

✔ Tips

- ■ Whatever you do, don't confuse the shadow color with the background color. It's a common mistake. Remember: you can set the background color from the Title Window Options dialog box. See the section "Background Color" earlier in this chapter.

- ■ Press Ⓧ to select the object color swatch; press Ⓒ to select the shadow color swatch. This action selects the color swatch, it doesn't open the color picker.

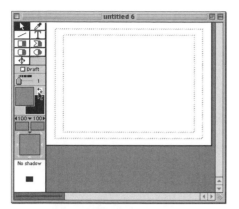

Figure 12.114 Click the swap button (the curved double arrow) to exchange the object and shadow colors.

Figure 12.115 Click the title window with the eyedropper tool to set the current object color. (Option)-click (Mac) or (Alt)-click (Windows) to set the current shadow color. Here, the eyedropper is used to select a color from the background and make it the object color of the selected text.

✔ Tips

■ Press (I) to select the eyedropper tool 🖋.

■ Use the eyedropper tool to match the colors of objects with colors in a background clip. See the section "Background Clips" earlier in this chapter.

■ Press (Z) to reset the object and shadow colors to their defaults. The default object color has a color gradient, and the default shadow color is set to 50 percent opacity.

Other Ways to Choose Colors

The title window offers several other ways to pick colors. You can swap the object and shadow colors, copy the color of one swatch to another, or pick a color from the title window with the eyedropper tool. Remember that you can choose a color before you create an object or change the color of a selected object.

To swap the object and shadow colors:

◆ Click the curved double arrow 🔁 between the object and shadow color swatches (**Figure 12.114**).

To copy the color from one swatch to another:

◆ Drag from one color swatch to another color swatch.

When you release the mouse button, the color is copied from the first swatch to the second. This method works with any color swatch in the title window.

To pick colors with the eyedropper tool:

1. Select the eyedropper tool 🖋 or press (I).

2. *Do either of the following:*

   ▲ To set the object color, click a color in the title window (**Figure 12.115**).

   or

   ▲ To set the shadow color, (Option)-click (Mac) or (Alt)-click (Windows) the title window.

Opacity

You can set the opacity level of any object or its shadow. As you would expect, objects lower in the stacking order show through semitransparent objects. When you superimpose a title over another clip (see Chapter 13), the clip in the background also shows through.

To set opacity:

1. *Do either of the following:*

▲ Select an object.

or

▲ Select a range of text.

2. *Do either of the following:*

▲ To set the opacity of the object, click the object color swatch.

or

▲ To set the opacity of the shadow, click the shadow color swatch.

3. Press and hold the overall opacity button (the triangle between the start and end opacity values) to reveal an opacity slider. Drag to select an overall opacity (**Figures 12.116** and **12.117**).

Both the start and end opacity values (the numbers on either side of the overall opacity button) display the same value. Releasing the mouse button sets the opacity slider value (**Figure 12.118**).

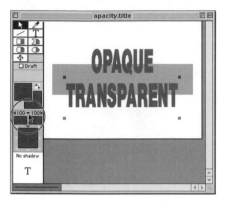

Figure 12.116 Press and hold the small center triangle to reveal a slider to control the overall opacity.

Figure 12.117 Drag the center slider to change the overall opacity of the selected objects.

Figure 12.118 The object or shadow color of the selected objects use the opacity value you set. Here, text with no shadow has an object color opacity of 60%.

OPACITY

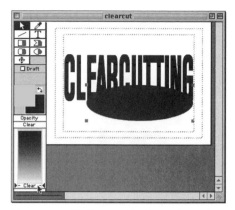

Figure 12.119 Setting an object's opacity to clear effectively cuts a hole through other objects. In this case, the oval is set to clear ...

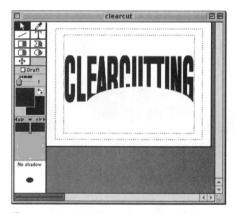

Figure 12.120 ... cutting out a portion of the text to reveal background objects or background clips.

✔ Tips

- When a semitransparent object looks darker than it should, it usually means that you are seeing through the object color to the shadow color. Simply remove the shadow.

- You can set an object's opacity to clear to make it completely transparent when you superimpose the title over video (see Chapter 13). A clear object cuts through an opaque object in the title (**Figures 12.119** and **12.120**).

Gradients

Both color and opacity can gradually change from one end of an object or shadow to the other in a *gradient*. The title window creates simple linear gradients in any of the eight compass directions. (If you need a more complex gradient, turn to Illustrator or Photoshop.) One more restriction: if a color (object or shadow) has both a color gradient and opacity gradient, both gradients must use the same direction.

To set a color gradient:

1. *Do either of the following:*
   ▲ Select an object.

   or

   ▲ Select a range of text.

2. *Do either of the following:*
   ▲ To make an object color gradient, click the object color swatch.

   or

   ▲ To make a shadow color gradient, click the shadow color swatch.

3. *Do any of the following:*
   ▲ To choose the starting color for the gradient, click the small swatch on the left, and choose a color in the color picker (**Figures 12.121** and **12.122**).
   ▲ To choose the ending color for the gradient, click the small swatch on the right and choose a color in the color picker.

   The color gradient you set is represented in the gradient swatch (the large bottom-most swatch). The selected title object also acquires the gradient.

4. To set the direction of the gradient, click one of the eight gradient direction buttons, which are the small triangles around the gradient swatch (**Figure 12.123**).

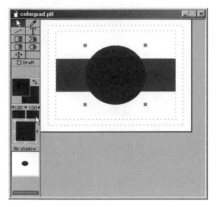

Figure 12.121 Click the swatch on the left to set the color of the beginning of the gradient. Click the right swatch to set the gradient end color.

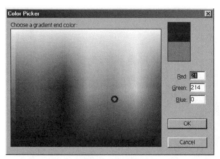

Figure 12.122 Choose a gradient color in the color picker.

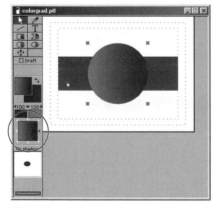

Figure 12.123 Click one of the small arrows around the gradient swatch to set the direction of the gradient. The direction arrow you select turns red, and the gradient swatch represents the gradient direction.

GRADIENTS

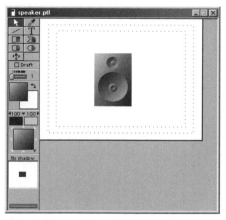

Figure 12.124 This icon of an audio speaker consists of several shapes with color gradients.

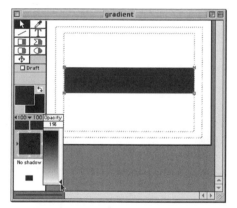

Figure 12.125 Press the opacity start button to reveal a slider, and drag to choose a starting opacity value. Do the same for the opacity end button.

The selected direction button turns from white to red. The gradient swatch and the selected objects in the drawing area display the color gradient in the direction you specified. The selected objects also reflect the gradient you set (**Figure 12.124**).

To set an opacity gradient:

1. *Do either of the following:*
   ▲ Select an object.
   or
   ▲ Select a range of text.

2. *Do either of the following:*
   ▲ Click the object color swatch.
   or
   ▲ Select the shadow color swatch.

3. *Do any of the following:*
   ▲ Press and hold the opacity start button (the triangle next to the opacity value on the left), and drag to choose an opacity from the slider (**Figure 12.125**).
   ▲ Press and hold the opacity end button (the triangle next to the opacity value on the right), and drag to choose an opacity from the slider.

   continues on next page

GRADIENTS

4. To set the direction of the opacity gradient, click one of the eight gradient direction buttons (the small triangles around the gradient swatch) (**Figure 12.126**).

The object displays the opacity gradient from starting opacity to ending opacity, in the direction you chose.

✔ Tips

- It can be difficult to see the difference between an opacity gradient and a color gradient, especially if there are no objects in the background to make the opacity setting apparent.

- Premiere's Tool Tips (the little labels that appear when the mouse pointer rests on an item or tool) sometimes use the term *transparency*, whereas I use the term *opacity*. I disagree with the Tool Tips to remain consistent with the sliders, which measure degrees of opacity (100 percent = opaque).

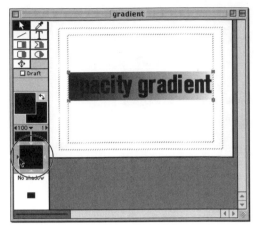

Figure 12.126 Click one of the small arrows around the gradient swatch to set the direction of the opacity gradient.

SUPER-IMPOSING CLIPS

In Chapter 5, you learned that you can have as many as 99 video tracks in the timeline. Here's where you start using them—at least, some of them.

By layering clips and adjusting their opacity, you can fade one image into another, or blend several images together. Other transparency settings allow you to make certain parts of an image transparent—based on the image's brightness, or color, for example. Or the transparent areas can be determined by the clip's alpha channel, or even by a separate clip. With Premiere's fade and transparency controls, you can superimpose a title over another clip, or composite a subject shot against a bluescreen with another background.

The Transparency Settings dialog box hasn't changed at all since earlier versions of the program. And of course, all the principles behind superimposing clips still hold true.

But as you learned in Chapter 6, "Editing in the Timeline," the timeline's superimpose tracks and fade controls have evolved. Starting with version 5, higher superimpose tracks appear on higher tracks, and are initially labeled Video 2 and up. Premiere 5 also introduced the ability to adjust the video fade controls in increments of 1 percent. Premiere 6 adds one more change to the timeline, requiring you to toggle between viewing effect keyframes and video fade handles. Even if you haven't used Premiere for a while, it should be easy to adapt to the changes.

Like all effects, superimposed clips must be previewed (see Chapter 9). The final results depend on the image quality of the source clips as well as on the preview or output quality settings. As usual, there is a direct correlation between quality and processing time.

Track Hierarchy

Tracks 2 and higher are known as *superimpose tracks*. If video clips are playing simultaneously in different tracks (and the monitor buttons are active), only the clip in the highest track is visible in the program view in the Monitor window, provided that you don't alter the clips' opacity levels. In other words, the superimpose tracks in Premiere work much like layers in Adobe Photoshop (or Illustrator or After Effects).

You can take advantage of track hierarchy for basic editing purposes. By placing a clip in a higher track, you can achieve an effect that looks like an overlay edit in program view without actually recording over a clip in the timeline (**Figure 13.1**).

Superimpose tracks allow you to layer video clips to accomplish fading and keying effects. You can also apply motion settings (see Chapter 13) to layers of video to create picture-in-picture effects and complex composites.

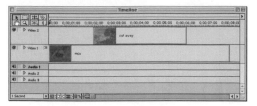

Figure 13.1 Because of the track hierarchy, placing a clip in a higher track can be an alternative to an overlay edit.

Figure 13.2 Fading a clip blends it with the clips in lower tracks.

Fading and Keying

You can superimpose clips in higher tracks over clips in lower tracks by using two methods, known as fading and keying.

Fading blends an entire clip with the clips in lower tracks (**Figure 13.2**). Fading can look similar to a cross-dissolve transition. With fading, however, it's easy to blend entire clips together, not just transition between them. And unlike a cross-dissolve (which occurs between two adjacent clips), you can fade multiple layers of clips at once.

Keying makes only certain parts of a clip transparent. The terms *key* and *keying* refer to their physical counterpart, the *keyhole*. This is because keying "cuts a hole" in an image, making it transparent. The hole is filled with another image—in this case, clips in lower tracks of the timeline. You can *key out*, or remove, parts of an image based on brightness or color. You can also base the key on a clip's alpha channel, or even on a separate image altogether (**Figure 13.3**).

You can also combine the effects of fading and keying—such as when you fade up a title over video.

Figure 13.3 Keying makes only certain elements transparent. By keying out the title's background, the title is keyed over another clip.

The Fade Control

You can reveal the opacity control for the clips in a superimpose track by expanding the track and selecting the fade switch (see Chapter 5). This reveals a red *fade line*, or *rubber band* control. The video fade line controls the opacity of a clip much the same way that the audio fade line controls the audio gain levels. Adding and adjusting control handles to the video fade line sets the opacity levels of the clip's image, allowing you to blend it with the clips in lower tracks. You can even use most of the same tools and techniques that you use with the audio fade line. The fade adjustment, scissors, and cross-fade tools, for example, all work with the video fade line.

Before you use the video fade controls, arrange clips in the timeline so that they overlap and expand the superimpose tracks.

To use a video fade handle:

1. Arrange clips in the timeline so that a clip in a superimpose track overlaps a clip in a lower track.

   The clip in the higher track acts as the foreground (higher layer of video), and clips in lower tracks act as the background (lower layers of video).

2. Expand the superimpose track to reveal the video fade line (**Figure 13.4**).

Expand —

Fade switch —

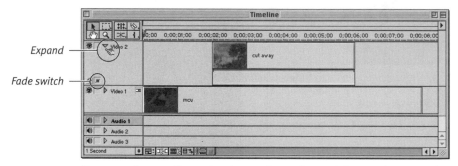

Figure 13.4 Arrange clips so that they overlap, and expand the superimpose tracks to reveal the fade line.

THE FADE CONTROL

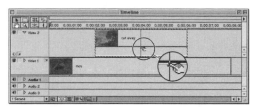

Figure 13.5 Click the fade line to create a handle.

Figure 13.6 Drag the fade handle down or up to control the opacity of the clip.

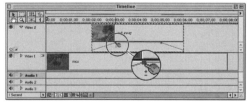

Figure 13.7 To remove a control handle, drag it completely outside the track.

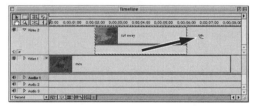

Figure 13.8 A gray finger icon indicates you can move a fade handle.

If the fade line is not visible, click the fade button ![fade button] to view the fade line instead of effect keyframes.

3. Position the pointer on the video fade line.

   The pointer changes to a white finger icon ![finger icon], indicating that you are about to create a new handle.

4. Click to create a control handle.

   A handle (red dot) appears on the video fade line (**Figure 13.5**).

5. Drag the fade handle down or up to control the opacity of the clip (**Figure 13.6**).

   The top of the fade area represents 100 percent opaque; the bottom represents 0 percent opaque.

To delete a fade handle:

◆ Drag a fade handle all the way outside the superimpose track (**Figure 13.7**).

   When you release the mouse button, the video fade handle disappears.

To move a video fade handle:

1. Position the pointer on a fade handle of a clip in an expanded superimpose track.

   The pointer changes to a gray finger icon ![gray finger icon], indicating that you are about to move a handle (**Figure 13.8**). If the finger is white, you'll create a new handle.

2. Drag the fade handle up or down to change the opacity value of the clip at that point, or side to side to change the handle's position in time.

To fade in increments of 1 percent:

1. Position the pointer on the video fade handle that you want to adjust.

   The pointer changes to a gray finger icon 🖐, indicating that you are about to move a fade handle.

2. Shift-drag the handle up or down.

   A numeric display appears, indicating the current opacity level. As you shift-drag, the opacity value changes in increments of 1 percent. You can Shift-drag beyond the top or bottom of the video track, enabling you to continue to change the opacity value. (**Figure 13.9**).

✔ Tips

- Unless otherwise noted, use the selection tool to accomplish the tasks in this chapter. If you can't seem to move a control handle, or if some other technique doesn't work, you may have the wrong tool selected.

- Premiere software and documentation use the terms "rubber band," "fade control," and "fader." This book favors the term "fade line."

- You can see the current position and level value update in the Info palette as you drag a handle (**Figure 13.10**).

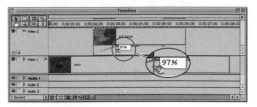

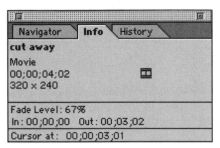

Figure 13.9 Shift-drag a handle to adjust the opacity in increments of 1 percent.

Figure 13.10 In the Info palette, you can view the exact position and value of a fade handle as you drag it.

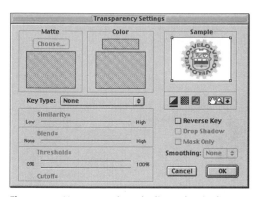

Figure 13.11 You can apply and adjust a key in the Transparency Settings dialog box.

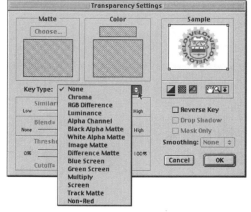

Figure 13.12 Premiere provides 15 key types, but they fall into four basic categories.

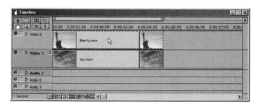

Figure 13.13 Select a clip in a superimpose track.

Keying

In addition to fading the entire image, you can key out particular areas of an image, making them transparent. You can apply and adjust a key effect (or simply, *key*) in the Transparency Settings dialog box (**Figure 13.11**).

You can key out parts of an image based on luminance, chrominance, an alpha channel, or a separate matte image. Although Premiere provides 15 key types, all fall into these four basic categories (**Figure 13.12**). You can use these key types in conjunction with a *garbage matte,* a method of cropping out the extraneous edges of an image.

This chapter covers key types by category, explaining the most commonly used key types in detail and summarizing the others. You can use the fade control in combination with any key.

To apply any key type:

1. Arrange clips in the timeline so that a clip in a superimpose track overlaps one or more clips in lower tracks.

    The clip in the higher track acts as the foreground, and clips in lower tracks act as the background.

2. Select a clip in a higher track to which you want to apply a transparency setting (**Figure 13.13**).

    continues on next page

KEYING

3. Choose Clip > Video Options >
Transparency (**Figure 13.14**).

The Transparency Settings dialog box
appears (**Figure 13.15**).

4. From the Key Type pull-down menu,
choose a key type (**Figure 13.16**).

See the following sections for information
about individual key types.

5. To adjust the parameters, drag any of the
sliders, depending on the key type that
you choose.

See **Table 13.1**, "Key Type Options," for a
summary of the options available for each
key type.

6. Preview and evaluate the effectiveness of
the key in the sample frame.

See the section, "To Preview Any Key
Type" for detailed instructions.

7. Click OK to apply the settings to the clip.

The Transparency Settings dialog box
closes. You must preview the appropriate
area of the timeline to see the effect in
the program view.

✔ Tips

■ The keyboard shortcut for Clip > Video
Options > Transparency is ⌘-G (Mac) or
Ctrl-G (Windows).

■ To apply transparency setting to a clip, it
must be located in a superimpose track.
The Transparency option is not available
for clips in the video track (single-track
editing) or A/B tracks (A/B roll editing).

Figure 13.14 Choose Clip > Video Options >
Transparency or press ⌘-G (Mac) or
Ctrl-G (Windows).

Figure 13.15 The Transparency Settings dialog box
appears.

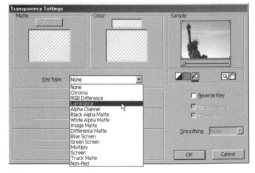

Figure 13.16 From the Key Type pull-down menu,
choose a key type and adjust its parameters.

Keying Controls

Every key type offers a different set of controls. If a control is unavailable, it is grayed-out. The following table summarizes the options that are available for each key type (Table 13.1).

Table 13.1

Key Type Options							
KEY TYPE	SIMILARITY	BLEND	THRESHOLD	CUTOFF	REVERSE KEY	DROP SHADOW	SMOOTHING
None					•		
Luminance Keys							
Luminance			•	•			
Multiply				•			
Screen				•			
Chrominance Keys							
Chroma	•	•	•	•		•	•
Blue screen			•	•			•
Green screen			•	•			•
RGB difference	•					•	•
Alpha Keys							
Alpha					•		
Black alpha matte							
White alpha matte							
Matte Keys							
Image matte					•		
Track matte					•		
Difference matte	•				•	•	•

Previewing Any Key

In the Transparency Settings dialog box, a sample image helps you analyze the effectiveness of the key. However, previewing the keyed image against the background image isn't always the best way to evaluate your settings. It can be difficult to discern pixels and identify transparent areas. For this reason, the preview includes several options to make your adjustments easier to make.

To preview any key type:

1. In the Transparency Settings dialog box, choose how you want to preview the key by clicking one of the icons below the sample frame:

   Black/White ◨ —to fill the transparent areas of a clip with black; click it again to see transparent areas as white (**Figure 13.17**).

   Checkerboard ▨ —to fill the transparent areas of the clip with a checkerboard pattern (**Figure 13.18**).

   Peel ◩ —to fill the transparent areas of the clip with the actual background image (**Figure 13.19**).

   The currently selected preview option icon appears underlined.

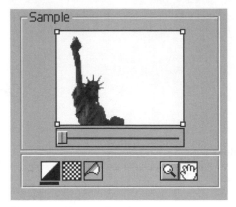

Figure 13.17 You can view the transparent areas in black or white …

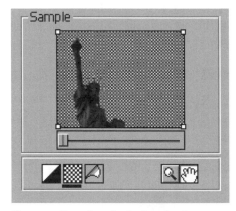

Figure 13.18 … or in a checkerboard pattern …

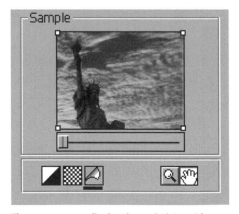

Figure 13.19 … or display the underlying video image.

Figure 13.20 Use the tools below the right side of the sample frame to take a closer look at the key or view it in the program view.

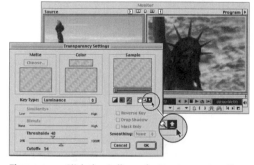

Figure 13.21 Click the Collapse button to preview the key in the program view of the Monitor window.

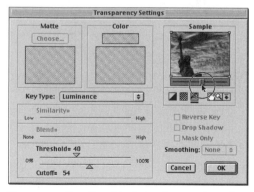

Figure 13.22 Drag the slider below the sample to view the key at different points in the clip.

2. To more closely evaluate the effectiveness of the key, select from the icons below the right side of the sample frame (**Figure 13.20**):

Zoom tool 🔍 —click the sample frame to view an area in more detail; (Option)-click (Mac) or (Alt)-click (Windows) to zoom out.

Hand tool 🖐 —drag in the sample frame to view different areas of the zoomed sample.

Collapse (in the Mac OS only) 🔽 — click to preview the key effect in the program view of the Monitor window; click again to preview the effect in the Transparency Settings dialog box (**Figure 13.21**).

3. To view the effectiveness of the key at different points in the clip, drag the slider below the sample frame (**Figure 13.22**).

4. Adjust the options for the currently selected key type, and repeat steps 1 through 3, as needed.

5. Click OK to apply the key and close the Transparency Settings dialog box.

✔ Tip

■ Here's another method you can use to better judge the transparency settings. Use a bright color, like a bright yellow or green, as a temporary background for the keyed clip. You can do this by placing a color matte (Chapter 2) in the track below the clip you're keying. This way, the color will show through when you click on the peel icon or preview in the program view. When you're finished, simply remove the temporary color matte from the timeline.

Using the Luminance-Based Keys

Luminance-based keys use luminance (or brightness) levels to define the transparent areas. You can choose to key out either the brightest or the darkest pixels contained in the image. Luminance-based key types include Luminance, Multiply, and Screen.

The luminance key isn't the only key type that uses luminance to define transparency, but it's probably the most commonly used (both in Premiere and in traditional editing suites). You may hear luminance keys generically referred to as *Luma keys*.

To use the luminance key:

1. Select a clip in a superimpose track, and choose Clip > Video Options > Transparency (**Figure 13.23**).

   The Transparency Settings dialog box appears.

2. From the Key Type pull-down menu of the Transparency Settings dialog box, choose Luminance (**Figure 13.24**).

3. In the Transparency Settings dialog box, drag the sliders to adjust the key:

   Threshold—to set the range of darker pixels that become transparent.

   Cutoff—to set the transparency of the areas defined by the Threshold value.

Figure 13.23 Select a clip in a superimpose track, and choose Clip > Video Options > Transparency.

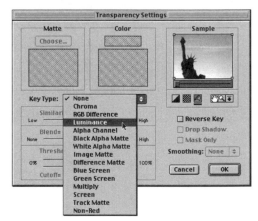

Figure 13.24 Choose Luminance from the Key Type pull-down menu.

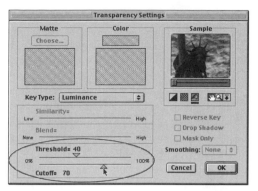

Figure 13.25 Drag the Threshold and Cutoff sliders, and preview the effects in the sample frame.

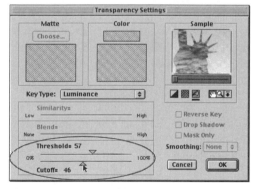

Figure 13.26 Reversing the relative positions of the threshold and cutoff sliders inverts the key.

4. View the effects of your adjustments in the sample frame (**Figure 13.25**).

When the relative positions of the threshold and cutoff are reversed, the key is reversed, and lighter areas become transparent (**Figure 13.26**).

5. When you are satisfied with your adjustments, click OK to close the Transparency Settings dialog box and apply the settings.

Using Multiply and Screen Keys

The multiply and screen keys calculate the clip's transparency based on luminance values taken from both the clip and the underlying image. Multiply determines transparency values by averaging the product of the luminance values of the clip and the underlying image. As a result, the clip becomes more transparent where brighter areas of both clips correspond. Black areas of the clip remain opaque (**Figure 13.27**). Screen uses inverse luminance values in its calculation. Therefore, Screen makes the clip more transparent where darker areas of both clips correspond. Pure white areas of the clip are always opaque (**Figure 13.28**). But the best way to understand these keys is to compare them.

To use the multiply or screen keys:

1. Select a clip in a superimpose track, and choose Clip > Video Options > Transparency (**Figure 13.29**).

   The Transparency Settings dialog box appears.

Figure 13.27 Multiply makes the clip more transparent where the bright areas of the clip and the underlying image correspond. In this image, the clouds show through more in areas where the statue's highlights and the clouds overlap.

Figure 13.28 Screen makes the clip more transparent where the dark areas of the clip and the underlying image correspond.

Figure 13.29 Select a clip in a superimpose track, and choose Clip › Video Options › Transparency.

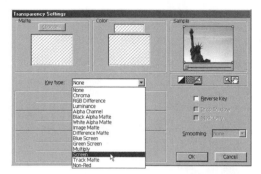

Figure 13.30 Choose Multiply or Screen (as shown here).

Figure 13.31 Adjust the Cutoff slider and preview the effects in the sample frame.

2. From the Key Type pull-down menu of the Transparency Settings dialog box, choose the appropriate option (**Figure 13.30**):

Multiply—makes the clip more transparent where brighter areas of both clips correspond.

Screen—makes the clip more transparent where darker areas of both clips correspond.

3. Drag the Cutoff slider to set the transparency levels.

4. Preview the key in the sample frame of the Transparency Settings dialog box (**Figure 13.31**).

5. Click OK to close the Transparency Settings dialog box and apply the settings.

USING MULTIPLY AND SCREEN KEYS

Chrominance-Based Keys

Chrominance-based keys use chrominance (or color) to define the transparent areas of a clip. Chrominance-based keys are commonly used to composite moving subjects that were shot against a colored background, usually a blue or green backdrop called a *bluescreen* or *greenscreen*, respectively. Provided the subject doesn't contain the key color, a chrominance-based key can remove the background while leaving the subject opaque. In fact, blue and green are standard key colors because they are relatively absent from human skin tones. Without the key color to differentiate the background from the subject, it would be difficult, if not impossible, to perfectly separate a moving subject from the background (**Figure 13.32**). Chrominance-based key types include Chroma, Blue Screen, Green Screen, RGB Difference, and Non-Red. The following sections explain in detail how to apply the chroma key and summarize the other color-based keys.

Figure 13.32 Chrominance-based keys are typically used to composite bluescreen footage.

Figure 13.33 Select a clip in a superimpose track, and choose Clip > Video Options > Transparency.

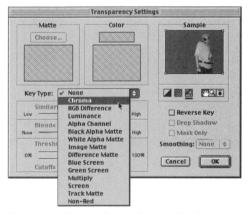

Figure 13.34 Choose Chroma from the Key Type pull-down menu.

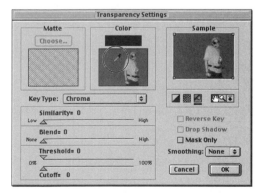

Figure 13.35 Choose a key color by clicking in the thumbnail image (shown here) or open the color picker by clicking the color swatch.

Using the Chroma Key

All the chrominance-based keys work essentially the same way, although the chroma key is the most flexible.

To use the chroma key:

1. Select a clip in a superimpose track, and choose Clip > Video Options > Transparency (**Figure 13.33**).

   The Transparency Settings dialog box appears.

2. From the Key Type pull-down menu of the Transparency Settings dialog box, choose Chroma (**Figure 13.34**).

3. In the Color section of the Transparency Settings dialog box, choose a key color by doing either of the following:

   ▲ To select a color from the thumbnail image, click in the thumbnail image.

   The eyedropper tool appears, and the selected color appears in the color swatch above the thumbnail (**Figure 13.35**).

   ▲ To choose a color from the color picker, click the color swatch over the thumbnail image.

   The color picker appears. Select a color and click OK to set the key color and return to the Transparency Settings dialog box.

   continues on next page

4. To adjust the key, drag the sliders:

   Similarity—to increase or decrease the range of colors similar to the key color that are keyed out.

   Blend—to blend the clip with the underlying clip.

   Threshold—to control the amount of shadows that you keep in the range of key colors.

   Cutoff—to darken or lighten shadows. Don't drag the Cutoff beyond the Threshold, or you will invert the gray and transparent pixels.

   Smoothing—to antialias (smooth) the edges of the opaque areas.

5. Preview the effects of your adjustments in the sample frame (**Figure 13.36**).

6. When you are satisfied with the adjustments, click OK to close the Transparency Settings dialog box and apply the settings.

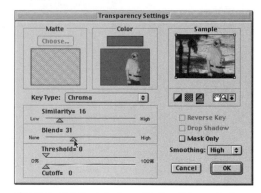

Figure 13.36 Adjust the key with the slider controls, and preview the effect in the sample frame.

✔ Tip

- Before you begin adjusting a chroma key, crop out extraneous portions of the image using a garbage matte, as explained in the section, "Using Garbage Mattes," later in this chapter. This way, you don't waste effort adjusting for parts of the background that can be eliminated at the outset.

Other Chrominance-Based Keys

The following section summarizes the other chrominance-based keys.

RGB Difference Key

The RGB difference key works like a simpler version of the chroma key. It provides only the similarity and smoothing sliders. You can also use the drop shadow option, which adds a 50 percent gray, 50 percent opaque shadow, offset 4 pixels to the right and 4 pixels down.

Blue Screen and Green Screen Keys

The blue screen and green screen keys are optimized for use with true chroma blue and true chroma green, respectively. However, they don't provide as many slider controls as the chroma key.

Non-Red Key

The non-red key makes blue and green areas (non-red) transparent. This key type also provides a blend slider.

Keys to the Kingdom

The results you get from chroma keying depend a great deal on the quality of your footage. Here are just a few things to consider if you plan to do bluescreen work:

◆ Shoot using the best format possible. For video, choose a format with the least compression and the greatest color depth.

◆ Use a high-quality bluescreen. A good bluescreen should be painted with paint specially formulated for bluescreen work. If possible, use a shadow-free cyclorama, a background constructed from hard materials with rounded corners to prevent shadows.

◆ Use good lighting techniques on the set. Preferably, work with someone experienced in lighting an evenly-lit shadow-free bluescreen. Use lighting to help separate the subject from the background, and reduce spill (blue light reflected on the subject).

◆ Use a high-quality capture device. If possible, transfer the footage uncompressed using a high-quality transfer method, such as SDI.

◆ Doing good bluescreen compositing is harder than it sounds. You may need to use software dedicated to the job, such as plug-ins, like Ultimatte's Primatte keyer, or those found in After Effects Production Bundle.

Alpha Keys

Alpha-based keys use the clip's alpha channel to define transparent areas of the image (**Figure 13.37**).

As you recall from chapter 2, an alpha channel can be a straight alpha channel (like the one you can save as the fourth channel of a Photoshop image), or it can be premultiplied with color (like the one you can save in titles you create in Premiere). The kind of alpha channel the clip contains determines the type of key that you choose. For more about alpha channels, see Chapter 2.

In the next chapter, "Motion Settings," you'll learn that when you apply a motion setting to a clip in a superimpose track, Premiere applies the appropriate alpha-based key automatically. Nevertheless, you should understand how each key works, just in case you need to override Premiere's choice.

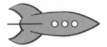

Figure 13.37 Alpha-based keys use the clip's alpha channel to define transparent areas of the image.

Using the Alpha Channel Key

Photoshop, Illustrator, and After Effects can all create images with a straight alpha channel—that is, the alpha channel contains all the transparency information. Use the alpha key for images that contain a straight alpha channel. For more about straight alpha channels versus premultiplied alpha channels, see Chapter 2.

To use the alpha channel key:

1. Select a clip in a superimpose track, and choose Clip > Video Options > Transparency (**Figure 13.38**).

   The Transparency Settings dialog box appears.

Figure 13.38 Select a clip in a superimpose track, and choose Clip > Video Options > Transparency.

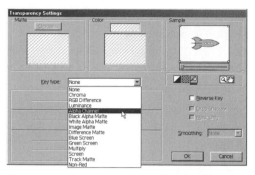

Figure 13.39 Choose Alpha channel from the Key type menu.

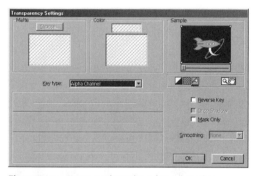

Figure 13.40 Areas are keyed out based on the straight alpha channel.

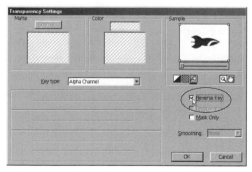

Figure 13.41 Check Reverse Key to reverse the opaque and transparent areas.

2. From the Key Type pull-down menu of the Transparency Settings dialog box, choose Alpha Channel (**Figure 13.39**).

Areas are keyed out based on the straight alpha channel (**Figure 13.40**). No slider controls are available.

3. Preview the key in the sample frame of the Transparency Settings dialog box.

4. Click OK to close the Transparency Settings dialog box and apply the settings.

✔ Tip

■ To invert the key, check the Reverse Key box. The opaque and transparent areas of the image are reversed (**Figure 13.41**).

USING THE ALPHA CHANNEL KEY

Using the Black and White Alpha Matte Keys

When the alpha channel is premultiplied, the transparency information is stored in all four channels of the image. This causes the edges of the opaque part of the image to blend into a background color. (For more about premultiplied alpha channels, see Chapter 2.) Use Black Alpha Matte or White Alpha Matte with images that contain an alpha channel premultiplied with a black or white background.

The alpha channel used by a Premiere title is premultiplied with a background color. Chapter 11 advises you to make the background of title clips black or white if you plan to superimpose the title over other clips. That way, the black alpha matte or white alpha matte keys will be most effective. If you're keying Premiere titles, don't forget another crucial step you learned in Chapter 11: In the Title Window Options, make sure Opacity is unchecked when you create the title. Otherwise, the title won't generate an alpha channel you can use for keying purposes.

To use the black alpha matte and white alpha matte keys:

1. Select a clip in a superimpose track, and choose Clip > Video Options > Transparency (**Figure 13.42**).

   The Transparency Settings dialog box appears.

2. In the Transparency Settings dialog box, choose one of the following options (**Figure 13.43**):

   Black Alpha Matte—if a clip has an alpha premultiplied with black, such as a title clip with a black background.

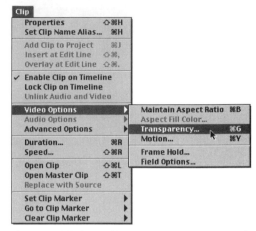

Figure 13.42 Select a clip in a superimpose track, and choose Clip > Video Options > Transparency.

Figure 13.43 Choose Black Alpha Matte if your clip's alpha is premultiplied with black; choose White Alpha Matte if your clip's alpha is premultiplied with white.

Figure 13.44 The alpha channel is keyed out.

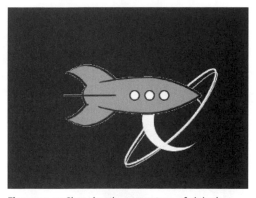

Figure 13.45 Choosing the wrong type of alpha key can result in an unattractive fringe, or halo around the opaque object. Choose a different alpha-based key type.

White Alpha Matte—if a clip has an alpha premultiplied with white, such as a title clip with a white background. Areas are keyed out based on the premultiplied alpha channel (**Figure 13.44**).

3. Preview the effect of the key in the sample frame of the Transparency Settings dialog box.

4. Click OK to close the Transparency Settings dialog box and apply the settings.

✔ Tip

■ If you use a regular alpha key on an image with a premultiplied alpha channel, you may see a black or white fringe, or halo around the edges of the opaque image (**Figure 13.45**).

Matte Keys

Matte-based keys use an external image to define transparent areas of a clip. A typical matte is a high-contrast grayscale image (sometimes called a *high-con*). By default, the white areas of the matte define opaque areas of the foreground clip (sometimes called the *beauty*); black areas of the matte define transparent parts of the foreground clip; and gray areas define semitransparent parts of the foreground clip. The matte itself never appears in the final output; it only defines areas of transparency. Sometimes the matte perfectly matches the shape of the beauty; other times, the matte cuts a shape out of the beauty (**Figures 13.46**, **13.47**, and **13.48**).

Matte-based key types include Image Matte and Track Matte. The difference matte key also falls into this category, although it creates its own matte by comparing two clips.

Figure 13.46 This matte's edges perfectly match the beauty.

Figure 13.47 This matte retains parts of the background color.

Figure 13.48 This matte is simply used as a stencil.

Using the Image Matte Key

The image matte key can use any grayscale still image as the matte, including a static title that you create in Premiere. Although you choose the matte image in the Transparency Settings dialog box, it does not have to be used in the timeline or even imported into the project.

To use the image matte key:

1. Select a clip in a superimpose track, and choose Clip > Video Options > Transparency (**Figure 13.49**).

   The Transparency Settings dialog box appears.

2. From the Key Type pull-down menu of the Transparency Settings dialog box, choose Image Matte (**Figure 13.50**).

3. In the Matte section of the Transparency Settings dialog box, click Choose (**Figure 13.51**).

   The Open File dialog box appears.

   continues on next page

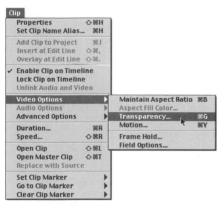

Figure 13.49 Select a clip in a superimpose track, and choose Clip > Video Options > Transparency.

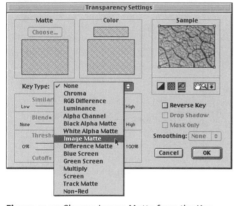

Figure 13.50 Choose Image Matte from the Key Type pull-down menu.

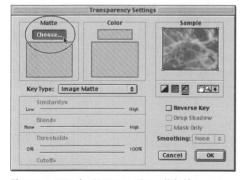

Figure 13.51 In the Matte section, click Choose to select a static matte.

USING THE IMAGE MATTE KEY

4. In the Open File dialog box, locate the still image that you want to use as the matte and click Open (**Figure 13.52**).

A thumbnail image of the matte appears in the Matte section of the Transparency Settings dialog box. Some areas are keyed out based on the alpha channel (**Figure 13.53**).

5. Preview the key in the sample frame of the Transparency Settings dialog box.

6. Click OK to exit the Transparency Settings dialog box and apply the settings.

✔ Tip

■ To reverse the opaque and transparent areas of the key, check Reverse Key (**Figure 13.54**).

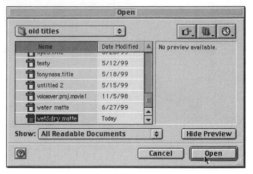

Figure 13.52 In the Open File dialog box, locate the still image that you want to use as the matte and click Open.

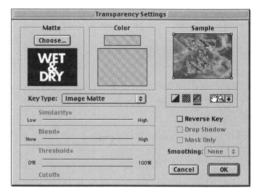

Figure 13.53 In the Matte section of the Transparency Settings dialog box, a thumbnail image of the matte appears.

Figure 13.54 Check Reverse Key to reverse the opaque and transparent areas of the key.

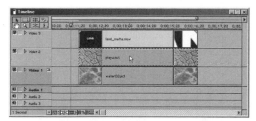

Figure 13.55 Stack the background, foreground, and matte clips in the timeline. Select the foreground clip.

Figure 13.56 Choose Clip > Video Options > Transparency.

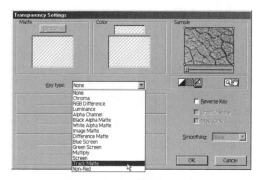

Figure 13.57 Choose Track Matte from the Key Type pull-down menu.

Using the Track Matte Key

The track matte key uses a moving matte, often called a *traveling matte*. The matte can be a high-contrast, grayscale video clip or an image that you animate with motion settings (Chapter 13), an effect (Chapter 10), or a text roll (Chapter 11). You can also create a matte from a clip by using the Transparency Settings dialog box. Unlike a still-image matte, a moving matte must be arranged in the timeline with the foreground and background clips.

To use the track matte key:

1. Arrange the clips for the track matte effect in the timeline:
   ▲ Position the background clip in a lower track.
   ▲ Position the foreground clip in the next-higher superimpose track.
   ▲ Position the moving matte in the superimpose track above the foreground clip.

2. Select the foreground clip (**Figure 13.55**).

3. Choose Clip > Video Options > Transparency (**Figure 13.56**).
   The Transparency Settings dialog box appears.

4. From the Key Type pull-down menu, choose Track Matte (**Figure 13.57**).

   continues on next page

The effects of the track matte key appear in the sample frame of the Transparency Settings dialog box (**Figure 13.58**).

5. Preview the key in the sample frame of the Transparency Settings dialog box.

6. Click OK to exit the Transparency Settings dialog box.

When you preview or export the appropriate area of the program, you'll see that the matte effect moves (**Figure 13.59**).

✔ Tip

- To reverse the transparent and opaque areas of the foreground image, check Reverse Key (**Figure 13.60**).

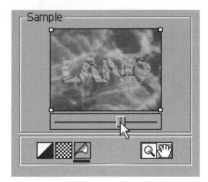

Figure 13.58 You can preview the first frame of the track matte key in the sample frame.

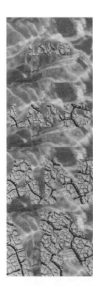

Figure 13.59 When you preview or export the appropriate area of the program, the matte effect moves.

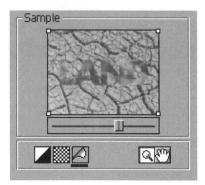

Figure 13.60 Reverse Key reverses the transparent and opaque areas of the key.

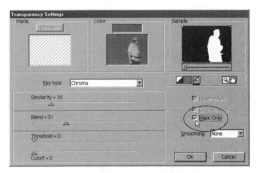

Figure 13.61 The Mask Only option uses the key type to create a black and white matte.

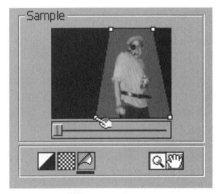

Figure 13.62 Use a garbage matte to throw away extraneous parts of an image before you apply a key …

Figure 13.63 … or use it to create a simple split screen effect.

Difference Matte Key

The difference matte key creates the transparent areas of a clip by comparing it with another still image and keying out the areas where the two clips match. The difference matte key is designed to remove a static background from behind a moving subject. By using a frame of a static background as the matte, you can key out the existing background and replace it with another. This key works only if the subject keeps moving and the camera remains static, however. This key type also provides the drop-shadow option.

Creating Mattes with the Mask Only Option

Mask Only is a checkbox available in the none, chroma, RGB difference, difference matte, blue screen, green screen, and non-red key types. The mask only option uses the key type to create a black and white matte (**Figure 13.61**). You can use the matte that you create with the track matte key.

Garbage Mattes

Garbage mattes earn their name because they are generally used to simply "throw out" extraneous areas of the frame. You create a garbage matte by dragging the corner handles of the sample frame to essentially crop the sides of the frame.

You can use a garbage matte in conjunction with other keys to eliminate unnecessary elements. For example, use a garbage matte to crop out the extraneous areas of the frame before you apply a chroma key. This way, you won't waste time adjusting the key for parts of the image you can exclude right away (**Figure 13.62**). You can also use a garbage matte to create a simple split-screen effect (**Figure 13.63**).

To create a garbage matte:

1. Select a clip in a superimpose track, and choose Clip > Video Options > Transparency (**Figure 13.64**).

   The Transparency Settings dialog box appears.

2. In the Sample section of the Transparency Settings dialog box, drag the handles of the image to key out unwanted areas of the clip (**Figure 13.65**).

✔ Tip

■ To smooth the edges of a split-screen effect, use the garbage matte in combination with the RGB difference key. Don't select a color; simply choose Low, Medium, or High from the Smoothing pull-down menu (**Figure 13.66**).

Figure 13.64 Select a clip in a superimpose track, and choose Clip > Video Options > Transparency.

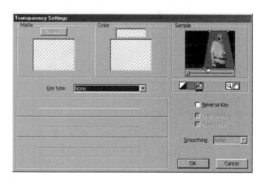

Figure 13.65 In the Sample section of the Transparency Settings dialog box, drag the handles of the image to key out unwanted areas of the clip.

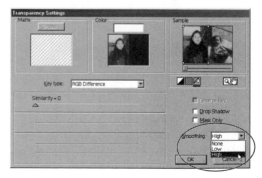

Figure 13.66 The RGB difference key provides a smoothing option you can use to smooth the edge of a garbage matte.

MOTION SETTINGS

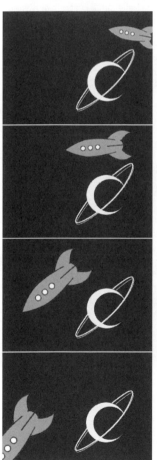

Motion settings allow you to move, rotate, zoom, and distort an image inside and outside the visible frame of the program view (**Figure 14.1**).

You can reposition a graphic to create a subtle logo "bug" in the corner of the screen, or fly titles and images wildly around the screen to promote a monster truck pull. By layering clips with motion settings, you can create a simple picture-in-picture effect, or compose several layers of video on the screen to create an elegant design. You can also create your own traveling mattes for track matte keys. As you learn about motion settings, try to look for ways to incorporate them with titles, effects, superimposing, or any other technique.

Figure 14.1
Motion settings allow you to reposition video or create two-dimensional animation.

Though motion settings help you to achieve all kinds of effects, you should be aware of one restriction: Motion settings are applied to the clip after they have been scaled to the output frame size. This prevents you from using motion settings to pan over an image larger than the screen size, simulating the camera pans commonly used in many documentaries. Instead, use the image pan effect (Chapter 11) to simulate these kinds of camera moves. Similarly, vector-based art (such as imported Illustrator files) is rasterized before motion settings are applied. Therefore, scaling the art above 100% with motion settings introduces aliasing, and pixels start to show. Then again, you would face a similar restriction if you were using a digital video effects (DVE) device in a traditional video suite.

Like the title window, the motion settings feature has required few changes from earlier versions. In the latest incarnation of Premiere, the controls in the Motion Settings dialog box have been slightly rearranged to accommodate a larger motion preview (**Figures 14.2** and **14.3**). Other than this welcome enhancement, everything works the same way as before.

Though that larger sample preview should give you an accurate idea of how the motion will look, you still have to render a preview (Chapter 9) to see the full effect in the program.

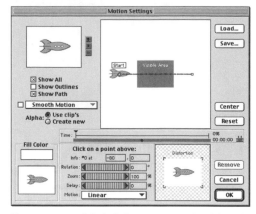

Figure 14.2 You'll find all the same controls of the old Motion Settings dialog box...

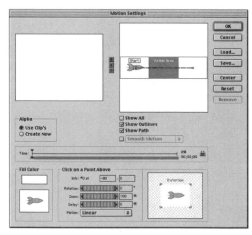

Figure 14.3 ...in the new Motion Settings dialog box, though they have been rearranged to accommodate a larger motion preview.

MOTION SETTINGS

Working with Keyframes (Again)

When you learned about effects in Chapter 11, you also learned about keyframes. As you recall, setting a keyframe defines the properties of an effect at a particular point in time. When the values of properties at each keyframe differ, Premiere calculates the value of the properties for all the frames in between. The result is an effect that changes over time.

Motion settings also use keyframes to define properties of a clip at certain frames—in this case, spatial properties, like position, rotation, scale, and distortion. Unlike effects, however, keyframes for motion settings appear in the Motion Settings dialog box, not in the timeline.

When you open the Motion Settings dialog box, it displays the default settings. The Start keyframe positions the clip offscreen left, and the Finish keyframe positions it offscreen right. Therefore, the default motion setting moves the clip through the screen horizontally, from offscreen left to offscreen right (**Figure 14.4**). Because even the most basic animation requires at least two keyframes, you can't delete the Start and Finish keyframes.

As with any form of animation, creating a motion setting revolves around repeatedly asking yourself the same basic question: What do I want the clip to look like at this point in time? Keyframes answer that question.

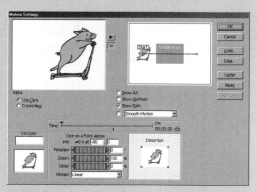

Figure 14.4 The default motion setting animates a clip horizontally through the visible area of the screen—offscreen left to offscreen right.

Applying Motion: An Overview

The following steps outline the basic process for applying a motion setting to a clip. Later sections describe each part of the process in more detail.

To add a motion setting to a clip:

1. In the timeline, select the clip to which you want to add motion (**Figure 14.5**).

2. Choose Clip > Video Options > Motion (**Figure 14.6**).

   The Motion Settings dialog box appears, and displays the default motion settings (**Figure 14.7**).

3. To add and adjust keyframes, *do any of the following:*

   ▲ To add keyframes spatially, click in the motion path.

   ▲ To add keyframes in time, click over the motion timeline.

   ▲ To move keyframes spatially, drag them in the motion path.

   ▲ To move keyframes in time, drag them in the timeline.

   For a more detailed explanation, see "Setting Keyframes," later in this chapter.

   ▲ To adjust the properties (position, rotation, distortion) at a selected keyframe, use the appropriate property controls at the bottom of the Motion Settings dialog box.

   For a more detailed explanation, see "Setting Keyframe Properties," later in this chapter.

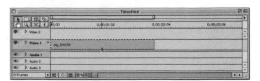

Figure 14.5 Select a clip in the timeline.

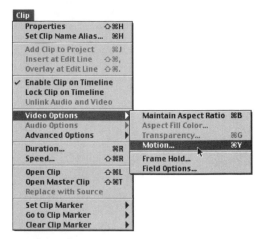

Figure 14.6 Choose Clip > Video Options > Motion.

Motion preview area *Motion path area— view keyframes spatially*

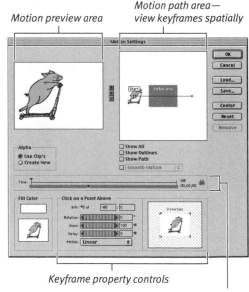

Keyframe property controls

Motion timeline—view keyframes in time

Figure 14.7 The Motion Settings dialog box contains controls to set keyframes in space and time, adjust the properties at each keyframe, and preview the motion.

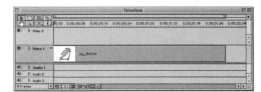

Figure 14.8 After you apply motion settings to a clip, it appears in the timeline with a red line at the bottom. Admittedly, it's hard to see when the clip is selected, (or when the illustration is in black and white).

4. Preview the motion using controls in the Motion Settings dialog box.

For details, see the section, "Previewing Motion," later in this chapter.

5. Repeat steps 3 and 4, as needed.

6. Click OK to close the Motion Settings dialog box and apply the motion settings to the clip.

The clip in the timeline displays a red line, indicating that you applied motion settings to it (**Figure 14.8**).

In order to see the motion effect in the program view, you must preview the appropriate area in the Timeline window, as explained in Chapter 9.

To remove a motion setting:

1. Select a clip in the timeline that has motion settings.

   Clips that have motion settings appear in the timeline with a red line (**Figure 14.9**).

2. Choose Clip > Video Options > Motion (**Figure 14.10**).

   The Motion Settings dialog box appears, displaying the default motion settings.

3. Click Remove to remove motion settings from the clip (**Figure 14.11**).

   In the Timeline window, the clip no longer displays a red line.

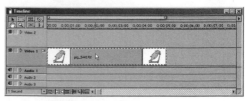

Figure 14.9 Select a clip containing a motion setting. It should display a red line.

Figure 14.10 Choose Clip > Video Options > Motion.

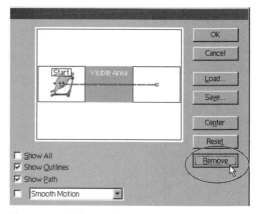

Figure 14.11 In the Motion Settings dialog box, click Remove to eliminate the Motion Settings.

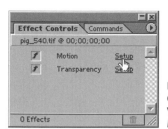

Figure 14.12
Choose Clip ›
Video Options ›
Motion.

✔ Tips

- The keyboard equivalent to Clip > Video Options > Motion is ⌘-Ⓨ (Mac) or Ctrl-Ⓨ (Windows).

- You can also access the Motion Settings dialog box from the Effect Controls palette. Next to Motion in a clip's Effect Controls palette, click either the box to the left, or the underlined word, Setup, to the right (**Figure 14.12**). Both open the Motion Settings dialog box.

Reverse Engineering

Sometimes it's easier to build a model if you've already seen the picture on the outside of the box. In much the same way, examining a finished motion setting can help you create your own. If the relatively minimal default settings are less than illuminating, you can load one of Premiere's preset motion settings files to study (**Figure 14.13**). See the section, "Saving and Loading Motion Settings" at the end of this chapter.

Once a motion setting is loaded:

- Press Tab to step through motion keyframes; they'll be highlighted in the motion path and in the motion timeline.

- Note the spatial position of keyframes in the motion path; note their position in time in the motion timeline.

- As you step through keyframes, note the values of properties, such as rotation and zoom.

- Press the spacebar to play and pause the sample preview.

If you're feeling bold, or if you already have experience with keyframe animation, you can modify the motion setting by changing the values at each keyframe. Otherwise, just press OK to apply the motion setting to the clip. After you preview it in the program, come back to this chapter to learn the process step-by-step.

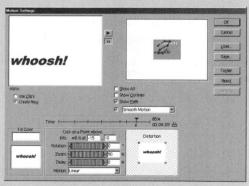

Figure 14.13 Premiere ships with 14 saved motion setting files you can load. Examining them can help you understand how motion settings work. This figure shows the "Whoosh 1" setting.

Previewing the Motion Setting

In the top left of the Motion Settings dialog box, a sample frame displays a preview of the motion setting (**Figure 14.14**). Though the motion preview closely approximates how the motion effect will look when it's rendered in the program, it may not play back as smoothly.

In Premiere 6, the sample preview is larger than in earlier versions. But if you're still not satisfied, you can also preview the motion in the program view of the Monitor window—without closing the Motion Settings dialog box.

Ordinarily, the sample preview illustrates the motion setting using only the first frame of the clip over a solid background. However, you can opt for a more accurate representation of the final effect and display clip playback, filters, and transparency, as well as any of the clips in the lower layers. Naturally, the added burden to your computer's processor may slow down the playback of the preview.

To preview the motion setting:

1. In the Motion Settings dialog box, *do any of the following*:

   ▲ To play an animation of the motion setting, press the play button ▶ (**Figure 14.15**).

   ▲ To pause the animated preview and view a static frame, press the pause button ▐▐ .

   ▲ Press the spacebar to toggle between play and pause.

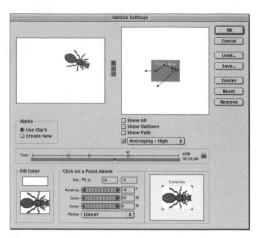

Figure 14.14 The motion preview area closely approximates how the motion will look when it's rendered in the program.

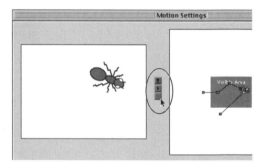

Figure 14.15 You can control the motion preview with standard play and pause buttons. The spacebar also toggles between play and pause.

PREVIEWING THE MOTION SETTING

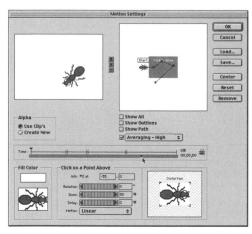

Figure 14.16 You can also control playback of the motion preview by dragging the arrow below the motion timeline.

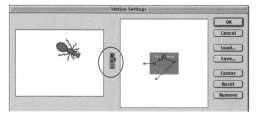

Figure 14.17 Click the collapse button...

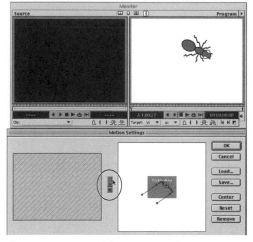

Figure 14.18 ...to send the preview to the program view of the Monitor window.

▲ To control playback manually, drag the small arrow under the timeline in the Motion Settings dialog box (**Figure 14.16**).

The frame displayed in the sample corresponds to the position of the small arrow under the motion timeline in the Motion Settings dialog box, as well as the edit line in the Timeline window.

To preview the motion in the program view:

◆ In the Motion Settings dialog box, click the collapse button ▣ (**Figure 14.17**).

The collapse button icon inverts, becoming the uncollapse button ▣ and the sample box turns gray. The motion preview appears in the program view (**Figure 14.18**). You may use the playback controls in the Motion Settings dialog box to preview the motion. Click the uncollapse button to return the image to the Motion Settings dialog box.

PREVIEWING THE MOTION SETTING

To display clip playback and other effects in the motion settings preview:

◆ In the Motion Settings dialog box, check Show All (**Figure 14.19**).

The motion settings preview displays clip playback, transitions, filters, transparency, and clips in lower layers (**Figure 14.20**). The additional processing this requires may cause the preview to play more slowly. Uncheck the Show All box to view the motion using the first frame of the clip against a solid background.

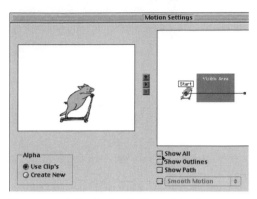

Figure 14.19 In the Motion Settings dialog box, checking Show All...

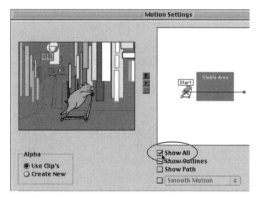

Figure 14.20 ...makes the motion preview display clip playback, transitions, filters, and clips in lower layers.

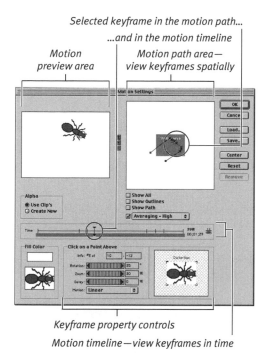

Selected keyframe in the motion path...

...and in the motion timeline

Motion preview area

Motion path area— view keyframes spatially

Keyframe property controls

Motion timeline—view keyframes in time

Figure 14.21 The motion path shows keyframes spatially; the motion timeline displays the same keyframes in time. The properties of the selected keyframes can be adjusted in the lower part of the dialog box.

Setting Keyframes

You can set motion keyframes in two areas of the Motion Settings dialog box: the motion path area, and the motion timeline. The properties of each keyframe—such as position, rotation, and so on—can be adjusted in the lower part of the Motion Settings dialog box (**Figure 14.21**).

In the large box at the top of the Motion Settings dialog box, you can add and adjust keyframes on a motion path. The motion path area indicates the position of the clip spatially. The gray visible area box corresponds to the visible viewing area of Program view. It's possible to position the clip inside and outside the visible area box. Keyframes in the motion path appear as dots, or handles. As you can see, the motion path makes it easy to see and manipulate the position of the image at a keyframe, but gives you little control over the timing of a keyframe.

For more precise control over timing, you can add and adjust keyframes in the motion timeline. The span of the motion timeline represents the entire duration of the clip, from in point to out point. In the motion timeline, keyframes appear as a vertical line; when a keyframe is selected, a triangle appears at the top of the line.

The keyframes in the motion path and the motion timeline are the same keyframes represented in different ways.

To add keyframes in the motion path:

1. Position the mouse pointer on the line of the motion path (**Figure 14.22**).

   The pointer turns into an add keyframe icon. It looks like a finger pointing diagonally. 👆

2. Click to add a keyframe on the motion path line.

   A dot represents the keyframe in the motion path (**Figure 14.23**). When the keyframe is selected, a thumbnail representation of the clip appears at the keyframe.

3. To change the position of the image at the keyframe, drag the point to a new position.

   The pointer becomes the move keyframe icon, which looks like a finger pointing up 👆 (**Figure 14.24**).

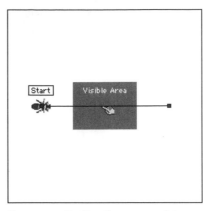

Figure 14.22 Position the mouse pointer on the line of the motion path...

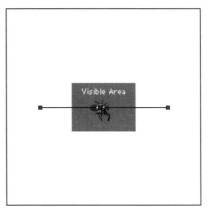

Figure 14.23 ...and click to add a keyframe. Here, the keyframe has been emphasized so you can see it better.

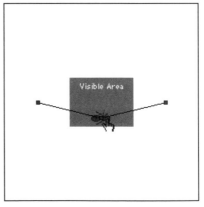

Figure 14.24 Drag the keyframe handle to move it.

Figure 14.25 Position the mouse pointer above the motion timeline until it becomes a triangle...

Figure 14.26 ...and click to add a keyframe. Keyframes in the timeline appear as vertical lines; the selected keyframe displays a triangle at the top of the line.

Figure 14.27 You can drag a keyframe to the right or left to change its position in time.

To add keyframes in the motion timeline:

1. Position the mouse pointer above the motion timeline.

   The pointer becomes a triangle (**Figure 14.25**).

2. Click to add a keyframe at the point in time indicated by the timeline.

   A keyframe appears, represented by a small vertical line. When the keyframe is selected, as it is now, a triangle appears at the top of the line (**Figure 14.26**).

3. Drag the keyframe to the right or left to change its position in time (**Figure 14.27**).

   A percentage display indicates the selected keyframe's relative position in time. For example, 50% equals halfway through the duration of the clip.

Selecting and Deleting Keyframes

You can select keyframes either directly in the motion path or the timeline, or by using keyboard shortcuts. You can delete any selected keyframe, except for the Start and Finish keyframes.

To select a keyframe:

In the Motion Settings dialog box, *do one of the following:*

◆ Click a point on the motion path.

◆ Click a keyframe in the motion timeline.

◆ Press ⟨Tab⟩ to select successive keyframes in order from Start to Finish.

◆ Press ⟨Shift⟩+⟨Tab⟩ to select successive keyframes in reverse order, from Finish to Start.

In the motion path, the selected keyframe appears highlighted; in the motion timeline, the selected keyframe appears as a triangle (**Figure 14.28**).

To delete a keyframe:

◆ Select a keyframe and then press the Delete key.

You may not delete the Start or Finish keyframes. Dragging a keyframe will only move it, not delete it.

✔ Tips

■ When selecting keyframes in the motion path, make sure the 🖑 appears. Clicking with the 🖐 will add a keyframe. Similarly, the 🖑 appears in the motion timeline. When a triangle appears over the timeline, clicking adds a keyframe.

■ If you don't want any motion, don't try to eliminate all the keyframes; simply click the Remove button to remove the motion setting altogether.

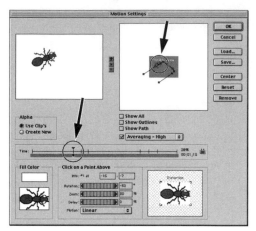

Figure 14.28 In the motion path, the selected keyframe appears highlighted; in the motion timeline, the selected keyframe appears as a triangle.

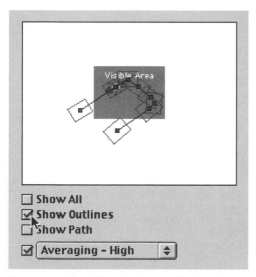

Figure 14.29 Check Show Outlines to display a framed outline representing the clip image at every keyframe in the motion path.

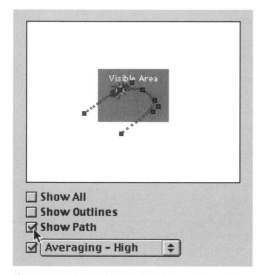

Figure 14.30 Check Show Path and the motion path displays a dotted line between keyframes. The spacing of the dots indicates speed. The path also reflects the selected smooth motion options.

Viewing Options in the Motion Path

Ordinarily, the motion path resembles a connect-the-dots representation of the motion setting. However, you can display additional information in the motion path to better analyze and adjust the clip's motion.

As well as dots that represent the positions of the keyframes, you can display a framed outline that shows the size and orientation of the image.

In addition to a simple line that represents the direction of motion, you can display a dotted path, which indicates the speed. Wider spacing between dots indicates faster speed between keyframes; tighter spacing represents slower speed.

To display frame outlines at keyframes in the motion path:

◆ Check Show Outlines

A frame outline representing the clip image appears at every keyframe in the motion path (**Figure 14.29**).

To display speed in the motion path:

◆ Check Show Path

The motion path displays dotted lines between keyframes. Dots that are closer together represent slower speed between keyframes; dots that are farther apart represent faster speed (**Figure 14.30**). The Show Path option also reflects the effects of smoothing options (see the section, "Smoothing Motion Using Spatial Interpolation.")

Viewing Time in the Motion Timeline

When you select a keyframe in the motion timeline, a display expresses its position in time as a percentage of the clip's duration. The Start keyframe is always at 0%; the Finish keyframe is always at 100%. A keyframe halfway through the clip would be 50%, and so on. Though this display is useful in relative terms, it can sometimes be difficult to determine what it means in terms of actual time.

Under the percentage display, the position of the selected keyframe is also expressed in minutes, seconds and frames. Depending on your choice, the display can indicate the time of the selected keyframe as measured from the beginning of the source clip (not its in point) or from the beginning of the program.

To position a keyframe at an exact time:

◆ To the right of the motion timeline, click the small red arrows to toggle the time display:

▲ **Touching arrows** —measures the position of the selected keyframe from the beginning of the source clip, not the in point (**Figure 14.31**).

▲ **Separated arrows** —measures the position of the selected keyframe from the beginning of the program, that is, the start of the timeline. (**Figure 14.32**).

✔ Tips

■ When you move a keyframe in the motion timeline, look at the time display to position it exactly.

■ As you drag a keyframe in the motion timeline, its position is also reflected by the edit line in the Timeline window.

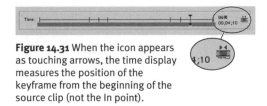

Figure 14.31 When the icon appears as touching arrows, the time display measures the position of the keyframe from the beginning of the source clip (not the In point).

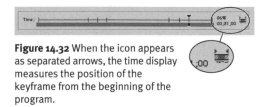

Figure 14.32 When the icon appears as separated arrows, the time display measures the position of the keyframe from the beginning of the program.

Setting Keyframe Properties

In previous sections, you learned how to use the motion path and motion timeline to create and adjust keyframes.

Though these controls enable you to define basic position and timing of keyframes, other controls allow you to specify various other properties of the clip at each keyframe: position, rotation, zoom, and distortion.

In addition to controlling the properties of the clip at each keyframe, you can also choose how Premiere calculates the values between keyframes, or its *interpolation* method. Setting a delay value for a keyframe postpones calculations, causing the motion to pause for a specified amount of time. Other temporal interpolation methods can cause movement to accelerate or decelerate from one keyframe to next. Changing the spatial interpolation can smooth the movement through keyframes, so that the clip takes a round turn, rather than a sharp corner.

The following sections explain how to set the value of these properties at each keyframe, and how to choose among the options that control how the values are interpolated.

✔ Tip

■ Use the standard copy and paste keyboard shortcuts to copy settings from one keyframe to another. Select a keyframe, press ⌘-Ⓒ (Mac) or Ⓒᵗʳˡ-Ⓒ (Windows) to copy its attributes. Create or select another keyframe and press ⌘-Ⓥ (Mac) or Ⓒᵗʳˡ-Ⓥ (Windows) to paste them to the keyframe.

Setting Position

True, you can set the position at a keyframe in the motion path. However, additional controls allow you to make more precise adjustments.

To set the spatial position at a keyframe:

1. In the Motion Settings dialog box, select a keyframe.

2. To change the spatial position of the selected keyframe, *do any of the following:*

   ▲ To change the position manually, drag the keyframe in the motion path (**Figure 14.33**).

   ▲ To nudge the position 1 pixel at a time, press an arrow key.

   ▲ To move the position 5 pixels at a time, press (Shift) + arrow key.

   ▲ To center the clip in the visible area (at coordinates 0,0), click the Center button (**Figure 14.34**).

   ▲ To set the position numerically, type X and Y coordinates in the boxes below the motion timeline (**Figure 14.35**).

✔ Tip

■ The coordinates in the Info boxes are expressed in the pixel dimensions of the sample image in the motion path area of the Motion Settings dialog box, which is 80×60. These numbers are scaled to your output size when the motion is rendered or exported. Therefore, a 1-pixel shift at the sample size equals a 4-pixel shift at an output size of 320×240 (4 times 80×60). To compensate for the difference, you can type fractional decimal values for the coordinates.

Figure 14.33 You can drag the position of a keyframe directly in the motion path.

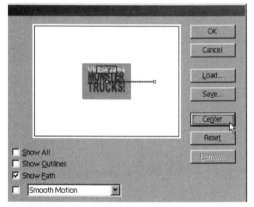

Figure 14.34 Click Center to position the clip at the center of the visible area for the current keyframe.

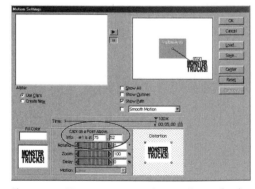

Figure 14.35 You can enter X and Y coordinates for the current keyframe's position, expressed in the pixel dimensions of the sample in the motion path area, 80 x 60 pixels.

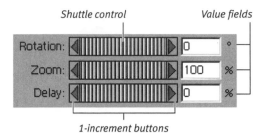

Shuttle control   *Value fields*

1-increment buttons

Figure 14.36 You can use the same type of controls to set values for rotation, zoom, and delay.

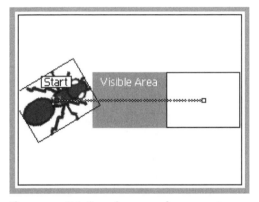

Figure 14.37 Rotation values range from –1440 to 1440 degrees. Here, the first keyframe Is rotated –30 degrees.

Figure 14.38 Zoom values range from 0% to 500%. Here, the image in Figure 14.37 has been scaled down to 50%.

Setting Rotation, Zoom, and Delay

Under the position coordinates, you can set values for each keyframe's rotation, zoom, and delay properties. All three properties use the same type of controls: including a slider, buttons, and a numeric value field (**Figure 14.36**).

To better understand rotation, it can be helpful to think of it as being rotational position or angle. The angle that you enter can range from –1440 degrees to 1440 degrees, allowing eight full rotations between keyframes (**Figure 14.37**).

Zoom increases or decreases the size of the clip at the keyframe. The size can range from 0 percent to 500 percent; 100 percent equals the clip at its normal size (**Figure 14.38**).

Delay pauses the clip at a keyframe for a specified period, expressed as a percentage of the clip's total duration. When you add a delay value, a blue line appears in the motion timeline, representing the length of the dclay. Delay saves you from having to set two keyframes with the same property values to create a pause in motion.

To set rotation, zoom, and delay:

1. In the Motion Settings dialog box, select a keyframe.

2. To set the rotation, zoom, or delay at the selected keyframe, *do any of the following:*

   ▲ To increase a value, drag a shuttle to the right.

   ▲ To decrease a value, drag a value shuttle control to the left.

   ▲ To change a value by a single increment, press the arrow keys on either side of a shuttle control.

   ▲ To enter a specific value, type a value in the box next to the property.

3. Repeat steps 1 and 2, as needed.

4. Preview your settings.

5. Click OK to apply the motion to the clip.

✔ Tips

■ When the coordinate, rotation, zoom, or delay value field is selected, pressing Tab advances to the next field. Press Return (Mac) or Enter (Windows) to set the value and deselect the property value area. When these fields are deselected, pressing Tab steps through the keyframes of the motion setting.

■ Remember that rotation is expressed as an angle, not as the amount of rotation from one keyframe to the next. To rotate a clip one full rotation clockwise and then remain at that angle, you make the three keyframes 0, 360, and 360. A common mistake would be to make the keyframes 0, 360, and 0. These settings would cause the clip to rotate first clockwise and then counterclockwise.

What's the Delay?

Strictly speaking, Delay isn't a physical property like Rotation and Zoom; it's a form of temporal interpolation. In other words, it determines how Premiere calculates value changes from one keyframe to the next. Rather than change the value using a simple linear progression, Premiere pauses the calculations for the time specified by delay value. But because you assign a delay value to a keyframe in the same way as rotation and zoom, this book explains all three in the same section.

Motion settings offer other interpolation options. These options can make the motion accelerate or decelerate, or cause the clip to take a smoother path from one keyframe to the next. For a detailed explanation of these options, see "Setting Interpolation Options," later in this chapter.

If Premiere won't accept a delay value, the value probably exceeds the remaining duration of the clip. Use a smaller value, or move the keyframe to an earlier position in time.

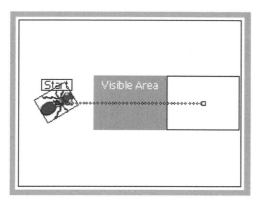

Figure 14.39 Drag one of the corner handles to distort the image at the current keyframe.

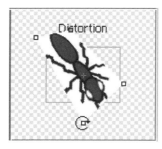

Figure 14.40
Option-drag (Mac) or Alt-drag (Windows) a corner handle to pivot the image around that point.

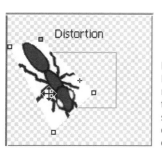

Figure 14.41
Position the mouse pointer in the center of the sample image and drag to move the entire image.

Setting Distortion

To the right of the property value sliders in the Motion Settings dialog box, you'll find a sample frame of your clip, labeled Distortion. The sample frame has four corner handles you can drag to distort the clip at each keyframe. Use it to skew, stretch, or even flip the image over.

Distortion doesn't have to result in a wacky effect. It's possible to use it more subtly. Because it can be used on a clip in a superimpose track, it can also be more convenient than using a similar wipe transition.

To distort a clip:

1. In the Motion Settings dialog box, select a keyframe.

2. In the Distortion section of the Motion Settings dialog box, do any of the following:
   ▲ Drag one of the corner handles to a new position (**Figure 14.39**).
   ▲ Option-drag (Mac) or Alt-drag (Windows) a corner handle to pivot the image around that point (**Figure 14.40**).
   ▲ Position the mouse pointer in the center of the sample image and drag to move the entire image (**Figure 14.41**).

3. Repeat steps 1 and 2, as needed.

4. Preview the motion setting, and click OK to apply it to the clip.

✔ Tips

■ Because the distortion settings do not have numerical controls, it can be especially useful to copy and paste distortion settings from one keyframe to the next.

■ Various effects can also distort a clip. In particular, check out the effects grouped in the distort category of the Effect Controls palette.

Resetting Attributes

If you decide against the rotation, zoom, delay, and distortion values you set for a keyframe, you can reset them to their default values with a single click of a button. The temporal interpolation option will also be reset to its default setting: Linear. Position and spatial interpolation options for the keyframe are retained, however.

To reset rotation, zoom, delay, and distortion settings for a keyframe:

1. In the Motion Settings dialog box, select a keyframe.

2. Click Reset (**Figure 14.42**).

   Rotation, zoom, delay, distortion, and temporal interpolation are reset to their default values for the selected keyframe.

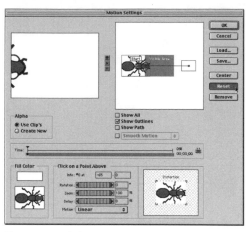

Figure 14.42 Click Reset to set the selected keyframe's rotation, zoom, delay, distortion, and motion options to their default values.

Speed Bumps

When you apply a motion setting to a clip, you apply it to the entire clip. The "entire clip" means the entire duration in the timeline, and the entire video frame. That sounds obvious enough. But if you don't fully appreciate this essential fact, it's easy to run into problems.

Like effects, motion settings are applied to the entire duration of a clip in the program, from in point to out point. In other words, the total duration of the motion equals the duration of the clip. If you lengthen the duration of the clip, the same motion takes a longer amount of time; if you shorten the duration, the same motion takes place in less time. And of course, the time it takes to travel a distance is the definition of speed.

Yet if you're new to animation, you may find this once familiar concept confounding. You may find yourself wanting the motion to look slower, lasting longer than the clip itself. Impossible, unless you increase the clip's duration: either by changing its in or out points, or by making it play in slow motion. At other times, you may want the motion to move faster, ending before the clip does. You can set a delay value for the second-to-last keyframe, so that the motion holds until the end of the clip. However, no matter what you try to do, the motion's Start keyframe will always be at the clip's in point; the Finish keyframe will always be at the out point.

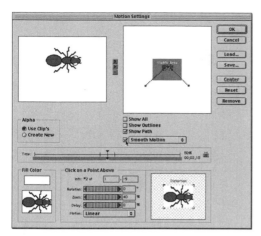

Figure 14.43 Check the box next to the Smooth Motion pull-down menu to activate it.

Smoothing Motion with Spatial Interpolation

Ordinarily, a clip proceeds to and from keyframes directly, in straight lines. You can smooth sharp changes in direction, rotation, and distortion by selecting one of the smooth motion options. These options cause the clip to follow a rounder, smoother course.

To choose a smooth motion option:

1. In the Motion Settings dialog box, check the box next to the Smooth Motion pull-down menu (**Figure 14.43**).

   The Smooth Motion pull-down menu becomes active.

continues on next page

Interpolation Options

The beauty of keyframes is that they save you work. If you set the keyframes, Premiere calculates the frames in between, a process known as *interpolation*. You won't find the word, "interpolation" in Premiere's documentation, but you will encounter the term in other animation programs, including Adobe's own After Effects. No harm in getting used to it now. By default, Premiere calculates the values between keyframes using a linear progression. Spatially, this linear interpolation method means that a clip proceeds from one position to the next in a straight line. Temporally, linear interpolation causes the clip to move from one position to the next at a constant rate, or speed.

As you might guess, simple linear interpolation can make motion seem somewhat mechanical. To make motion appear more natural, you would have to set many more keyframes—and in effect defeat their labor-saving purpose. Fortunately, Premiere offers a few other, more sophisticated interpolation methods. Temporally, this means motion can accelerate or decelerate from one keyframe to the next. Spatially, interpolation options allow movement to follow a smoother, rounder course through keyframe positions.

2. From the Smooth Motion pull-down menu, choose a smoothing option (**Figure 14.44**):

Smooth Motion—for the smallest amount of smoothing.

Averaging-Low—for a moderate amount of smoothing.

Averaging-High—for a high amount of smoothing.

If the Show Paths option is checked, you can see the effects of the smooth motion option in the motion path (**Figure 14.45**).

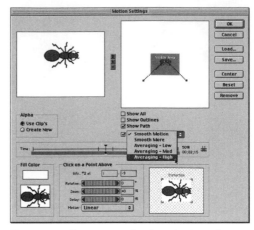

Figure 14.44 Choose an option from the Smooth Motion pull-down menu.

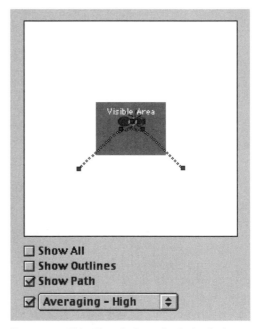

Figure 14.45 If the Show Paths option is checked, you can see the effects of the smooth motion option in the motion path.

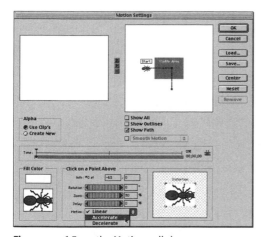

Figure 14.46 From the Motion pull-down menu, choose one of the three motion options.

Figure 14.47 If the Show Paths option is checked, you can see changes in speed in the motion path.

Creating Acceleration or Deceleration

Ordinarily, motion proceeds from one keyframe to the next at a constant rate. Motion options change Premiere's temporal interpolation method, so that the rate can change between keyframes. In other words, movement can accelerate or decelerate from one keyframe to the next. This way, motion can ease into or out of a position, which can look more natural. Note that these options don't change the time between keyframes. Whether it accelerates, decelerates, or moves at a constant speed, the clip traverses the distance between keyframes in the same amount of time.

To select a motion option:

1. In the Motion Settings dialog box, select a keyframe.

2. From the Motion pull-down menu at the bottom of the Motion Settings dialog box, choose one of the three interpolation options (**Figure 14.46**):

   Linear—motion proceeds from the selected keyframe to the next keyframe at a constant rate, in a linear progression.

   Accelerate—motion proceeds from the selected keyframe to the next keyframe slowly at first, then more quickly.

   Decelerate—motion proceeds from the selected keyframe to the next keyframe quickly at first, then more slowly.

   Regardless of the option you choose, the time between keyframes remains the same. If the Show Paths option is checked, you can see changes in speed in the motion path (**Figure 14.47**).

Setting the Fill Color

When a clip containing a motion setting does not fill the visible frame, the empty part of the frame is filled with a solid color. You can select a *fill color* either from the sample frame or from a color picker.

To set the fill color:

In the Fill Color area in the lower left of the Motion Settings dialog box, *do one of the following:*

◆ To select a color from the clip image, click in the sample frame.

The eyedropper tool appears, and the selected color appears in the Fill Color swatch and in the preview area of the Motion Settings dialog box (**Figure 14.48**).

◆ To pick a color from the color picker, click in the color swatch (**Figure 14.49**).

The color picker appears. Select a color and click OK to close the color picker and return to the Motion Settings dialog box. The fill color appears in the sample preview.

✔ Tip

■ If the fill color you select doesn't appear in the preview sample, press Tab to step through the keyframes. This should make the sample preview update and show the fill color.

Figure 14.48 To select a color from the clip image, click in the sample frame.

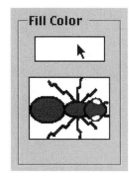

Figure 14.49 To pick a color from the color picker, click in the color swatch.

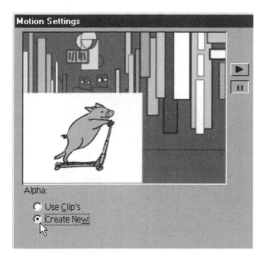

Figure 14.50 Create New generates an alpha channel to cut out the frame of the clip and ignores any alpha channel information contained in the clip.

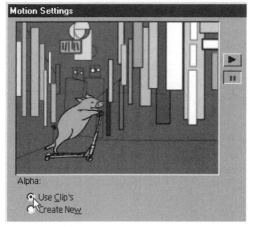

Figure 14.51 Use Clip's recognizes the alpha channel contained in the clip.

Setting Alpha Channel Options

Adding a motion setting to a clip frequently means that you're also superimposing it over other clips in the program. Conveniently, the Motion Settings feature supplies an alpha channel that you can use to key out the parts of the frame left empty by the moving clip.

However, if the clip already contains an alpha channel, you must specify whether to use that channel or the alpha channel generated by the motion setting. Do this by selecting an alpha channel option in the Motion Settings dialog box.

To select an alpha channel option:

In the Motion Settings dialog box, select the appropriate radio button:

Alpha: Create New—to create an alpha channel that matches the frame of the clip, ignoring any existing alpha channel (**Figure 14.50**).

Alpha: Use Clip's—to use the clip's alpha channel (**Figure 14.51**).

✔ Tips

- If the clip is in a superimpose track when you add the motion setting, Premiere applies the appropriate alpha channel key type automatically. Premiere even knows when the motion setting has been applied to a title clip, and applies a black alpha matte or white alpha matte key, whichever is appropriate. However, if you want to use another keying method, such as a color key, you must set it manually.

- If you're frustrated by the fact that motion settings don't include controls to soften the edges of a clip's frame, apply the same motion settings to a soft-edged matte, and use the matte key effects.

Saving and Loading Motion Settings

If you're particularly fond of a motion setting (or if you've worked particularly hard to create it), you can save it as a separate motion settings file. Later, you can instantly apply your motion settings to a clip in any project.

Premiere also ships with several preset motion-settings files, which are located in the Motion Settings folder inside the Premiere folder. These settings not only provide preset effects but also serve as useful examples for you to examine or modify. Don't forget that you can also use saved motion settings with the motion transition (see Chapter 8).

To save a motion setting:

1. Create a motion setting, as explained in the preceding sections.

2. In the Motion Settings dialog box, click Save (**Figure 14.52**).

   A Save Motion Settings dialog box appears.

3. In the Save Motion Settings dialog box, specify a name and location for the motion setting file (**Figure 14.53**).

   If you want to be able to use your saved motion setting on a Windows system, its name shouldn't exceed eight characters, and should include .PMT at the end.

4. Click Save.

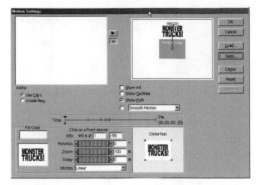

Figure 14.52 In the Motion Settings dialog box, click Save to save a motion setting as a file.

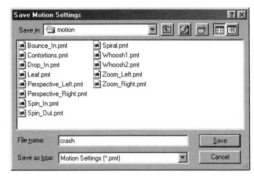

Figure 14.53 In the Save Motion Settings dialog box, specify a name and location for the motion setting file.

SAVING AND LOADING MOTION SETTINGS

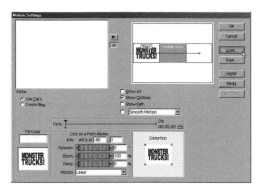

Figure 14.54 To use a saved motion setting, click Load in the Motion Settings dialog box.

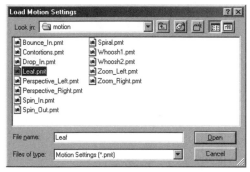

Figure 14.55 In the Open dialog box, locate and choose a motion-settings file and click Open.

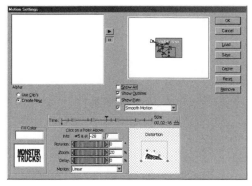

Figure 14.56 The motion settings you selected become the current motion settings.

To load a motion setting:

1. In the Motion Settings dialog box, click Load (**Figure 14.54**).

   An Open dialog box appears.

2. In the Open dialog box, locate and choose a motion-settings file (**Figure 14.55**).

   The motion settings that are included with Premiere are located in the Motion Settings folder, which is in the Premiere folder.

3. Click Open.

   The motion settings you selected become the current motion settings (**Figure 14.56**).

4. If you want, modify the keyframes and other settings.

5. Click OK to apply the motion settings to the clip.

✔ Tips

- You can copy and paste motion settings from one clip in the timeline to another by using the Paste Custom command. (See Chapter 6.)

- You can also load motion settings into the motion transition. (See Chapter 8.)

15

CREATING OUTPUT

At the beginning of the editing process, you asked yourself, "What is my final output goal?" Now it's time to deliver.

Depending on your needs, you can output your program to videotape, as a digital file, or both. If your computer has a video capture card, or a FireWire or iLink, you can output the program directly from the timeline to a video camera or video tape recorder. Alternatively, you may want to create a stand-alone movie file to burn to a CD-ROM, or present via the Web.

On the other hand, the edited Premiere program may not represent your completed work. An exported movie may serve as source material for other programs—such as a Power Point presentation, After Effects composition, or even another Premiere project. If you are using Premiere as an offline editing tool, you can export an edit decision list (EDL) for use with a traditional online editing suite.

It can be difficult to master every aspect of the export process. The number of options can be daunting, and the minutiae of issues such as compression and video standards can be difficult to grasp—or, at very least, boring. Luckily, recent developments have made export relatively simple. If you're working in an all-DV editing environment, it couldn't get much easier. Unlike using a capture card, the process doesn't require you to install hardware or software, or to familiarize yourself with hardware-specific settings. If exporting to Web formats is your goal, the Media Cleaner and Real Media plug-ins provide simple presets optimized for your target format, whether it's a CD-ROM, streaming media, or MP3.

Choosing Export Options and Settings

You can export footage from the timeline or from an individual clip. When you export from the timeline, you can export the entire program, or just the area below the work area bar. Similarly, you can export an entire clip or just the area between its in and out points. Because the two procedures are essentially the same, the following sections focus on exporting from the timeline.

The settings that determine the characteristics of the footage you export depend on the export option you choose. When you print to video or export to tape, playback is based on the settings from the source clip or project settings. When you export a movie file, you select settings in the Export Movie dialog box. When you use a plug-in export option— such as Media Cleaner or Real Media— you choose settings in dialog boxes unique to the plug-in.

✔ Tip

- Exporting Clip Sequences and Fast-Start QuickTime Movie features is obsolete in Premiere 6.

Considering Output Goals

Your output goal helps determine the settings you choose. Though you've thought of it from the beginning of your project (right?), the considerations are worth reviewing.

Videotape—Exporting to tape is simultaneously the easiest and most difficult export option. It's simple in that it can be straightforward: your capture, project, and export settings all match. Video formats demand a lot from your system, however. For DV, your system must meet minimum requirements. In particular, your hard drives must be able to sustain the minimum data rate for playing back DV footage—approximately 3.6 MB/sec. For other types of device, such as a Matrox or Pinnacle capture card, you need to familiarize yourself with the requirements of your hardware. If you're preparing your videotape for television broadcast, it may have to comply to stringent standards for video signal and format. Be sure to check with the presenter or a postproduction facility to learn the requirements.

CD-ROM—When you optimize a movie to play from a CD-ROM, your primary goal is compatibility. You also should answer the following questions:

◆ Does the movie need to be cross-platform-compatible?

◆ What movie player software will be used?

◆ What is the slowest possible CD drive that will be playing the movie?

◆ Will the movie be copied from CD to play back from a hard drive? If so, what is the slowest hard drive that will be playing back the movie?

◆ What image quality do you require?

◆ What is the total running time of the movie, and will you be able to reduce the file size to fit onto a typical CD-ROM, which holds 650 MB?

Web—When you optimize movies for Web delivery, file size (and its conjoined twin, data rate) is the primary concern. To stream a movie, you need to limit the movie's data rate to the slowest anticipated connection speed. Even for fast Internet connections, that's a big limitation. You'll have to decide whether the loss in quality is worth the immediate playback capability. The limitations are more forgiving for movies that can be downloaded. In this case, file size influences how long the viewer will have to wait before watching your movie. Though a *progressive download* format will start playing before the movie is fully downloaded to the viewer's hard drive, file size remains an impediment, especially if the movie is more than, say, one minute in duration.

Other Programs—If you're exporting footage from Premiere to use in another program, the factors you should consider depend on the particular format and program. Nevertheless, you should bear in mind several common issues. Make sure you know the file formats and compression types that the program accepts. If you want to retain transparency, choose a codec that supports an alpha channel (such as Uncompressed in Windows, Apple None, or Animation). When you are exporting still frames acquired on video, be aware that video resolution translates into a mere 72 dpi, which is appropriate only for relatively small, low-quality printouts. When you are exporting a still-image sequence, use the naming convention for image sequences that your system uses.

Exporting File Types

Premiere exports various file formats for video, audio, or image sequences. The formats that you can export depend on whether you are using the Macintosh or Windows version of Premiere. The formats that each platform opens and plays, however, depend on your particular system. You can also add formats via plug-in software extensions.

✔ Tip

- Formats such as Windows Media and QuickTime are known as media *architectures*, which include a growing number of individual compression schemes, or *codecs*. Cinepak, for example, is a codec supported by both QuickTime and Windows Media. For more information about compression and codecs, see Chapter 18.

Formats for Export

Video/audio formats
- ◆ Animated GIF
- ◆ DV Stream
- ◆ Microsoft AVI
- ◆ QuickTime
- ◆ MPEG
- ◆ RealMedia
- ◆ Windows Media
- ◆ ASF

Audio-only formats
- ◆ AIFF
- ◆ MP3
- ◆ Windows Audio Waveform (Windows only)

Still-image formats
- ◆ Filmstrip
- ◆ FLC/FLI (Windows)
- ◆ GIF/GIF Sequence
- ◆ PICT/PICT Sequence (Mac OS only)
- ◆ Targa/Targa Sequence
- ◆ TIFF/TIFF Sequence
- ◆ Windows Bitmap/Windows Bitmap Sequence (Windows only)

EXPORTING FILE TYPES

Recording to Tape

If your computer can output a video signal, you can record your program to videotape by using either the Print to Video or Export to Tape command. The term *print* really isn't far from the truth; in effect, you're creating a "hard copy" of your video file. You can print to video in three ways: directly from the program, from a single clip, or from a storyboard.

When you record directly from the program or storyboard, the settings that you specify in the Project Settings dialog box (see Chapter 2) determine the characteristics of the final video, such as the frame size and compression.

You determine the qualities of a clip, on the other hand, when you capture it (see Chapter 16) or create it from a program (as explained in "Creating a Movie" later in this chapter).

If you're using device control to control the operation of the camera or deck, you can choose the Export to Tape command. Otherwise, choose the Print to Video command and operate the camera or deck manually. Either way, the Print to Video and Export to Tape commands won't prompt you to choose settings.

When you are exporting the program in the timeline, you may want to double-check the project settings (see Chapter 2). Also, make sure that the program is ready for export by replacing any offline files with the original footage (see Chapter 2) and rendering any transitions and effects (see Chapter 9).

To print to video:

1. *Do either of the following:*

   ▲ To export the program from the timeline, select the Timeline window or Monitor window.

   or

   ▲ To export a clip, open a video clip.

2. To define the footage you want to export, *do either of the following:*

   ▲ In the program, set the work area bar over the range in the timeline you want to export.

   or

   ▲ In a clip, set the in and out points to define the frames you want to export.

3. Choose either of the following:

   File > Export Timeline > Print to Video—to export from the timeline (**Figure 15.1**).

   File > Export Clip > Print to Video—to export a clip.

   The Print to Video dialog box appears (**Figure 15.2**).

4. *Do any of the following:*

   ▲ To play NTSC color bars before the program begins, enter the number of seconds in the Color bars for field.

   ▲ To play a black video before the program begins (but after the color bars), enter the number of seconds in the Play black for field.

Figure 15.1 Choose File > Export Timeline > Print to Video.

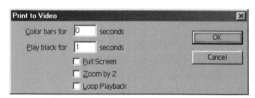

Figure 15.2 The Print to Video dialog box appears.

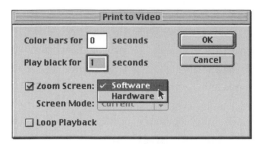

Figure 15.3 Choose an option from the Zoom Screen pull-down menu.

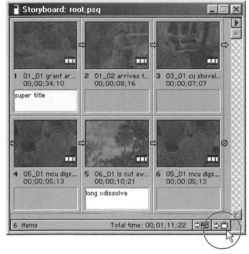

Figure 15.4 To export a storyboard, click the print to video button in the Storyboard window.

▲ To play the video back at double normal size, select Zoom Screen and choose an option from the Zoom Screen pull-down menu (**Figure 15.3**):

Software—to use software (such as QuickTime) to zoom the image size.

Hardware—to use your hardware capture card to zoom the image size.

This option can be useful if the normal size of the image is less than full-screen. When this option is selected, a 320x240 movie plays back at 640x480.

▲ To play the program or clip repeatedly, check Loop Playback.

5. If available, choose an option from the Screen Mode pull-down menu:

Current—to play back video on the main computer screen.

NTSC—to use an attached television monitor.

This option is available when certain capture card hardware plug-ins are installed. Check the documentation for your hardware.

6. Prepare your recording device, and click OK in the Print to Video dialog box to begin playing back the program.

To stop playback, press ⌘-. (Mac) or Ctrl-. (Windows).

✔ Tips

■ To export a storyboard, click the print to video button ⮕🖥 in the Storyboard window (**Figure 15.4**).

■ Even if your computer isn't connected to a VCR, you can use the Print to Video command to present the video over a blank screen.

RECORDING TO TAPE

Printing to Tape

If you have a recording device connected, you can choose to print to tape. When you use a compatible camera or deck, Premiere can activate your deck automatically. You can even choose where on the tape to start recording, if you can provide a timecode number at the start time. Typically, you use a *black and coded* tape—a tape with a black video signal and timecode.

The following example uses a DV camera as the recording device. Options may vary according to your hardware.

To print to tape:

1. *Do either of the following:*
   ▲ To export the program from the timeline, select the Timeline window or Monitor window.

   or

   ▲ To export a clip, open a video clip.

2. To define the footage you want to export, *do either of the following:*
   ▲ In the program, set the work area bar over the range in the timeline you want to export.

   or

   ▲ In a clip, set the in and out points to define the frames you want to export.

3. Choose either of the following:

   File > Export Timeline > Export to Tape—to export from the timeline (**Figure 15.5**).

   File > Export Clip > Export to Tape—to export a clip.

   The Export to Tape dialog box appears (**Figure 15.6**).

   This dialog box may vary depending on the type of hardware you're using.

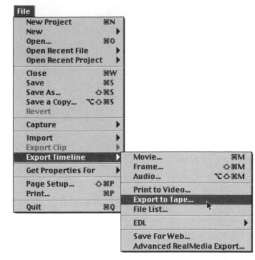

Figure 15.5 Choose File > Export Timeline > Export to Tape.

Figure 15.6 The Export to Tape dialog box appears. Because I'm using DV, this is the DV Export to Tape dialog box: the dialog box you see may be different, depending on the hardware you are using.

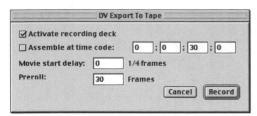

Figure 15.7 In the Export to Tape dialog box, specify whether you want Premiere to activate the recording device and where you want the program to start on the tape. Also enter a delay and a preroll.

4. *Do any of the following:*

▲ **Activate recording deck**—automatically triggers record mode in a controllable deck or camera.

▲ **Assemble at time code**—allows you to enter the timecode number on the tape where you want recording to start.

The tape must already have a timecode signal. Therefore, you can't use a blank tape.

5. Enter values for the following:

Movie start delay—sets the number of $1/4$ frames to delay playback after you click the OK button.

Preroll—sets the number of frames the camera or deck rewinds from the start time for the tape to get up to speed (**Figure 15.7**).

6. Click OK.

Playback begins. If you are controlling the recording device manually, make sure that you trigger record mode. If you checked Activate recording deck, Premiere triggers the recording device automatically.

Creating a Movie

You can create a single, independent file from all or part of the program in the timeline. You can also create a movie from a clip. This is useful if you want to make a movie from only one portion of a clip or create a version that uses a different format or compression type.

Just as you specify capture and project settings, you must specify the characteristics of the exported movie, such as frame size, frame rate, compression, and audio quality. The settings that you choose are determined not only by your output goal, but also by the capabilities of your playback device.

Because you are already familiar with video, audio, keyframe, and rendering settings from Chapter 2, this chapter concentrates on the settings that are unique to output. For more in-depth explanations about compression and other technical considerations, see Chapter 18.

To export a video file:

1. *Do either of the following:*

▲ To export the program from the timeline, select the Timeline window or Monitor window.

or

▲ To export a clip, open a video clip.

2. To define the footage you want to export, *do either of the following:*

▲ In the program, set the work area bar over the range in the timeline you want to export.

or

▲ In a clip, set the in and out points to define the frames you want to export.

3. Choose either of the following:

File > Export Timeline > Movie—to export from the timeline (**Figure 15.8**).

Figure 15.8 Choose File > Export Timeline > Movie to export all or part of the program in the timeline. You can also export all or a portion of a single clip.

Figure 15.9 The Export Movie dialog box appears. To change the current settings, click the Settings button.

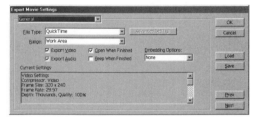

Figure 15.10 The General panel of the Export Movie Settings dialog box appears.

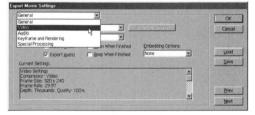

Figure 15.11 To change the current export settings, specify settings in the other panels of the Export Movie Settings dialog box by choosing a category from the pull-down menu.

File > Export Clip > Movie—to export a clip.

The Export Movie dialog box appears. The bottom of the dialog box summarizes the current export settings (**Figure 15.9**).

4. To change the current export settings, click the Settings button.

   The General panel of the Export Movie Settings dialog box appears. It looks similar to the Project Settings dialog box but has a few important differences (**Figure 15.10**).

5. To change the current export settings, specify settings in the other panels of the Export Movie Settings dialog box by choosing a category from the pull-down menu (**Figure 15.11**):

   General—to specify the range of the timeline you want to export, which tracks to include, and whether to embed a link.

   Video—to specify settings that control aspects of the video image, such as frame size and frame rate.

   Audio—to specify settings that control aspects of the audio, such as sample rate and bit depth.

   Keyframe and Rendering—to specify keyframe options (which control how a codec uses frame differencing) and rendering options (which control which elements are included in export, as well as video field dominance).

   Special Processing—to specify additional options, particularly for optimizing the exported movie for CD-ROM.

   The following sections explain each category in detail.

   continues on next page

6. Click OK to exit the Export Movie Settings dialog box.

You return to the Export Movie dialog box. The current export settings are summarized in the Export Movie dialog box.

7. Specify a name and destination for your file, and click OK to begin rendering the movie.

A progress bar appears, displaying an estimate of the processing time required to make the movie (**Figure 15.12**).

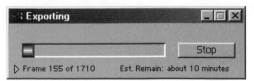

Figure 15.12 In the Export Movie dialog box, specify a name and destination for your file, and click OK. A progress bar appears, displaying an estimate of the processing time.

✔ Tips

■ You can also open the Export Movie dialog box to export from the timeline by pressing ⌘-M (Mac) or Ctrl-M (Windows).

■ Consult your Premiere user guide to find out about *batch processing*, which enables you to export multiple files from the same project.

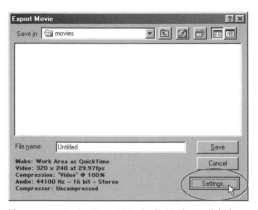

Figure 15.13 In the Export Movie dialog box, click the Settings button to change the current settings.

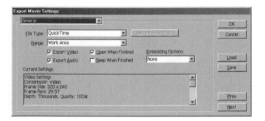

Figure 15.14 The General panel of the Export Movie Settings dialog box appears.

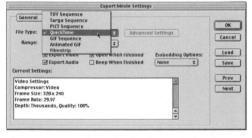

Figure 15.15 Specify a video file format in the File Type pull-down menu. This figure shows the Mac options.

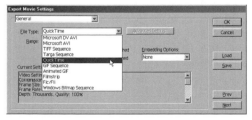

Figure 15.16 This figure shows the File Type options for Windows.

Specifying the General Export Settings

In the General panel of the Export Movie Settings dialog box, you can specify the range of timeline you want to export, which tracks to include, and whether to open the movie when it's finished. And you can have Premiere make a beep sound when the movie's done.

A new option lets you embed a project link. Choosing this option links the movie with the project from which it was exported. When you use the movie in After Effects or Premiere, you can use the Edit Original command to open the project that originated the movie to make any needed changes. All the project references must be available on the hard drive, of course, and you'll have to re-render any changes. Nevertheless, this feature does improve workflow when changes must be made.

To specify general export settings:

1. In the Export Movie dialog box, click the Settings button to change the current settings (**Figure 15.13**).

   The General panel of the Export Movie Settings dialog box appears (**Figure 15.14**).

2. To specify a video file format, such as QuickTime or AVI, choose an option from the File Type pull-down menu (**Figures 15.15** and **15.16**).

   The available options depend on your platform, as well as on the extensions you have installed on your system.

3. Specify the range of the program that you want to export by choosing one of the following options from the Range pull-down menu:

   Work Area—to export only the part of the program below the work area bar.

continues on next page

Entire Program—to export the entire program from the timeline.

4. Specify the tracks you want to export by checking one or both of the following options:

   Export Video—includes video tracks in the exported file.

   Export Audio—includes audio tracks in the exported file.

   Leave an option unchecked to exclude the video or audio from the exported file.

5. Set the following options:

   Open When Finished—opens the rendered movie automatically upon completion.

   Beep When Finished—alerts you that the rendering process is complete by making a beep.

   If you don't want to use these options, leave them unchecked.

6. Choose an option from the Embedding pull-down menu (**Figure 15.17**):

   None—doesn't link the movie to the project from which it was exported.

   Project Link—embeds a link in the movie, which links it to the project from which it was exported.

   When you play the movie in After Effects or Premiere, you can choose the Edit Original command to open the original project.

7. *Do either of the following:*

   ▲ To close the Export Movie Settings dialog box and return to the Export Movie dialog box, click OK.

   or

   ▲ To specify settings in another category, click the Next or Previous button, or choose the category from the pull-down menu (**Figure 15.18**).

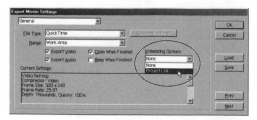

Figure 15.17 Choose an option from the Embedding pull-down menu.

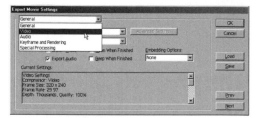

Figure 15.18 To specify settings in another category, click the Next or Previous button, or choose the category from the pull-down menu. To close the dialog box and return to the Export Movie Settings dialog box, click OK.

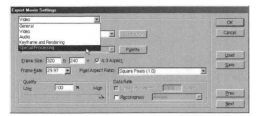

Figure 15.19 From the pull-down menu in the Export Movie Settings dialog box, choose Special Processing.

Figure 15.20 A summary of the special processing options appears in the Export Movie Settings dialog box. To change the settings, click the Modify button.

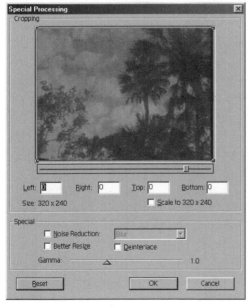

Figure 15.21 The Special Processing dialog box appears.

Using Special Processing Options

In the Export Movie Settings dialog box, special processing options allow you to further control the characteristics of the final movie. These options are particularly useful if you are preparing movies that require limited data rates—for CD-ROM or Web playback, for example.

Admittedly, Premiere 6 includes plug-in options (Media Cleaner and Real Media) that have presets optimized for CD-ROM and Web delivery. Nevertheless, the special processing options permit you to fine-tune various settings yourself, using the standard Export dialog box. You can crop the movie; optimize resizing; and add noise-reduction, deinterlacing, and gamma-correction filters. Premiere dynamically previews these options, as well as the effects of any other filters and transitions.

The following task explains how to access the special processing options. Specific options are covered in the following sections.

To access special processing options:

1. In the Export Movie dialog box, click the Settings button to change the current settings.

   The General panel of the Export Movie Settings dialog box appears.

2. From the pull-down menu, choose Special Processing (**Figure 15.19**).

   The Export Movie Settings dialog box displays a summary of the special processing options (**Figure 15.20**).

3. Click the Modify button.

   The Special Processing dialog box appears (**Figure 15.21**).

   continues on next page

457

4. Set the special processing options, as explained in the following sections.

5. Drag the slider below the sample frame to preview the effects of the options that you choose.

6. Click OK to return to the Export Movie Settings dialog box.

7. *Do either of the following:*

▲ To close the Export Movie Settings dialog box and return to the Export Movie dialog box, click OK.

or

▲ To specify settings in another category, click the Next or Previous button, or choose the category from the pull-down menu.

Resizing

If the final-output frame size is smaller than the frame size of the source clips, the Better Resize option resizes the final movie with the same interpolation method used by Adobe After Effects. Otherwise, Premiere uses a lower-quality method.

To optimize resizing:

◆ In the Special Processing dialog box, check the Better Resize checkbox (**Figure 15.22**).

Cropping

Full-screen video often contains black edges. These edges are not visible when displayed on an overscanned video monitor (see "Overscan and Safe Zones," in Chapter 18), but they appear on a computer screen, especially when the image frame size is less than full-screen.

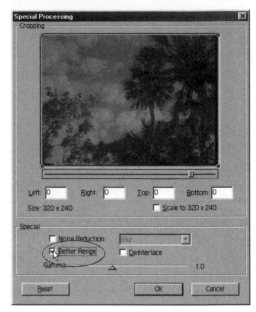

Figure 15.22 In the Special Processing dialog box, check the Better Resize checkbox.

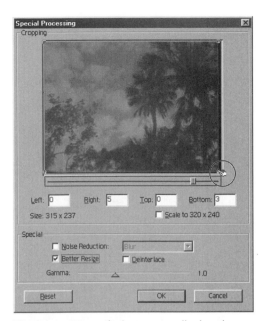

Figure 15.23 To crop the image manually, drag the corner handles of the sample frame. Alternatively, enter the number of pixels you want to crop from the top, bottom, right, and left sides of the image in the corresponding boxes.

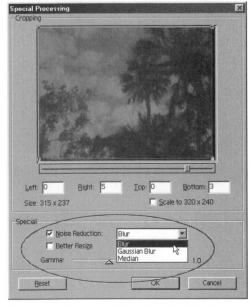

Figure 15.24 Choose an option from the Noise Reduction pull-down menu.

To crop the video:

◆ In the Special Processing dialog box, *do any of the following:*

   To crop the image manually, drag the corner handles of the sample frame (**Figure 15.23**).

   To crop the image numerically, enter the number of pixels by which you want to crop the top, bottom, right, and left sides of the final movie in the corresponding fields below the sample frame.

Noise-Reduction Filter

The noise-reduction filter adds a blur to the movie, softening the image and creating the illusion of slightly higher resolution when used with certain codecs at low data rates.

To apply the noise-reduction filter:

1. In the Special Processing dialog box, check the Noise Reduction checkbox.

2. From the Noise Reduction pull-down menu, choose one of the following options (**Figure 15.24**):

   Blur—creates the most subtle effect of the three options. Blur averages pixels next to the hard edges and shaded areas.

   Gaussian Blur—produces a hazier effect.

   Median—creates the strongest blur while preserving the hard edges.

✔ Tip

■ The noise-reduction filter especially improves the apparent image quality when you use Cinepak compression.

Deinterlace Filter

Many capture boards digitize two interlaced frames of video. If you want to render the movie smaller than full-screen, you should remove one field by using the deinterlace filter. This filter removes the secondary field from each frame and doubles the dominant field. If you don't choose this option, the video is deinterlaced by means of a lower-quality method, and the movie may appear to flicker. See Chapter 18 for a complete explanation of fields, interlacing, and field dominance.

To add the deinterlace filter:

◆ In the Special Processing dialog box, check the Deinterlace checkbox (**Figure 15.25**).

Gamma Adjustment

Brightness levels of midtones (middle gray levels) differ between Macintosh and Windows platforms. A movie created on a Mac appears darker on a Windows system, and vice versa. You can add the gamma filter to compensate for this difference. The gamma filter adjusts the midtones without affecting the black and white areas.

To adjust the gamma:

1. In the Special Processing dialog box, drag the Gamma slider (**Figure 15.26**).

2. Preview the changes to the midtone brightness levels in the sample frame.

✔ Tip

■ A gamma setting of 0.7 or 0.8 helps a Mac-compressed clip look good on either a Mac or Windows computer.

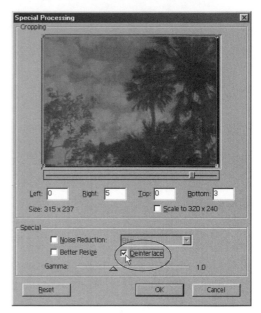

Figure 15.25 In the Special Processing dialog box, check the Deinterlace checkbox.

Figure 15.26 In the Special Processing dialog box, drag the Gamma slider. A setting of 0.7 or 0.8 makes a Mac clip look good on either Mac or Windows systems.

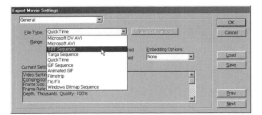

Figure 15.27 From the File Type pull-down menu, choose a still-image sequence format.

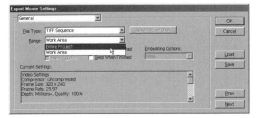

Figure 15.28 Specify the range of the program that you want to export by making a choice from the Range pull-down menu.

Exporting Still-Image Sequences

You can export a program or clip as a sequence of still images. Premiere numbers the frames automatically, and if you want, you can specify the starting frame number. Many animation and 3-D programs can import video images only as a numbered sequence of still-image files.

To export a still-image sequence:

1. In the Export Movie dialog box, click the Settings button.

   The General panel of the Export Movie Settings dialog box opens.

2. From the File Type pull-down menu, choose a still-image sequence format (**Figure 15.27**).

   Available still image formats depend on the platform you're using. TIFF Sequence, Targa Sequence, and GIF Sequence are available for both Mac and Windows.

3. Specify the range of the program that you want to export by making a choice from the Range pull-down menu (**Figure 15.28**):

   Work Area—to export only the part of the program below the work area bar.

   Entire Project—to export the entire program from the timeline.

   continues on next page

4. Set the following options:

Open When Finished—opens the rendered movie automatically upon completion.

Beep When Finished—alerts you that the rendering process is complete by making a beep.

If you don't want to use these options, leave them unchecked.

5. To specify settings in another category, click the Next or Previous button, or choose the category from the pull-down menu.

If necessary, specify the Video, Rendering, and Special Processing settings. If you are exporting a GIF sequence or animated GIF, click Advanced Settings in the Export Movie Settings dialog box. (See the following section for more details.)

6. In the Export Movie Settings dialog box, click OK.

The Export Movie Settings dialog box closes, and you return to the Export Movie dialog box.

7. Specify a destination and file name, and click OK (**Figure 15.29**).

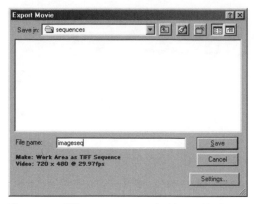

Figure 15.29 When you return to the Export Movie dialog box, specify a destination and file name, and click OK.

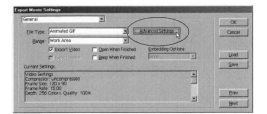

Figure 15.30 In the General panel of the Export Movie Settings dialog box, click Advanced Settings.

Figure 15.31 The Advanced GIF Options dialog box appears.

Exporting GIF Sequences and Animated GIFs

You can export GIF sequences and animated GIFs from Premiere as you would any other image format, except that additional options are available.

To specify settings for animated GIFs and GIF sequences:

1. In the General panel of the Export Movie Settings dialog box, from the File Type pull-down menu, choose Animated GIF or GIF Sequence.

   The Advanced Settings button becomes available for use.

2. Click Advanced Settings (**Figure 15.30**).

   The Advanced GIF Options dialog box appears (**Figure 15.31**).

3. To simulate colors that are not available in the Web-safe colors palette by dithering (or mixing) pixels of available colors, check the Dithering checkbox.

   Although dithered colors look grainy, they can make the limited color range appear to be greater and improve the appearance of color gradients. When Dithering is unchecked, unavailable colors are replaced with the next-closest colors, often resulting in banding, or abrupt color transitions.

   continues on next page

4. From the Transparency pull-down menu, choose one of the following options (**Figure 15.32**):

None—exports the animated GIF or GIF sequence as opaque.

Hard—makes one color in the image transparent.

Soft—makes one color in the image transparent with soft edges.

Click Color to open the color picker and choose the color that becomes transparent.

5. To make an animated GIF play continuously, check the Looping checkbox.

Leave this option unchecked to make the animated GIF play once and then stop. This option is available only when you are exporting an animated GIF.

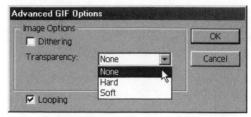

Figure 15.32 Choose an option from the Transparency pull-down menu. To make the GIF play continuously, check Looping.

Figure 15.33 A filmstrip file in Photoshop looks like a filmstrip: a single still image that contains the frames of video arranged in a long column. In this example, Photoshop tools are being used to paint out the trail of an airplane.

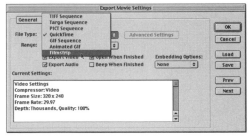

Figure 15.34 In the General panel of the Export Movie Settings dialog box, choose Filmstrip from the Format pull-down menu.

Exporting Filmstrip Files

You can export a clip or any part of the program as a filmstrip file. The filmstrip format allows you to use Adobe Photoshop to paint directly onto the frames of video—a technique similar to *rotoscoping* in traditional film postproduction. Unlike Premiere, however, Photoshop manipulates files directly. Be aware that the changes you make in the filmstrip file are permanent.

Appropriately enough, a filmstrip file in Photoshop looks like a filmstrip: a single still image that contains the frames of video arranged in a long column (**Figure 15.33**). A frame number, reel name, and timecode are displayed below each frame. If the frames of the filmstrip exceed 30,000 pixels in height, the frames continue in another column until the file reaches the maximum image dimensions for Photoshop.

After you alter the filmstrip file in Photoshop, you can import the file into Premiere and convert it back to a video file.

To export a filmstrip:

1. In the Export Movie dialog box, click Settings.

   The General panel of the Export Movie Settings dialog box appears.

2. From the Format pull-down menu, choose Filmstrip (**Figure 15.34**).

   continues on next page

3. From the Range pull-down menu, choose one of the following (**Figure 15.35**):

   Work Area—to export only the part of the program below the work area bar.

   Entire Program—to export the entire program from the timeline.

4. Set the following options:

   Open When Finished—opens the rendered movie automatically.

   Beep When Finished—beeps when the rendering process is complete.

   If you don't want to use these options, leave them unchecked.

5. To specify settings in another category, click the Next or Previous button, or choose the category from the menu.

   When you are exporting video that contains interlaced fields (like most full-screen video), make sure to specify the dominant field in the Keyframe and Rendering panel of the Movie Export Settings dialog box. See "Specifying Keyframe and Rendering Options" in Chapter 2.

6. In the Export Movie Settings dialog box, click OK.

   The Export Movie Settings dialog box closes, and you return to the Export Movie dialog box.

7. Specify a destination and file name for the filmstrip file, and click OK.

   Premiere renders a filmstrip file.

8. Open the filmstrip file in Photoshop, and edit as needed.

   When you're finished, you can import the filmstrip file back into Premiere, which will re-interpret the file as motion video.

Figure 15.35 Specify the range of frames that you want to export as a filmstrip and whether you want Premiere to open the file when it's finished.

Using Filmstrips

Although you should consult your Adobe Photoshop user guide for more details on how to use filmstrip files, here are a few important guidelines:

◆ Don't crop or resize the filmstrip.

◆ You can manipulate the Red, Green, Blue, and Alpha channels of the filmstrip, but Premiere won't recognize any additional channels.

◆ You can paint on the gray borders between the frames of a filmstrip, but they won't appear when the filmstrip is converted back to a video file.

◆ Your source video should match or exceed your final output quality. Don't waste your time painstakingly rotoscoping a shot at draft quality.

Figure 15.36 To export a frame in a clip, cue the current frame to the frame that you want to export.

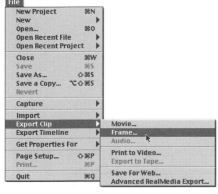

Figure 15.37 Choose File > Export Clip > Frame to export a frame in the program. You can also export a frame from the timeline.

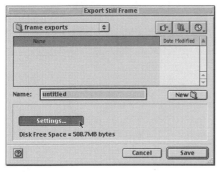

Figure 15.38 In the Export Still Frame dialog box, click Settings.

Exporting Single Still Images

You can export the current frame of video from the program or source clip as a single still-image file.

To export a single frame:

1. *Do either of the following:*
   ▲ To export a frame in the program, cue the current frame to the frame that you want to export (indicated by the current frame in the program view or the edit line in the timeline).

   or

   ▲ To export a frame in a clip, cue the current frame to the frame that you want to export (**Figure 15.36**).

2. Choose either of the following:
   File > Export Clip > Frame—to export a frame from a source clip (**Figure 15.37**).
   File > Export Timeline > Frame— to export a frame from the program.
   The Export Still Frame dialog box appears.

3. Click Settings (**Figure 15.38**).
   The General panel of the Export Still Frame Settings dialog box appears.

4. From the File Type pull-down menu, choose a still-image format (**Figure 15.39**).
   The available options depend on the platform you're using. TIFF is common to both Mac and Windows.

5. *Do any of the following:*
   ▲ To open the exported still image automatically, check Open When Finished.
   ▲ To specify options for GIF images, click Advanced Options.

   continues on next page

EXPORTING SINGLE STILL IMAGES

6. To specify settings in another category, click the Next or Previous button, or choose the category from the pull-down menu.

If necessary, specify the Video, Keyframe and Rendering, and Special Processing settings.

7. Click OK.

The Export Still Frame Settings dialog box closes, and you return to the Export Still Frame dialog box.

8. Specify a name and destination for the still image, and click Save (**Figure 15.40**).

The frame you specified is exported as a still-frame file, in the format and location you set.

✔ Tips

■ If you plan to print the still image, you should know that standard-resolution video always translates to 72 dpi, no matter what format you shot it in. This is fine for small, low-resolution printouts. But for most purposes, printing shops ask for a minimum of 300 dpi. If you want to create a press kit or other printed materials, make sure to take production stills with a film camera or a high-quality digital still camera.

■ If you plan to use the image in a still-image editing program (such as Photoshop), simply export the highest image quality possible. Don't resize the image, use special processing options, or even deinterlace it. Photoshop's tool set is superior for any image editing you may want to do.

■ In Photoshop, always deinterlace video images before you resize them, not the other way around.

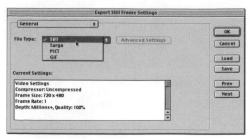

Figure 15.39 In the General panel of the Export Still Frame Settings dialog box, from the File Type pull-down menu, choose a still-image format. Also, check whether you want Premiere to open the still image file.

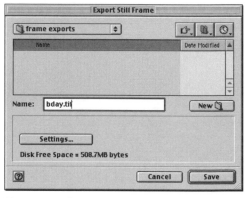

Figure 15.40 After you specify other settings, click OK to return to the Export Still Frame dialog box. Specify a name and destination for the file, and click Save.

Using Export Plug-Ins

Premiere 6 includes two extremely useful plug-in modules for optimizing exported video for low-data rate media, such as CD-ROM or the Web.

Media Cleaner EZ provides a list of preset export settings you can choose according to your output goal, whether it's for CD-ROM, Web streaming, or progressive download. Media Cleaner EZ also includes a wizard feature that asks you simple questions to determine the settings you need.

If you plan to stream your video in the popular RealMedia format, Premiere incorporates an Advanced RealMedia Export feature as well.

Both plug-in modules are programs in their own right and fall outside the scope of this chapter. The following tasks explain how to access these features but don't explain the details of their dialog boxes. You'll find ample documentation with Premiere. Both plug-ins are simple to use when you know your options.

To use plug-in export options:

1. *Do either of the following:*
   ▲ To export the program from the time-line, select the Timeline window or Monitor window.

   or

   ▲ To export a clip, open a video clip.

2. Define the footage you want to export by doing either of the following:
   ▲ In the program, set the work area bar over the range in the timeline you want to export.
   ▲ In a clip, set the in and out points to define the frames you want to export.

continues on next page

3. Choose any of the following:

▲ To use **Media Cleaner EZ**, choose File > Export Timeline > Save for Web or File > Export Clip > Save for Web.

▲ To use **RealMedia**, choose File > Export Timeline > Advanced RealMedia Export or File > Export Clip > Advanced RealMedia Export.

▲ To use **Windows Media** (Windows only), choose File > Export Timeline > Windows Media or File > Export Clip > Windows Media.

Depending on your choice, Media Cleaner EZ, Advanced RealMedia Export, or Windows Media launches (**Figures 15.41**, **15.42**, and **15.43**).

✔ Tip

■ You can apply what you learn about choosing settings in Premiere to any digital video application. Even so, both the Media Cleaner EZ and RealMedia plug-ins come with their own documentation.

Figure 15.41 If you chose Save for Web, Media Cleaner EZ launches. Media Cleaner optimizes settings based on the output goal you choose from the pull-down menu.

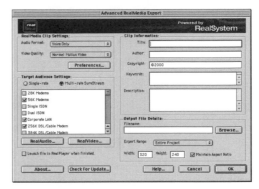

Figure 15.42 Use the Advanced RealMedia Export dialog box to prepare movies for streaming over the Web in the RealMedia format.

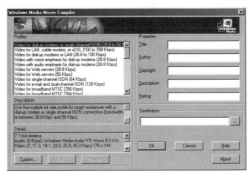

Figure 15.43 Use the Windows Media Movie Compiler dialog box to prepare movies for streaming in the Windows Media format.

USING EXPORT PLUG-INS

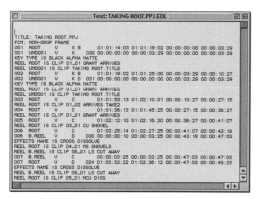

Figure 15.44 An EDL describes your edited program as a list of editing events. Though it may look confusing at first, the trained eye sees a detailed list: source and program in and out points, transition types and durations, notes, and B-roll information.

Exporting an Edit Decision List

As you learned in the introduction to the book, the primary goal of an offline edit is to generate an edit decision list, or EDL. An *EDL* describes your edited program as a list of editing events (**Figure 15.44**). Exporting an EDL enables you to transfer your offline editing decisions to an online editing controller. Premiere even allows you to export an EDL in a format that is compatible with several common online-edit controllers. Because these EDL formats come in the form of plug-ins, you can add other Premiere-compatible EDL formats in the future.

Most EDLs must be stored on $3\frac{1}{2}$-inch floppy disks formatted for MS-DOS. Fortunately for Mac users, the Mac OS includes PC Exchange, which allows you to read, format, and save to MS-DOS–format disks. (If you're working on a recent model of Mac, of course, you may need to use an add-on floppy drive.)

This section explains how to export a generic EDL. Creating an EDL in a specific format falls outside the scope of this chapter, because it requires an explanation of online editing and of how an edit controller interprets the information in the EDL. Besides, you can find a thorough discussion of specific EDL options (such as B-rolls and wipe codes) in the Adobe Premiere 6 User Guide or by consulting an online editor (the person, not the machine). Always keep in close contact with your online editing facility to ensure that you are prepared for online editing.

To export a generic EDL:

1. Choose File > Export Timeline > EDL > Generic EDL (**Figure 15.45**).

   The Save Generic EDL As dialog box appears.

2. In the Save Generic EDL As dialog box, specify a file name and destination for the EDL file, and click Save (**Figure 15.46**).

   The EDL file is saved to the destination you specified.

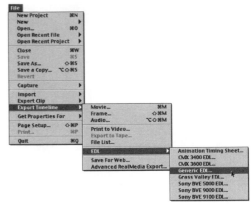

Figure 15.45 Choose File > Export Timeline > EDL > Generic EDL.

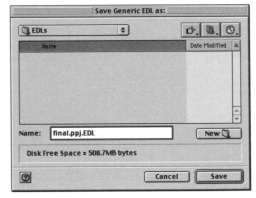

Figure 15.46 In the Save Generic EDL As dialog box, specify a file name and destination for the EDL file, and click Save.

16

Capturing Video

You don't have to shoot your own video footage to create a program in Premiere. As explained in Chapter 2, you can import a wide range of digitally stored content, including stills, audio, and of course, video. Maybe you've already started using the files in Premiere's Sample folder. But chances are, you're eager to edit your own video footage. Usually, this means getting the video from a tape to your hard drive—a process known as video *capture*.

In Premiere 6, all the controls you'll need for capture are integrated into an enhanced Movie Capture window. As in previous versions of Premiere, you can set up the capture window to control a camera or deck. But now, Premiere takes full advantage of DV devices, and presets for controlling most DV cameras and decks are built-in. The capture window also incorporates tabbed panels for viewing the current capture settings, and for logging clips into a batch list. Speaking of batch lists: the batch list window also shows improvements over the one found in previous versions of Premiere. Like the Movie Capture window, the batch list window's refinements include a pull-down menu that eliminates the need for one in the menu bar.

This chapter illustrates the capture process using a DV video source. Though your particular capture device may slightly alter your choices and dialog boxes, the overall process doesn't vary. Consult the documentation that came with your hardware to learn about your special options. Chapter 18 also offers guidance on selecting and understanding capture settings.

Understanding Capture

It's not enough to have your video in a digital form; it also has to be in a format that's practical to use for editing. As a digital file, every frame of standard (as opposed to high-definition) video consumes nearly 1MB. Capturing and playing back approximately 30 frames per second (the standard frame rate) is impossible for most processors and drives; the *data rate*, or flow of information, is simply too high. Never mind the storage capacity you'd need to hold such enormous files.

Some professionals do use equipment that can process digital video in a relatively pristine, or *uncompressed,* form. However, most users either don't require or can't afford this level of quality, and use equipment that *compresses* the video for use on the computer. Compression is one way to reduce the file size (and thereby the data rate) of the video, making it easier to store, process, and play back. Other audio and video settings, such as frame size and frame rate, also affect the data rate. Along with your final output goal, the equipment you use helps determine the video and audio settings you'll choose for capturing video.

UNDERSTANDING CAPTURE

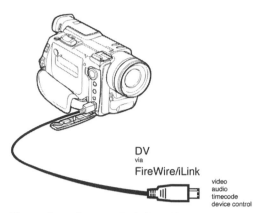

Figure 16.1 DV footage—including video, audio and timecode—can be transferred over a single FireWire/ iLink connection. DV standards vary very little, so choosing settings is easy.

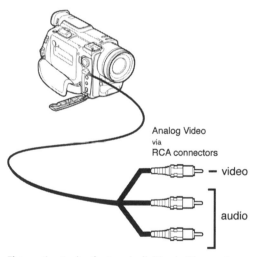

Figure 16.2 Analog footage is digitized with a capture card installed in your computer's expansion slot. Usually, separate cables deliver video and audio. A professional deck and a separate device control cable are often required to deliver timecode. Settings vary according to each capture card.

Capturing DV vs. Digitizing Analog

If you're using the increasingly popular DV format, the capture process couldn't get much easier. DV cameras compress the video in the camera, and record the resulting DV signal onto any of several DV tape formats— most commonly, miniDV. If your computer is equipped with a port—commonly known as FireWire, iLink, or IEEE-1394—you can easily transfer footage from a DV camera or deck to your hard disk in much the same way you would copy files from one disk to another. A single cable delivers the video, audio, and timecode information (**Figure 16.1**). Assuming your system is fast enough to play back DV (with its relatively lenient 3.6 MB/sec data rate), you're in business. The DV standard is just that: standard. It narrows down what would otherwise be an intimidating selection of video and audio settings into a single set of options.

Despite the pervasiveness of DV, video and audio are still commonly recorded, stored, and delivered via an analog signal. Common formats include VHS and Hi8 videotape and conventional audiocassette tapes. To use analog media, most computers require a video capture card—add-on hardware that you can install in one of the expansion slots of your computer. The capture card *digitizes* analog video and audio, converting it to a digital form that can be stored on your computer (**Figure 16.2**). Usually, separate cables deliver the video, audio, and timecode (if timecode is present), and the video is digitized using some version of a type of compression known as Motion-JPEG (MJPEG). However, capture cards can use other compression standards, or even digitize the video in an uncompressed format. The capabilities, requirements, and prices of capture cards vary widely.

✔ Tips

■ Not all capture cards certified to work with Premiere 5.1c have been certified to work with Premiere 6. Be sure to check Adobe's Web site for an updated list of certified capture devices.

■ Most capture cards digitize footage to some version of the MJPEG compression standard. However, you can also get capture devices that convert analog sources into the DV format.

■ Because DV uses a fixed data rate, it doesn't lend itself to the offline-online editing strategy you read about in Chapter 1. When putting together a DV editing system, it's probably best to get enough drive space for your needs: about 1 GB for every 4 minutes, 40 seconds.

Preparing for Capture

As you have already discovered, digital video thrives on a fast processor, speedy drives, and even additional (and often expensive) hardware.

In addition to using powerful hardware, you can take certain steps to maximize your computer's performance:

◆ Quit all other applications.

◆ Turn off file-sharing software, at least temporarily.

◆ Disable other unnecessary operating-system features.

◆ Choose a fast, large disk or disk array as your scratch disk for digitizing.

◆ Defragment hard disks with a reliable disk utility to optimize their performance.

◆ Select compression settings that do not exceed the capabilities of your system.

Using the Movie Capture Window

Figure 16.3
Choose File › Capture › Movie Capture.

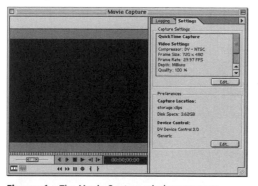

Figure 16.4 The Movie Capture window appears.

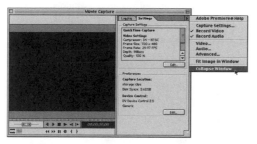

Figure 16.5 From the Movie Capture window's pull-down menu, choose Collapse Window.

In Premiere 6, the Movie Capture window includes two tabbed palettes: Logging and Settings. Clicking the Logging tab reveals controls you can use to define the part of the video you want to capture, or to log the in and out points to a batch list for capturing later. Settings that were once only available from the menu bar can now be accessed from the Settings panel. By clicking the Settings tab, you can view and change capture settings, or set up the scratch disks and device control.

If you want, you can hide the tabbed panels and access other options from the Movie Capture window's new pull-down menu.

To open the Movie Capture window:

◆ Choose File > Capture > Movie Capture (**Figure 16.3**).

The Movie Capture window appears (**Figure 16.4**).

To hide and show tabbed panels:

◆ *Do either of the following:*

To hide the tabbed panels, choose Collapse Window from the Movie Capture window's pull-down menu, (**Figure 16.5**).

continues on next page

USING THE MOVIE CAPTURE WINDOW

The Logging and Settings panels disappear (**Figure 16.6**).

or

To show hidden tabbed panels, choose Expand Window from the Movie Capture window's pull-down menu.

To fit the video image in the Movie Capture window:

◆ From the Movie Capture window's pull-down menu, choose Fit Image in Window (**Figure 16.7**).

The image area of the Movie Capture window increases to fill the window (**Figure 16.8**).

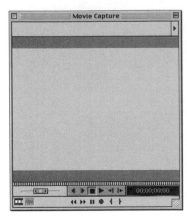

Figure 16.6 The Logging and Settings panels disappear.

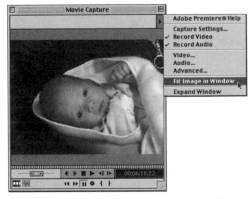

Figure 16.7 From the Movie Capture window pull-down menu, choose Fit Image in Window.

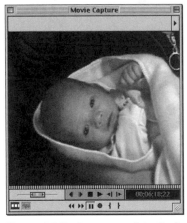

Figure 16.8 The image area of the Movie Capture window increases to fill the window.

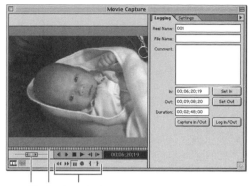

Playback controls

Figure 16.9 When you enable device control, Premiere's Movie Capture window includes buttons that allow you to control the camera or deck from within Premiere.

Understanding Capture Options

At minimum, video capture requires a video source (a camera or deck) and a capture device (a FireWire/iLink port or capture card). For more professional-level editing, you may use additional options, such as device control and timecode. These options not only make features such as automated capture—or batch capture—available, but also make it possible to employ an offline/online editing strategy, as described in Chapter 1.

Device control, timecode, and batch capture are summarized below. Later sections put these concepts into practice.

Device Control As the name indicates, *device control* gives Premiere a means of controlling an external device—usually, a videotape deck or camera (though it could also control a digital disk recorder or DAT player, for example). When you enable device control, Premiere's Movie Capture window includes buttons that allow you to control the camera or deck from within Premiere (**Figure 16.9**). Device control can also activate a camera or deck to record your finished program (see Chapter 15). Premiere can control most DV devices through the FireWire/iLink interface; other cameras and decks may require add-on hardware and software.

continues on next page

Timecode Each videotape has a signal encoded on it called a timecode that identifies each frame of video with a unique number—expressed in hours, minutes, seconds, and frames. Using timecode as a frame-accurate reference, it's possible to create a *batch list*, a list of shots defined by timecoded start and end times. Combined with device control, Premiere can use timecode to capture clips in the batch list automatically. Similarly, timecode makes it possible to recapture clips at a different quality, as when you replace offline-quality clips with those captured at output quality. (See Chapter 1 about the offline-online editing strategy.) Timecode is always included in the DV signal; but for most video formats, timecode is considered a professional option.

Batch Capture With device control and timecoded source tapes, Premiere can capture clips automatically, a process known as *batch capture*. Device control enables Premiere to cue and play the tape in the camera or deck; timecode makes it possible for Premiere to locate the exact shot logged in the batch list (**Figure 16.10**). When you finish an offline edit, you can use a batch list generated from the final program to recapture only the clips required to recreate the program, this time at final-output quality. (See Chapter 17 for more about online editing in Premiere.)

UNDERSTANDING CAPTURE OPTIONS

Reel Name	In Point	Out Point	Duration	File Name	Log Comment	Settings
florida01_2	00;00;10;12	00;03;58;21	00;03;48;10	dad_baby2		
florida01_2	00;00;10;12	00;02;19;26	00;02;09;15	dad_baby	long ms	
florida01_2	00;04;04;10	00;04;38;23	00;00;34;14	caty_baby		
florida01_2	00;04;04;10	00;05;35;00	00;01;30;21	3generations	dad,lani,baby	

Batch Capture: florida01_2.pbl

Total Duration: 00;08;03;04 — Uncaptured Duration: 00;08;03;04

Figure 16.10 With device control and timecoded source tapes, Premiere can batch capture clips from a batch list.

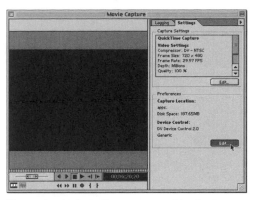

Figure 16.11 In the Preferences area of the Settings panel of the Movie Capture window, click the Edit button.

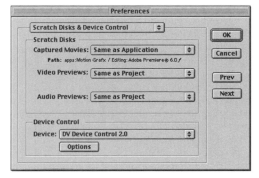

Figure 16.12 The Scratch Disks & Device Control panel of the Preferences dialog box appears.

Choosing a Scratch Disk

In Chapter 9, you learned to designate the disks Premiere uses to save video and audio preview files. You can also designate a scratch disk for capture. Choose your fastest disk, because it's most capable of capturing all the frames successfully.

To set the scratch disk:

1. In the Movie Capture window, click the Settings tab.

   The Movie Capture window's Settings panel appears. In the panel, a summary of the capture settings and capture preferences appears. (If the tabbed panels are not visible, see "To hide and show tabbed panels," earlier in this chapter.)

2. In the Preferences area of the Settings panel of the Movie Capture window, click the Edit button (**Figure 16.11**).

   The Scratch Disks & Device Control panel of the Preferences dialog box appears (**Figure 16.12**).

   continues on next page

3. Choose an option from the Captured Movies pull-down menu (**Figure 16.13**):

Same as Application—to capture clips to the folder in which the Premiere application is located.

Select Folder—to open a dialog box in order to select a folder on any disk.

If you choose Select Folder, a Choose a Folder dialog box appears. In the dialog box, select a folder and click Choose. To achieve the best results, choose a fast disk or disk array.

4. Click OK to close the Preferences dialog box.

✔ Tip

■ The maximum size for a single file is determined by your operating system and file type. In the past, file sizes could never exceed 2 GB. The Mac OS no longer limits file sizes, as long as you are using OS 9 or later and QuickTime 4.1 or later. In Windows, you may be able to capture files larger than 2 GB, depending on the DV camera or capture card you're using. However, AVI files are still limited to either 1 or 2 GB, depending on your capture device.

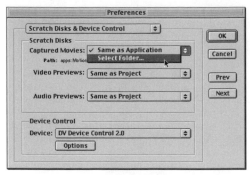

Figure 16.13 Specify the disk and folder you want to use for capturing clips.

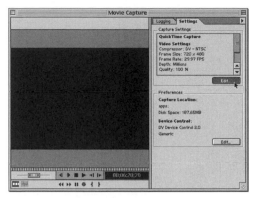

Figure 16.14 In the Settings section of the Movie Capture window's settings panel, click the Edit button.

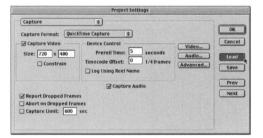

Figure 16.15 In the Capture panel of the Project Settings dialog box, click Load.

Choosing Capture Settings

Before you capture, you must specify the characteristics of the digitized clips, such as the file format, frame size, frame rate, and so on. The process is much the same as selecting project settings, which you learned about in Chapter 2.

In fact, when capturing from DV, you can use one of the DV project presets to set your capture settings. (If you already have a DV project open, you don't have to do anything more.) If you're using a capture card, you'll probably have to choose the video and audio settings manually, according to the particular card and type of editing you're doing. Either way, your capture settings and project settings usually match.

This section provides general instructions for selecting settings. To help you pick specific settings, consult the documentation that comes with your capture card and software. You can also go to Chapter 18 for a detailed explanation of what each capture setting means.

To choose capture settings for DV:

1. In the Movie Capture window, click the Settings tab.

    The Settings panel appears.

2. In the Settings section of the Movie Capture window's settings panel, click the Edit button (**Figure 16.14**).

    The Capture panel of the Project Settings dialog box appears.

3. In the Capture panel of the Project Settings dialog box, click Load (**Figure 16.15**).

    continues on next page

CHOOSING CAPTURE SETTINGS

The Load Project Settings dialog box appears (**Figure 16.16**).

4. In the Available Presets panel of the Load Project Settings dialog box, choose the DV standard that matches your source material:

DV - NTSC folder—contains presets for DV footage shot in NTSC, the video standard used in North America, Japan, and other countries.

DV - PAL folder—contains presets for DV footage shot in PAL, the standard in most of Europe.

These folders each contain the following four options:

Standard 32kHz—for DV footage shot in television's standard 4:3 aspect ratio, using 32kHz audio, one of two audio sample rates supported by most DV cameras.

Standard 48kHz—for DV footage shot in television's standard 4:3 aspect ratio, using 48kHz audio.

Widescreen 32kHz—for DV footage shot in a 16:9 aspect ratio, which is supported by some DV cameras and equipment, using 32kHz audio.

Widescreen 48kHz—for DV footage shot in a 16:9 aspect ratio, which is supported by some DV cameras and equipment, using 48kHz audio.

5. Click OK to close the Load Project Settings dialog box, and click OK to close the Project Settings dialog box.

You return to the Movie Capture dialog box. Your settings are summarized in the Capture Settings section of the Settings tabbed panel.

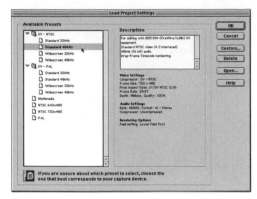

Figure 16.16 In the Load Project Settings dialog box, choose the DV preset that matches your source material.

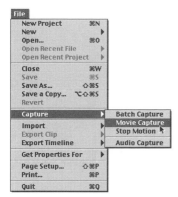

Figure 16.17
Choose File >
Capture > Movie
Capture.

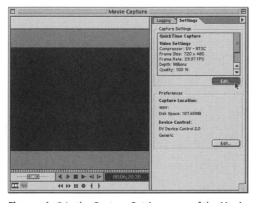

Figure 16.18 In the Capture Settings area of the Movie Capture window, click Edit.

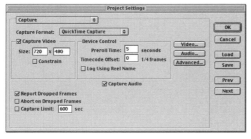

Figure 16.19 The Capture panel of the Project Settings dialog box appears.

To choose capture settings for capture cards:

1. Choose File > Capture > Movie Capture (**Figure 16.17**).

   The Movie Capture window appears.

2. In the Movie Capture window, click the Settings tab.

   The Capture Window's settings panel appears. In the panel, a summary of the capture settings and capture preferences appears.

3. In the Capture Settings area of the settings panel, click Edit (**Figure 16.18**).

   The Capture panel of the Project Settings dialog box appears (**Figure 16.19**).

4. From the Capture Format pull-down menu, choose a video format, such as QuickTime or .AVI.

   Your choice can change the options that are available in other parts of the Capture Settings dialog box and in the dialog boxes that appear when you click the Video, Audio, and Advanced buttons.

5. In the Capture panel of the Project Settings dialog box, choose any of the following options:

   Capture Video—to capture video from the source tape.

   continues on next page

CHOOSING CAPTURE SETTINGS

Capture Audio—to capture audio from the source tape (**Figure 16.20**).

For QuickTime capture, type the pixel width and height of the captured video in the Size boxes in the Capture Video area, and check Constrain to constrain the numbers that you type in the Size boxes to the aspect ratio supported by your capture card (usually, 4:3).

For AVI capture, choose a frame rate for digitizing video from the Rate pull-down menu. Choose 29.97 fps for NTSC video or 25 fps for PAL and SECAM.

6. At the bottom of the Capture panel, check any of the optional settings that you want to enable.

    These settings are explained in detail in the following section, "Optional Settings."

7. Click any of the following buttons to access options that are specific to your capture device:

    Video—to access settings related to video, such as the video source, video codec, and so on.

    Audio—to access settings related to audio, such as audio source, audio codec, and so on.

    Advanced—to access advanced settings, such as audio block size (interleave) options.

    See Chapter 18 for an explanation of the various capture settings.

8. Click OK to exit the capture settings.

    If you opened the dialog box from the Movie Capture window, you return to the Movie Capture window. The settings you specified are summarized in the Capture Settings area of the Movie Capture window. You are ready to begin capturing clips, using the methods explained in the following sections.

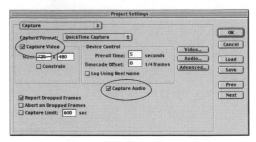

Figure 16.20 Check Capture Video to capture the video image, and Capture Audio to capture the sound.

✔ Tip

- If you're choosing settings manually, you can save your settings as a preset. See Chapter 2 to review how to save your settings.

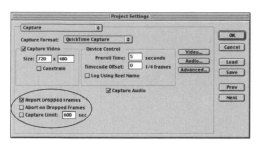

Figure 16.21 At the bottom of the Capture panel of the Project Settings dialog box, you can choose several optional settings.

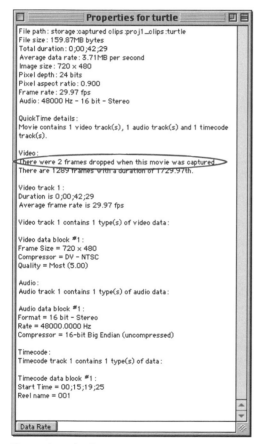

Figure 16.22 Checking Report Dropped Frames will instruct Premiere to alert you if frames are dropped during capture. Dropped frames are reported in a Clip Properties window, shown here.

Optional Settings

At the bottom of the Capture panel of the Project Settings dialog box, you can choose several optional settings (**Figure 16.21**):

Report Dropped Frames—to have Premiere alert you when at least one frame of the clip has not been digitized successfully. If frames are dropped, Premiere opens a Clip Properties window for the clip. This window notes the dropped frames (**Figure 16.22**). If no frames are dropped, no report appears.

Abort on Dropped Frames—to have Premiere automatically stop digitizing when a frame is dropped during capture.

Capture Limit—to limit the number of seconds that Premiere can digitize in a single capture. This option can help prevent the error messages that result when you try to exceed the file-size limit for your system. See the tip in the section, "Choosing a Scratch Disk," earlier in this chapter.

✔ Tip

■ Some capture devices drop the very first frame of captured video but digitize the rest of the frames successfully. If this is the case, Abort on Dropped Frames prevents you from capturing anything. Report Dropped Frames, on the other hand, tells you how many frames were dropped. If only one frame was dropped, the capture probably was successful; you can keep the clip if it looks good when you play it back. If more than one dropped frames are reported, however, you should recheck your settings and attempt to capture the clip again.

Hardware-Specific Settings

Near the right side of the Capture panel, the Video, Audio, and Advanced buttons enable you to access options that are specific to your capture device (**Figure 16.23**). Though the options can vary from one capture card to the next, the general categories are similar. Consult the documentation included with your capture card for specific instructions. See Chapter 18 for additional information on compression settings.

Video Settings—control the attributes of the captured source video (**Figure 16.24**). A pull-down menu in the Video Settings dialog box gives you access to four categories: Compression, Image, Source, and a hardware-specific category.

Audio Settings—control the attributes of the captured audio. The pull-down menu in the Audio Settings dialog box gives you access to four categories: Compression, Image, Source, and a hardware-specific category. The audio settings also include a control for adjusting audio gain levels (**Figure 16.25**).

Advanced Settings—control various options that are specific to each capture card. Typically, this panel opens controls for audio block size (see Chapter 18) (**Figure 16.26**).

VFW Settings—control options specific to capturing Video for Windows format (Windows only).

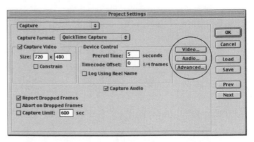

Figure 16.23 The Video, Audio, and Advanced buttons enable you to access options that are specific to your capture device.

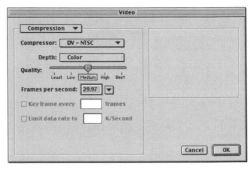

Figure 16.24 Video settings control the attributes of the captured source video.

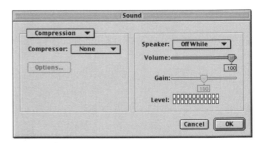

Figure 16.25 Audio settings control the attributes of the captured audio.

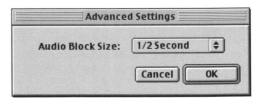

Figure 16.26 Advanced settings typically open a dialog box for controlling audio block size, or interleave.

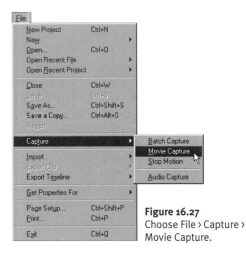

Figure 16.27
Choose File > Capture >
Movie Capture.

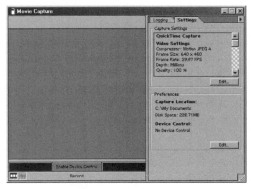

Figure 16.28 The Movie Capture window appears, but doesn't display playback controls.

Capturing Without Device Control

If your system is not equipped with device control, use Premiere's basic capture window and the playback controls on the videotape deck.

To capture without device control:

1. Choose File > Capture > Movie Capture (**Figure 16.27**).

   If prompted, disable AppleTalk (Mac OS only). The Movie Capture window opens (**Figure 16.28**).

2. Under the video display, click the icons to toggle video and audio capture on and off:

   ▦—indicates video capture is enabled;
   ▦—indicates video capture is disabled.
   ▨—indicates audio capture is enabled;
   ▨—indicates audio capture is disabled.

3. Using the controls of your videotape deck, play the tape for several seconds before you begin capturing, allowing the deck to reach normal speed. If the system is configured properly, the video should appear in the preview area of the Movie Capture window.

continues on next page

4. Under the video image in the Movie Capture Window, click Record.

Premiere begins capturing.

5. To stop capturing, click the mouse again. You should also stop playback on the camera or deck.

If a project is open, the clip appears in the selected bin of the Project window. If no project is open, the captured clip appears in a clip window (**Figure 16.29**). If you want, use the playback controls on the clip to check the clip.

✔ Tip

■ If no image appears in the Movie Capture window, make sure that you selected your capture device and its correct video input for the video options of the Capture panel of the Project Settings dialog box. If the settings are correct, check the cable connections between your deck and your capture card. Lastly, be sure the tape actually contains video.

Figure 16.29 The captured clip appears in a Clip window.

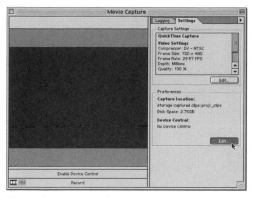

Figure 16.30 In the Preferences section of the Settings panel, click the Edit button.

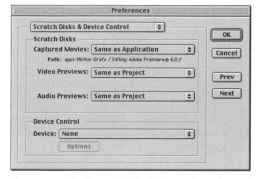

Figure 16.31 The Scratch Disks & Device Control panel of the Preferences dialog box appears.

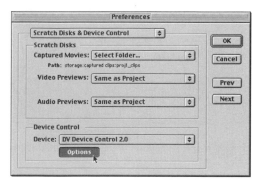

Figure 16.32 Choose the device controller that you are using in the Device pull-down menu.

Using Device Control

DV devices can be controlled via the same FireWire/iLink cable that delivers the video and audio, and the plug-ins to control most DV cameras and decks come built into Premiere.

If you're not using a DV setup, device control usually includes two components: a hardware cable to connect your computer to your deck and a software plug-in to put in the Premiere Plug-Ins folder. Consult the documentation that came with your device control equipment to make sure that the equipment is set up properly.

To enable device control:

1. Make sure your device control hardware is connected.

2. In the Movie Capture window, click the Settings tab.

   The Settings panel appears.

3. *Do either of the following:*

   ▲ In the Preferences section of the Settings panel, click the Edit button (**Figure 16.30**).

   or

   ▲ Under the video preview area, click the Enable Device Control button.

   The Scratch Disks & Device Control panel of the Preferences dialog box appears (**Figure 16.31**).

4. In the Scratch Disks & Device Control panel of the Preferences dialog box, choose the device controller that you are using in the Device pull-down menu (**Figure 16.32**).

5. To access additional options included with your device controller, click the Options button.

USING DEVICE CONTROL

To set DV device control options:

1. In the Preferences section of the Movie Capture window, click the Edit button.

   The Scratch Disks & Device Control panel of the Preferences dialog box opens.

2. In the Device Control area of the dialog box, click the Options button (**Figure 16.33**).

   The Device Control Options dialog box appears (**Figure 16.34**). The dialog box may vary, according to the device control plug-in you selected in the Device pull-down menu of the Scratch Disks & Device Control dialog box.

3. In the Device Control Options dialog box, select the options appropriate to your system from the pull-down menus:

   Video Standard—the video standard used by your equipment. NTSC is the standard used in North America and Japan. PAL is the standard used in most of Europe.

   Device Brand—the brand of the camera or deck you're using. If your brand doesn't appear on the menu, choose Generic (**Figure 16.35**).

   Device Model—the model of the camera or deck you're using. If your particular model doesn't appear in the menu, choose a closely related model, or choose Generic.

   Timecode Format—the counting method used by your tape and playback device. Most MiniDV equipment records Drop-Frame timecode. Other DV devices may offer a choice between Drop-Frame and Non Drop-Frame timecode. (See "Drop-Frame and Non Drop-Frame Timecode," in Chapter 18.)

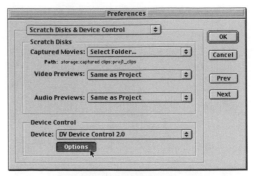

Figure 16.33 In the Device Control area of the dialog box, click the Options button.

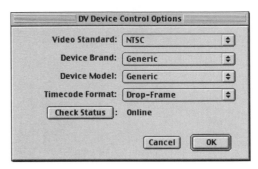

Figure 16.34 The Device Control Options dialog box appears.

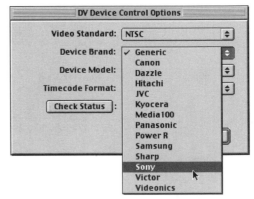

Figure 16.35 Choose the brand of device you're using in the Device Brand pull-down menu.

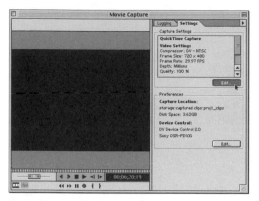

Figure 16.36 In the Capture Settings area of the settings panel, click Edit.

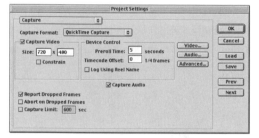

Figure 16.37 The Capture panel of the Project Settings dialog box appears.

✔ **Tip**

■ Use the Timecode Offset feature only if the timecode encoded on the captured clips does not match the timecode on the source tape. Check for possible discrepancies the first time you use your capture card, and use the Timecode Offset feature to calibrate your equipment.

4. Click the Check Status button to see if the device control is ready:

Online—indicates the device is connected and ready to use.

Offline—indicates the device is not connected, or not ready to use.

5. Click OK to close the Device Control Options dialog box.

To set other device control options:

1. In the Movie Capture window, click the Settings tab.

The capture window's settings panel appears.

2. In the Capture Settings area of the Settings panel, click Edit (**Figure 16.36**).

The Capture panel of the Project Settings dialog box appears (**Figure 16.37**).

3. In the Device Control section of the dialog box, specify the following options:

Preroll Time—enter the number of seconds the deck or camera rewinds before a specified in point. Preroll allows the deck to reach normal playback speed before digitizing begins.

Timecode Offset—enter the number of $\frac{1}{4}$ frames to compensate for discrepancies between the timecode on the tape and on the captured clips. Use this feature according to the documentation included with your capture device and device controller.

Log Using Reel Name—check this option if you want Premiere to automatically enter the reel name and timecode as the name of the clips that you log to a batch list.

4. Click OK to close the dialog box and return to the Movie Capture window.

Capturing with Device Control

Device control allows you to control a camera or deck from within Premiere (**Figure 16.38**). More importantly, device control can also help Premiere read timecode from source tapes so that matching timecode information can be encoded into the captured clips. Later sections in this chapter explain how to use device control to log shots from timecoded tapes to create a batch list, and to batch capture the shots on the list.

To simply control a camera or deck, device control doesn't require that your tapes contain timecode, nor that your device can read timecode. It's even possible for some device controllers to use your deck's counter numbers to capture a specified shot, though it won't be frame-accurate. Unlike timecode, counter numbers are arbitrary, and can be reset at any time. Counter numbers won't be encoded onto the captured clip, and can't be used for batch lists or for batch capturing.

To capture using device control:

1. Set up device control, as explained in "Using Device Control" earlier in this chapter and according to the documentation that shipped with the device controller.

2. Choose File > Capture > Movie Capture.

   If device control is set up properly, the Movie Capture window will appear with buttons to control the deck.

3. In the Movie Capture window, click the Logging tab.

   The Logging panel appears (**Figure 16.39**).

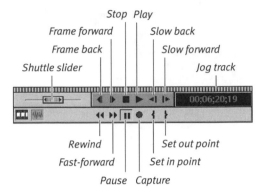

Figure 16.38 Device control allows you to control a camera or deck from within Premiere. The specific capabilities depend on your device and device controller.

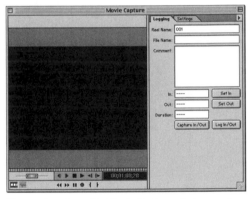

Figure 16.39 Open the Movie Capture window, and click the Logging tab.

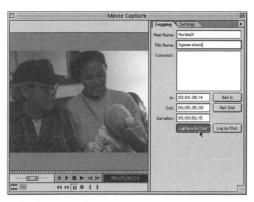

Figure 16.40 After setting the in point and out point, click the Capture In/Out button to capture the clip you defined.

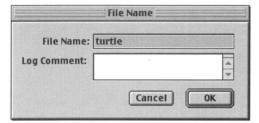

Figure 16.41 In the File Name dialog box, enter a name for the clip, and click OK.

✔ Tips

■ If your deck isn't reaching normal speed before the in point, the device-control software may issue an error message. Try increasing the preroll time in the device-control section of the Capture panel. See "To set other device control options," earlier in this chapter.

■ To cue the tape to the edit mark you set, Option-click (Mac) or Alt-click (Windows) the Set In or Set Out buttons.

■ Premiere also has a stop motion feature, that can be used to achieve time-lapse effects or assist in stop motion animation. See your user guide and online help for more details.

4. Use the playback controls in the Movie Capture window to cue the tape to the starting point, and *do either of the following*:

▲ In the Logging panel, click the Set In button.

or

▲ In the Movie Capture window's playback controls, click the set in button ⧉.

The current time appears as the in point for the capture.

5. Use the controls in the Movie Capture window to cue the tape to the ending point, and *do either of the following*:

▲ In the Logging panel, click the set out button.

or

▲ In the Movie Capture window's playback controls, click the set out button ⧉.

The current time appears as the out point for the capture.

6. In the Logging panel of the Movie Capture window, click the Capture In/Out button (**Figure 16.40**).

Premiere captures the video you defined with in and out points automatically. When it cues the tape, Premiere uses the preroll you specified in the Capture settings (see "To set other device control options," earlier in this chapter). When digitizing is complete, a File Name dialog box appears.

7. In the File Name dialog box, enter a name for the clip, and click OK (**Figure 16.41**).

The captured clip appears in the selected bin of the Project window. If no project is open, the clip appears in a Clip window.

Creating a Batch List

You can log clips to a batch list in two ways. When you use device control, you can create a batch list as you view the timecoded tape in Premiere's Movie Capture window. If the tape is unavailable (or if a timecode-capable deck is unavailable), you can log a batch list manually. To log manually, you'll need a written list of accurate timecode starting and ending numbers ready. Logging manually can help you remain productive (saving you time and money) if you do not always have access to a system that has a deck and device control.

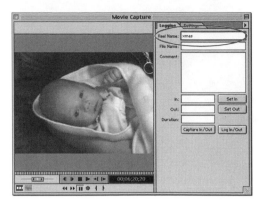

Figure 16.42 For Reel Name, enter the name of the tape you're using.

To generate a batch list with device control:

1. Set up device control, as explained in the section "Using Device Control," earlier in this chapter.

2. Choose File > Capture > Movie Capture. The Movie Capture window appears.

3. In the Movie Capture window, click the Logging tab.
   The Logging panel appears.

4. For Reel Name, enter the name of the reel, or tape, you're using (**Figure 16.42**).
   Each tape you use should have a unique reel name.

5. Use the playback controls in the Movie Capture window to cue the tape to the frame where you want to start digitizing, and click the Set In button.
   The current timecode appears in the In display.

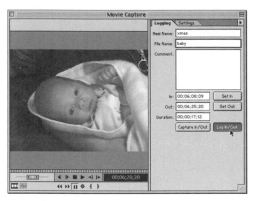

Figure 16.43 After defining the clip, click the Log In/Out button.

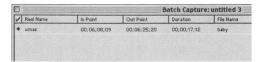

Figure 16.44 A File Name dialog box appears. If you want, enter a comment and click OK.

Figure 16.45 The specified clip appears in an untitled batch list window.

6. Use the deck controls in the Movie Capture window to cue the tape to the frame you want to stop digitizing, and click the Set Out button.

The current timecode appears in the Out display.

7. Click Log In/Out (**Figure 16.43**).

A File Name dialog box appears (**Figure 16.44**).

8. In the File Name dialog box, enter a name for the clip.

If you want, enter a comment or short note you want logged with the clip.

9. Click OK to add the clip to a batch list.

The specified clip appears in an untitled batch list window (**Figure 16.45**).

10. Repeat steps 5 through 9 for every clip you want to capture from this tape, or reel.

If you change tapes, make sure to enter a new Reel name.

11. With the Batch Capture window selected, choose File > Save.

The Save Batch List dialog box appears.

12. In the Save Batch List dialog box, specify a filename and destination for the batch list and click Save.

When using the Mac OS, add the .PBL extension to keep the batch list file cross-platform compatible.

CREATING A BATCH LIST

To generate a batch list manually:

1. Choose File > Capture > Batch Capture (**Figure 16.46**).

   An untitled Batch Capture window appears.

2. In the Batch Capture window, click the add button 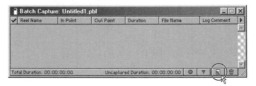 (**Figure 16.47**).

   The Clip Capture Parameters dialog box opens (**Figure 16.48**).

3. In the Clip Capture Parameters dialog box, specify the following options:

   Reel Name—enter the name of the tape from which you will digitize the clip.

   File Name—enter a name for the clip.

   Comment—enter comments that you want to include in the batch list, if any.

   In Time—enter the timecode in point for the clip.

   Out Time—enter the timecode out point for the clip.

   You don't have to type the colons between fields of the timecode number; you can substitute periods or use no punctuation. To the right of the number that you type, Premiere displays how the number will be interpreted in hours, minutes, seconds, and frames.

4. From the Frame Rate pull-down menu, choose the frame rate of the source tape:

   30 fps—for NTSC

   25 fps—for PAL

   Choose the frame rate of the tape's video standard, not the final frame rate of the clip. The frame rate for all NTSC video is approximately 30 fps, even if it was transferred from film.

Figure 16.46 Choose File > Capture > Batch Capture.

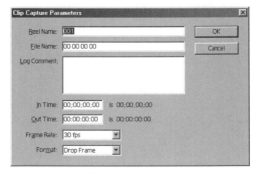

Figure 16.47 In the Batch Capture window, click the Add button.

Figure 16.48 The Clip Capture Parameters window opens.

CREATING A BATCH LIST

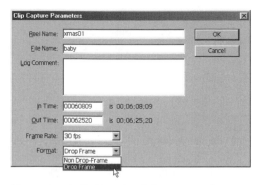

Figure 16.49 In the Format pull-down menu, choose the counting method used by your source tape.

Figure 16.50 The clip information you entered appears in the Batch Capture window.

5. From the Format pull-down menu, choose the counting method used by the time-code on the source tape (**Figure 16.49**):

Non-Drop Frame—if the source uses non-drop-frame timecode.

Drop Frame—if the source uses drop-frame timecode.

6. Click OK to close the Clip Capture Parameters dialog box.

The clip information you entered appears in the Batch Capture window (**Figure 16.50**).

7. Repeat steps 2 through 6 until you have logged all the clips for your batch list.

8. Choose File > Save As.

The Save Batch List dialog box appears.

9. Specify a file name and destination for the batch list, and click Save.

✔ Tip

- As you create a batch list, save often. Logging can be tedious and time-consuming; protect your work from system crashes.

CREATING A BATCH LIST

Editing a Batch List

Once items are in a batch list, you can change them, remove them, rearrange them, or even copy them to another list.

To change items in a batch list:

1. In a Batch Capture window, double-click an item (**Figure 16.51**).

   The Clip Capture Parameters window for the clip appears.

2. In the Clip Capture Parameters window, change any of the information about the clip, such as its reel name, or in and out points (**Figure 16.52**)

3. Click OK.

   The Clip Capture Parameters window closes, and the changes to the item appear in the batch list (**Figure 16.53**).

4. Choose File > Save to save the changes to the batch list.

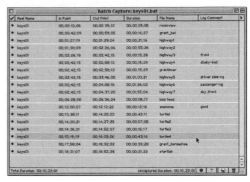

Figure 16.51 In a Batch Capture window, double-click an item.

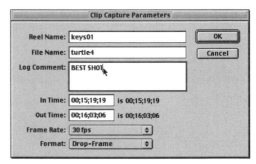

Figure 16.52 In the Clip Capture Parameters window, change any of the information about the clip and click OK.

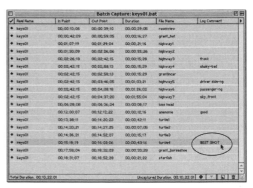

Figure 16.53 The changes to the item appear in the batch list.

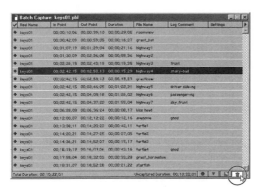

Figure 16.54 In a batch list, select an item and click the delete button.

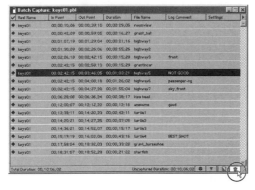

Figure 16.55 The item is removed from the list.

Figure 16.56 Click and drag an item in the batch list...

Figure 16.57 ...to move it to a new position in the list.

To delete items from a batch list:

◆ In a batch list, select an item and click the delete button 🗑 (**Figure 16.54**). The item is removed from the list (**Figure 16.55**).

To rearrange items in the batch list:

◆ Drag an item in the batch list to another position in the list (**Figures 16.56**) and **16.57**).

To sort items in the batch list chronologically by in point:

◆ In a batch list window, click the sort button 🔽 (**Figure 16.58**).

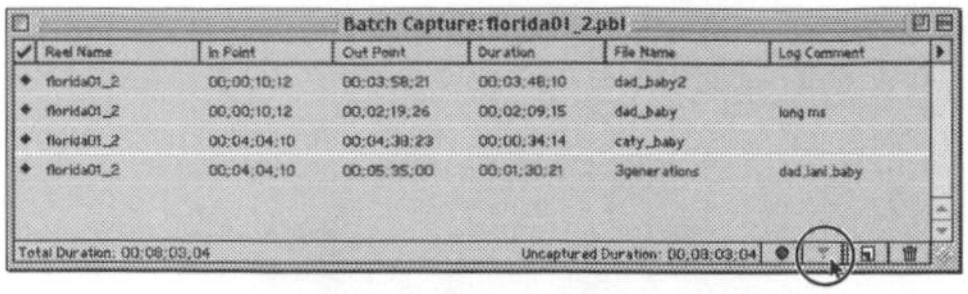

To copy items from one batch list to another:

1. Open two or more batch lists.

2. In one batch list window, select one or more items.

   [Shift]-click to select multiple items in the list.

3. Drag the selected items to another batch list window (**Figure 16.59**).

   The items are copied to the second batch list window (**Figure 16.60**).

Figure 16.58 Click the sort button to arrange the items by in point.

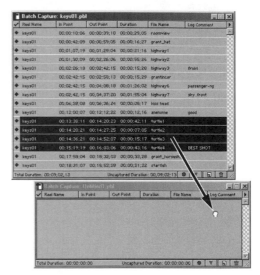

Figure 16.59 Drag the selected items to another batch list window.

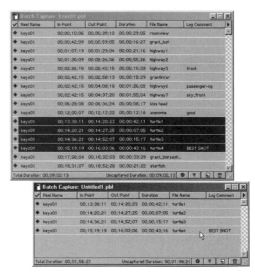

Figure 16.60 The items are copied to the second batch list window.

EDITING A BATCH LIST

Figure 16.61 In the batch list window pull-down menu, choose Attach Settings.

Figure 16.62 Find the project preset settings file you want to attach to the clips and click Open.

Figure 16.63 The settings appear in the Settings column of the batch list window.

Attaching Capture Settings to Items in a Batch List

In Chapter 2, you learned how to choose and to save preset project settings, which include the capture settings reviewed in this chapter (see "Choosing Capture Settings," earlier in this chapter). The presets included with Premiere are saved in the Settings folder, located in the Premiere application folder.

These preset capture settings can be attached, or assigned, to items in a batch list. This way, the clips you batch capture can use different settings from each another or from the currently selected capture settings. This feature is most useful if you're using a capture card that supports various capture settings. For example, you can easily attach lower-quality settings to items in a batch list that you're using for an offline edit, and attach higher-quality settings to a trimmed batch list at your output quality. By simply attaching settings, you never have to revisit or recheck the capture settings before you capture each batch list. (For more about trimmed batch lists and online editing, see Chapter 15.)

To attach settings to selected items in a batch list:

1. Select one or more items in a batch list.

2. In the batch list window pull-down menu, choose Attach Settings (**Figure 16.61**). The Open dialog box appears.

3. In the Open dialog box, find the project preset settings file you want to attach to the clips and click Open (**Figure 16.62**). Settings are typically stored in the Settings folder, which is located inside the Premiere folder. When you click Open, the settings appear in the Settings column of the batch list window (**Figure 16.63**).

To remove settings from selected items in a batch list:

1. Select one or more items in a batch list that have settings attached.

    Settings appear in the Settings column of the Batch Capture window, across from each item in the list.

2. In the Batch Capture window's pull-down menu, choose Remove Settings (**Figure 16.64**).

    The settings no longer appear in the Settings column (**Figure 16.65**).

✔ Tip

- The batch list uses the capture settings attached to the items in the list. Otherwise, it uses the currently selected capture settings. You can open the Capture panel of the Project Settings dialog box by selecting Recording Setting from the batch list window's pull-down menu.

Figure 16.64 Select one or more items in a batch list and choose Remove Settings from the Batch List pull-down menu.

Figure 16.65 The settings no longer appear in the Settings column.

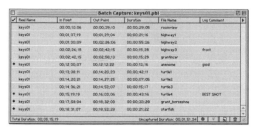

Figure 16.66 Icons indicate the status of items in the batch list, and buttons allow you to sort and capture items.

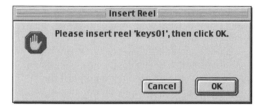

Figure 16.67 Premiere prompts you to insert the tape, or reel, associated with the first item in the batch list.

Using Batch Capture

Before you batch-capture, check the scratch disk, available disk space, capture settings, device-control settings, and deck, if necessary. (These topics are covered earlier in this chapter.) If everything is set properly, you need to attend to the batch capture only when you are required to change source tapes.

To batch-capture clips:

1. Open a project and select a bin to store the captured clips.

   If you don't specify a bin in a project, Premiere will prompt you to create an external bin on the hard drive.

2. Open a batch list (**Figure 16.66**), and if necessary, click to the left of any clip in the list to change its icon, and thereby its capture status:

   No icon—indicates that the clip will not be captured when you click Capture.

   Diamond ⬦—indicates that the clip will be captured when you click Capture.

   Check ☑—indicates that the clip has been captured.

   X ☒—indicates that an error occurred during capture.

3. Click the Capture button ⬦.

   Premiere prompts you to insert the tape, or reel, associated with the first item in the batch list (**Figure 16.67**).

   continues on next page

USING BATCH CAPTURE

4. Supply the appropriate tape and click OK.

As each clip is captured, the diamond icon will change into a check (**Figure 16.68**). If an error occurs, the diamond will change into an X. Clips are saved onto the disk you specified as the scratch disk for capturing (see "Specifying a Scratch Disk," earlier in this chapter). If prompted again, insert the appropriate tape and click OK to continue capturing. To stop capture, press Esc.

5. With the batch list window selected, choose File > Save.

The current status of the items in the list is saved.

✔ Tips

■ Sometimes, it's useful to add *handles*, or additional frames before the specified in and out points of the clips. This can give you extra footage you need for transitions, for example. Choose Handles from the Batch Capture window pull-down menu.

■ A gap (unrecorded area) in the tape, or a discontinuity (or *break*) in the tape's timecode can cause the batch capture process to be aborted. Understand how your camera works in order to avoid these problems while you shoot. Otherwise, you may have to copy, or dub, your camera original to another tape. Alternatively, you can capture the items where the timecode is continuous, and cue the tape manually to prevent Premiere from encountering the gap or timecode break.

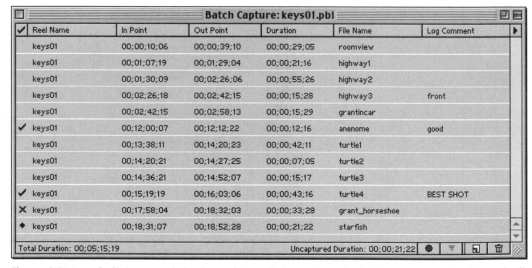

✓	Reel Name	In Point	Out Point	Duration	File Name	Log Comment	▶
	keys01	00;00;10;06	00;00;39;10	00;00;29;05	roomview		
	keys01	00;01;07;19	00;01;29;04	00;00;21;16	highway1		
	keys01	00;01;30;09	00;02;26;06	00;00;55;26	highway2		
	keys01	00;02;26;18	00;02;42;15	00;00;15;28	highway3	front	
	keys01	00;02;42;15	00;02;58;13	00;00;15;29	grantincar		
✓	keys01	00;12;00;07	00;12;12;22	00;00;12;16	anenome	good	
	keys01	00;13;38;11	00;14;20;23	00;00;42;11	turtle1		
	keys01	00;14;20;21	00;14;27;25	00;00;07;05	turtle2		
	keys01	00;14;36;21	00;14;52;07	00;00;15;17	turtle3		
✓	keys01	00;15;19;19	00;16;03;06	00;00;43;16	turtle4	BEST SHOT	
X	keys01	00;17;58;04	00;18;32;03	00;00;33;28	grant_horseshoe		
◆	keys01	00;18;31;07	00;18;52;28	00;00;21;22	starfish		

Batch Capture: keys01.pbl

Total Duration: 00;05;15;19 — Uncaptured Duration: 00;00;21;22

Figure 16.68 As each clip is captured, the diamond icon will change into a check. If an error occurs, the diamond will change into an X.

Figure 16.69 Choose Clip > Advanced Options > Timecode.

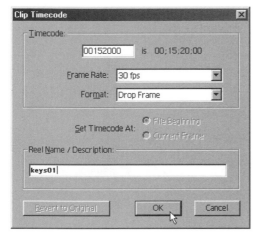

Figure 16.70 The Clip Timecode dialog box appears. Enter timecode information that matches the timecode visible in the window dub.

Adding Timecode Manually

Even if your equipment doesn't support timecode, you can still add timecode to a captured clip manually. You should set the timecode manually when you capture from a timecode window dub.

Many productions use timecode *window dubs* to avoid over-using the precious original tapes—and to avoid the costs of buying or renting an expensive professional deck. To make a window dub, the camera originals are copied onto a more inexpensive and expendable tape format, such as VHS. The window dub doesn't usually contain the timecode from the original tape, but it does record a display of the source tape's timecode as part of the video image. As part of the video image, the so-called "burned-in" timecode isn't meant to be read by video equipment, but by humans like you. In a traditional offline edit, an editor can generate an edit decision list (EDL) manually by transcribing the burned-in timecode numbers from the beginning and ending of each shot in the program.

In Premiere, adding timecode to the captured clips manually allows you to generate the EDL automatically—or to create a batch list for recapturing clips from the camera original tapes.

To set timecode manually:

1. Select or open a clip.

2. Choose Clip > Advanced Options > Timecode (**Figure 16.69**).

   The Clip Timecode dialog box appears (**Figure 16.70**).

   continues on next page

3. *Do either of the following:*

▲ Type the timecode number that matches the frame that's currently visible in the clip.

or

▲ Type the timecode number that matches the timecode number of the first frame of the clip.

Refer to the timecode window (burned-in timecode) that is visible in the clip.

4. From the Frame Rate pull-down menu, choose the frame rate that matches the source tape:

24—for film

25—for PAL standard video

30—for NTSC standard video

5. From the Format pull-down menu, choose the format that matches the source tape:

Drop Frame—for drop-frame timecode

Non Drop-Frame—for non drop-frame timecode

See Chapter 18 for an explanation of drop-frame and non drop-frame timecode.

6. In the Set Timecode At section, click the appropriate radio button:

File Beginning—to set the timecode for the first frame of the clip.

Current Frame—to set the timecode for the current frame.

7. In the Reel Name/Description box, type the name of the clip's source tape.

8. Click OK to close the Clip Timecode dialog box and apply the changes.

The timecode of the clip and the timecode window display should match (**Figure 16.71**). You can change the reel name and timecode (or revert to the clip's original reel name and timecode) at any time.

Figure 16.71 The timecode of the clip and the timecode window display should match.

✔ Tip

■ The timecode and reel name that you specify is used by Premiere but not encoded into the source movie file. As long as you work with this project, however, the timecode reference will be useful for generating accurate EDLs and batch lists.

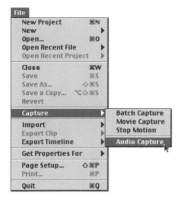

Figure 16.72
Choose File ›
Capture › Audio
Capture.

Figure 16.73
The Audio Recorder
window appears.

Figure 16.74 To open a
Sound Settings dialog
box, choose Audio
Capture › Sound Input.

Analog Audio Capture

If your computer is equipped with a sound-recording device, you can digitize audio in an audio-only format, such as .AIFF or .WAV. Unlike video capture cards, audio input is a built-in feature of most computers.

On the Mac OS, you can capture an audio-only clip directly from Premiere. On the Windows platform, you must use a separate audio capture program, such as Microsoft Windows Sound Recorder.

To capture audio using the Mac OS:

1. Choose File > Capture > Audio Capture (**Figure 16.72**).

   The Audio Recorder window appears (**Figure 16.73**), and the Audio Capture menu appears in the menu bar.

2. Choose Audio Capture > Sound Input (**Figure 16.74**).

   The Sound Settings dialog box appears.

3. In the Sound Settings dialog box, select the characteristics of the audio.

   See the next section, "To select audio capture options."

4. Click OK to close the dialog box.

   You return to the Audio Capture window.

5. In the Audio Capture window, click Record to start recording, and click Stop to stop recording.

   An audio clip window opens, and the clip appears in the selected bin of the Project window.

To select audio recording options:

1. With the Audio Recorder window active, choose Audio Capture > Sound Input (**Figure 16.75**).

   The Sound Settings dialog box appears (**Figure 16.76**).

2. From the Source pull-down menu, choose the audio source that you are using (such as the built-in microphone input of your computer).

3. From the Sample Rate pull-down menu, choose a sample rate:

   22050 Hz—suitable for voices only, or multimedia projects.

   44100 Hz—comparable to the sample rate of CD audio.

4. From the Format pull-down menu, choose a bit depth:

   8 Bits—produces less dynamic range, and results in a smaller file.

   16 Bits—produces more dynamic range, comparable to CD audio.

5. From the pull-down menu next to the Format pull-down menu, choose an option:

   Stereo—preserves two discrete channels of audio, if present.

   Mono—mixes stereo channels into a single channel of audio, and results in a smaller file.

Figure 16.75 With the Audio Recorder window active, choose Audio Capture > Sound Input.

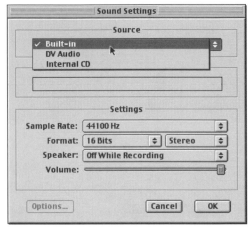

Figure 16.76 In the Sound Settings dialog box, specify the settings you want for the captured audio.

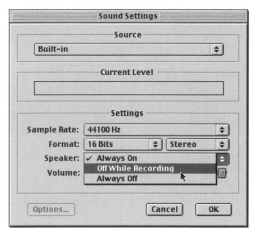

Figure 16.77 Specify how you want the speakers to function during digitizing in the Speaker pull-down menu.

✔ Tips

■ For more detailed information about audio settings, see Chapter 18.

■ After you capture audio, check the waveform display in the audio clip window. If the waveform looks small and flat, you may need to increase the audio levels. If the waveform seems to extend beyond the top or bottom of the window, the audio levels are too loud. You should adjust the audio levels and capture the file again.

6. From the Speaker pull-down menu, make a choice to specify how you want the speakers to function during digitizing (**Figure 16.77**):

Always On—speakers are always on; sound should be monitored with headphones.

Off While Recording—speakers are on except when recording; this prevents feedback during recording.

Always Off—speakers are always off; audio cannot be monitored before or during recording.

7. Drag the Volume slider to adjust the incoming audio levels.

The Volume slider does not adjust the recording levels. However, some audio hardware does provide a slider to adjust gain.

In the Current Levels area of the dialog box, monitor the levels displayed in the audio meter. Adjust the volume so that the meter registers a strong signal without peaking into the red too often. The audio must already be playing for you to see the levels.

8. To choose hardware-specific options, click Option (if available).

9. Click OK to close the Sound Settings dialog box and return to the Audio Recorder window.

ANALOG AUDIO CAPTURE

PREMIERE ONLINE

Chapter 1 outlined the offline/online editing process, in which you edit your program at low quality (offline edit) and complete it at high quality (online edit).

Typically, the online edit takes place in a traditional online editing suite, complete with all the professional (and expensive) gear available to finish the program at the highest possible quality. This kind of online edit uses your Premiere-generated edit decision list (EDL) as the blueprint for quickly re-creating the program from your source tapes—or, in some cases, a pristine, uncompressed digital version of the source footage. This offline/online editing strategy was developed to save money by staying out of the online suite. The time-consuming editing is accomplished on less inexpensive gear, making your stay in an expensive online suite quick and efficient.

You can accomplish the offline and online edit on the same system, however. For the offline edit, you can digitize clips at relatively low quality. When you finish editing, you simply recapture the clips—this time, at a higher, final-output quality. Fortunately, you don't have to recapture all the source clips— just the clips that you use in the final program.

This type of offline/online strategy is designed to save money by saving hard disk space. Capturing at a lower quality maximizes the amount of footage you can store on a hard disk. After you narrow down the footage to just what you need in the program, recapturing the clips at higher quality becomes more feasible. This method is suitable for editors who use capture cards that allow for different quality settings but who don't have ample disk space for raw footage. Because most capture cards compress the footage, you can't achieve the same quality you would get by using the source tapes in an online suite. For many applications, however, the card's image quality is more than adequate.

As you know, using any offline/online strategy means using timecode. The clips that you use in the offline edit must have timecode that matches the timecode on the source tapes. When you recapture the clips for online editing, you need your timecoded source tapes, a deck that can read the timecode, and device control. In addition, your capture card and drives must be able to capture and play back the clips at your desired output quality.

What if you work at output quality from beginning to end? In that case, the intricacies of offline and online editing don't apply to you. Nevertheless, this chapter may contain a few useful techniques for creating hard disk space and doing some housekeeping before you archive your finished project.

DV Offline?

Because DV is relatively inexpensive to shoot and to edit, many people are able to avoid the offline-online process. However, even those using DV sometimes consider the offline strategy.

In some productions, the *shooting ratio*—the ratio of the footage shot to the amount used in the final program—can be very high. A documentary might have a shooting ratio of 20:1 or more. Digitizing at a low quality could allow you to use more footage before exceeding your hard drive space. However, most capture cards allow you to scale the amount of compression (and thereby the file size), DV does not: the video is encoded in the camera, at DV's fixed 3.4MB/sec data rate. Though you can install a variety of DV codecs on your computer to decode the DV, they can't change its data rate.

Instead of adopting an offline strategy, it's often better to invest in additional storage. If a new hard drive isn't an option, you can try to buy a copy of ProMax's DV Toolkit, which does include a low-resolution codec for capturing DV. But because the DV Toolkit's primary purpose was to provide a better DV codec than had been available, it was discontinued with the introduction of QuickTime 5. If you can't capture with a lo-res codec, you'll have to recompress your DV files after you capture them. This can be a time-consuming extra step, and you won't be able to preview the video through a DV camera or deck on a video monitor; the clips won't be DV clips anymore. But the recompressed clips will act as stand-ins, or proxies, for the original DV clips, and they'll take up less storage space. Whether the trouble is worth what you save on hard drives is another question.

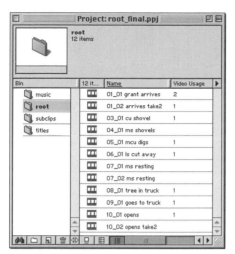

Figure 17.1 Select a Project or Bin window.

Figure 17.2 Choose Project > Remove Unused Clips, or press ⌘-Ⓤ (Mac) or Ctrl-Ⓤ (Windows).

Figure 17.3 Clips that are not used in the program are removed from the window.

Purging Unused Clips

The final program rarely uses all the clips that you imported into the program. As a matter of housekeeping (and in preparation for online editing), you can remove the clips that you didn't use in the program. Although icons in the Project and Bin windows show you which clips are in the timeline, Premiere can identify these clips automatically and delete them from your project and bins.

To remove unused clips:

1. Select a Project or Bin window (**Figure 17.1**).

2. Choose Project > Remove Unused Clips, or press ⌘-Ⓤ (Mac) or Ctrl-Ⓤ (Windows) (**Figure 17.2**).

   Clips that are not used in the program are removed from the window. Unused clips in other windows and nested bins remain untouched (**Figure 17.3**).

3. Repeat steps 1 and 2 to remove unused clips from other bins and nested bins.

4. Save the file by doing either of the following:
   - ▲ Choose File > Save to save the changes.
   - ▲ Choose File > Save As to save the project under a new name.

   The references to files not used in the timeline are removed. You can delete them from the hard disk without affecting the project.

Creating a File List

You can export a list of the files used in your project. This list can make a handy reference. If you want, the list can include the exact locations of the files.

To export a file list:

1. Choose File > Export Timeline > File List (**Figure 17.4**).

   The Save File List dialog box appears.

2. Specify a name and destination for the file list.

   To include the locations of the files on your hard disk, check the Include full path names checkbox (**Figure 17.5**).

3. Click Save.

   The file list is saved under the name and in the location you specified. You can open the file in Premiere and in most text-editing programs.

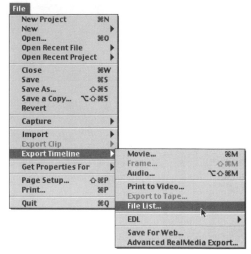

Figure 17.4 Choose File > Export Timeline > File List.

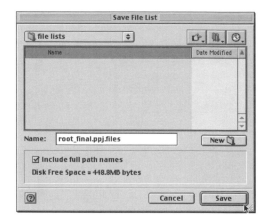

Figure 17.5 In the Save File List dialog box, specify a name and destination for the file list. To include the locations of the files on your hard disk, check Include full path names.

Figure 17.6 With a project open, choose Project > Utilities > Project Trimmer.

Figure 17.7 The Project Trimmer dialog box appears. Specify the options, and click Create Project.

Trimming a Project

The Project Trimmer command automatically prepares your project for recapturing clips by creating a trimmed project and a trimmed batch list.

A *trimmed project* is an exact duplicate of your project, except that it adds a number to the names of all the clips. The new name differentiates the clips of a trimmed project from those of the original project.

Because they're created from the trimmed project, clips in the *trimmed batch list* also have a number appended to their file names. More important, a trimmed batch list includes only the portions of the clips that you used in the program. High-quality video files can be extremely large; batch-digitizing from a trimmed batch list uses your disk space efficiently by capturing only what you need to create the program.

After you capture the clips in the trimmed batch list, open the trimmed project. The project retains all your editing decisions but refers to the new, high-quality video files. Fine-tune or export the program as needed.

To create a trimmed project and trimmed batch list:

1. With a project open, choose Project > Utilities > Project Trimmer (**Figure 17.6**).

   Premiere prompts you to save the project before creating a trimmed version.

2. In the warning dialog box, click OK to confirm that you want to create a trimmed version.

   The Project Trimmer dialog box appears (**Figure 17.7**).

continues on next page

TRIMMING A PROJECT

3. Specify the following options:

Create Trimmed Batch List—check to generate a trimmed batch list after creating a trimmed project.

Copy Trimmed Source Files—check to create trimmed copies of the source files.

For the online process described in this chapter, leave this checkbox unchecked.

Keep frame handles—enter the number of frames that you want to include as *handles* (frames before the in point and after the out point of each trimmed clip).

Handles give you flexibility to fine-tune the program after you recapture clips.

4. Click Create Project.

A Save New Project dialog box appears.

5. In the Save New Project dialog box, specify a filename and location for the trimmed project (**Figure 17.8**), and click Save.

A Save Batch List dialog box appears.

6. In the Save Batch List dialog box, specify a filename and location for the trimmed batch list (**Figure 17.9**), and click Save.

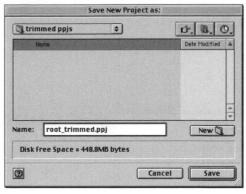

Figure 17.8 In the first Save dialog box, specify a filename and location for the trimmed project, and click Save.

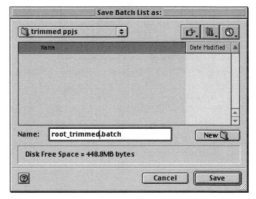

Figure 17.9 In the next Save dialog box, specify a filename and location for the trimmed batch list, and click Save.

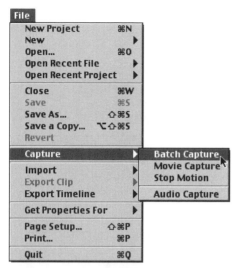

Figure 17.10 Choose File > Capture > Batch Capture to create a new batch list.

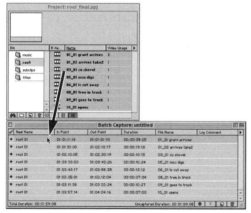

Figure 17.11 Drag clips from the Project window to the batch list; then save the batch list.

Creating a Batch List Manually

If prefer to manage your batch list yourself, you can create a batch list manually. Unlike the Project Trimmer method, this method does not trim or rename your clips, so differentiating them from the original clips is more difficult. To prevent confusion, you may want to delete the original source files (if the timecode is good, you have nothing to fear). If you prefer to keep the original files around, make sure that you keep the recaptured files in a separate, easy-to-identify folder.

To create a batch list from a project or bin:

1. Remove unused clips, as explained in "Purging Unused Clips" earlier in this chapter.

   This step prevents you from recapturing clips that aren't necessary in your program.

2. Choose File > Capture > Batch Capture to create a new batch list (**Figure 17.10**).

3. In a Project or Bin window, select the clips to add to the batch list.

4. Drag the selected clips into the Batch Capture window.

   The clips appear in the batch list. The durations of the clips reflect the duration of the entire clip, not the duration with in and out points (**Figure 17.11**).

5. Repeat steps 3 and 4 for other clips.

6. With the Batch Capture window active, choose File > Save.

7. In the Save dialog box, specify a filename and destination for the batch list.

Replacing Clip References

When you offline-edit in Premiere, the clips in your project refer to low-quality video files. When you recapture clips for your online version, you want the project to refer to the new, high-quality clips.

If you use the Project Trimmer before you recapture, the clips in the trimmed project and trimmed batch list are renamed. In this way, the clips in the trimmed project refer to files captured from the trimmed batch list.

If you decide not to use the Project Trimmer and opt to create a batch list manually, the clips are not renamed. Even after you recapture the clips at higher quality, the project may continue to refer to the lower-quality versions (even if they're not currently on the hard disk). You must get the project to refer to the new clips instead of the old ones.

One way to do this is to delete or move the low-quality clips and then reopen the project. When Premiere prompts you to locate the source files, simply locate the new high-quality sources.

On the other hand, you can use the Replace Clips command to accomplish the same task much more easily. Replace Clips allows you to change the clip references, effectively replacing one file with another. (The process is a lot like replacing an offline file with the proper reference.) Then you can fine-tune, preview, or export the final program.

To replace clips:

1. With the Project window active, choose Project > Replace Clips (**Figure 17.12**).

   Premiere alerts you that the command cannot be undone and will delete preview files (**Figure 17.13**).

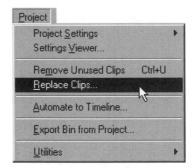

Figure 17.12 With the Project window active, choose Project > Replace Clips.

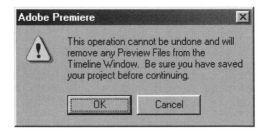

Figure 17.13 Premiere alerts you that the command cannot be undone and will delete preview files. Click OK to confirm that you want to replace clips.

REPLACING CLIP REFERENCES

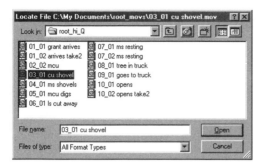

Figure 17.14 The Locate Files dialog box appears, prompting you to locate a file. Locate the files to update the file references for the clips.

2. Click OK to continue to replace clips.

   The Locate File dialog box appears, prompting you to locate a file (**Figure 17.14**).

3. Locate the requested files.

   If you are replacing lower-quality files with higher-quality versions, make sure that you locate the correct version.

VIDEO AND AUDIO SETTINGS

At every major step in the editing process—capture, edit, and output—you encounter settings that control the basic attributes of the video and audio. The settings you choose for one step of the process may not be the best choices for another.

To make intelligent choices, you should have a basic understanding of topics such as frame rates, frame sizes, compression, and audio quality. You should familiarize yourself not only with how these settings relate to video displayed on computers, but also with how they relate to video displayed on television.

This chapter helps you choose settings in Premiere, but it also helps you understand some of the fundamental principles of all digital video. Of course, it can offer only brief explanations of the matters directly referenced in Premiere.

Choosing Settings

Perhaps the greatest advantage of using a DV-based editing system is the way in which it simplifies your choice of settings. The DV format is so consistent that systems like Premiere can include presets, sparing you the hassle of choosing video and audio settings manually. Ignorance is indeed bliss.

If you are using a hardware capture card, your choices are simpler not because they're universal, but because they're specific. The settings supported by your card are the most obvious choices for capture, playback, and export—especially if your goal is to produce a videotape of your final program. The documentation included with your capture card is your best guide.

If you're editing on a different system from the one that you used for capture, however, you need to understand a broader range of options. Files that rely on a hardware card won't play back on systems that don't have the same hardware. In fact, the files won't even open on other systems unless they have a software version of the capture card's compression scheme, or *codec* (see "Codecs" later in this chapter).

Similarly, if you want to export a final movie to play back on other devices—such as on another hard disk, on a CD-ROM, or via the Internet—you need to know which settings are most appropriate for each use.

Guidelines to Choosing Settings

The settings that you choose depend on your particular needs, but a few general principles apply:

◆ When you capture, choose settings to digitize at the highest quality possible without dropping frames.

◆ For editing, use settings that your system can process quickly and play back smoothly.

◆ When you export to tape, choose the settings that match or approach the quality of your source files, yet play back smoothly.

◆ When you create a final movie, choose settings based on the specifications of the playback device. When playback devices vary, use settings that don't exceed the least-capable device.

Figure 18.1 You choose a timebase when you capture video, create an offline file, and specify project settings (shown here). Because Premiere uses the timebase to make time calculations, choose the correct timebase, and don't change it.

Timebase

The timebase of a project determines how Premiere calculates time divisions, expressed in frames per second, or *fps* (**Figure 18.1**). The timebase shouldn't be confused with the frame rate—the rate at which the program displays frames.

If you're using standard video in North America, choose 29.97 as the timebase for your project settings. Set the correct timebase before you start editing, and don't change it. Changing the timebase in the middle of a project affects Premiere's time calculations, causing existing edit marks and markers to shift and changing the durations of clips.

✔ Tip

- A few dialog boxes in Premiere (such as the Clip Capture parameters dialog box) prompt you to select a frame rate, when strictly speaking they should say timebase. Don't be confused; just choose the option that most closely matches the timebase standard you're using.

Timebase Standards

The timebase is derived from the following film and video standards:

- ◆ 24 fps for film
- ◆ 25 fps for PAL and SECAM video (standards common in most countries outside North America)
- ◆ 29.97 fps for NTSC video (the standard in North America, Central America, Japan, and other countries)
- ◆ 30 fps for other video types

TIMEBASE

Frame Rate

Frame rate refers to both the number of frames per second contained in a source clip and to the number of frames per second displayed by the program or exported movie. The frame rate of source video is determined when it is recorded or rendered. You determine the frame rate of a program in the Project Settings dialog box and the frame rate of an exported movie in the Export Settings dialog box (**Figure 18.2**).

Regardless of a source clip's frame rate, it is displayed in the program and timeline at the frame rate determined by the project settings. A 15-fps source, however, does not play back more smoothly when set to play back at 30 fps; each frame of the source is simply displayed twice. Similarly, a 30-fps source in a program set for 15-fps displays only every other frame in the program view and in the timeline.

Whenever possible, you should make sure that the timebase, source frame rate, and project frame rate agree. If you choose to preview or export a movie at a lower frame rate, choose an even division of the full frame rate. A rate of 29.97 fps or 30 fps, for example, is considered to be full-motion for NTSC video. Choose 15 fps or 10 fps when you want to use a lower frame rate. Choosing a different frame rate does not affect the speed of the clip—only how smoothly (or choppily) it plays back.

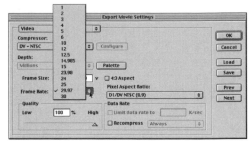

Figure 18.2 You choose frame rates when you specify settings for capture, a project, and export (shown here).

Timecode

Timecode is a method of counting video frames, developed by the Society of Motion Picture and Television Engineers (SMPTE). SMPTE timecode is counted in hours, minutes, seconds, and frames. It counts 30 frames per second, from zero up to just under one day, or 23:59:59:29. Therefore, there's a timecode hour 0 but no timecode hour 24.

The advantage of timecode is that it provides an *absolute address* for each frame of video—that is, each frame has a unique and unchanging number. The number acts as an address or identity. Just as a street address helps you find a specific place, timecode helps you find a specific frame.

Timecode makes offline/online editing possible. By keeping track of timecode numbers (and the reel, or tape, that they're on), you can easily re-create an offline edit.

Without timecode, frames can be counted sequentially, but they cannot be identified specifically. Without timecode, you have no way to refer to a frame of video accurately—and consequently, you have no way to create an EDL (see Chapter 15) or recapture a particular clip (see Chapter 17).

A great deal of consumer video equipment does not read or record timecode. Even if you are using a timecode display in your project, timecode isn't necessarily present in the source clip or the source tape.

DV cameras, however, do record timecode (typically drop-frame timecode; see the following section). Computer programs like Premiere can read the timecode without using additional equipment.

✔ Tip

- Most consumer-level cameras start at timecode 00;00;00;00. In many cases, turning off the camera for more than a few minutes resets the timecode, so that the next shot on the same tape restarts at 00;00;00;00. Check the documentation included with your camera to see how it handles timecode.

TIMECODE

Drop-Frame and Non-Drop-Frame Timecode

Although the timebase of NTSC video is a constant 29.97 fps, SMPTE timecode counts it in two different ways: drop-frame and non-drop-frame.

Non-Drop-Frame Timecode—Even though the true timebase of NTSC video is 29.97, non-drop-frame (NDF) timecode counts 30 fps. Over time, however, the discrepancy results in a small but significant difference between the duration indicated by the timecode and the actual elapsed time (**Figure 18.3**). Nevertheless, NDF timecode is easy to understand and usually is used for source tapes. Video equipment displays NDF timecode with colons between the numbers.

Drop-Frame Timecode—To compensate for the discrepancy caused by the 30-fps counting scheme, SMPTE developed drop-frame timecode (DF). Drop-frame timecode also counts 30 fps, but it skips two frame numbers (not actual video frames) at the end of every minute, except for every 10th minute (**Figure 18.4**).

As confusing as this sounds, DF timecode displays durations that very closely match actual time. Premiere and other video equipment display drop-frame timecode with semicolons between numbers.

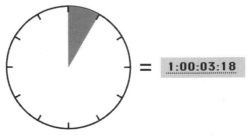

Figure 18.3 Every hour of real-time, non-drop-frame timecode has counted an extra 3 seconds and 18 frames.

Figure 18.4 Drop-frame timecode skips two frame numbers at the end of every minute, except for every 10th minute.

Figure 18.5 You can change the source display in the Monitor window options, or you can change the program display in the Timeline window options or the Project Settings dialog box (shown here). You can also cycle through the options directly in the Monitor or Timeline window.

Time Displays

In the Monitor and Clip windows, you can choose among several time displays (**Figure 18.5**). Choose the time display that is best suited for your project. Your options are:

24-fps Timecode—counts for standard film frame rates.

25-fps Timecode—counts for PAL and SECAM (common standards in most countries outside North America).

30-fps Drop-Frame (DF) Timecode—counts for NTSC video (the standard in North America, Japan, and other countries) in drop-frame format. It displays with semicolons between numbers.

30-fps Non-Drop-Frame (NDF) Timecode—counts for NTSC video (the standard in North America, Japan, and other countries) in non-drop-frame format. It displays with colons between numbers.

Frames/Samples—counts video frames and audio samples.

Feet/Frames 16mm—counts for 16mm motion-picture film, which has 40 frames per foot.

Feet/Frames 35mm—counts for 35mm motion-picture film, which has 16 frames per foot.

The time display is a counting system and doesn't affect the timebase or frame rate, so you can change the time display at any time. The display represents a clip's timecode if it is present in the source or stamped manually (see Chapter 16). If no timecode is present, the display merely starts counting from zero.

✔ Tip

■ Most consumer DV cameras record drop-frame timecode.

Interlaced and Progressive Scan Video

One important difference between television and computers lies in how they display frames of video. Television monitors display interlaced video, whereas computer monitors use a progressive scan.

In a *progressive scan*, the horizontal lines of each frame are displayed from the top of the screen to the bottom in a single pass.

Interlaced video divides each frame into two fields. Each field includes every other horizontal line (scan line) in the frame. A television displays one field first, drawing alternating scan lines from the top of the image to the bottom (**Figure 18.6**). Returning to the top, it then displays the alternate field, filling in the gaps to complete the frame (**Figure 18.7**). In NTSC video, each frame displays approximately ¹⁄₃₀ of a second; each field displays every ¹⁄₆₀ of a second.

The field that contains the topmost scan line is called *field 1*, the odd field, or the upper field. The other field is known as *field 2*, the even field, or the lower field. Your video equipment and the settings that you choose determine which field is the *dominant* field—the field that is displayed first (**Figure 18.8**).

As you would expect, video cameras record interlaced images. Capture cards designed to work with NTSC video also digitize and export interlaced video fields. Similarly, some software programs (many animation programs, for example) support field rendering—the capability to export noninterlaced source material as interlaced video.

Figure 18.6 Interlaced displays present a single field that includes every other line of the image ...

Figure 18.7 ...and then interlaces the opposite field to create a full frame.

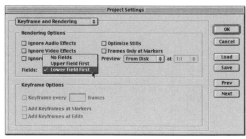

Figure 18.8 Choose the correct field dominance in the Keyframe and Rendering panels of the Project, Export, or Capture Settings dialog boxes.

✔ Tips

- Some DV cameras also offer progressive-scan video. Before you embrace progressive-scan video, make sure that you understand its practical implications. Some cameras can capture 30 fps in progressive mode; others can record only 15 fps. Progressive-scan video might be appropriate for projects destined only for presentation on computer screens. But if there's a chance that you want to present the project on television, it's probably best to stick with interlaced video.

- Because its frame rate is similar to film, the PAL video standard shot in progressive-scan mode might make the transition to film better than interlaced video. Even so, research the pros and cons of this technique before you invest your time and money.

You can display interlaced video on a progressive-scan monitor, and you can display noninterlaced source material on a video monitor. But the natures of interlaced and noninterlaced images have several practical implications. Read on.

Interlacing Problems

Problems arising from the nature of interlaced and noninterlaced images are some of the most pervasive and least understood.

Because video cameras capture each field of a frame at different moments in time, moving objects may be in one position in one field and in a different position in the next field. You'd never notice the difference as the video is playing, but it becomes quite apparent when you view a single interlaced frame. The way interlacing makes a moving object look when viewed as a still frame is described as *combing* or *field artifacts*. Interlacing can also become apparent when you make a clip play in slow motion.

Conversely, certain graphic elements that look good on a progressive-scan monitor display poorly on an interlaced monitor. Due to interlacing, thin horizontal lines (or patterns containing thin horizontals) appear to flicker or vibrate. If a line is thin enough, it actually disappears with every scan of its field.

Disagreement between the field dominance of a video playback device and a recording device can cause movement in the frame to appear staggered or stuttered in the recorded image. That's because the fields have been recorded in the wrong order; the field dominance was reversed inadvertently. Applying the backward video effect also reverses field order.

Fortunately, there are solutions for all these field-related problems.

Solving Interlacing Problems

You can solve most interlacing problems by choosing the appropriate field option in the Keyframe and Rendering panel of the appropriate settings dialog box (Capture, Project, or Export) (**Figure 18.9**). Select the field dominance that matches your footage or recording device. Or select None, if your footage isn't interlaced.

If you intend to export interlaced video for display on computer monitors, you should deinterlace it. *Deinterlacing* converts two fields into a single frame, either by duplicating one field or blending the two. Some codecs deinterlace the video automatically. You can also select a deinterlacing feature in the Special Processing dialog box. (**Figure 18.10**). You can open the Special Processing dialog box by clicking the Modify button in the Special Processing panel of the Export Settings dialog box. See Chapter 15 for more information about export.

You can solve other field rendering problems by using the Field Options command. Applying this command allows you to deinterlace clips that have been slowed, interlace noninterlaced footage, or reduce flicker due to interlacing.

To use the Field Options command:

1. Select a clip in the timeline that requires field processing.

2. Choose Clip > Video Options > Field Options (**Figure 18.11**).

   The Field Options dialog box appears.

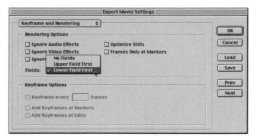

Figure 18.9 Most interlacing problems can be solved by choosing the appropriate field option in the Keyframe and Rendering panel of the appropriate Settings dialog box.

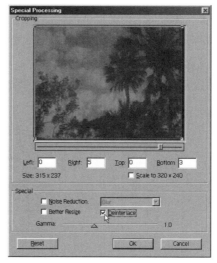

Figure 18.10 You can also select a deinterlacing feature in the Special Processing Options tab of the Export Settings dialog box.

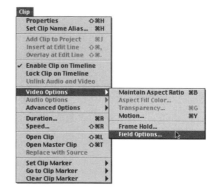

Figure 18.11 Choose Clip > Video Options > Field Options.

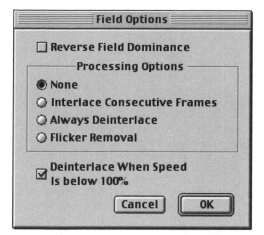

Figure 18.12 In the Field Options dialog box, specify the appropriate options, and click OK to apply the changes to the clip.

3. Specify the following options (**Figure 18.12**):

Reverse Field Dominance—to eliminate the stuttering effect evident in clips that use the wrong field dominance or clips with the backwards video effect.

Deinterlace When Speed Is Below 100%—deinterlaces the clip when played at a slower speed than normal, eliminating combing.

4. In the Processing Options section, choose the appropriate option:

None—doesn't execute field processing.

Interlace Consecutive Frames—interlaces frames that aren't interlaced.

Always Deinterlace—deinterlaces the clip, regardless of its playback speed.

Flicker Removal—blurs the image so that thin horizontal details don't flicker due to interlacing.

5. Click OK to close the dialog box and apply the changes.

✔ Tips

■ Many DV cameras offer a progressive-scan feature for capturing still images. For stills, a progressive-scan feature can save you the step of deinterlacing frames of video later. This feature may not be all that it's cracked up to be, however. Generally, still images captured in video cameras don't exceed the quality of the video. For high-quality stills (for printing, for example), rely on a digital still-camera or a good, old-fashioned film still-camera.

■ Avoid using light typefaces, thin lines, and tight patterns in images that are destined for television. If necessary, choose the Flicker Removal option in the Field Options dialog box.

SOLVING INTERLACING PROBLEMS

Overscan and Safe Zones

The methods used to scan the image onto the screen—progressive and interlaced—are just one important difference between computer and television monitors. Whereas computer monitors display the entire video image, televisions *overscan* the video image, cropping off the outer edges of the screen. To make matters worse, the amount of overscan differs slightly from television to television.

To ensure that important elements (such as titles) remain visible when displayed on a television screen, make sure that you keep these elements within television's so-called *safe zones*. You can view safe-zone guides in the source and program views of the Monitor window (see Chapter 4) and in the title window (see Chapter 12).

In video, the inner 90% of the complete image is considered to be *action-safe*—that is, everything within that area is likely to appear on most television screens. The inner 80% is considered to be *title-safe*. Because you can't afford to let any of the title's content be lost, the title-safe area defines a necessary safety margin. The safe-zone guides are for your reference only; they aren't added to the source image and don't appear in the program output (**Figures 18.13** and **18.14**).

Figure 18.13 This identification looks fine when you can see the entire image.

Figure 18.14 When the image is overscanned, you may lose important elements.

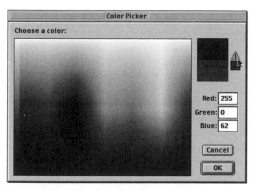

Figure 18.15 Click the warning icon to shift the color to a video-safe color on export.

Safe Colors

Yet another difference between computers and video lies in how they display colors. Video's native color model has a much narrower range, or *gamut*, than the RGB model used by computers and by Premiere. As a result, computers allow you to select much more saturated colors than video allows. Anything more saturated than video's *safe* colors will appear to be noisy or even bleed into areas where they don't belong when they're displayed on a video monitor.

In the color picker, a warning sign appears when you've selected a color that's not a video-safe color. Click the warning sign to shift the color to a safe color automatically when Premiere renders the color (**Figure 18.15**). You can adjust a clip's brightness and color levels for video by applying the broadcast colors effect. (See Chapter 11 to learn how to add effects to clips.)

Frame Size

Frame size refers to the number of pixels used to describe the video image. The number of pixels that equals full-screen video depends on the standard used by your capture or playback device. The most common frame sizes for full-screen video are as follows:

640×480—full-screen, square-pixel standard for computers, used by some lower-end capture cards.

720×486—nonsquare pixels used by standard-resolution professional video.

720×480—nonsquare pixels used by DV standard.

720×576—PAL video standard.

When you use frame sizes smaller than full-screen video, choose an even fraction of the full-screen pixel size (**Figure 18.16**), such as 640×480, 320×240, 240×180, or 160×120. Uneven fractions of frame sizes are more difficult for the computer to process.

✔ Tips

■ In video, it's common to refer to frame size as resolution. The term *resolution*, however, has a slightly different meaning for video than it does for print media. Although the number of pixels in full-screen video can differ, you can think of the display size as being fixed; it's full-screen, regardless of the size of the television screen. Therefore, it's best to think of digital video in terms of pixel dimensions, not pixels-per-inch (ppi).

■ People who are accustomed to print media are often disappointed to learn that standard-definition video always translates to a mere 72 dpi. If you want to print large, high-quality images of your video (for a press kit or poster) take production stills with a megapixel or film still camera.

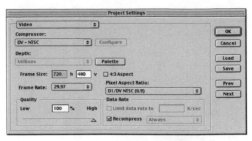

Figure 18.16 Set the frame size in the Video panels of the Capture, Project (shown here), or Export Settings dialog boxes.

Figure 18.17 Video in the 4:3 aspect ratio is still prevalent.

Figure 18.18 Increasingly, video is shown in 16:9 aspect ratio, which matches a common motion-picture aspect ratio. Premiere supports both 4:3 and 16:9.

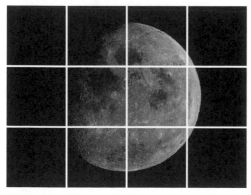

Figure 18.19 This example illustrates how square pixels can be used to form an image with a 4:3 aspect ratio.

Image Aspect Ratios

Aspect ratio refers to the dimensions of the video frame, expressed as a ratio between the width and the height (horizontal and vertical aspects). Most video uses a 4:3 aspect ratio, but with the advent of new video standards, the 16:9 aspect ratio is becoming more common (**Figures 18.17** and **18.18**).

Although video frame-size formats may differ, they maintain the same 4:3 aspect ratio. A 640×480 frame size, for example, uses square pixels to form an image with a 4:3 aspect ratio (**Figure 18.19**). A 720×486 frame size (D-1 resolution) uses non-square pixels to achieve the same 4:3 ratio (**Figure 18.20**). The image aspect ratios are the same; the pixel aspect ratios are different.

Pixel Aspect Ratio

When the aspect ratio of a source clip doesn't match the aspect ratio of the program, you can maintain the original aspect ratio of the source or change it to conform to the aspect ratio of the program. As discussed in Chapter 4, changing the aspect ratio of the source results in a distorted image.

Image distortion also occurs when a source clip uses a different pixel aspect ratio from the one used by your display monitor. An animation rendered at D-1 resolution (720×486 non-square pixels), for example, appears distorted when you display it on a typical computer monitor, which displays square pixels (**Figure 18.21**). Conversely, a 640×480 image appears distorted when it is displayed at D-1 resolution, which uses non-square pixels. Some programs and software codecs (see "Codecs" later in this chapter) correct for this type of distortion automatically; otherwise, you have to correct it by resizing the image. Better yet, prevent the problem by using consistent image aspect and pixel aspect ratios.

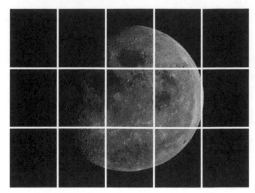

Figure 18.20 This example illustrates how non-square pixels form an image with a 4:3 aspect ratio.

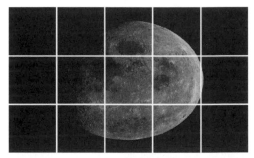

Figure 18.21 An image created with nonsquare pixels appears distorted when displayed with square pixels.

Figure 18.22 You can choose the image bit depth in the Video panels of the Project, Export, or Capture Settings dialog boxes. Click the Palette button to create or use a limited, optimized color palette.

Image Bit Depth

Computers store information in discrete quantities, called bits. *Bit depth* indicates the number of bits used to describe a single pixel. A higher bit depth produces more colors in an image and, consequently, higher picture quality. The RGB color format assigns 8 bits for each color channel—red, green, and blue—for 24-bit color. A 24-bit image contains millions of colors. If an alpha channel is present, it also uses 8 bits, for a total of 32 bits—often referred to as Millions of Colors +. Regardless of the bit depth of the source clips, Premiere always uses 32 bits to process video.

You can choose the image bit depth in the Video panels of the Project, Export, or Capture Settings dialog boxes (**Figure 18.22**). Depending on the codec you use, you can choose any (or none) of the following bit depths:

256 (8-bit color)—produces a grainy appearance.

Thousands (16-bit color)—suitable for some multimedia (or for people who enjoy the retro-aesthetic of a severely limited palette).

Millions (24-bit color)—produces the best image quality.

Millions+ (32-bit color)—preserves the alpha channel.

Palette—create a custom palette. If you are forced to work with older displays with limited bit-depth, you can get the most from your limited number of colors by clicking the Palette button and creating a palette which contains only the colors that appear most in the image.

IMAGE BIT DEPTH

Compression

Simply put, *compression* is the science of storing large amounts of data in small packages. Without compression, digital video would be impractical for all but the most powerful computer systems. A single uncompressed frame of full-screen video consumes nearly 1 MB of storage. Capturing and playing back 30 uncompressed frames per second is beyond the capability of most hard disks and processors; the data rate (or flow of information) is simply too high.

Fortunately, various compression schemes have been devised to reduce the file size and data rates of digital video and audio. In addition, add-on capture cards and fast drives can enable your computer to process relatively high-quality, high-data-rate video files. The DV format accomplishes its compression in the camera, reducing the data rate to a level most modern computers can handle without extra hardware.

✔ Tips

- Technically speaking, even footage shot in the professional Betacam SP format undergoes certain types of compression when it's recorded. When it comes to editing, *uncompressed* usually means avoiding any additional compression. Uncompressed nonlinear editing systems are available but generally are used only for high-end broadcast work.

- You could fill books—others have—on the topic of compression. This chapter merely touches on the subject enough to ground your knowledge of editing with Premiere.

Cards and Codecs

Some capture cards also offer a software-only version of the codec. Although the software codec usually can't enable you to play back the clip smoothly, it does allow you to open and process the file on computers that don't have the necessary hardware.

Codec technology changes rapidly. Visit the Web sites of codec developers to stay up to date.

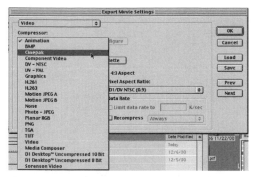

Figure 18.23 Choose one of the codecs available for your system in the Video panels of the Capture, Project (shown here), or Export Settings dialog boxes.

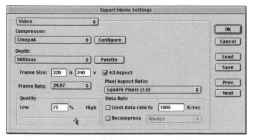

Figure 18.24 Within each codec, you usually can control how much compression is applied by using a quality slider. You can find this slider in the Keyframe and Rendering panel of the Capture, Project or Export Settings (shown here) dialog box.

Codecs

Codec stands for *compressor/decompressor*. *Compressor* refers to encoding a file and is synonymous with capture and rendering. *Decompressor* refers to decoding a file and is associated with playback. Codec denotes a particular compression scheme—a method of compressing and decompressing a file.

In general, you have a choice of software and hardware codecs. QuickTime and Video for Windows include several software-based codecs; others are available as software plug-ins (**Figure 18.23**).

For most high-quality video capture and playback, however, you need a hardware-assisted codec. If your hardware capture card and its software are installed properly, its codec appears in the Compressor menu of the Video panels of the Settings dialog boxes.

Within each codec, you usually can control how much compression is applied by using a quality slider (**Figure 18.24**), or you can define a top limit for the data rate (see "Data Rates" later in this chapter). You may also be able to specify whether you capture two interlaced fields or noninterlaced video.

For exporting to videotape, choosing a codec is relatively easy. For movie output, your choice becomes more difficult. Fortunately, plug-in tools such as Media Cleaner and RealMedia simplify your choices.

Video Codecs

Premiere offers the following video codecs if you choose QuickTime as your editing mode (in the Project Settings dialog box) or as the file type (in the Export Settings dialog box).

- **Animation**—designed for images that contain large areas of flat color, such as cartoon animations. Lossless at its 100 percent quality setting, it's suitable for interim storage of title sequences and animations.
- **Cinepak**—compresses 24-bit video for data rates suitable for CD-ROM playback or Internet download; can be played back on older computers.
- **Component Video**—used for capture and as an interim storage format but not for video delivery.
- **DV-PAL** and **DV-NTSC**—used to transfer video from a DV deck to Premiere or to transfer DV video across platforms and between computers with a FireWire or iLink connection.
- **Graphics**—intended for 8-bit images; compresses smaller than the animation codec.
- **H.261** and **H.263**—used for videoconferencing at low data rates.
- **Motion JPEG A** and **Motion JPEG B**—used to transfer video captured with a hardware capture card.
- **None**—a pristine interim storage format, usually too large to be played back smoothly.
- **Photo-JPEG**—best for still images, especially those without a lot of edges or sharp detail.
- **Planar RGB**—a lossless codec similar to animation, best suited for images that have large areas of solid color.
- **Video**—designed for video content in thousands of colors; good for previewing edits.
- **Sorenson Video**—although slow to compress, yields high compression with high quality for data rates ideal for Internet download; plays back best on computers with faster processors.

These are the video codecs Premiere offers if you choose Video for Windows as your editing mode (Project Settings dialog box) or Microsoft .AVI as the file type (Export Settings). The DV formats are available when you select MS DV as the editing mode or file type. (Video for Windows is built into Windows 95, but Microsoft no longer supports it and is replacing it with DirectShow/ActiveMovie. The .AVI format is being replaced by .ASF.)

- **Cinepak**—compresses 24-bit video for data rates suitable for CD-ROM playback or Internet download, and for playback on older computers.
- **Intel Indeo 5.04**—used for video distributed over the Internet for computers with fast (Pentium II) processors and designed to work with the Intel Audio Software codec.
- **Intel Indeo Video R3.2**—compresses 24-bit video for data rates suitable for CD-ROM playback; comparable in quality to Cinepak.
- **Microsoft DV (NTSC)** and **Microsoft DV (PAL)**—used to transfer video from a DV deck to Premiere or to transfer DV video across platforms and between computers with an iLink or FireWire connection.
- **Microsoft RLE**—designed for images that contain large areas of flat color, such as cartoon animations. Lossless at its 100 percent quality setting, it's suitable for interim storage of title sequences and animations.
- **Microsoft Video 1**—compresses analog video at 8 or 16 bits.
- **None**—a pristine interim storage format, usually too large to be played back smoothly.

CODECS

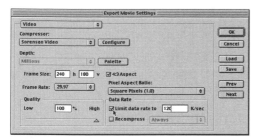

Figure 18.25 Some video codecs allow you to define the maximum data rate the clip can use.

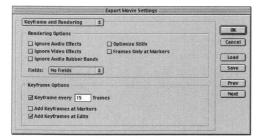

Figure 18.26 In the Keyframe and Rendering panel of the Project or Export Settings (shown here) dialog box, specify keyframing options (if the codec provides for them).

✔ Tips

- The codec helps determine your degree of control of the data rate, but Premiere's Data Rate graph provides a powerful tool for viewing and evaluating the data rate of a clip. It's invaluable when you need to troubleshoot playback problems you may experience. See your user guide or the online help system to find out how to open and interpret the Data Rate graph.

- Working with keyframes intelligently requires a strong understanding of the codec and compression, as well as a great deal of experimentation.

Data Rates

The file size of a clip relates directly to its data rate—the amount of information that the computer must process each second as it plays back the clip. Most of the video and audio settings you choose influence the data rate of clips. In addition, some video codecs allow you to define the maximum data rate for the frames of the clip (**Figure 18.25**). You set a data rate according to the limitations of the playback device and the specifications of the codec.

Keyframes

Many codecs—especially codecs designed for low data rates—use keyframes to optimize compression while maintaining the highest possible image quality. Keyframes are essential to a compression technique called frame differencing. (The term *keyframe* in this context has a different meaning than when it's used in reference to animation. See Chapter 11 and Chapter 14 for more information about using keyframes in animation.)

In *frame differencing*, keyframes act as reference frames, with which subsequent frames are compared. Rather than describe every frame completely, frame differencing achieves more efficient compression by describing only the changes between keyframes.

Keyframes are most effective when the image differs greatly from the preceding frame. Some codecs allow you to set the frequency of keyframes or to insert keyframes at markers and edits in the timeline window (**Figure 18.26**). Some codecs may insert keyframes automatically when the image changes significantly. A greater number of keyframes tends to increase image quality, as well as file size. Fewer keyframes usually results in decreased file size but lower image quality. But this isn't always the case; learn about the particular codec.

Audio Sample Rate

Analog signals are described by a continuous fluctuation of voltage. The analog signal is converted to a digital signal by being measured periodically, or *sampled*. If you think of the original audio as a curve, the digital audio would look like a connect-the-dots version of that curve (**Figures 18.27** and **18.28**). The more dots (or samples) you have, the more accurately you can reproduce the original curve.

Sample rate describes the number of times audio is sampled to approximate the original analog sound. Sample rates are measured in samples per second, or hertz (Hz). 1,000 hertz is called a kilohertz, or kHz. Sample rates are expressed in both Hz and kHz. The higher the sample rate, the larger the file.

Premiere offers most standard sample rates, depending on your system. Choose the sample rate that is most appropriate for your purposes (**Figure 18.29**). Your options are:

48000 Hz—equivalent to DAT or Digital Betacam; not always supported by sound or video cards; used by some DV cameras.

44100 Hz—equivalent to CD, appropriate for music; used by some DV cameras.

32000 Hz—the same bit rate used by some DV cameras.

22050 Hz—a good compromise between file size and quality.

11025 Hz—adequate for narration.

8000 Hz—achieves low data rates; suitable for the Internet.

5000 Hz—achieves the lowest data rates but delivers the poorest quality; suitable for the Internet.

Figure 18.27 You can think of analog audio as being a continuous curve. Analog is more detailed but more difficult to copy exactly.

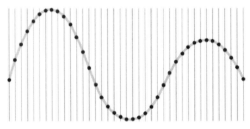

Figure 18.28 Digital audio samples, or measures, the audio at discrete intervals. This way, it can closely approximate the original curve. Because each sample has a defined value, digital audio can be copied exactly.

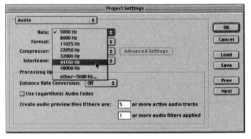

Figure 18.29 You can find options for audio sample rate and bit depth in the Audio panels of the Capture, Project (shown here) and Export Settings dialog boxes. Your camera may offer a choice of sample rates. You also have a choice of sample rates when you extract audio from a CD.

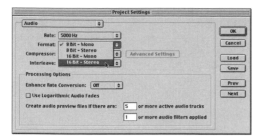

Figure 18.30 You specify an audio bit depth and channel options by making choices from the Format pull-down menu in the Audio panels of the Capture, Project, and Export Settings dialog boxes.

✔ Tips

■ In conjunction with audio compression, some audio codecs reduce the sample rate and bit depth even lower than the standard options.

■ You can find several effects that manipulate audio channels in the Audio palette. You can also manipulate channels by using the Pan controls in the timeline or in the Audio Mixer window. Effects are covered in Chapter 11; audio mixing is covered in Chapter 10.

Audio Bit Depth and Channels

Audio bit depth describes the number of bits used to describe each audio sample. Bit depth affects the range of sound that the audio file can reproduce, from silence to the loudest sound. This range is known as the signal-to-noise (s/n) ratio, which can be measured in decibels (dB).

Premiere and many other programs express this range as bit depth and allow you to choose the one that is most appropriate for your needs (**Figure 18.30**).

You also can choose between stereophonic audio and monophonic audio. In a *stereophonic* recording, audio is mixed differently in the left channel and the right channel. When the audio is played through stereo speakers, the separate channels give the sound a sense of space. A *monophonic* recording distributes the audio evenly between the two channels and plays back the same sounds through the left and right speakers.

In Premiere, both stereo and mono audio files appear as a single clip in a track. You specify whether you want to use mono or stereo in the Audio panels of the Capture, Project, and Export Settings dialog boxes.

AUDIO BIT DEPTH AND CHANNELS

Audio Format Options

◆ **8 bit - Mono**—equivalent to 48 dB; similar to FM broadcast in monophonic sound.

◆ **8 bit - Stereo**— equivalent to 48 dB; similar to FM broadcast in stereophonic sound.

◆ **16 bit - Mono**—equivalent to 96 dB; used by CD audio in monophonic sound.

◆ **16 bit - Stereo**— equivalent to 96 dB; used by CD audio in stereophonic sound.

Audio Interleave

In the Audio panels of the Capture, Project and Export Settings dialog boxes, you can specify the amount of audio interleave by clicking the Advanced Settings button (**Figure 18.31**). *Audio interleave* (also called *audio blocks*) determines how often audio information is loaded into RAM and inserted, or interleaved, among frames of video. Previous versions of Premiere referred to audio interleave as audio blocks, because blocks of audio are interleaved with blocks of video. Usually, an interleave value of 1 second results in smooth playback. If the audio falters during playback, however, you should adjust the interleave value. A low value needs less RAM but requires the computer to process audio more often. A large value results in larger audio blocks that are processed less often but require more RAM.

Audio Fades

You can specify how Premiere processes audio fades in the Audio panels of the Project and Export Settings dialog boxes. Ordinarily, Premiere processes audio fades according to a linear progression. When you choose logarithmic audio fades, however, Premiere processes the audio according to a logarithmic scale, which more closely approximates the way the human ear perceives audio-gain increases and decreases (**Figure 18.32**). Logarithmic fades sound more natural but require more processing time.

The Enhance Rate Conversion pull-down menu sets the level of quality used in converting audio to a higher sample rate (*upsampling*) or to a lower sample rate (*downsampling*) (**Figure 18.33**). The better the conversion method, the slower the processing time.

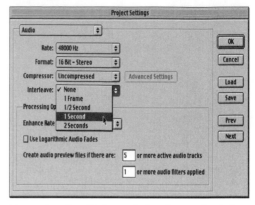

Figure 18.31 Specify the audio interleave value in the Audio panels of the Capture, Project, or Export Settings dialog boxes. In most cases, 1 second works fine.

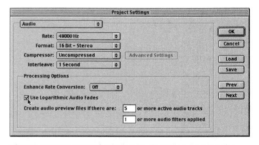

Figure 18.32 Logarithmic audio fades more closely approximate the way the human ear perceives audio-gain increases and decreases.

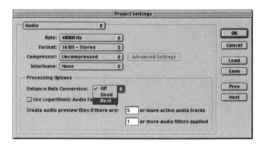

Figure 18.33 Choose the quality of the method used to upsample or downsample audio from the Enhance Rate Conversion pull-down menu.

AUDIO INTERLEAVE AND AUDIO FADES

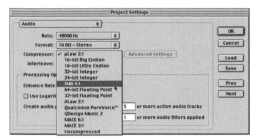

Figure 18.34 To lower file sizes and data rates, choose an audio codec from the Compressor pull-down menu of the Audio panel.

Audio Compression

If you plan to export your program to videotape, you probably don't need to compress the audio. Audio file sizes and data rates, however, often exceed the limitations of other applications, such as CD-ROMs or Internet delivery.

Audio codecs are designed for the type of audio used in your program or clip, such as voice or music. Some codecs achieve a specific compression ratio, which is part of the codec's name (MACE 3:1, for example). Choose the codec that is best suited for your purposes (**Figure 18.34**).

QuickTime Audio Codecs

Premiere offers the following audio codecs if you choose QuickTime as your capture format (in the Capture dialog box), editing mode (in the Project Settings dialog box) or file type (in the Export Settings dialog box):

μLaw 2:1—used for digital telephony in North America and Japan; the standard audio format on some platforms, such as UNIX workstations.

16-Bit Big Endian and **16-Bit Little Endian**—useful for hardware and software engineers in preparing processor-specific audio, but not useful for video editing.

24-Bit Integer and **32-Bit Integer**—useful for hardware and software engineers in preparing processor-specific audio, but not useful for video editing.

IMA 4:1—used for cross-platform audio for multimedia.

32-Bit Floating Point and **64-Bit Floating Point**—useful for hardware and software engineers in preparing processor-specific audio, but not useful for video editing.

ALaw 2:1—used primarily for digital telephony in Europe.

Qualcomm PureVoice—designed for speech at 8 kHz.

Qdesign Music Codec 2—compresses high-quality music for the Internet; capable of delivering CD-quality audio over a 28.8-Kbps connection.

MACE 3:1 and **MACE 6:1**—general-purpose audio codecs; MACE 3:1 achieves less compression and higher quality than MACE 6:1.

Uncompressed—no compression applied.

Video for Windows Audio Codecs

Premiere offers the following audio codecs if you choose Video for Windows as your capture format (in the Capture dialog box) editing mode (in the Project Settings dialog box) or Microsoft .AVI as the file type (in the Export Settings dialog box):

MPEG Layer-3 Codec—commonly known as MP3, a popular high-quality codec suitable for music.

ACELP.net—used for speech encoding and decoded at 8 Kbps.

WM-AUDIO—Windows Media Audio, a high-quality Web audio codec, better than MP3 at a given data rate.

Intel Audio Software—intended to deliver music and speech over the Internet. This codec is designed to work with the Intel Video Software codec; its maximum compression ratio is 8:1.

Microsoft G.723.1—used for video conferencing over standard phone lines; optimized for real-time encoding and decoding.

TrueSpeech—designed for speech over the Internet at low data rates.

Microsoft CCITT G.711—for medium- to high-bit-rate voice encoding.

Microsoft GSM 6.10—used in Europe for telephony.

MS-ADPCM—a Microsoft implementation of a common format that is capable of storing CD-quality audio.

Microsoft IMA ADPCM—useful for cross-platform multimedia.

L&H Codecs—Lernout & Hauspie codecs, designed for encoding speech at low bit rates (4.8 Kbps).

Uncompressed—no compression applied.

INDEX

INDEX

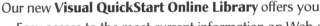